Ignorance, Thy Name Is Bucky

Other *Get Fuzzy* Books

The Dog Is Not a Toy (House Rule #4)

Fuzzy Logic: Get Fuzzy 2

The Get Fuzzy Experience: Are You Bucksperienced

I Would Have Bought You a Cat, But . . .

Blueprint for Disaster

Say Cheesy

Scrum Bums

I'm Ready for My Movie Contract

Take Our Cat, Please!

Treasuries

Groovitude: A Get Fuzzy Treasury

Bucky Katt's Big Book of Fun

Loserpalooza

The Potpourrifc Great Big Grab Bag of Get Fuzzy

Ignorance, Thy Name Is Bucky

a **GET FUZZY** collection by darby conley

**Andrews McMeel
Publishing, LLC**

Kansas City

Get Fuzzy is distributed internationally by United Feature Syndicate, Inc.

09 10 11 12 13 RR2 10 9 8 7 6 5 4 3 2 1

ISBN-13: 978-0-7407-8098-1
ISBN-10: 0-7407-8098-0

Library of Congress Control Number: 2008936280
www.andrewsmcmeel.com

Get Fuzzy can be viewed on the Internet at
www.comics.com.

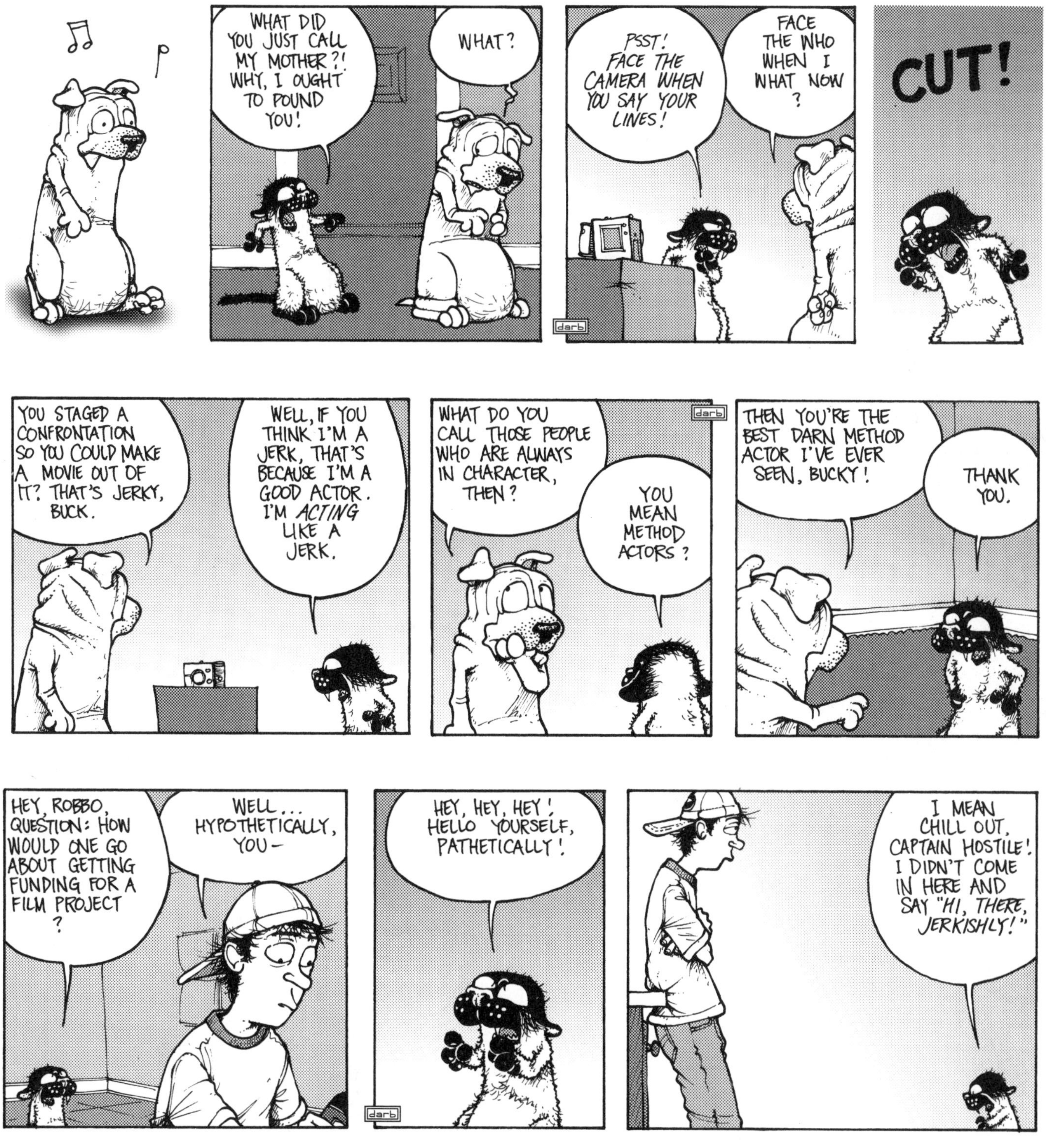
WHAT DID YOU JUST CALL MY MOTHER?! WHY, I OUGHT TO POUND YOU!
WHAT?
PSST! FACE THE CAMERA WHEN YOU SAY YOUR LINES!
FACE THE WHO WHEN I WHAT NOW?
CUT!
YOU STAGED A CONFRONTATION SO YOU COULD MAKE A MOVIE OUT OF IT? THAT'S JERKY, BUCK.
WELL, IF YOU THINK I'M A JERK, THAT'S BECAUSE I'M A GOOD ACTOR. I'M *ACTING* LIKE A JERK.
WHAT DO YOU CALL THOSE PEOPLE WHO ARE ALWAYS IN CHARACTER, THEN?
YOU MEAN METHOD ACTORS?
THEN YOU'RE THE BEST DARN METHOD ACTOR I'VE EVER SEEN, BUCKY!
THANK YOU.
HEY, ROBBO, QUESTION: HOW WOULD ONE GO ABOUT GETTING FUNDING FOR A FILM PROJECT?
WELL... HYPOTHETICALLY, YOU–
HEY, HEY, HEY! HELLO YOURSELF, PATHETICALLY!
I MEAN CHILL OUT, CAPTAIN HOSTILE! I DIDN'T COME IN HERE AND SAY "*HI, THERE, JERKISHLY!*"

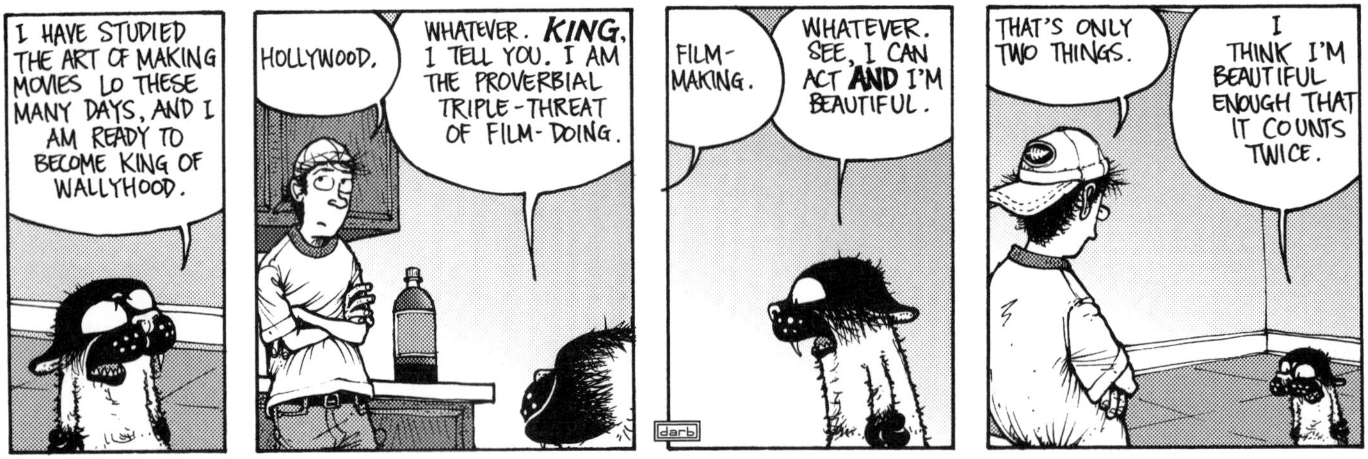
I HAVE STUDIED THE ART OF MAKING MOVIES LO THESE MANY DAYS, AND I AM READY TO BECOME KING OF WALLYHOOD.
HOLLYWOOD.
WHATEVER. **KING**, I TELL YOU. I AM THE PROVERBIAL TRIPLE-THREAT OF FILM-DOING.
FILM-MAKING.
WHATEVER. SEE, I CAN ACT **AND** I'M BEAUTIFUL.
THAT'S ONLY TWO THINGS.
I THINK I'M BEAUTIFUL ENOUGH THAT IT COUNTS TWICE.
darb

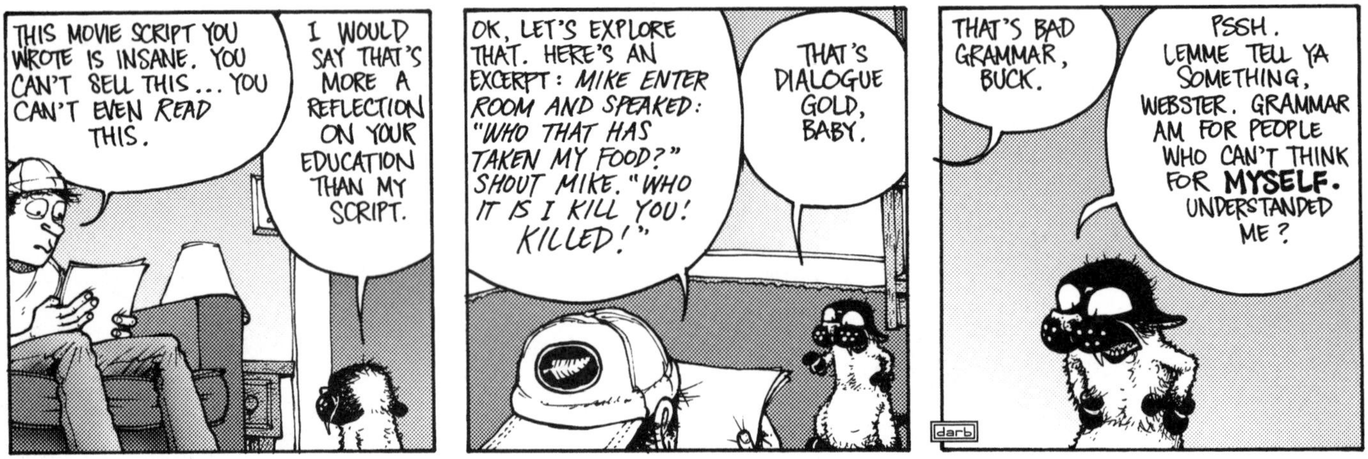
THIS MOVIE SCRIPT YOU WROTE IS INSANE. YOU CAN'T SELL THIS... YOU CAN'T EVEN *READ* THIS.
I WOULD SAY THAT'S MORE A REFLECTION ON YOUR EDUCATION THAN MY SCRIPT.
OK, LET'S EXPLORE THAT. HERE'S AN EXCERPT: *MIKE ENTER ROOM AND SPEAKED: "WHO THAT HAS TAKEN MY FOOD?" SHOUT MIKE. "WHO IT IS I KILL YOU! KILLED!"*
THAT'S DIALOGUE GOLD, BABY.
THAT'S BAD GRAMMAR, BUCK.
PSSH. LEMME TELL YA SOMETHING, WEBSTER. GRAMMAR AM FOR PEOPLE WHO CAN'T THINK FOR **MYSELF.** UNDERSTANDED ME?
darb

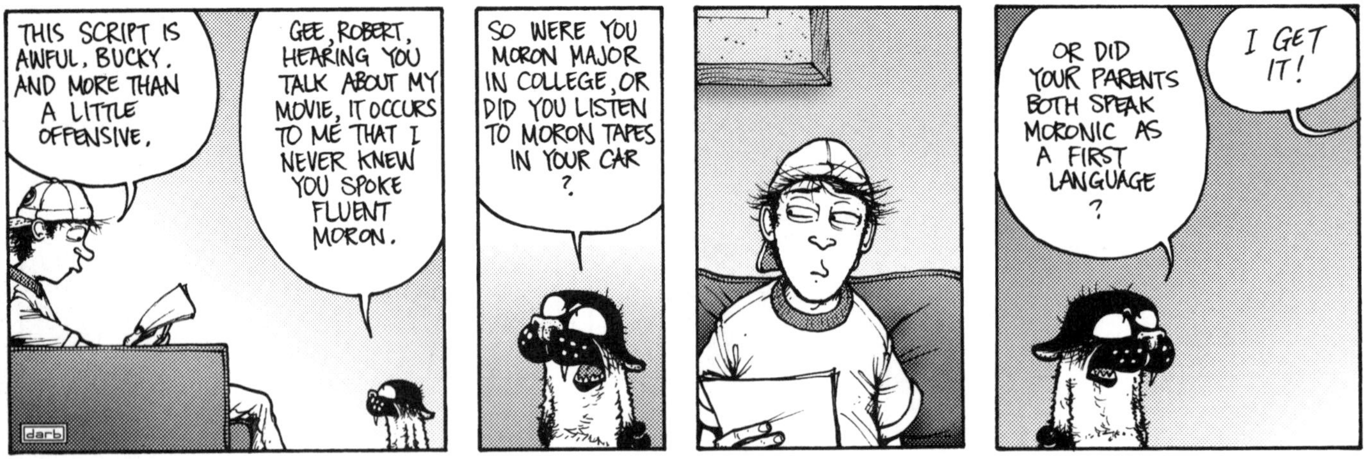
THIS SCRIPT IS AWFUL, BUCKY. AND MORE THAN A LITTLE OFFENSIVE.
GEE, ROBERT, HEARING YOU TALK ABOUT MY MOVIE, IT OCCURS TO ME THAT I NEVER KNEW YOU SPOKE FLUENT MORON.
SO WERE YOU MORON MAJOR IN COLLEGE, OR DID YOU LISTEN TO MORON TAPES IN YOUR CAR?
OR DID YOUR PARENTS BOTH SPEAK MORONIC AS A FIRST LANGUAGE?
I GET IT!
darb

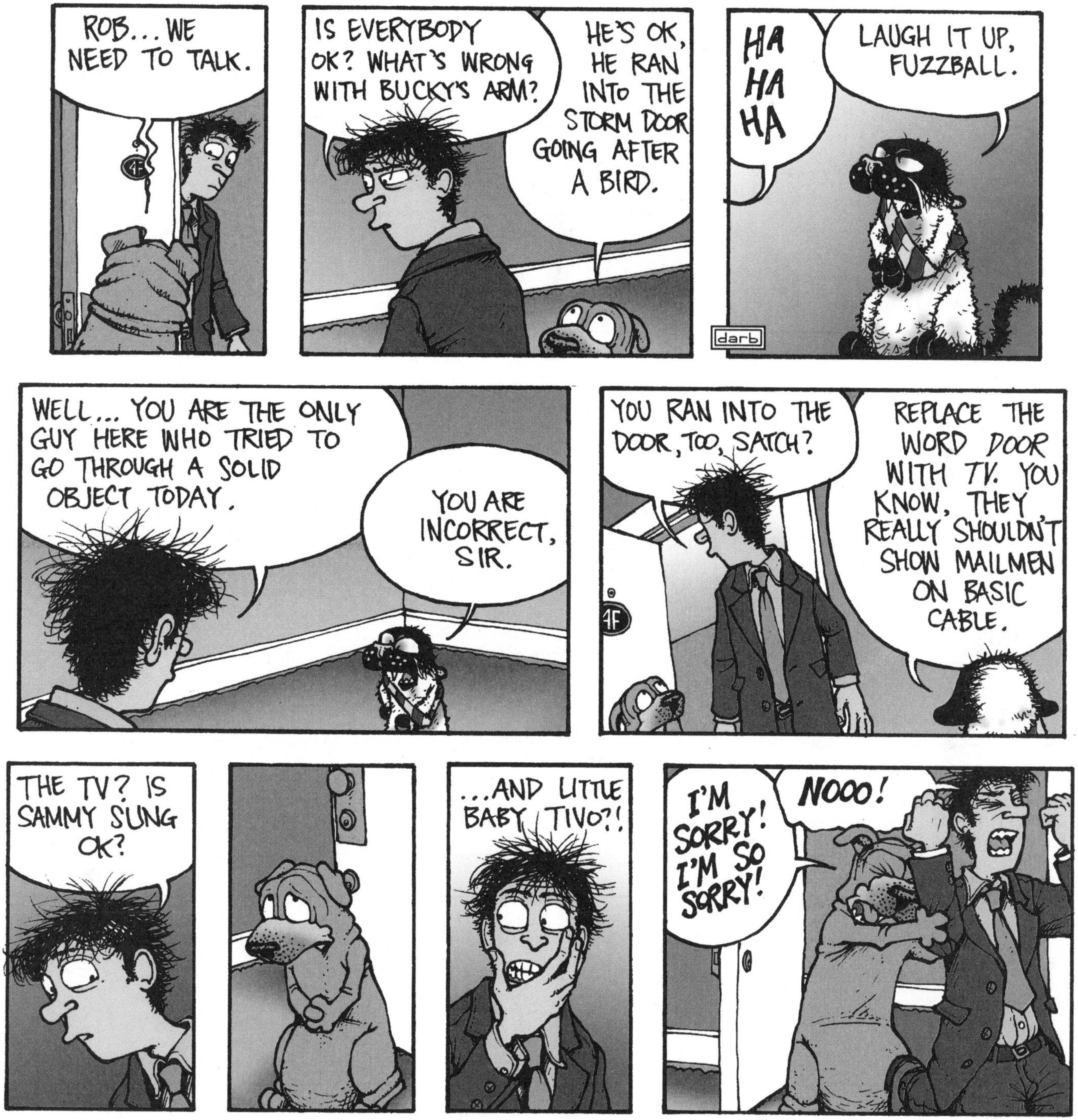
ROB... WE NEED TO TALK.
IS EVERYBODY OK? WHAT'S WRONG WITH BUCKY'S ARM?
HE'S OK, HE RAN INTO THE STORM DOOR GOING AFTER A BIRD.
HA HA HA
LAUGH IT UP, FUZZBALL.
darb
WELL... YOU ARE THE ONLY GUY HERE WHO TRIED TO GO THROUGH A SOLID OBJECT TODAY.
YOU ARE INCORRECT, SIR.
YOU RAN INTO THE DOOR, TOO, SATCH?
REPLACE THE WORD *DOOR* WITH *TV*. YOU KNOW, THEY REALLY SHOULDN'T SHOW MAILMEN ON BASIC CABLE.
THE TV? IS SAMMY SUNG OK?
...AND LITTLE BABY TIVO?!
I'M SORRY! I'M SO SORRY!
NOOO!

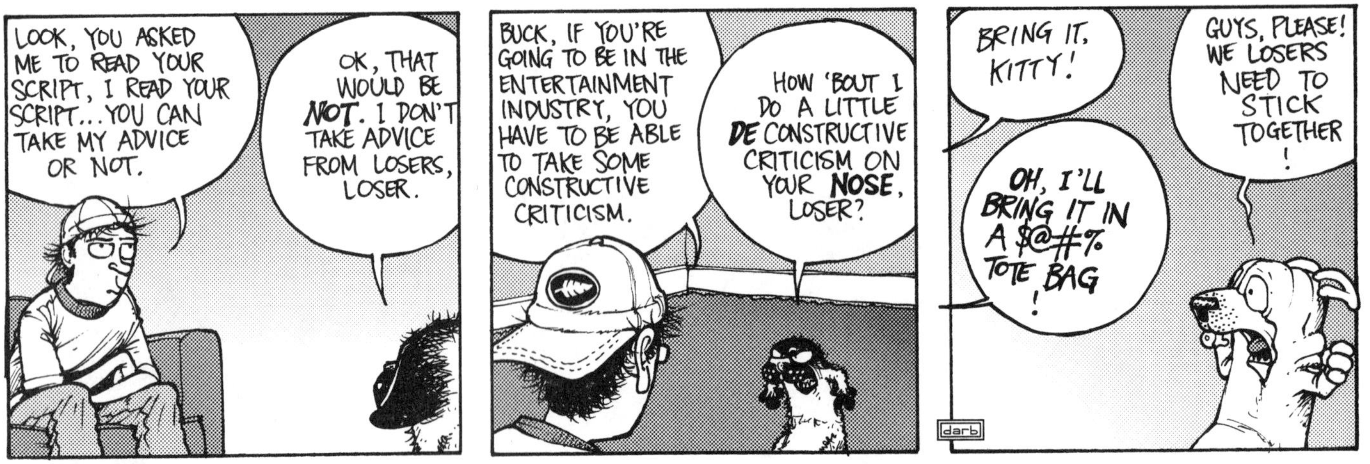
LOOK, YOU ASKED ME TO READ YOUR SCRIPT, I READ YOUR SCRIPT... YOU CAN TAKE MY ADVICE OR NOT.
OK, THAT WOULD BE NOT. I DON'T TAKE ADVICE FROM LOSERS, LOSER.
BUCK, IF YOU'RE GOING TO BE IN THE ENTERTAINMENT INDUSTRY, YOU HAVE TO BE ABLE TO TAKE SOME CONSTRUCTIVE CRITICISM.
HOW 'BOUT I DO A LITTLE DECONSTRUCTIVE CRITICISM ON YOUR NOSE, LOSER?
BRING IT, KITTY!
OH, I'LL BRING IT IN A $@#% TOTE BAG!
GUYS, PLEASE! WE LOSERS NEED TO STICK TOGETHER!

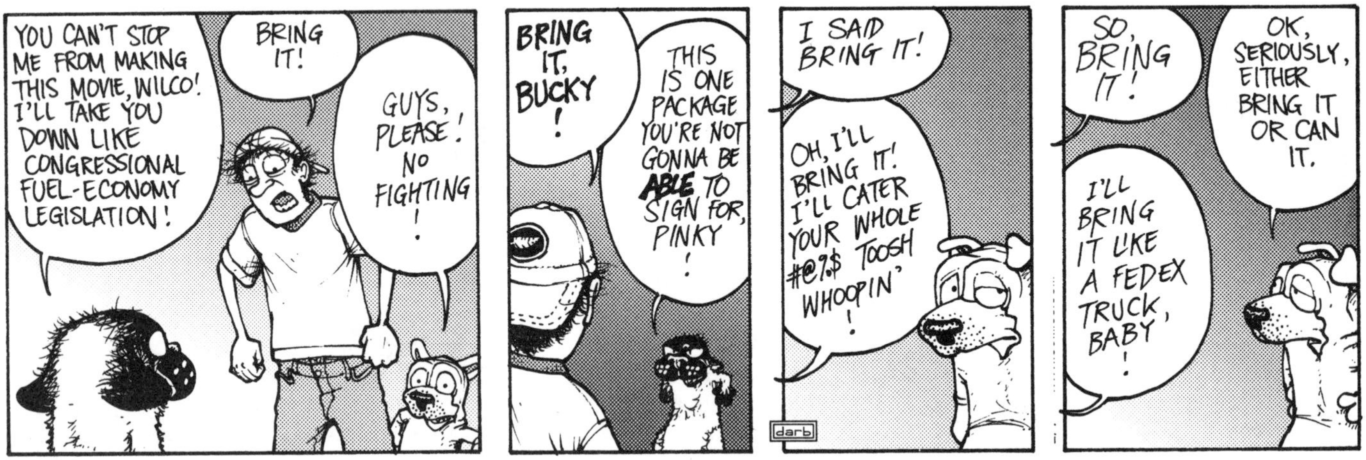
YOU CAN'T STOP ME FROM MAKING THIS MOVIE, WILCO! I'LL TAKE YOU DOWN LIKE CONGRESSIONAL FUEL-ECONOMY LEGISLATION!
BRING IT!
GUYS, PLEASE! NO FIGHTING!
BRING IT, BUCKY!
THIS IS ONE PACKAGE YOU'RE NOT GONNA BE ABLE TO SIGN FOR, PINKY!
I SAID BRING IT!
OH, I'LL BRING IT! I'LL CATER YOUR WHOLE #@%$ TOOSH WHOOPIN'!
SO, BRING IT!
OK, SERIOUSLY, EITHER BRING IT OR CAN IT.
I'LL BRING IT LIKE A FEDEX TRUCK, BABY!

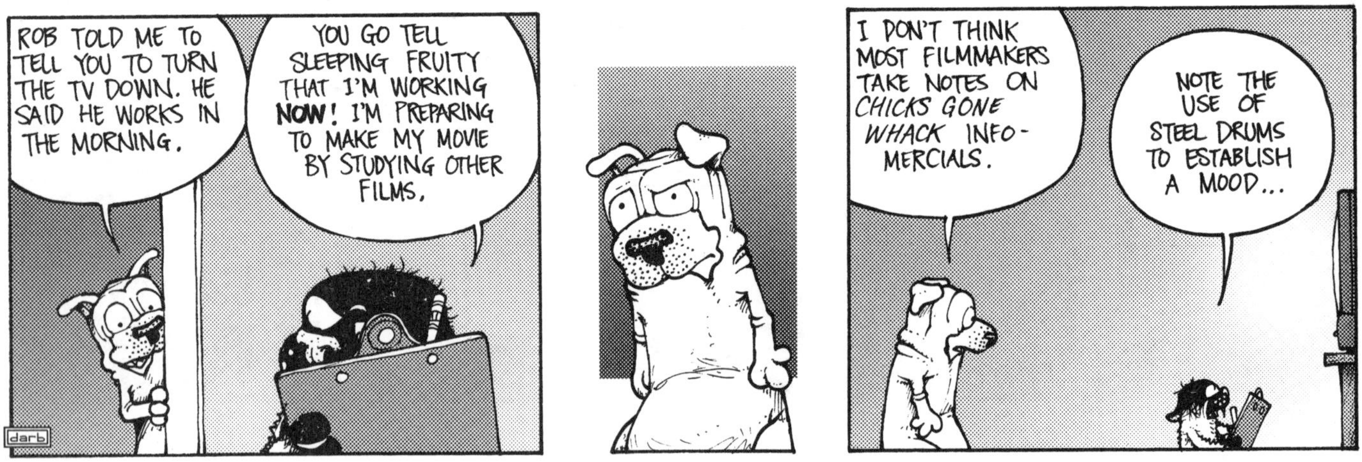
ROB TOLD ME TO TELL YOU TO TURN THE TV DOWN. HE SAID HE WORKS IN THE MORNING.
YOU GO TELL SLEEPING FRUITY THAT I'M WORKING NOW! I'M PREPARING TO MAKE MY MOVIE BY STUDYING OTHER FILMS.
I DON'T THINK MOST FILMMAKERS TAKE NOTES ON CHICKS GONE WHACK INFO-MERCIALS.
NOTE THE USE OF STEEL DRUMS TO ESTABLISH A MOOD...

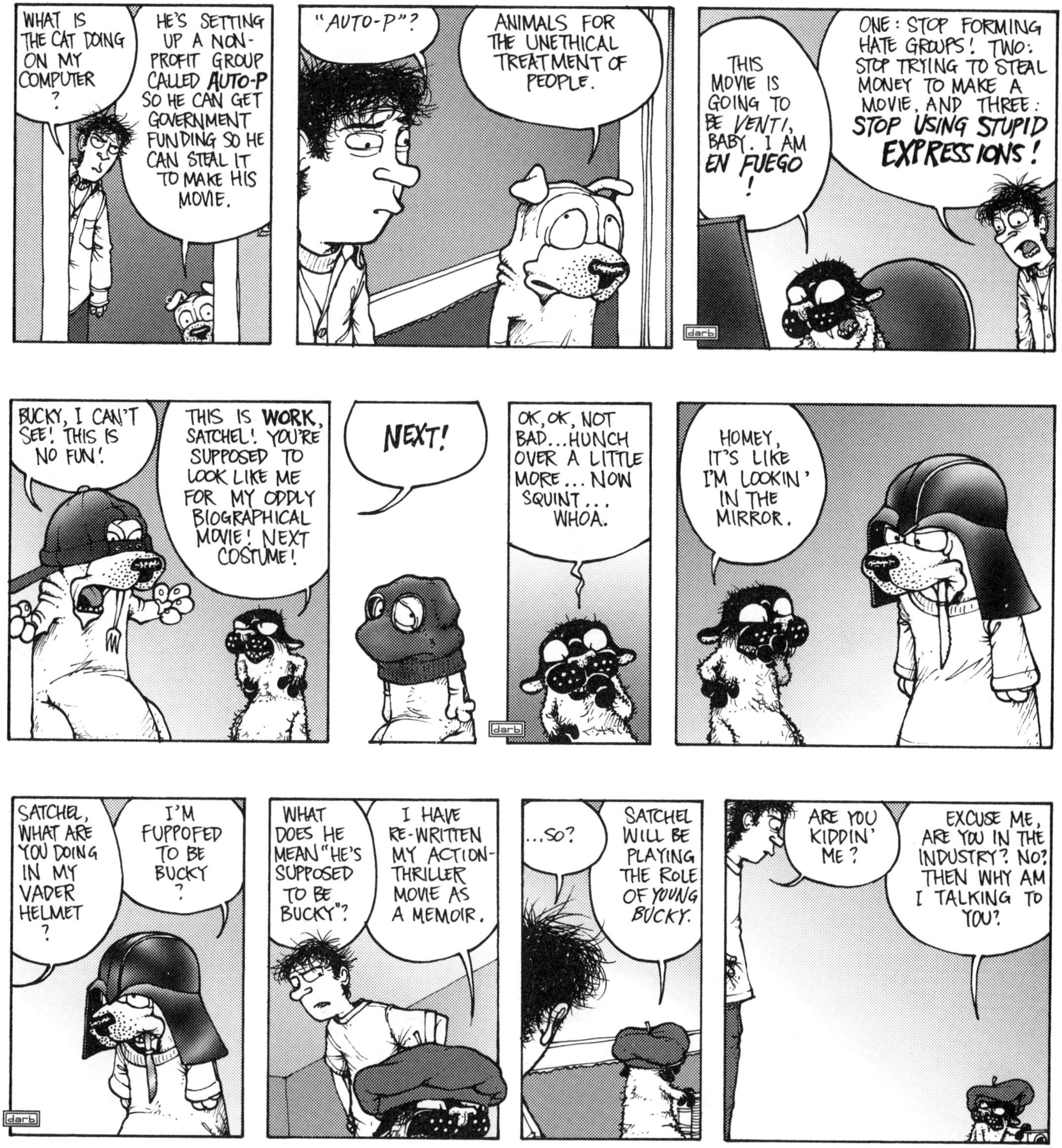
WHAT IS THE CAT DOING ON MY COMPUTER ?
HE'S SETTING UP A NON-PROFIT GROUP CALLED AUTO-P SO HE CAN GET GOVERNMENT FUNDING SO HE CAN STEAL IT TO MAKE HIS MOVIE.
"AUTO-P"?
ANIMALS FOR THE UNETHICAL TREATMENT OF PEOPLE.
THIS MOVIE IS GOING TO BE VENTI, BABY. I AM EN FUEGO !
ONE: STOP FORMING HATE GROUPS! TWO: STOP TRYING TO STEAL MONEY TO MAKE A MOVIE, AND THREE: STOP USING STUPID EXPRESSIONS!
darb
BUCKY, I CAN'T SEE! THIS IS NO FUN!
THIS IS WORK, SATCHEL! YOU'RE SUPPOSED TO LOOK LIKE ME FOR MY ODDLY BIOGRAPHICAL MOVIE! NEXT COSTUME!
NEXT!
darb
OK, OK, NOT BAD... HUNCH OVER A LITTLE MORE... NOW SQUINT... WHOA.
HOMEY, IT'S LIKE I'M LOOKIN' IN THE MIRROR.
SATCHEL, WHAT ARE YOU DOING IN MY VADER HELMET ?
I'M FUPPOFED TO BE BUCKY ?
darb
WHAT DOES HE MEAN "HE'S SUPPOSED TO BE BUCKY"?
I HAVE RE-WRITTEN MY ACTION-THRILLER MOVIE AS A MEMOIR.
...SO?
SATCHEL WILL BE PLAYING THE ROLE OF YOUNG BUCKY.
ARE YOU KIDDIN' ME ?
EXCUSE ME, ARE YOU IN THE INDUSTRY? NO? THEN WHY AM I TALKING TO YOU?

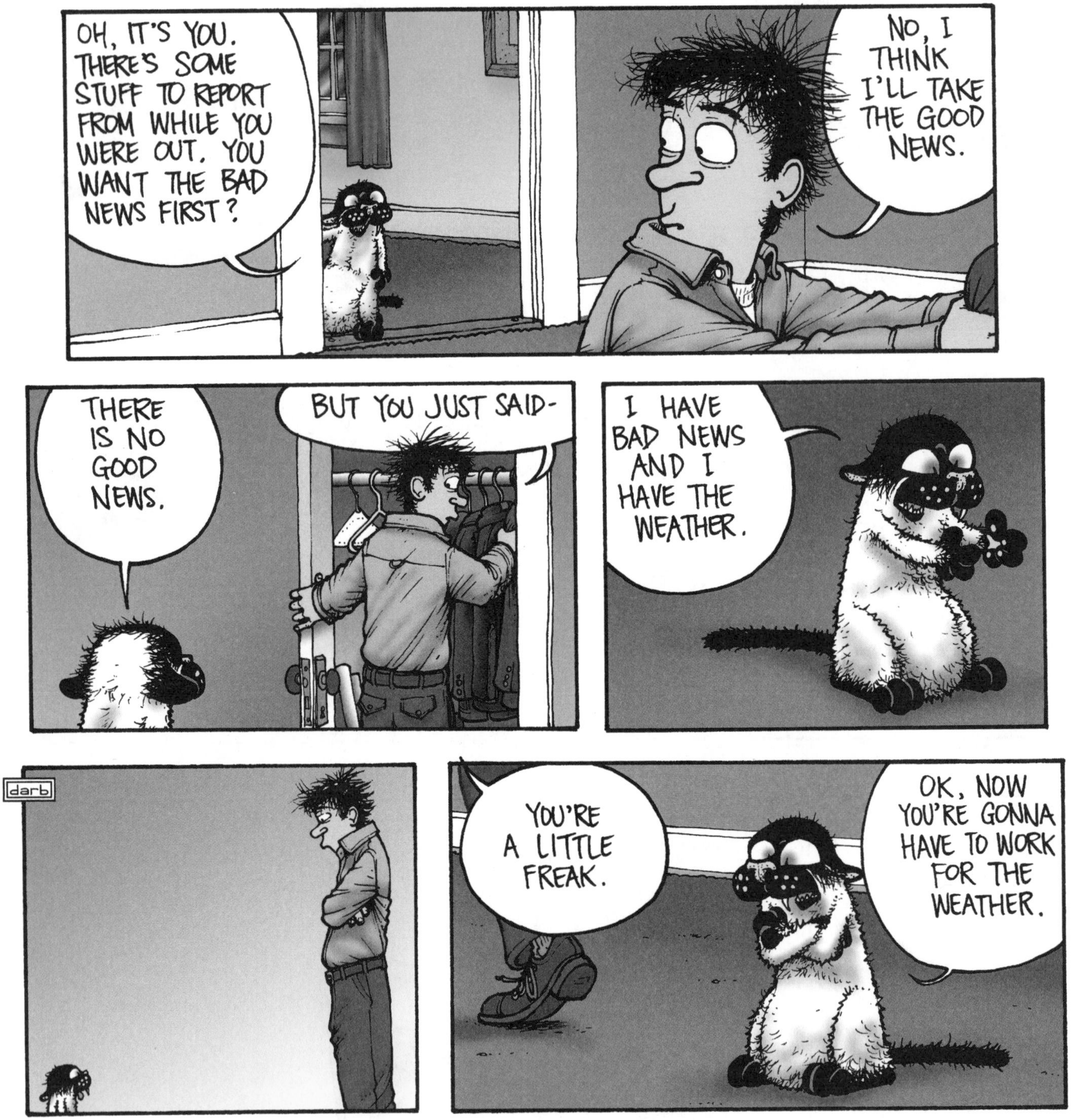
OH, IT'S YOU. THERE'S SOME STUFF TO REPORT FROM WHILE YOU WERE OUT. YOU WANT THE BAD NEWS FIRST?
NO, I THINK I'LL TAKE THE GOOD NEWS.
THERE IS NO GOOD NEWS.
BUT YOU JUST SAID-
I HAVE BAD NEWS AND I HAVE THE WEATHER.
darb
YOU'RE A LITTLE FREAK.
OK, NOW YOU'RE GONNA HAVE TO WORK FOR THE WEATHER.

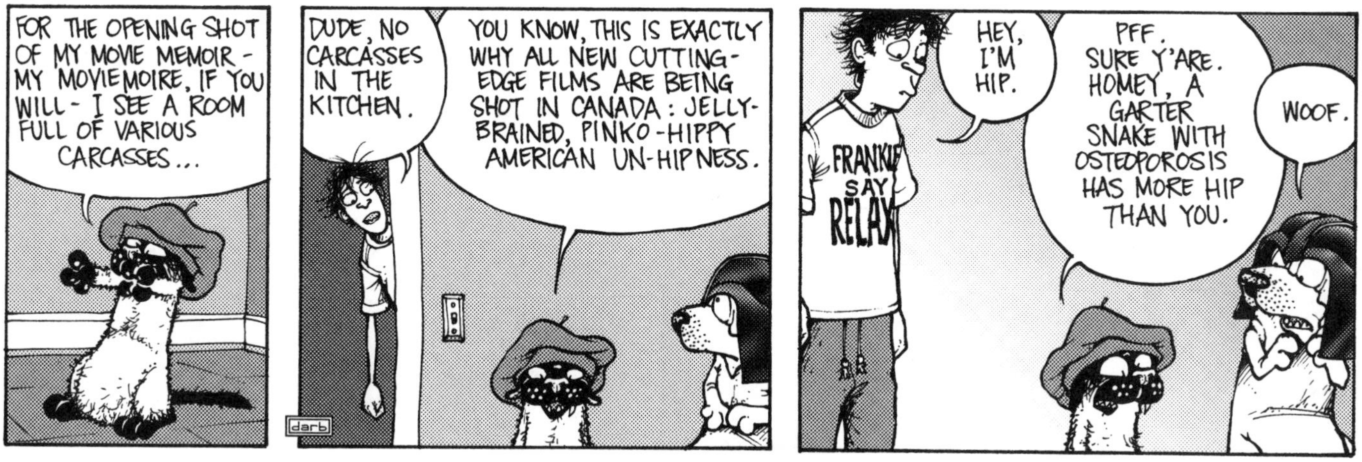
FOR THE OPENING SHOT OF MY MOVIE MEMOIR - MY MOVIEMOIRE, IF YOU WILL - I SEE A ROOM FULL OF VARIOUS CARCASSES...
DUDE, NO CARCASSES IN THE KITCHEN.
YOU KNOW, THIS IS EXACTLY WHY ALL NEW CUTTING-EDGE FILMS ARE BEING SHOT IN CANADA: JELLY-BRAINED, PINKO-HIPPY AMERICAN UN-HIPNESS.
darb
FRANKIE SAY RELAX
HEY, I'M HIP.
PFF. SURE Y'ARE. HOMEY, A GARTER SNAKE WITH OSTEOPOROSIS HAS MORE HIP THAN YOU.
WOOF.

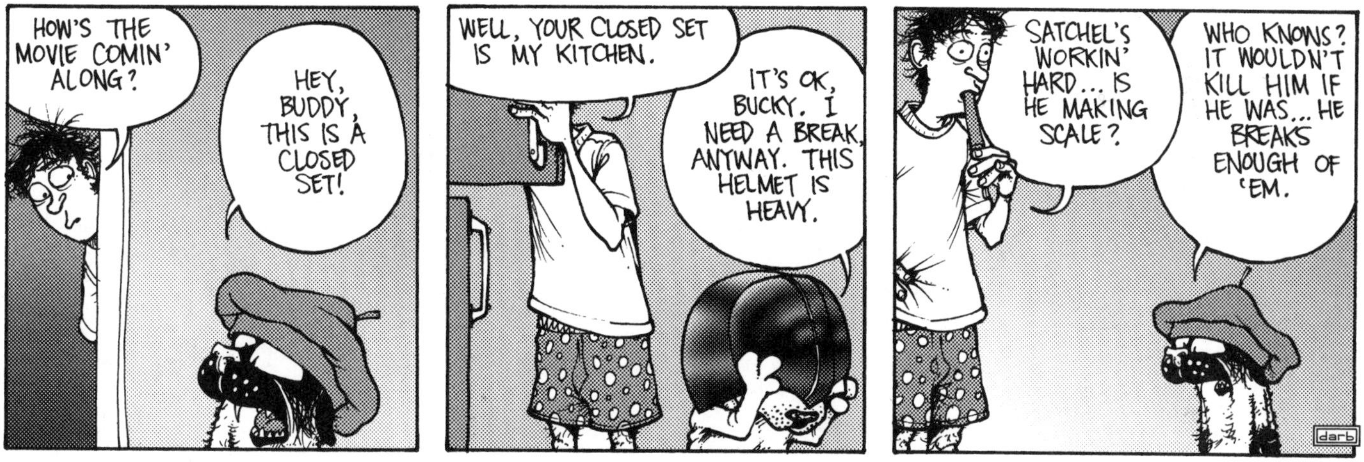
HOW'S THE MOVIE COMIN' ALONG?
HEY, BUDDY, THIS IS A CLOSED SET!
WELL, YOUR CLOSED SET IS MY KITCHEN.
IT'S OK, BUCKY. I NEED A BREAK, ANYWAY. THIS HELMET IS HEAVY.
SATCHEL'S WORKIN' HARD... IS HE MAKING SCALE?
WHO KNOWS? IT WOULDN'T KILL HIM IF HE WAS... HE BREAKS ENOUGH OF 'EM.
darb

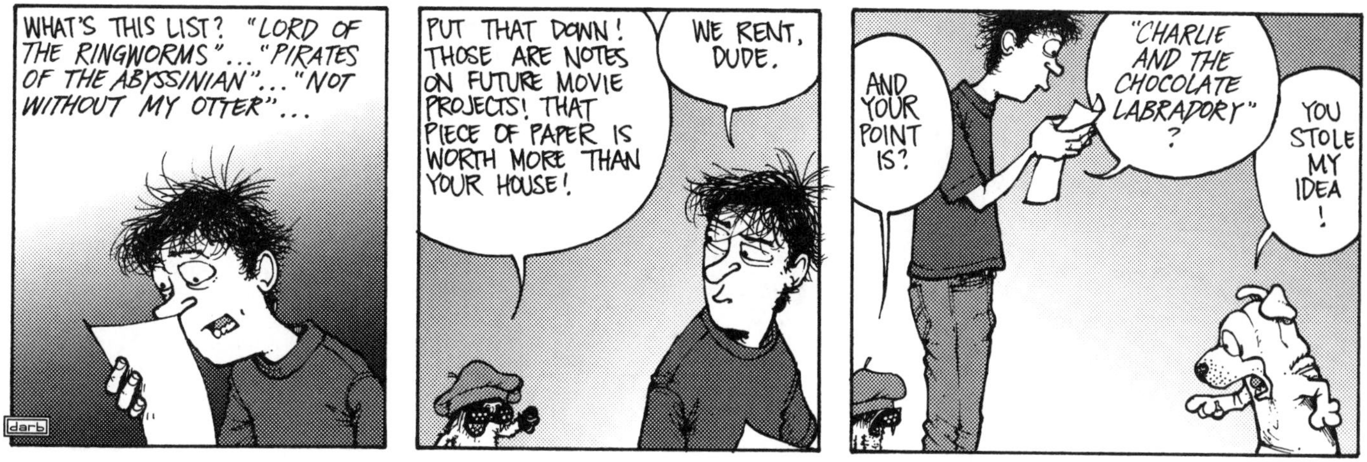
WHAT'S THIS LIST? "LORD OF THE RINGWORMS"... "PIRATES OF THE ABYSSINIAN"... "NOT WITHOUT MY OTTER"...
darb
PUT THAT DOWN! THOSE ARE NOTES ON FUTURE MOVIE PROJECTS! THAT PIECE OF PAPER IS WORTH MORE THAN YOUR HOUSE!
WE RENT, DUDE.
AND YOUR POINT IS?
"CHARLIE AND THE CHOCOLATE LABRADORY"?
YOU STOLE MY IDEA!

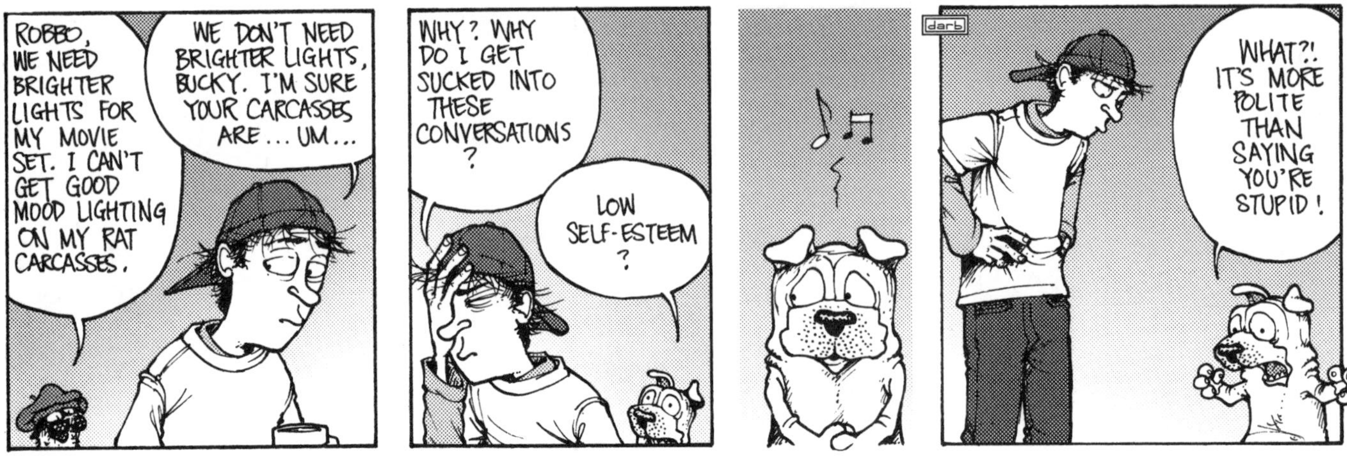
ROBBO, WE NEED BRIGHTER LIGHTS FOR MY MOVIE SET. I CAN'T GET GOOD MOOD LIGHTING ON MY RAT CARCASSES.
WE DON'T NEED BRIGHTER LIGHTS, BUCKY. I'M SURE YOUR CARCASSES ARE... UM...
WHY? WHY DO I GET SUCKED INTO THESE CONVERSATIONS?
LOW SELF-ESTEEM?
WHAT?! IT'S MORE POLITE THAN SAYING YOU'RE STUPID!
darb

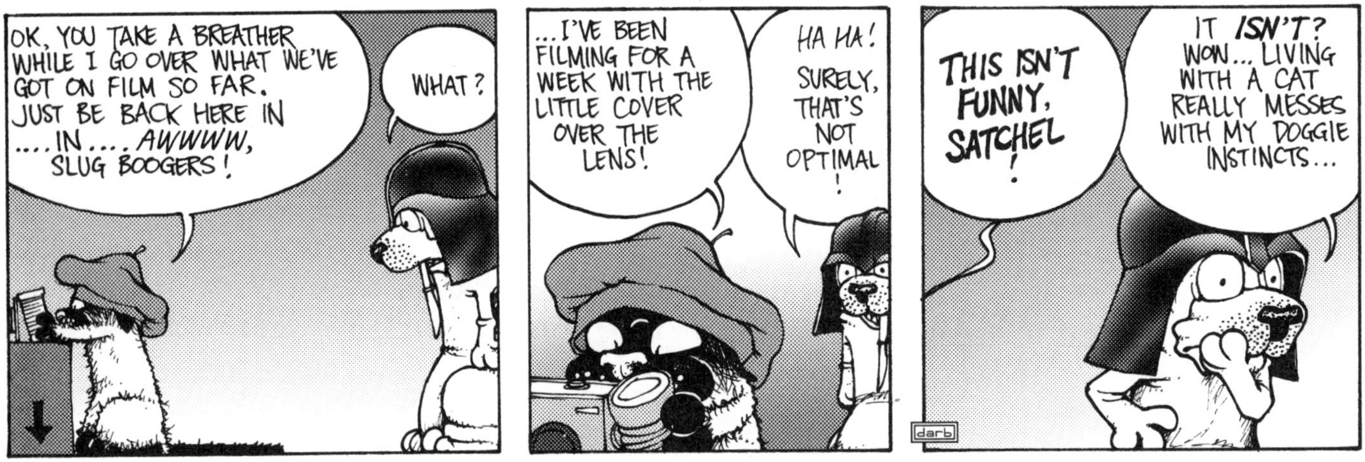
OK, YOU TAKE A BREATHER WHILE I GO OVER WHAT WE'VE GOT ON FILM SO FAR. JUST BE BACK HERE IN ....IN.... AWWWW, SLUG BOOGERS!
WHAT?
...I'VE BEEN FILMING FOR A WEEK WITH THE LITTLE COVER OVER THE LENS!
HA HA! SURELY, THAT'S NOT OPTIMAL!
THIS ISN'T FUNNY, SATCHEL!
IT ISN'T? WOW... LIVING WITH A CAT REALLY MESSES WITH MY DOGGIE INSTINCTS...
darb

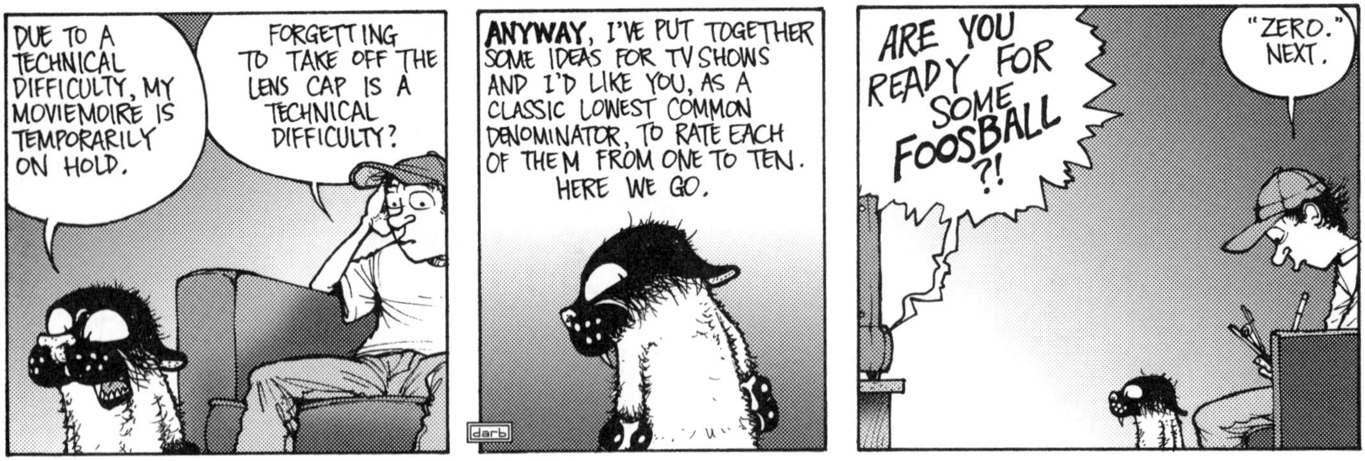
DUE TO A TECHNICAL DIFFICULTY, MY MOVIEMOIRE IS TEMPORARILY ON HOLD.
FORGETTING TO TAKE OFF THE LENS CAP IS A TECHNICAL DIFFICULTY?
ANYWAY, I'VE PUT TOGETHER SOME IDEAS FOR TV SHOWS AND I'D LIKE YOU, AS A CLASSIC LOWEST COMMON DENOMINATOR, TO RATE EACH OF THEM FROM ONE TO TEN. HERE WE GO.
ARE YOU READY FOR SOME FOOSBALL?!
"ZERO." NEXT.
darb

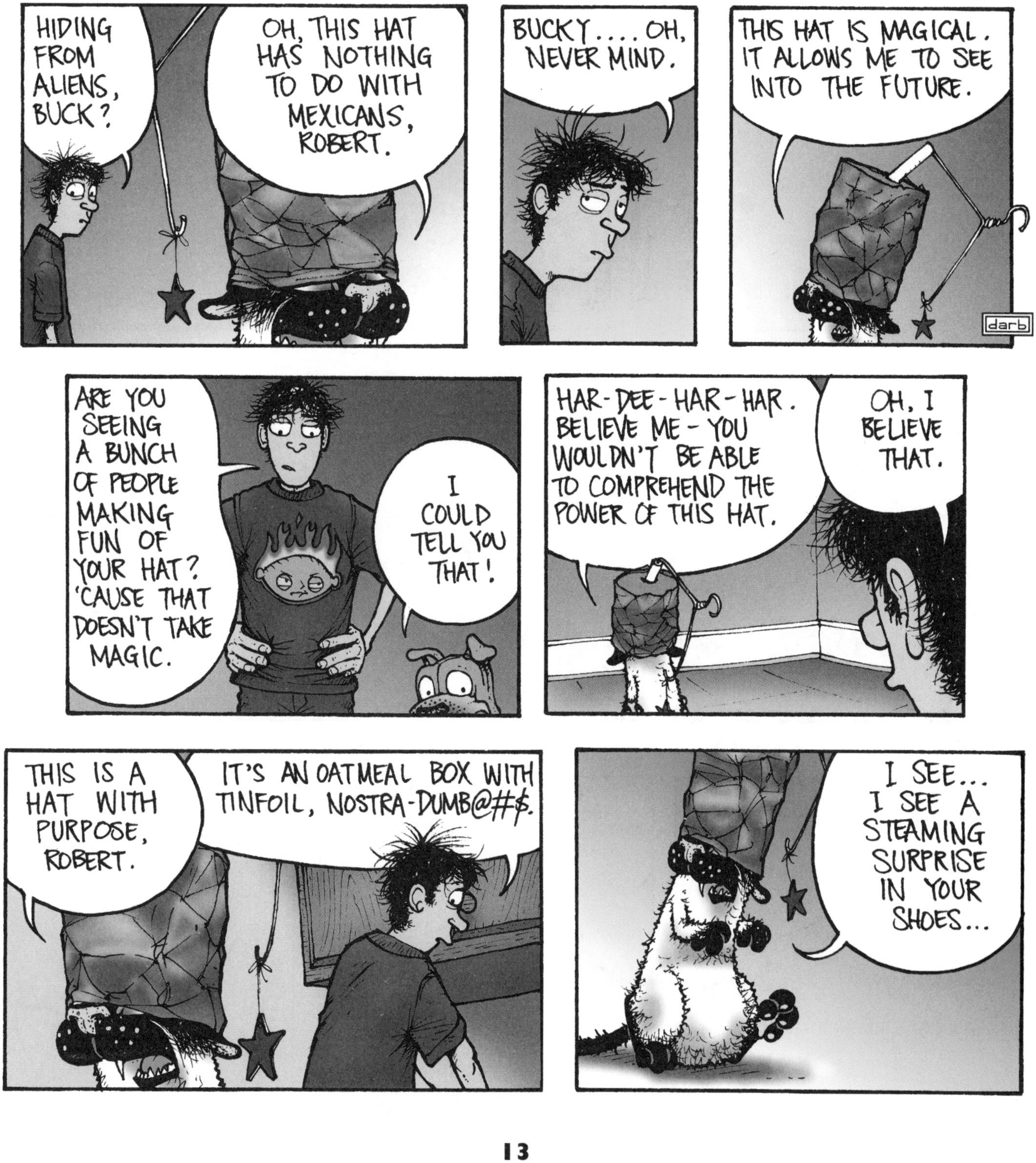
HIDING FROM ALIENS, BUCK?
OH, THIS HAT HAS NOTHING TO DO WITH MEXICANS, ROBERT.
BUCKY.... OH, NEVER MIND.
THIS HAT IS MAGICAL. IT ALLOWS ME TO SEE INTO THE FUTURE.
darb
ARE YOU SEEING A BUNCH OF PEOPLE MAKING FUN OF YOUR HAT? 'CAUSE THAT DOESN'T TAKE MAGIC.
I COULD TELL YOU THAT!
HAR-DEE-HAR-HAR. BELIEVE ME - YOU WOULDN'T BE ABLE TO COMPREHEND THE POWER OF THIS HAT.
OH, I BELIEVE THAT.
THIS IS A HAT WITH PURPOSE, ROBERT.
IT'S AN OATMEAL BOX WITH TINFOIL, NOSTRA-DUMB@#$.
I SEE... I SEE A STEAMING SURPRISE IN YOUR SHOES...

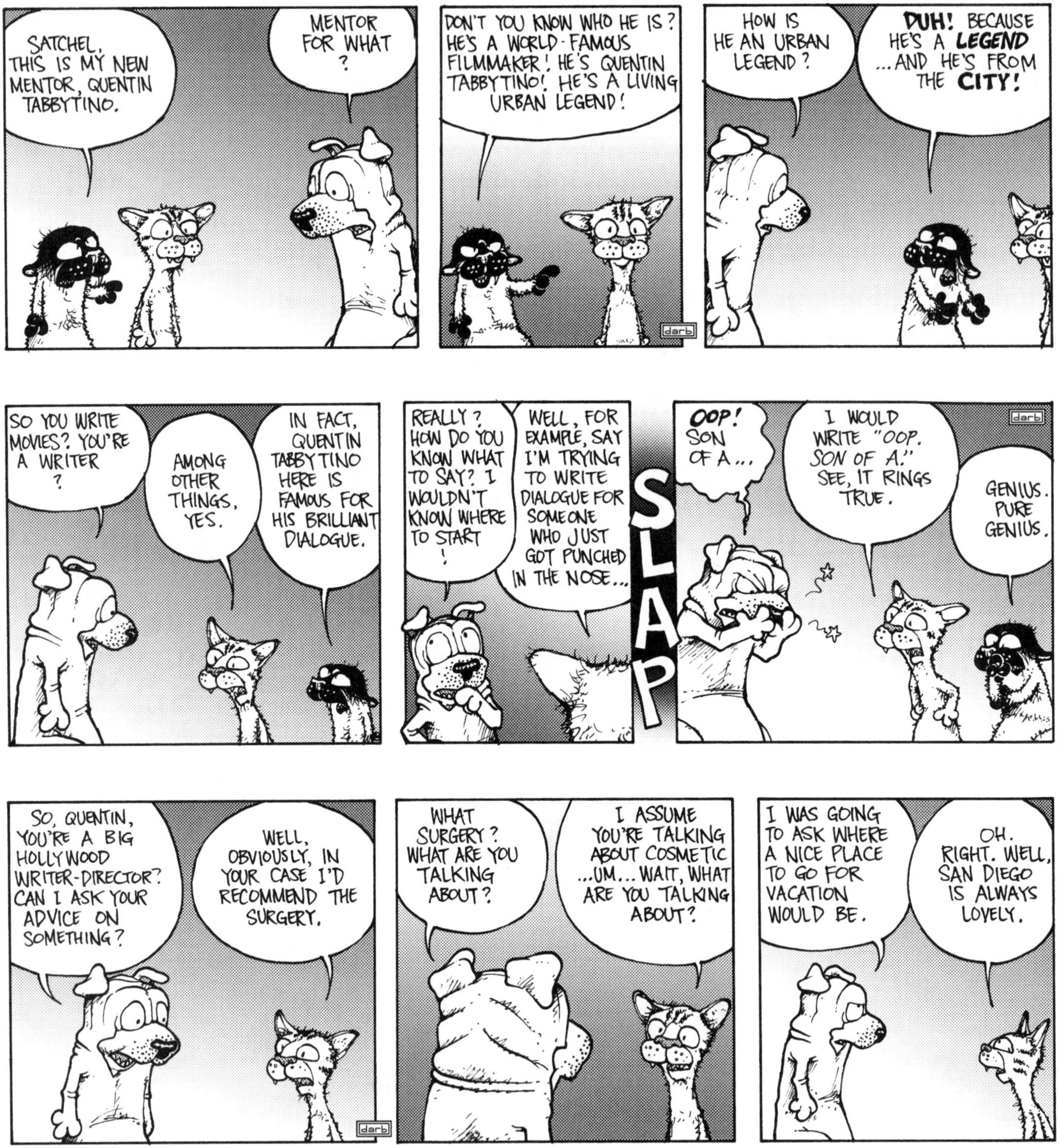
SATCHEL, THIS IS MY NEW MENTOR, QUENTIN TABBYTINO.
MENTOR FOR WHAT ?
DON'T YOU KNOW WHO HE IS ? HE'S A WORLD-FAMOUS FILMMAKER! HE'S QUENTIN TABBYTINO! HE'S A LIVING URBAN LEGEND!
HOW IS HE AN URBAN LEGEND ?
DUH! BECAUSE HE'S A LEGEND ...AND HE'S FROM THE CITY!
darb
SO YOU WRITE MOVIES? YOU'RE A WRITER ?
AMONG OTHER THINGS, YES.
IN FACT, QUENTIN TABBYTINO HERE IS FAMOUS FOR HIS BRILLIANT DIALOGUE.
REALLY ? HOW DO YOU KNOW WHAT TO SAY? I WOULDN'T KNOW WHERE TO START !
WELL, FOR EXAMPLE, SAY I'M TRYING TO WRITE DIALOGUE FOR SOMEONE WHO JUST GOT PUNCHED IN THE NOSE...
SLAP
OOP! SON OF A...
I WOULD WRITE "OOP. SON OF A." SEE, IT RINGS TRUE.
GENIUS. PURE GENIUS.
darb
SO, QUENTIN, YOU'RE A BIG HOLLYWOOD WRITER-DIRECTOR? CAN I ASK YOUR ADVICE ON SOMETHING ?
WELL, OBVIOUSLY, IN YOUR CASE I'D RECOMMEND THE SURGERY.
WHAT SURGERY ? WHAT ARE YOU TALKING ABOUT ?
I ASSUME YOU'RE TALKING ABOUT COSMETIC ...UM... WAIT, WHAT ARE YOU TALKING ABOUT ?
I WAS GOING TO ASK WHERE A NICE PLACE TO GO FOR VACATION WOULD BE.
OH. RIGHT. WELL, SAN DIEGO IS ALWAYS LOVELY.
darb

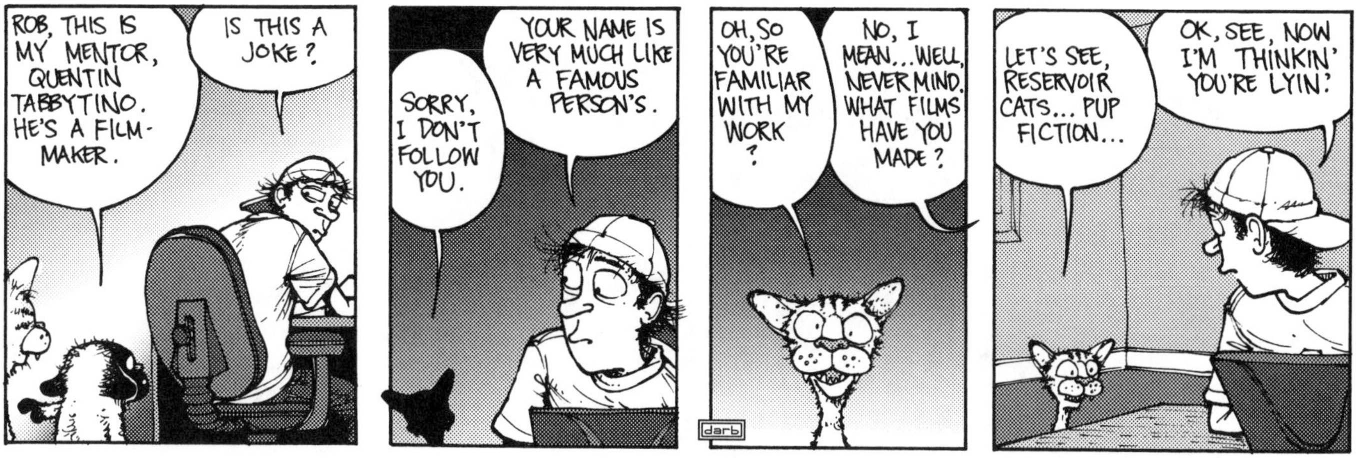
ROB, THIS IS MY MENTOR, QUENTIN TABBYTINO. HE'S A FILM-MAKER.
IS THIS A JOKE?
YOUR NAME IS VERY MUCH LIKE A FAMOUS PERSON'S.
SORRY, I DON'T FOLLOW YOU.
OH, SO YOU'RE FAMILIAR WITH MY WORK ?
NO, I MEAN... WELL, NEVERMIND. WHAT FILMS HAVE YOU MADE?
darb
LET'S SEE, RESERVOIR CATS... PUP FICTION...
OK, SEE, NOW I'M THINKIN' YOU'RE LYIN'.

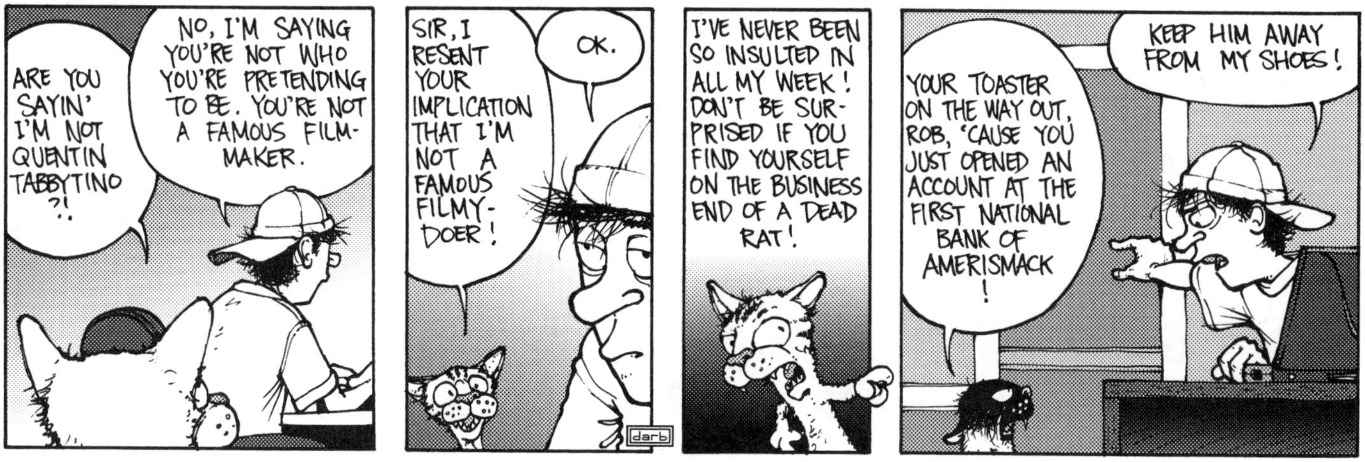
ARE YOU SAYIN' I'M NOT QUENTIN TABBYTINO ?!
NO, I'M SAYING YOU'RE NOT WHO YOU'RE PRETENDING TO BE. YOU'RE NOT A FAMOUS FILM-MAKER.
SIR, I RESENT YOUR IMPLICATION THAT I'M NOT A FAMOUS FILMY-DOER!
OK.
darb
I'VE NEVER BEEN SO INSULTED IN ALL MY WEEK! DON'T BE SUR-PRISED IF YOU FIND YOURSELF ON THE BUSINESS END OF A DEAD RAT!
KEEP HIM AWAY FROM MY SHOES!
YOUR TOASTER ON THE WAY OUT, ROB, 'CAUSE YOU JUST OPENED AN ACCOUNT AT THE FIRST NATIONAL BANK OF AMERISMACK !

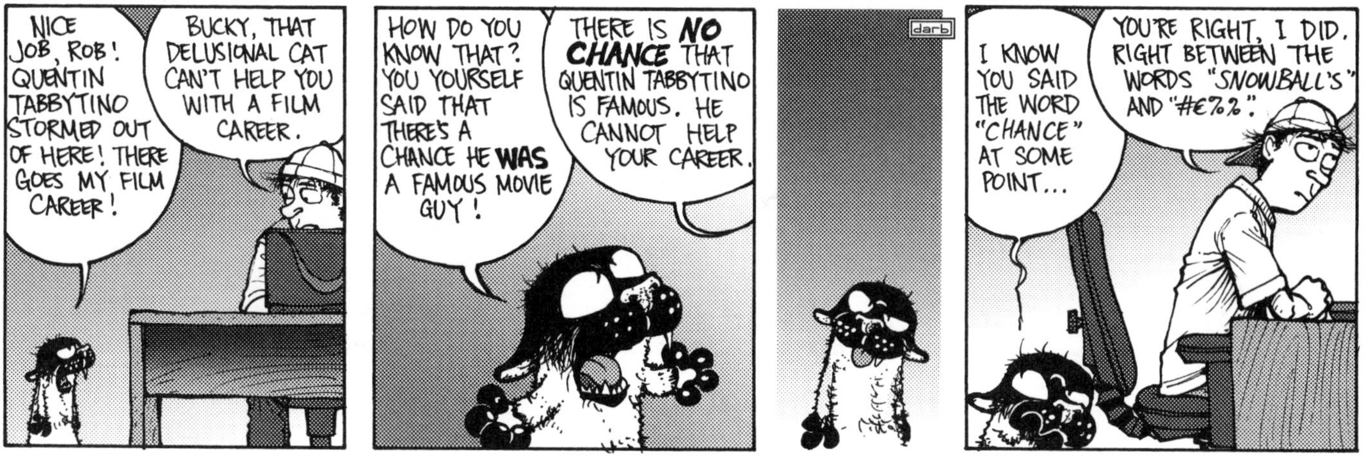
NICE JOB, ROB! QUENTIN TABBYTINO STORMED OUT OF HERE! THERE GOES MY FILM CAREER!
BUCKY, THAT DELUSIONAL CAT CAN'T HELP YOU WITH A FILM CAREER.
HOW DO YOU KNOW THAT? YOU YOURSELF SAID THAT THERE'S A CHANCE HE **WAS** A FAMOUS MOVIE GUY!
THERE IS ***NO CHANCE*** THAT QUENTIN TABBYTINO IS FAMOUS. HE CANNOT HELP YOUR CAREER.
darb
I KNOW YOU SAID THE WORD "*CHANCE*" AT SOME POINT...
YOU'RE RIGHT, I DID. RIGHT BETWEEN THE WORDS "*SNOWBALL'S*" AND "#€%%".

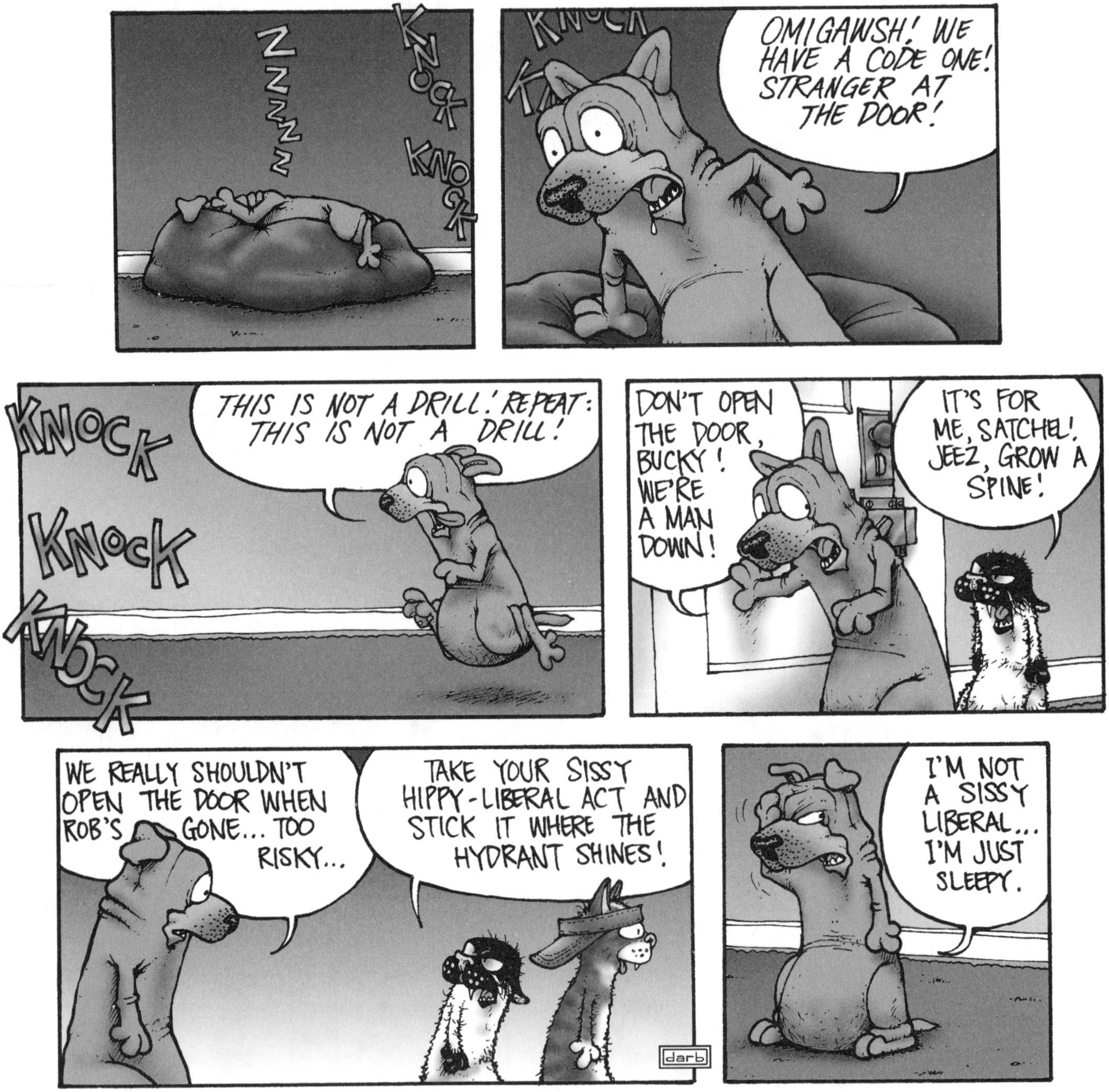
ZZZZZ
KNOCK
KNOCK
OMIGAWSH! WE HAVE A CODE ONE! STRANGER AT THE DOOR!
THIS IS NOT A DRILL! REPEAT: THIS IS NOT A DRILL!
KNOCK
KNOCK
KNOCK
DON'T OPEN THE DOOR, BUCKY! WE'RE A MAN DOWN!
IT'S FOR ME, SATCHEL! JEEZ, GROW A SPINE!
WE REALLY SHOULDN'T OPEN THE DOOR WHEN ROB'S GONE... TOO RISKY...
TAKE YOUR SISSY HIPPY-LIBERAL ACT AND STICK IT WHERE THE HYDRANT SHINES!
darb
I'M NOT A SISSY LIBERAL... I'M JUST SLEEPY.

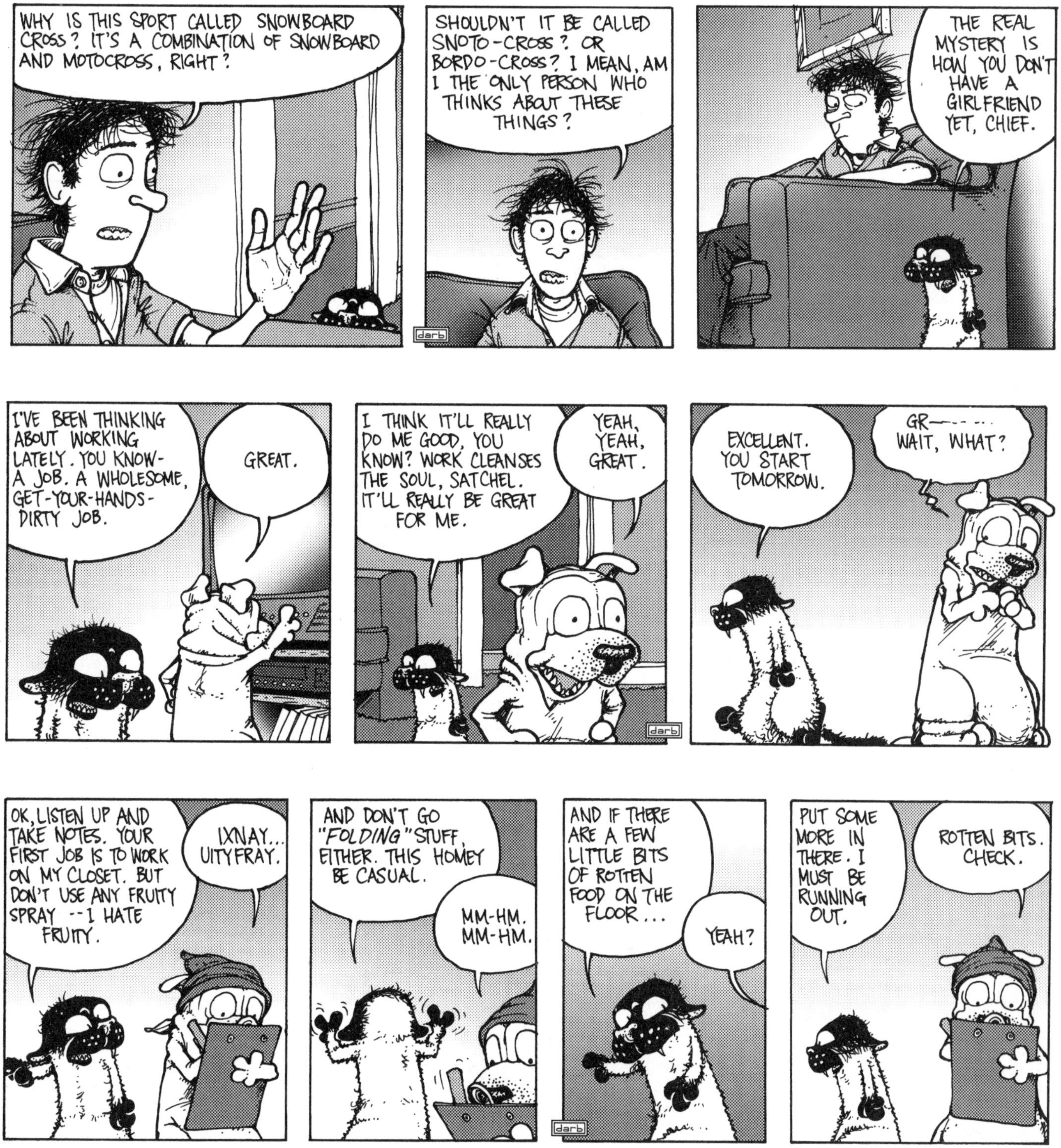
WHY IS THIS SPORT CALLED SNOWBOARD CROSS? IT'S A COMBINATION OF SNOWBOARD AND MOTOCROSS, RIGHT?
SHOULDN'T IT BE CALLED SNOTO-CROSS? OR BORDO-CROSS? I MEAN, AM I THE ONLY PERSON WHO THINKS ABOUT THESE THINGS?
darb
THE REAL MYSTERY IS HOW YOU DON'T HAVE A GIRLFRIEND YET, CHIEF.
I'VE BEEN THINKING ABOUT WORKING LATELY. YOU KNOW- A JOB. A WHOLESOME, GET-YOUR-HANDS-DIRTY JOB.
GREAT.
I THINK IT'LL REALLY DO ME GOOD, YOU KNOW? WORK CLEANSES THE SOUL, SATCHEL. IT'LL REALLY BE GREAT FOR ME.
YEAH, YEAH, GREAT.
darb
EXCELLENT. YOU START TOMORROW.
GR—— - - .. WAIT, WHAT?
OK, LISTEN UP AND TAKE NOTES. YOUR FIRST JOB IS TO WORK ON MY CLOSET. BUT DON'T USE ANY FRUITY SPRAY --I HATE FRUITY.
IXNAY... UITYFRAY.
AND DON'T GO "FOLDING" STUFF, EITHER. THIS HOMEY BE CASUAL.
MM-HM. MM-HM.
AND IF THERE ARE A FEW LITTLE BITS OF ROTTEN FOOD ON THE FLOOR...
YEAH?
darb
PUT SOME MORE IN THERE. I MUST BE RUNNING OUT.
ROTTEN BITS. CHECK.

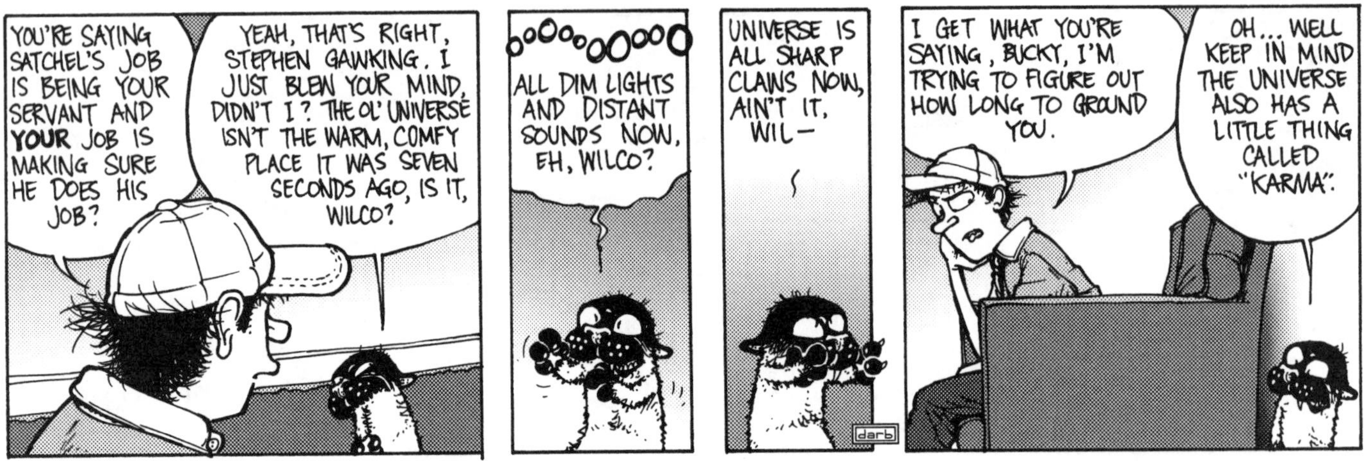
YOU'RE SAYING SATCHEL'S JOB IS BEING YOUR SERVANT AND **YOUR** JOB IS MAKING SURE HE DOES HIS JOB?
YEAH, THAT'S RIGHT, STEPHEN GAWKING. I JUST BLEW YOUR MIND, DIDN'T I? THE OL' UNIVERSE ISN'T THE WARM, COMFY PLACE IT WAS SEVEN SECONDS AGO, IS IT, WILCO?
oOOooOOOoO
ALL DIM LIGHTS AND DISTANT SOUNDS NOW, EH, WILCO?
UNIVERSE IS ALL SHARP CLAWS NOW, AIN'T IT, WIL—
I GET WHAT YOU'RE SAYING, BUCKY, I'M TRYING TO FIGURE OUT HOW LONG TO GROUND YOU.
OH... WELL KEEP IN MIND THE UNIVERSE ALSO HAS A LITTLE THING CALLED "KARMA".
darb

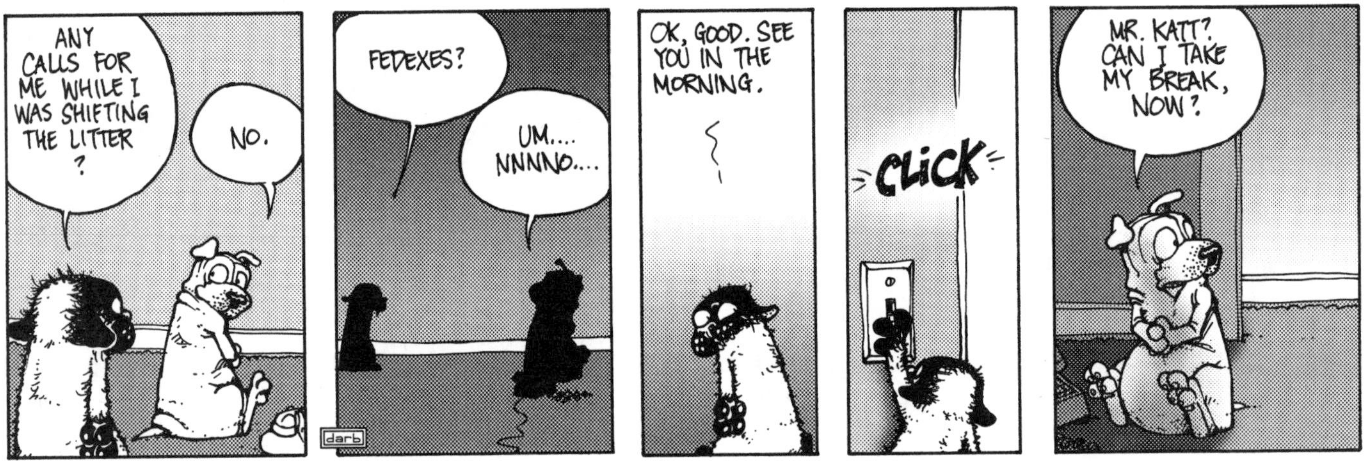
ANY CALLS FOR ME WHILE I WAS SHIFTING THE LITTER?
NO.
darb
FEDEXES?
UM.... NNNNO....
OK, GOOD. SEE YOU IN THE MORNING.
CLICK
MR. KATT? CAN I TAKE MY BREAK, NOW?

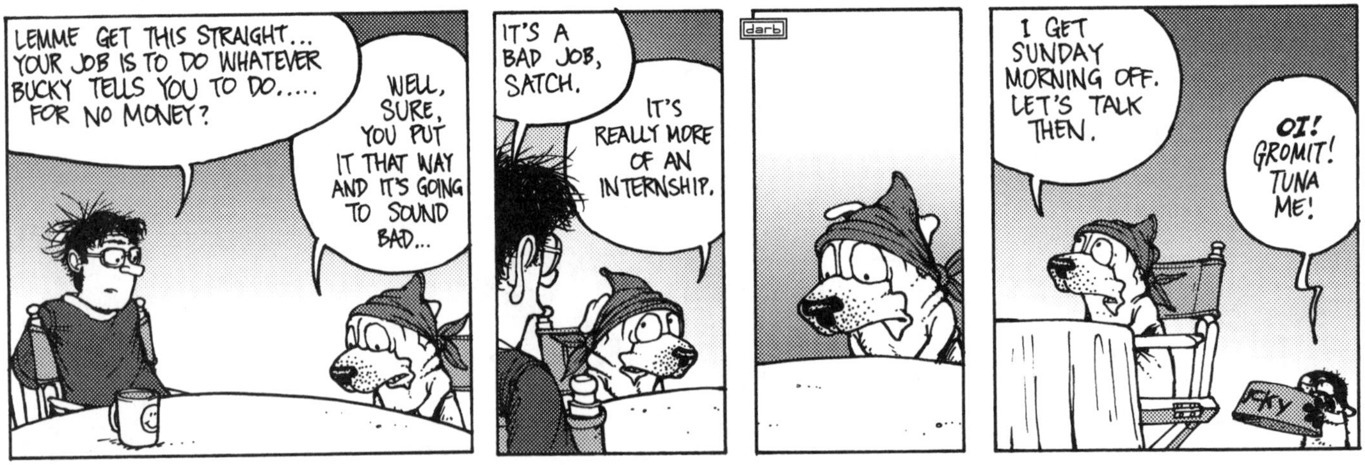
LEMME GET THIS STRAIGHT... YOUR JOB IS TO DO WHATEVER BUCKY TELLS YOU TO DO..... FOR NO MONEY?
WELL, SURE, YOU PUT IT THAT WAY AND IT'S GOING TO SOUND BAD...
IT'S A BAD JOB, SATCH.
IT'S REALLY MORE OF AN INTERNSHIP.
darb
I GET SUNDAY MORNING OFF. LET'S TALK THEN.
OI! GROMIT! TUNA ME!

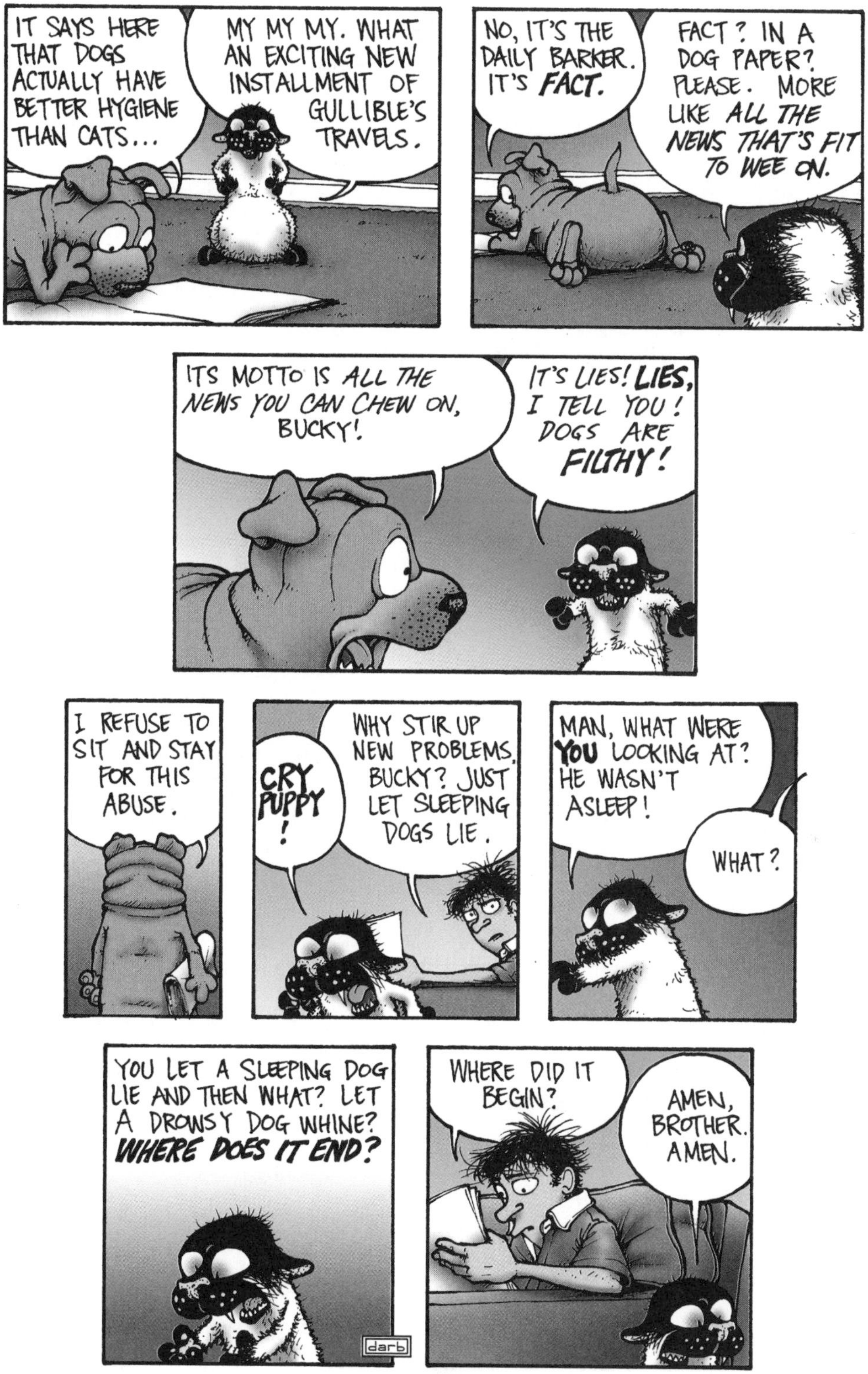
IT SAYS HERE THAT DOGS ACTUALLY HAVE BETTER HYGIENE THAN CATS...
MY MY MY. WHAT AN EXCITING NEW INSTALLMENT OF GULLIBLE'S TRAVELS.
NO, IT'S THE DAILY BARKER. IT'S *FACT*.
FACT? IN A DOG PAPER? PLEASE. MORE LIKE *ALL THE NEWS THAT'S FIT TO WEE ON*.
ITS MOTTO IS *ALL THE NEWS YOU CAN CHEW ON*, BUCKY!
IT'S LIES! **LIES**, I TELL YOU! DOGS ARE ***FILTHY***!
I REFUSE TO SIT AND STAY FOR THIS ABUSE.
CRY PUPPY!
WHY STIR UP NEW PROBLEMS, BUCKY? JUST LET SLEEPING DOGS LIE.
MAN, WHAT WERE **YOU** LOOKING AT? HE WASN'T ASLEEP!
WHAT?
YOU LET A SLEEPING DOG LIE AND THEN WHAT? LET A DROWSY DOG WHINE? ***WHERE DOES IT END?***
darb
WHERE DID IT BEGIN?
AMEN, BROTHER. AMEN.

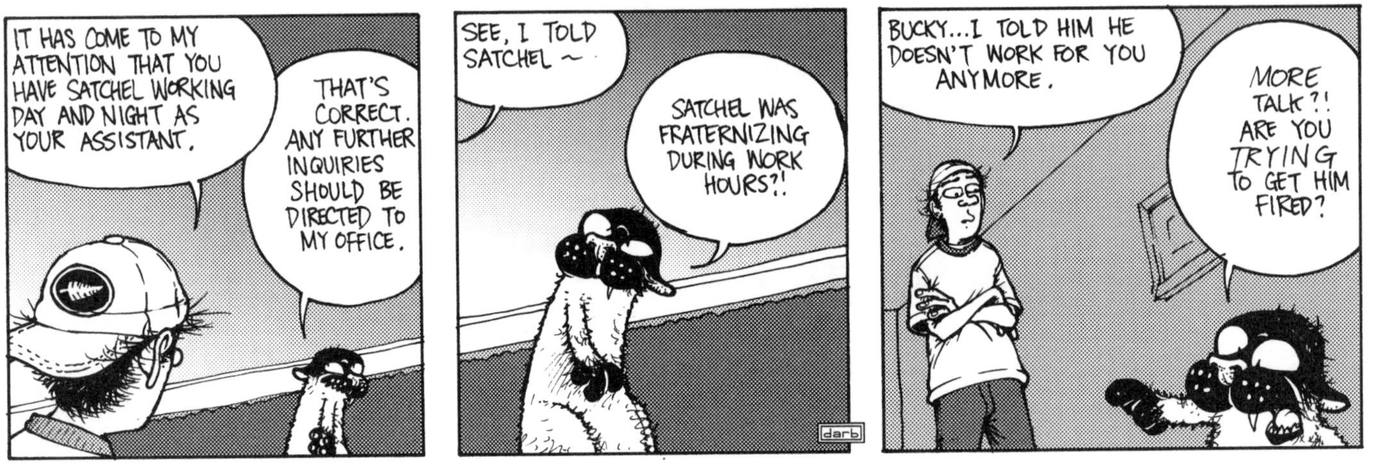
IT HAS COME TO MY ATTENTION THAT YOU HAVE SATCHEL WORKING DAY AND NIGHT AS YOUR ASSISTANT.
THAT'S CORRECT. ANY FURTHER INQUIRIES SHOULD BE DIRECTED TO MY OFFICE.
SEE, I TOLD SATCHEL ~
SATCHEL WAS FRATERNIZING DURING WORK HOURS?!
BUCKY...I TOLD HIM HE DOESN'T WORK FOR YOU ANYMORE.
MORE TALK?! ARE YOU TRYING TO GET HIM FIRED?
darb

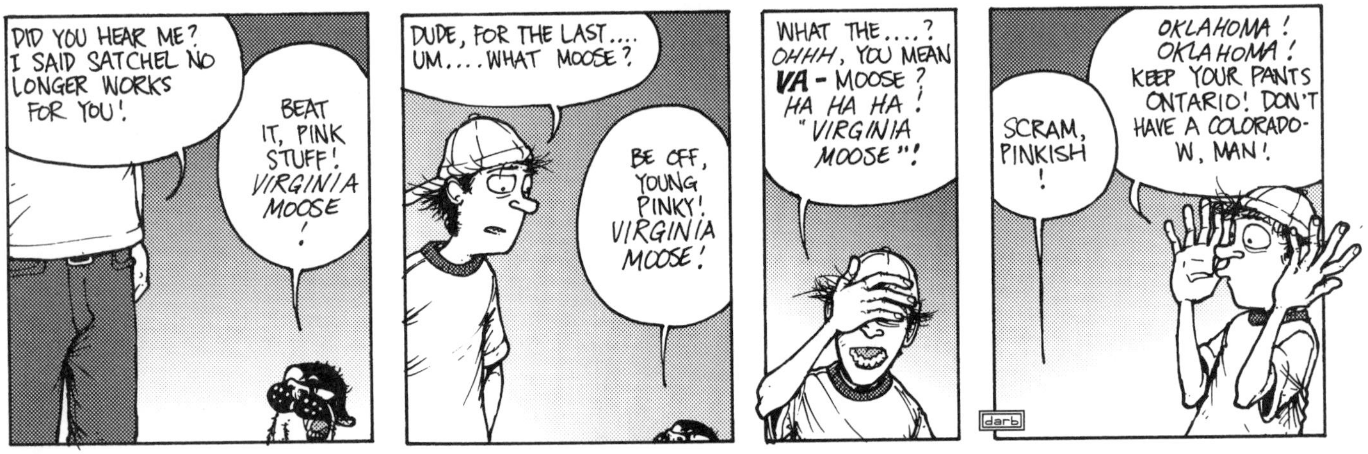
DID YOU HEAR ME? I SAID SATCHEL NO LONGER WORKS FOR YOU!
BEAT IT, PINK STUFF! VIRGINIA MOOSE!
DUDE, FOR THE LAST.... UM....WHAT MOOSE?
BE OFF, YOUNG PINKY! VIRGINIA MOOSE!
WHAT THE....? OHHH, YOU MEAN VA-MOOSE? HA HA HA! "VIRGINIA MOOSE"!
SCRAM, PINKISH!
OKLAHOMA! OKLAHOMA! KEEP YOUR PANTS ONTARIO! DON'T HAVE A COLORADO-W, MAN!
darb

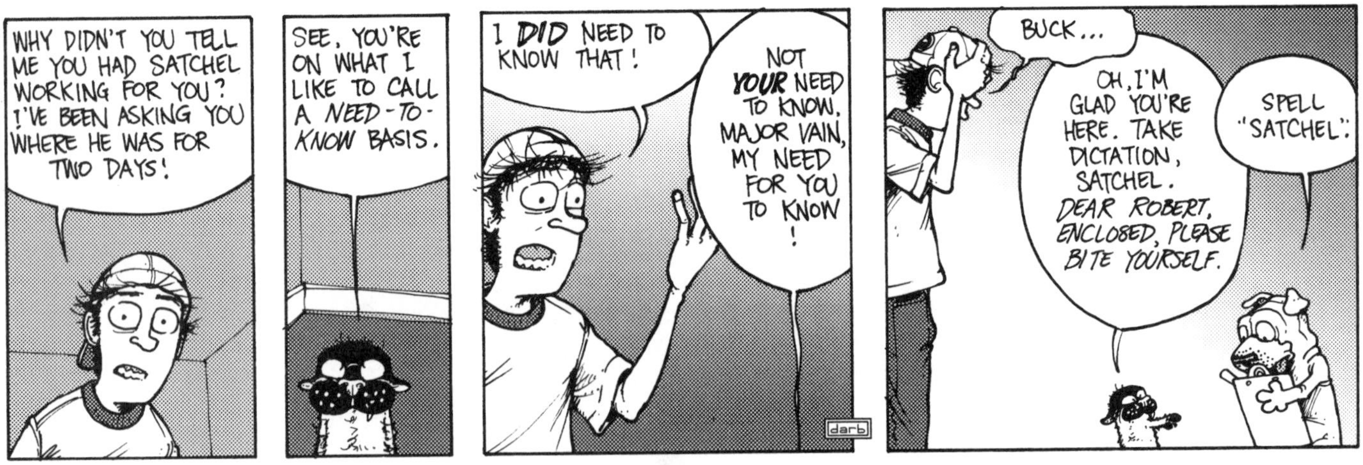
WHY DIDN'T YOU TELL ME YOU HAD SATCHEL WORKING FOR YOU? I'VE BEEN ASKING YOU WHERE HE WAS FOR TWO DAYS!
SEE, YOU'RE ON WHAT I LIKE TO CALL A NEED-TO-KNOW BASIS.
I DID NEED TO KNOW THAT!
NOT YOUR NEED TO KNOW, MAJOR VAIN, MY NEED FOR YOU TO KNOW!
darb
BUCK...
OH, I'M GLAD YOU'RE HERE. TAKE DICTATION, SATCHEL. DEAR ROBERT, ENCLOSED, PLEASE BITE YOURSELF.
SPELL "SATCHEL".

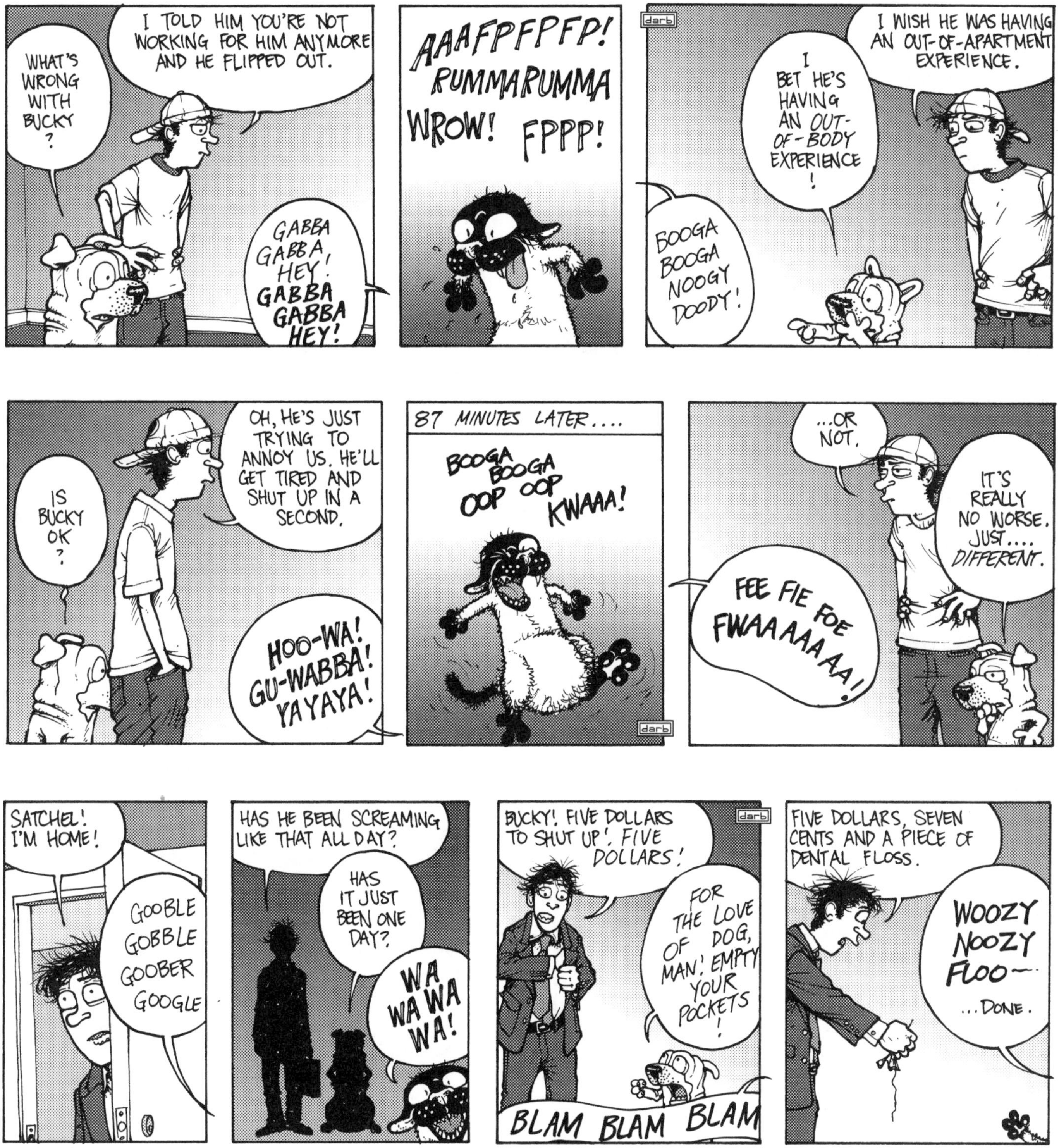
WHAT'S WRONG WITH BUCKY?
I TOLD HIM YOU'RE NOT WORKING FOR HIM ANYMORE AND HE FLIPPED OUT.
GABBA GABBA, HEY! GABBA GABBA HEY!
AAAFPFPFP! RUMMARUMMA WROW! FPPP!
I BET HE'S HAVING AN OUT-OF-BODY EXPERIENCE!
I WISH HE WAS HAVING AN OUT-OF-APARTMENT EXPERIENCE.
BOOGA BOOGA NOOGY DOODY!
IS BUCKY OK?
OH, HE'S JUST TRYING TO ANNOY US. HE'LL GET TIRED AND SHUT UP IN A SECOND.
HOO-WA! GU-WABBA! YAYAYA!
87 MINUTES LATER....
BOOGA BOOGA OOP OOP KWAAA!
...OR NOT.
IT'S REALLY NO WORSE. JUST.... DIFFERENT.
FEE FIE FOE FWAAAAAAAA!
SATCHEL! I'M HOME!
GOOBLE GOBBLE GOOBER GOOGLE
HAS HE BEEN SCREAMING LIKE THAT ALL DAY?
HAS IT JUST BEEN ONE DAY?
WA WA WA WA!
BUCKY! FIVE DOLLARS TO SHUT UP! FIVE DOLLARS!
FOR THE LOVE OF DOG, MAN! EMPTY YOUR POCKETS!
BLAM BLAM BLAM
FIVE DOLLARS, SEVEN CENTS AND A PIECE OF DENTAL FLOSS.
WOOZY NOOZY FLOO~
...DONE.

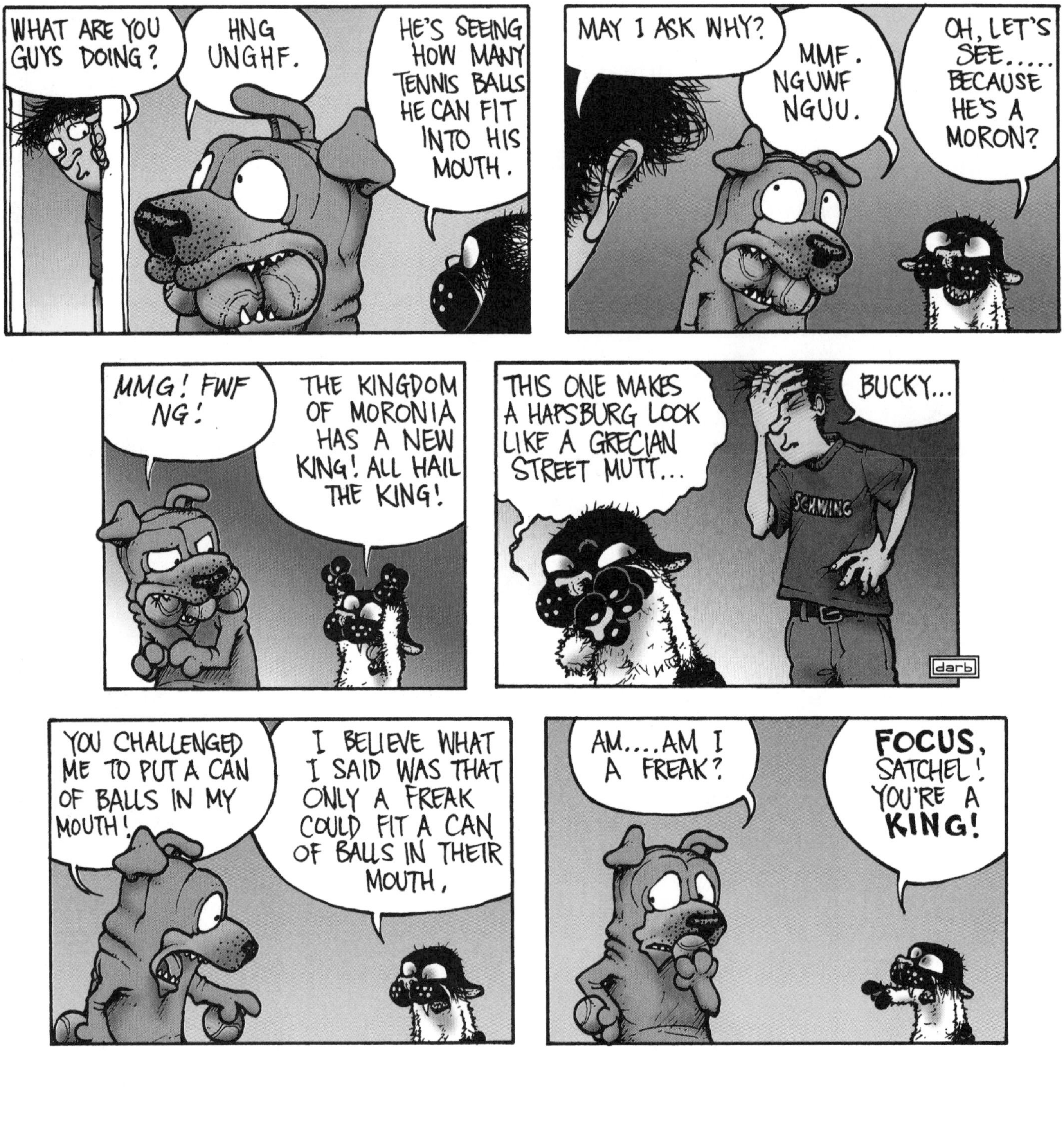
WHAT ARE YOU GUYS DOING?
HNG UNGHF.
HE'S SEEING HOW MANY TENNIS BALLS HE CAN FIT INTO HIS MOUTH.
MAY I ASK WHY?
MMF. NGUWF NGUU.
OH, LET'S SEE..... BECAUSE HE'S A MORON?
MMG! FWF NG!
THE KINGDOM OF MORONIA HAS A NEW KING! ALL HAIL THE KING!
THIS ONE MAKES A HAPSBURG LOOK LIKE A GRECIAN STREET MUTT...
BUCKY...
SCHWING
darb
YOU CHALLENGED ME TO PUT A CAN OF BALLS IN MY MOUTH!
I BELIEVE WHAT I SAID WAS THAT ONLY A FREAK COULD FIT A CAN OF BALLS IN THEIR MOUTH.
AM....AM I A FREAK?
FOCUS, SATCHEL! YOU'RE A **KING**!

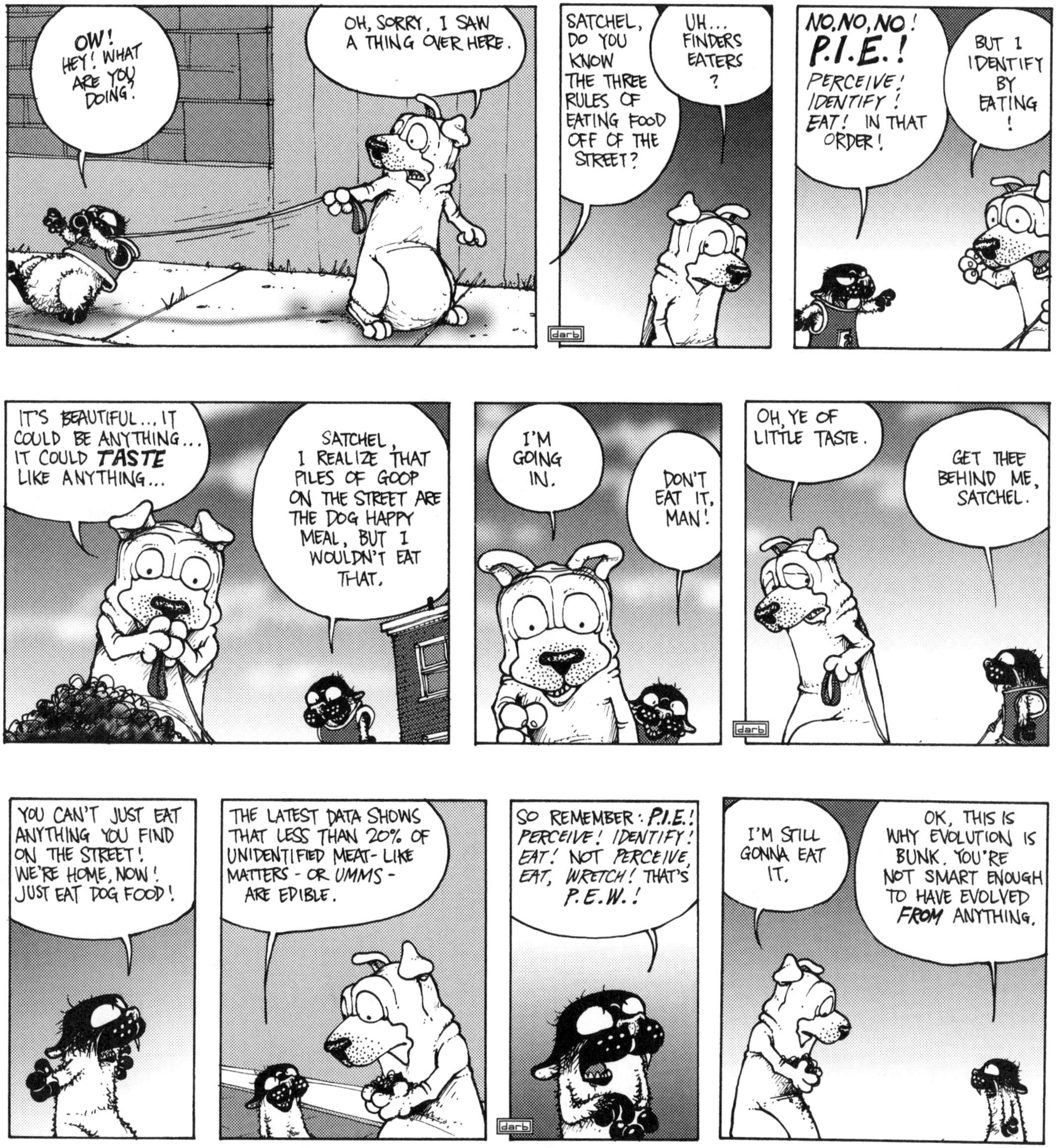
OW! HEY! WHAT ARE YOU DOING?
OH, SORRY. I SAW A THING OVER HERE.
SATCHEL, DO YOU KNOW THE THREE RULES OF EATING FOOD OFF OF THE STREET?
UH... FINDERS EATERS ?
NO, NO, NO! P.I.E.! PERCEIVE! IDENTIFY! EAT! IN THAT ORDER!
BUT I IDENTIFY BY EATING !
IT'S BEAUTIFUL... IT COULD BE ANYTHING... IT COULD TASTE LIKE ANYTHING...
SATCHEL, I REALIZE THAT PILES OF GOOP ON THE STREET ARE THE DOG HAPPY MEAL, BUT I WOULDN'T EAT THAT.
I'M GOING IN.
DON'T EAT IT, MAN!
OH, YE OF LITTLE TASTE.
GET THEE BEHIND ME, SATCHEL.
YOU CAN'T JUST EAT ANYTHING YOU FIND ON THE STREET! WE'RE HOME, NOW! JUST EAT DOG FOOD!
THE LATEST DATA SHOWS THAT LESS THAN 20% OF UNIDENTIFIED MEAT-LIKE MATTERS - OR UMMS - ARE EDIBLE.
SO REMEMBER: P.I.E.! PERCEIVE! IDENTIFY! EAT! NOT PERCEIVE, EAT, WRETCH! THAT'S P.E.W.!
I'M STILL GONNA EAT IT.
OK, THIS IS WHY EVOLUTION IS BUNK. YOU'RE NOT SMART ENOUGH TO HAVE EVOLVED FROM ANYTHING.

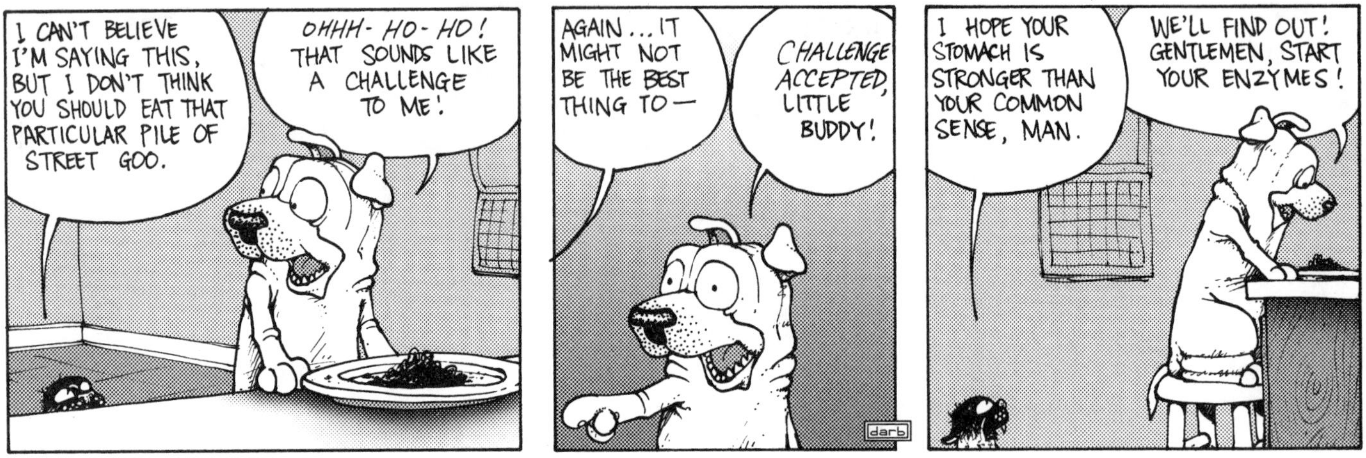
I CAN'T BELIEVE I'M SAYING THIS, BUT I DON'T THINK YOU SHOULD EAT THAT PARTICULAR PILE OF STREET GOO.
OHHH-HO-HO! THAT SOUNDS LIKE A CHALLENGE TO ME!
AGAIN... IT MIGHT NOT BE THE BEST THING TO—
CHALLENGE ACCEPTED, LITTLE BUDDY!
I HOPE YOUR STOMACH IS STRONGER THAN YOUR COMMON SENSE, MAN.
WE'LL FIND OUT! GENTLEMEN, START YOUR ENZYMES!
darb

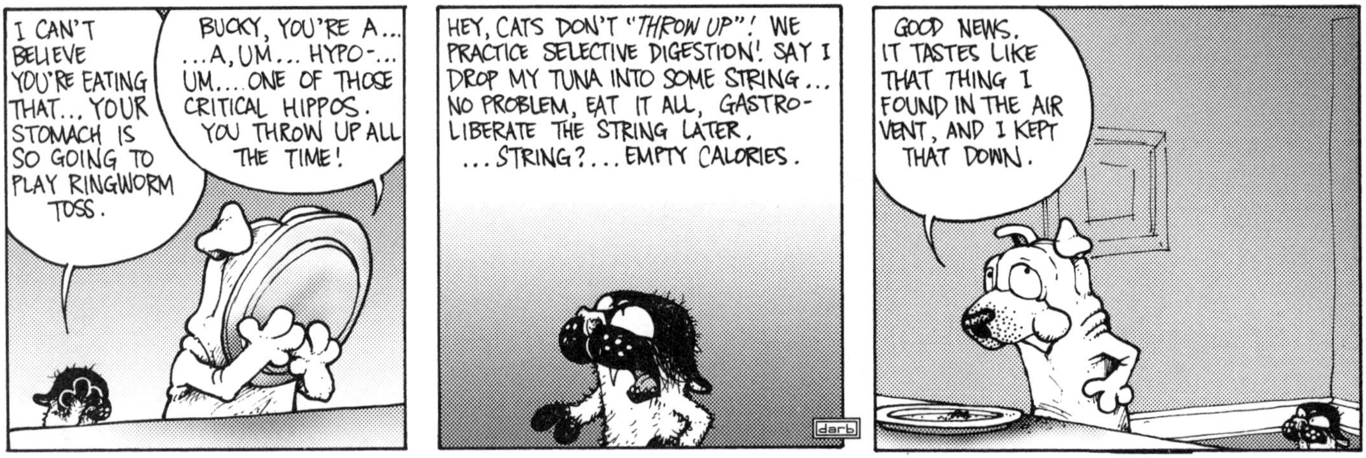
I CAN'T BELIEVE YOU'RE EATING THAT... YOUR STOMACH IS SO GOING TO PLAY RINGWORM TOSS.
BUCKY, YOU'RE A... ...A, UM... HYPO-... UM.... ONE OF THOSE CRITICAL HIPPOS. YOU THROW UP ALL THE TIME!
HEY, CATS DON'T "THROW UP"! WE PRACTICE SELECTIVE DIGESTION! SAY I DROP MY TUNA INTO SOME STRING... NO PROBLEM, EAT IT ALL, GASTRO-LIBERATE THE STRING LATER. ...STRING?... EMPTY CALORIES.
GOOD NEWS. IT TASTES LIKE THAT THING I FOUND IN THE AIR VENT, AND I KEPT THAT DOWN.
darb

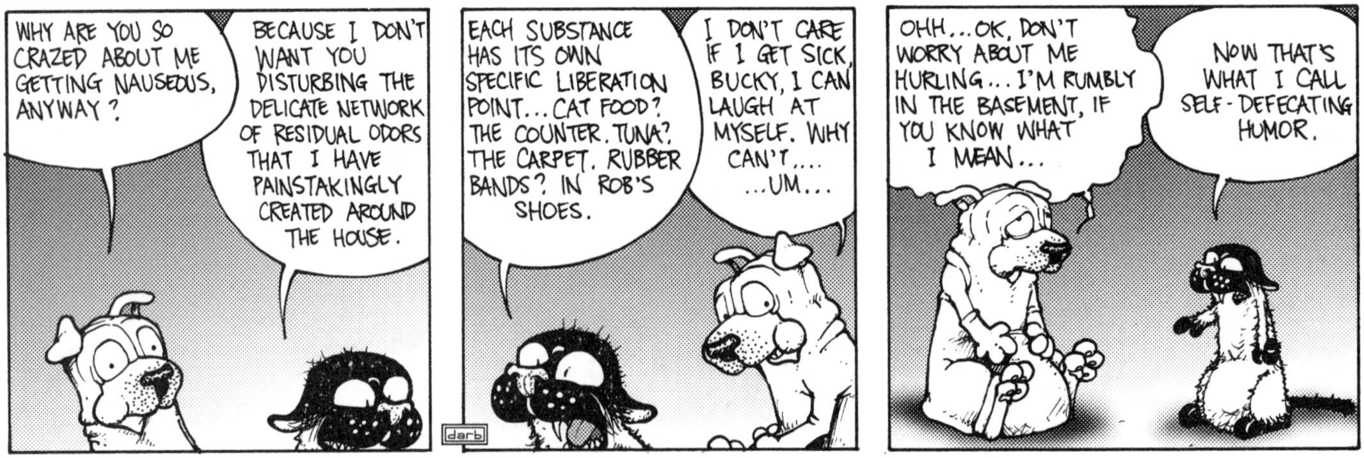
WHY ARE YOU SO CRAZED ABOUT ME GETTING NAUSEOUS, ANYWAY?
BECAUSE I DON'T WANT YOU DISTURBING THE DELICATE NETWORK OF RESIDUAL ODORS THAT I HAVE PAINSTAKINGLY CREATED AROUND THE HOUSE.
EACH SUBSTANCE HAS ITS OWN SPECIFIC LIBERATION POINT... CAT FOOD? THE COUNTER. TUNA? THE CARPET. RUBBER BANDS? IN ROB'S SHOES.
I DON'T CARE IF I GET SICK, BUCKY, I CAN LAUGH AT MYSELF. WHY CAN'T.... ...UM...
OHH...OK, DON'T WORRY ABOUT ME HURLING... I'M RUMBLY IN THE BASEMENT, IF YOU KNOW WHAT I MEAN...
NOW THAT'S WHAT I CALL SELF-DEFECATING HUMOR.
darb

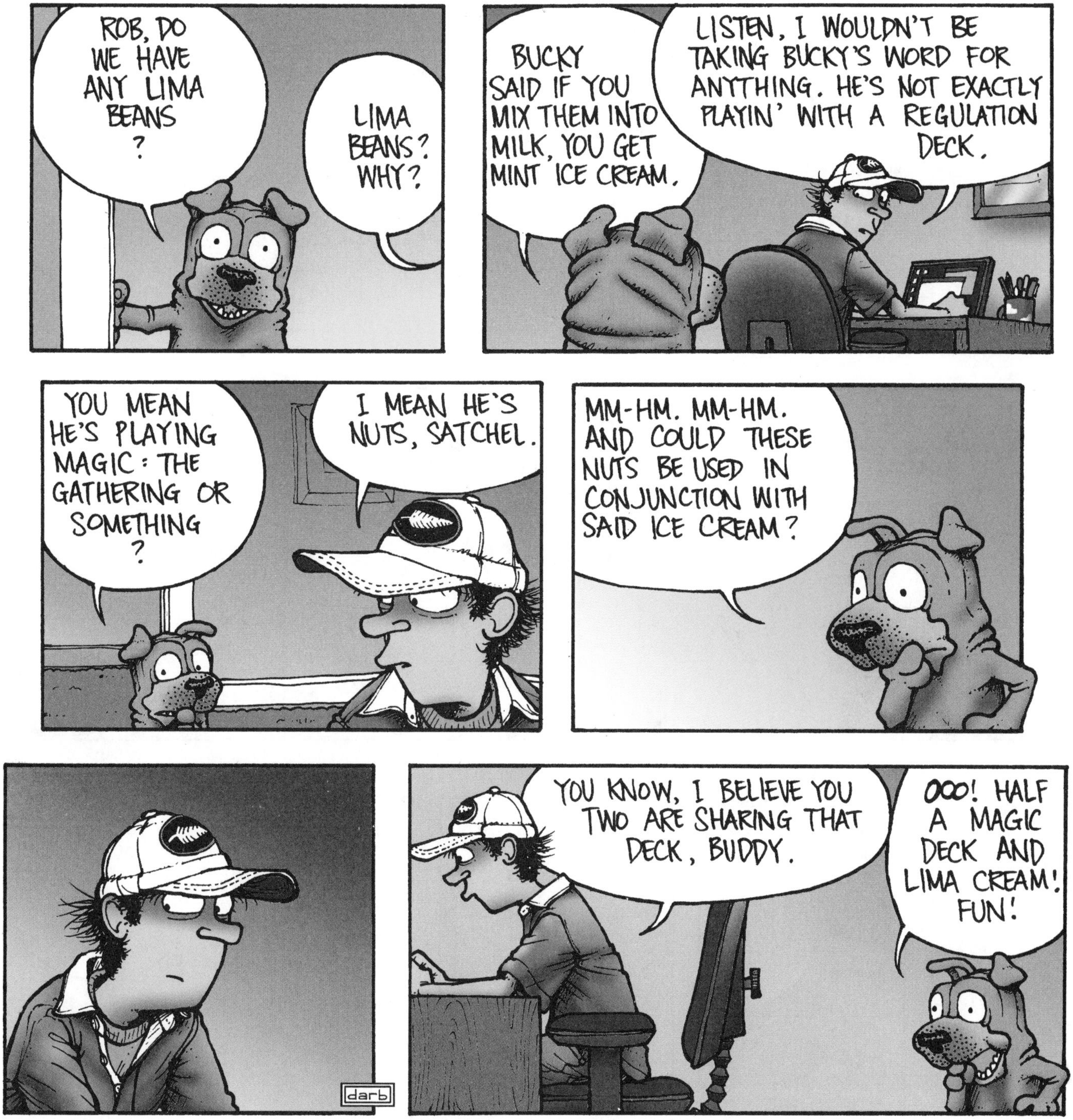
ROB, DO WE HAVE ANY LIMA BEANS ?
LIMA BEANS? WHY?
BUCKY SAID IF YOU MIX THEM INTO MILK, YOU GET MINT ICE CREAM.
LISTEN, I WOULDN'T BE TAKING BUCKY'S WORD FOR ANYTHING. HE'S NOT EXACTLY PLAYIN' WITH A REGULATION DECK.
YOU MEAN HE'S PLAYING MAGIC: THE GATHERING OR SOMETHING ?
I MEAN HE'S NUTS, SATCHEL.
MM-HM. MM-HM. AND COULD THESE NUTS BE USED IN CONJUNCTION WITH SAID ICE CREAM?
darb
YOU KNOW, I BELIEVE YOU TWO ARE SHARING THAT DECK, BUDDY.
OOO! HALF A MAGIC DECK AND LIMA CREAM! FUN!

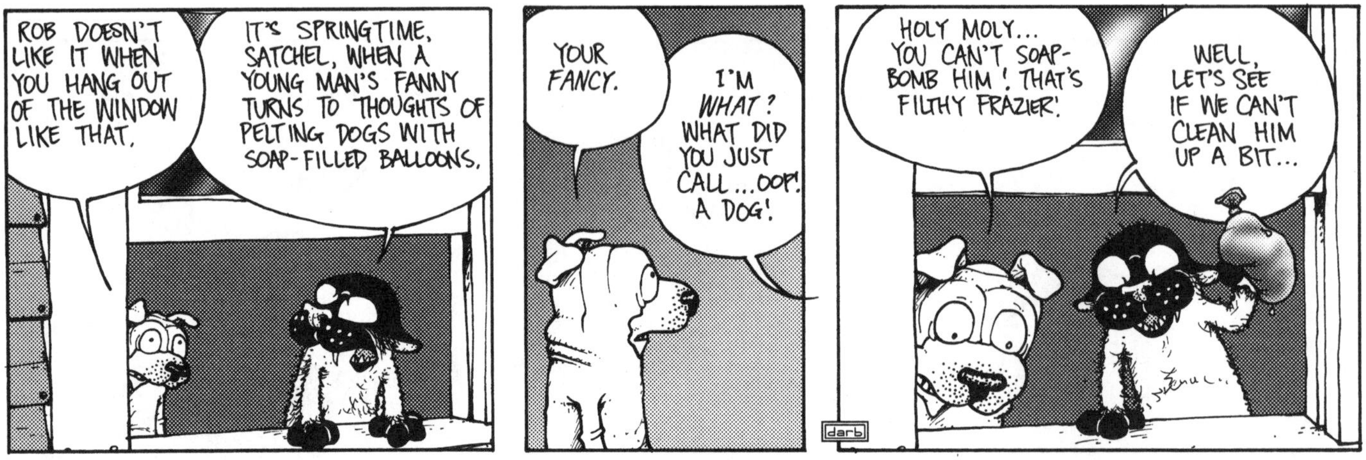
ROB DOESN'T LIKE IT WHEN YOU HANG OUT OF THE WINDOW LIKE THAT.
IT'S SPRINGTIME, SATCHEL, WHEN A YOUNG MAN'S FANNY TURNS TO THOUGHTS OF PELTING DOGS WITH SOAP-FILLED BALLOONS.
YOUR *FANCY.*
I'M *WHAT?* WHAT DID YOU JUST CALL...OOP! A DOG!
HOLY MOLY... YOU CAN'T SOAP-BOMB HIM! THAT'S FILTHY FRAZIER!
WELL, LET'S SEE IF WE CAN'T CLEAN HIM UP A BIT...

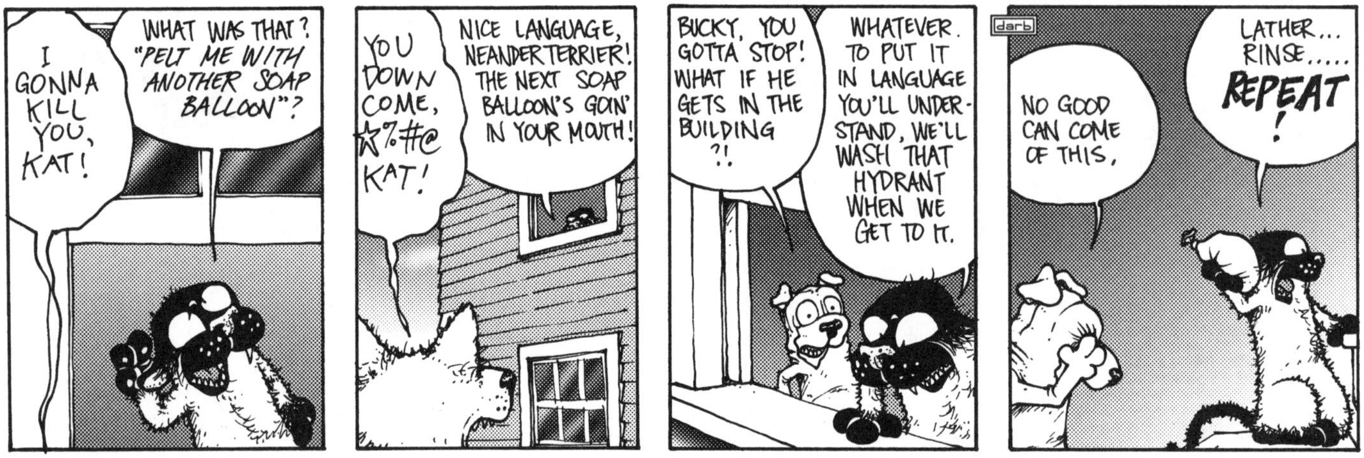
I GONNA KILL YOU, KAT!
WHAT WAS THAT? *"PELT ME WITH ANOTHER SOAP BALLOON"?*
YOU DOWN COME, ☆%#@ KAT!
NICE LANGUAGE, NEANDERTERRIER! THE NEXT SOAP BALLOON'S GOIN' IN YOUR MOUTH!
BUCKY, YOU GOTTA STOP! WHAT IF HE GETS IN THE BUILDING ?!
WHATEVER. TO PUT IT IN LANGUAGE YOU'LL UNDERSTAND, WE'LL WASH THAT HYDRANT WHEN WE GET TO IT.
NO GOOD CAN COME OF THIS.
LATHER... RINSE..... **REPEAT** !

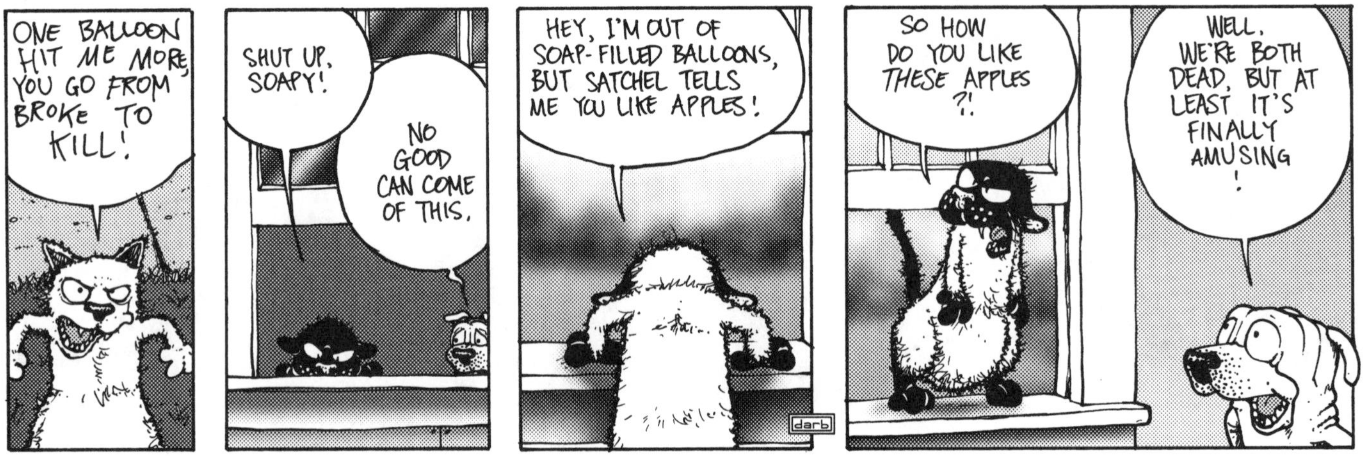
ONE BALLOON HIT *ME* MORE, YOU GO *FROM* BROKE TO KILL!
SHUT UP, SOAPY!
NO GOOD CAN COME OF THIS.
HEY, I'M OUT OF SOAP-FILLED BALLOONS, BUT SATCHEL TELLS ME YOU LIKE APPLES!
SO HOW DO YOU LIKE *THESE* APPLES ?!
WELL, WE'RE BOTH DEAD, BUT AT LEAST IT'S FINALLY AMUSING !

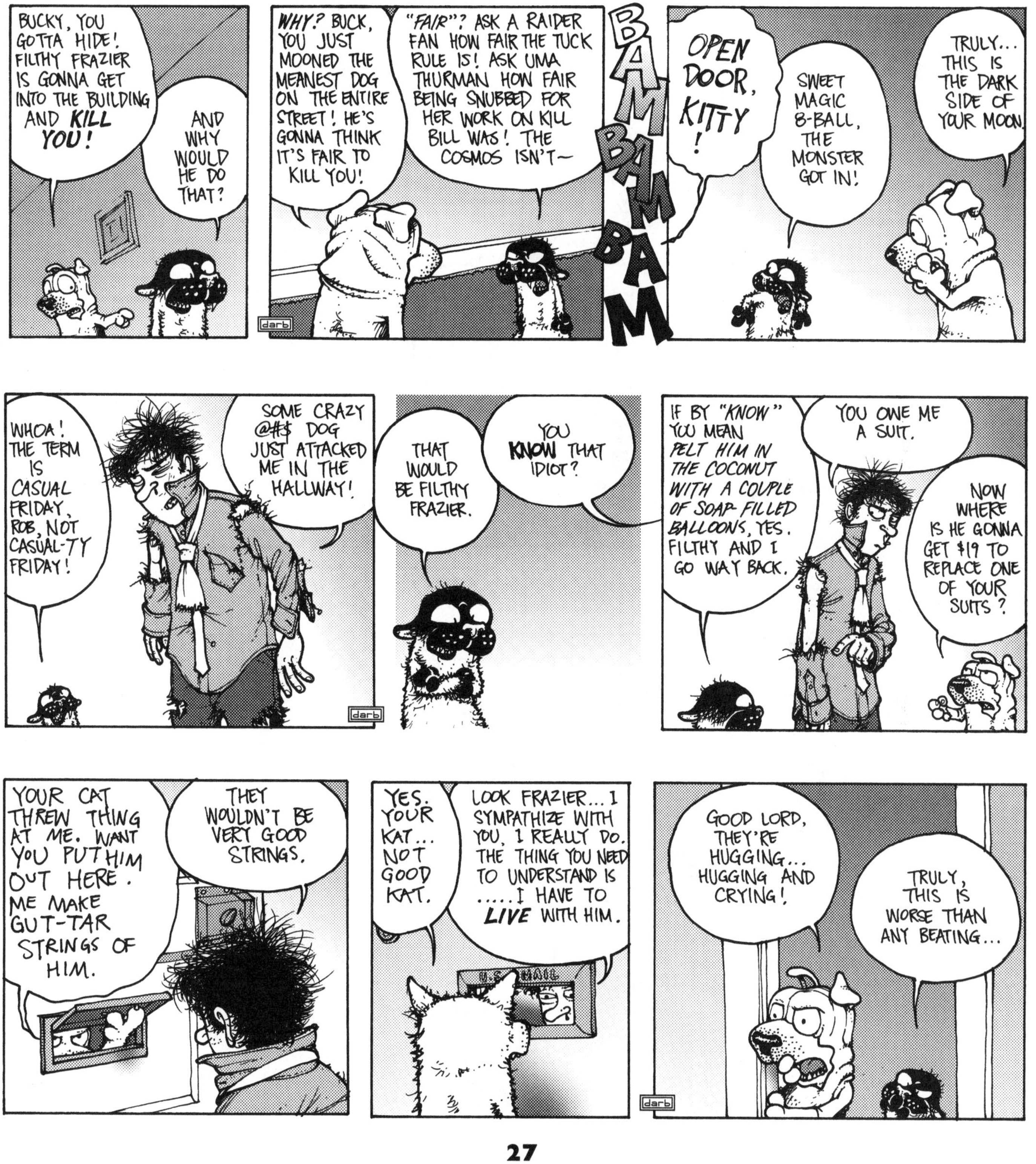
BUCKY, YOU GOTTA HIDE! FILTHY FRAZIER IS GONNA GET INTO THE BUILDING AND **KILL YOU!**
AND WHY WOULD HE DO THAT?
darb
WHY? BUCK, YOU JUST MOONED THE MEANEST DOG ON THE ENTIRE STREET! HE'S GONNA THINK IT'S FAIR TO KILL YOU!
"*FAIR*"? ASK A RAIDER FAN HOW FAIR THE TUCK RULE IS! ASK UMA THURMAN HOW FAIR BEING SNUBBED FOR HER WORK ON KILL BILL WAS! THE COSMOS ISN'T~
BAM BAM BAM BAM
OPEN DOOR, KITTY!
SWEET MAGIC 8-BALL, THE MONSTER GOT IN!
TRULY... THIS IS THE DARK SIDE OF YOUR MOON.
WHOA! THE TERM IS CASUAL FRIDAY, ROB, NOT CASUAL-TY FRIDAY!
SOME CRAZY @#$ DOG JUST ATTACKED ME IN THE HALLWAY!
darb
THAT WOULD BE FILTHY FRAZIER.
YOU **KNOW** THAT IDIOT?
IF BY "*KNOW*" YOU MEAN *PELT HIM IN THE COCONUT WITH A COUPLE OF SOAP-FILLED BALLOONS*, YES. FILTHY AND I GO WAY BACK.
YOU OWE ME A SUIT.
NOW WHERE IS HE GONNA GET $19 TO REPLACE ONE OF YOUR SUITS?
YOUR CAT THREW THING AT ME. WANT YOU PUT HIM OUT HERE. ME MAKE GUT-TAR STRINGS OF HIM.
THEY WOULDN'T BE VERY GOOD STRINGS.
YES. YOUR KAT... NOT GOOD KAT.
LOOK FRAZIER... I SYMPATHIZE WITH YOU, I REALLY DO. THE THING YOU NEED TO UNDERSTAND IS .....I HAVE TO **LIVE** WITH HIM.
U.S. MAIL
darb
GOOD LORD, THEY'RE HUGGING... HUGGING AND CRYING!
TRULY, THIS IS WORSE THAN ANY BEATING...

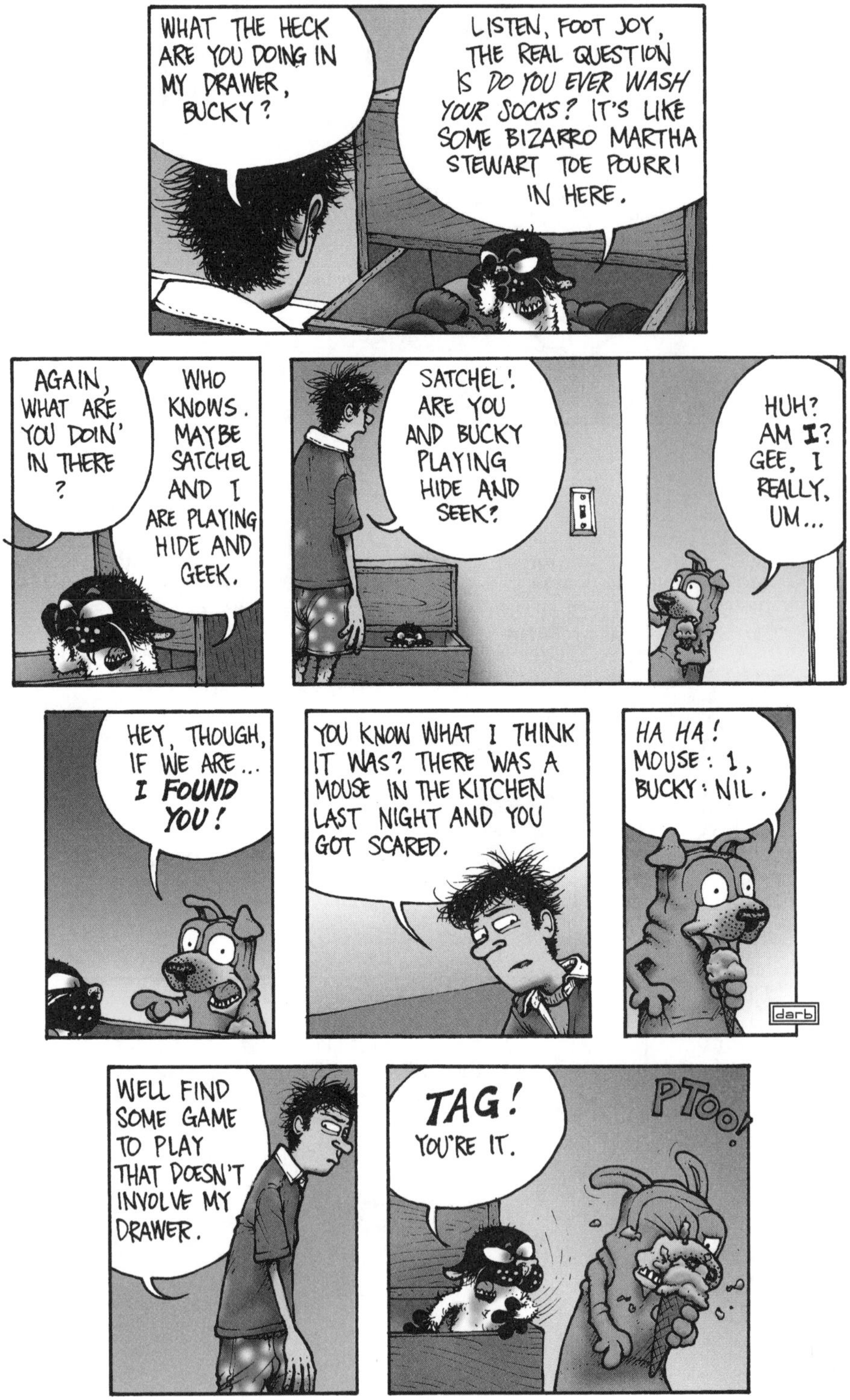
WHAT THE HECK ARE YOU DOING IN MY DRAWER, BUCKY?
LISTEN, FOOT JOY, THE REAL QUESTION IS *DO YOU EVER WASH YOUR SOCKS?* IT'S LIKE SOME BIZARRO MARTHA STEWART TOE POURRI IN HERE.
AGAIN, WHAT ARE YOU DOIN' IN THERE ?
WHO KNOWS. MAYBE SATCHEL AND I ARE PLAYING HIDE AND GEEK.
SATCHEL! ARE YOU AND BUCKY PLAYING HIDE AND SEEK?
HUH? AM **I**? GEE, I REALLY, UM...
HEY, THOUGH, IF WE ARE... ***I FOUND YOU!***
YOU KNOW WHAT I THINK IT WAS? THERE WAS A MOUSE IN THE KITCHEN LAST NIGHT AND YOU GOT SCARED.
HA HA! MOUSE: 1, BUCKY: NIL.
darb
WELL FIND SOME GAME TO PLAY THAT DOESN'T INVOLVE MY DRAWER.
TAG! YOU'RE IT.
PTOO!

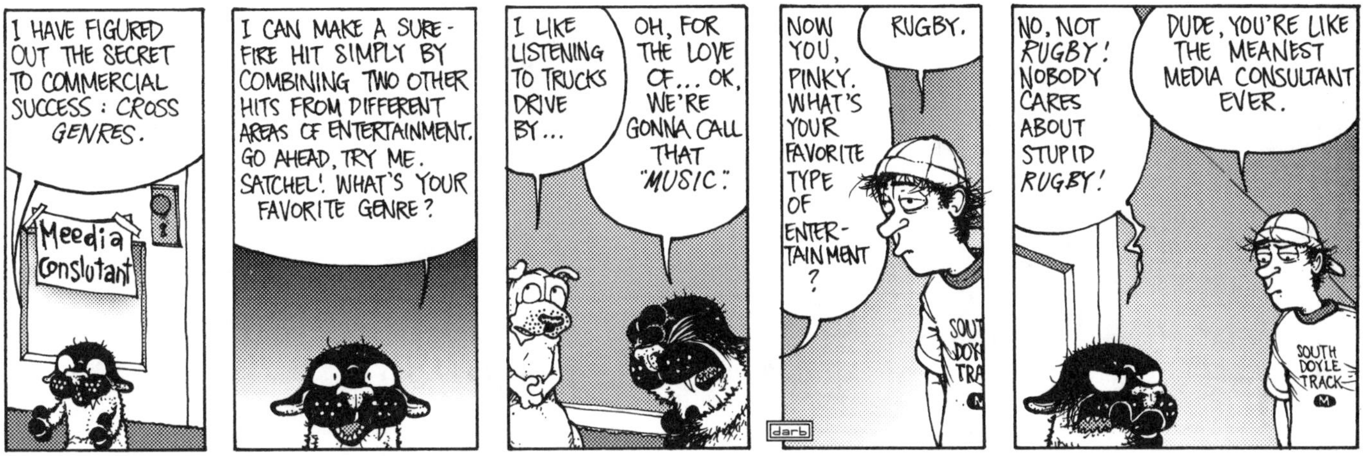
I HAVE FIGURED OUT THE SECRET TO COMMERCIAL SUCCESS: CROSS GENRES.
Meedia Conslutant
I CAN MAKE A SURE-FIRE HIT SIMPLY BY COMBINING TWO OTHER HITS FROM DIFFERENT AREAS OF ENTERTAINMENT. GO AHEAD, TRY ME. SATCHEL! WHAT'S YOUR FAVORITE GENRE?
I LIKE LISTENING TO TRUCKS DRIVE BY...
OH, FOR THE LOVE OF... OK, WE'RE GONNA CALL THAT "MUSIC."
NOW YOU, PINKY. WHAT'S YOUR FAVORITE TYPE OF ENTERTAINMENT?
RUGBY.
NO, NOT RUGBY! NOBODY CARES ABOUT STUPID RUGBY!
DUDE, YOU'RE LIKE THE MEANEST MEDIA CONSULTANT EVER.

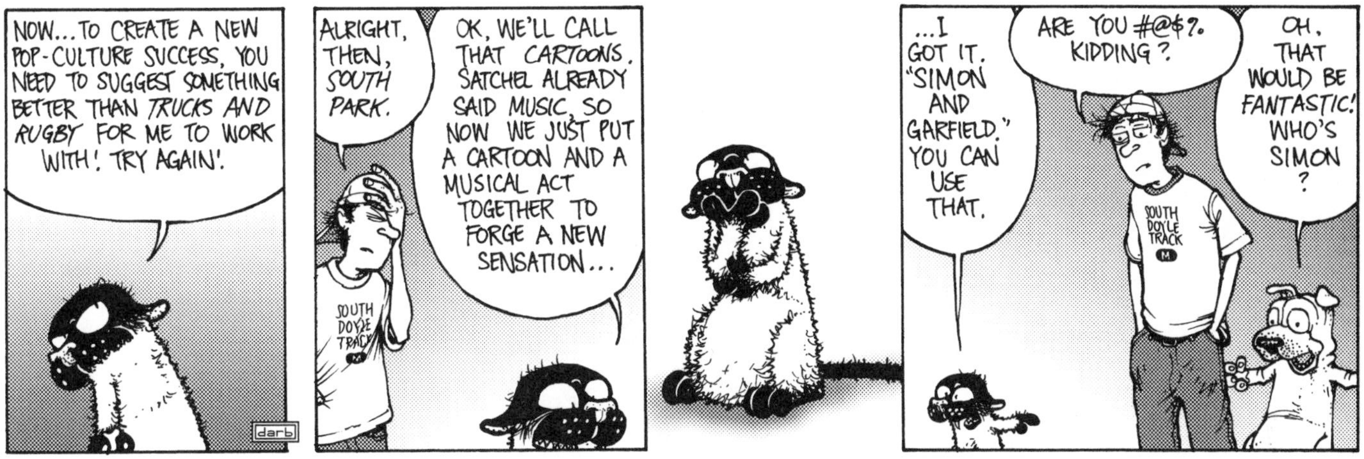
NOW... TO CREATE A NEW POP-CULTURE SUCCESS, YOU NEED TO SUGGEST SOMETHING BETTER THAN TRUCKS AND RUGBY FOR ME TO WORK WITH! TRY AGAIN!
ALRIGHT, THEN, SOUTH PARK.
OK, WE'LL CALL THAT CARTOONS. SATCHEL ALREADY SAID MUSIC, SO NOW WE JUST PUT A CARTOON AND A MUSICAL ACT TOGETHER TO FORGE A NEW SENSATION...
...I GOT IT. "SIMON AND GARFIELD." YOU CAN USE THAT.
ARE YOU #@$%. KIDDING?
OH. THAT WOULD BE FANTASTIC! WHO'S SIMON?

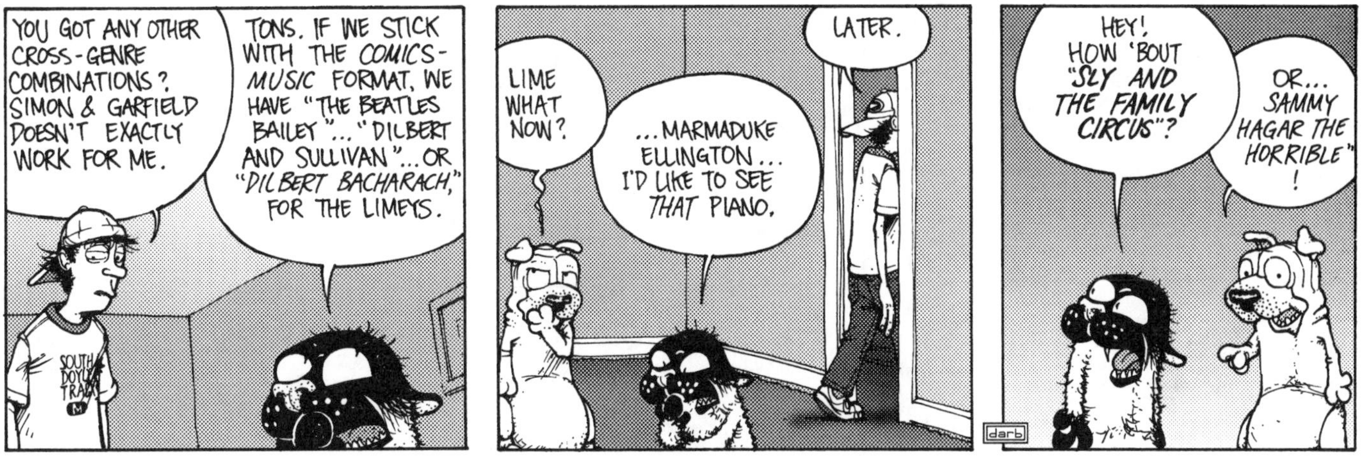
YOU GOT ANY OTHER CROSS-GENRE COMBINATIONS? SIMON & GARFIELD DOESN'T EXACTLY WORK FOR ME.
TONS. IF WE STICK WITH THE COMICS-MUSIC FORMAT, WE HAVE "THE BEATLES BAILEY"... "DILBERT AND SULLIVAN"... OR "DILBERT BACHARACH," FOR THE LIMEYS.
LIME WHAT NOW?
...MARMADUKE ELLINGTON... I'D LIKE TO SEE THAT PIANO.
LATER.
HEY! HOW 'BOUT "SLY AND THE FAMILY CIRCUS"?
OR... "SAMMY HAGAR THE HORRIBLE"!

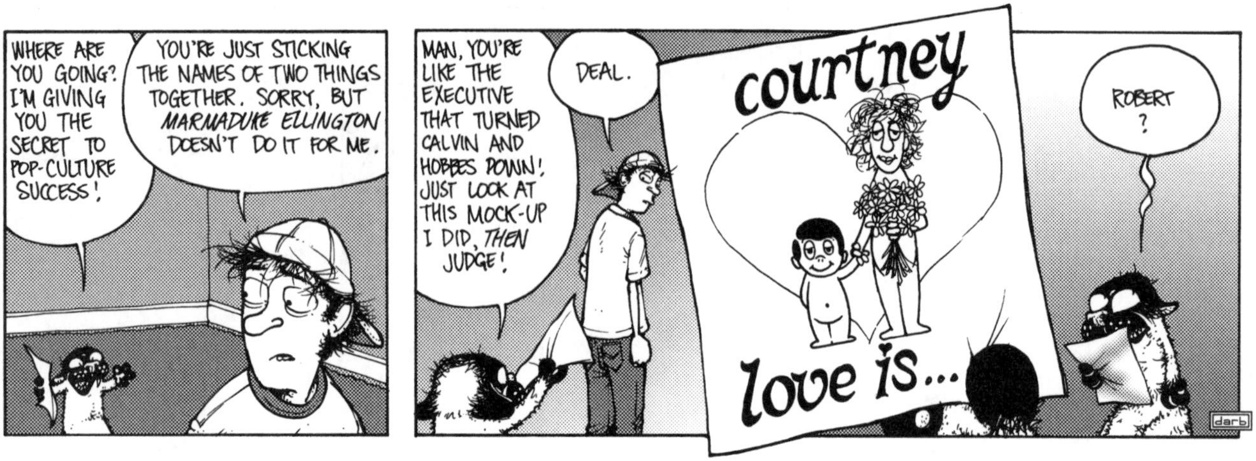
WHERE ARE YOU GOING? I'M GIVING YOU THE SECRET TO POP-CULTURE SUCCESS!
YOU'RE JUST STICKING THE NAMES OF TWO THINGS TOGETHER. SORRY, BUT *MARMADUKE ELLINGTON* DOESN'T DO IT FOR ME.
MAN, YOU'RE LIKE THE EXECUTIVE THAT TURNED CALVIN AND HOBBES DOWN! JUST LOOK AT THIS MOCK-UP I DID, *THEN* JUDGE!
DEAL.
courtney
love is...
ROBERT ?
darb

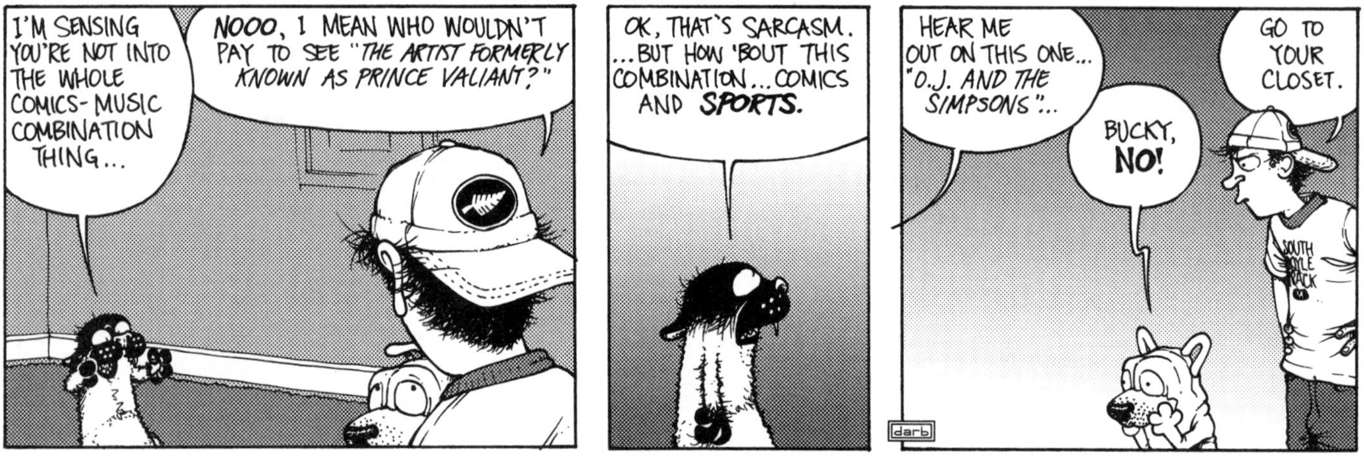
I'M SENSING YOU'RE NOT INTO THE WHOLE COMICS-MUSIC COMBINATION THING...
NOOO, I MEAN WHO WOULDN'T PAY TO SEE "*THE ARTIST FORMERLY KNOWN AS PRINCE VALIANT?*"
OK, THAT'S SARCASM. ...BUT HOW 'BOUT THIS COMBINATION... COMICS AND **SPORTS.**
darb
HEAR ME OUT ON THIS ONE... "*O.J. AND THE SIMPSONS*"...
BUCKY, **NO!**
GO TO YOUR CLOSET.

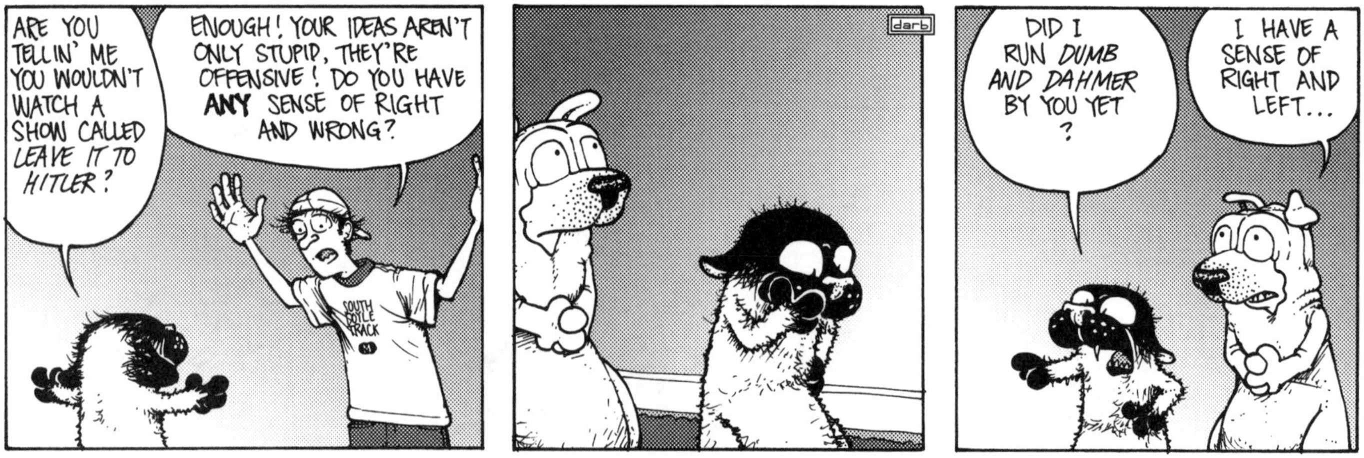
ARE YOU TELLIN' ME YOU WOULDN'T WATCH A SHOW CALLED *LEAVE IT TO HITLER*?
ENOUGH! YOUR IDEAS AREN'T ONLY STUPID, THEY'RE OFFENSIVE! DO YOU HAVE **ANY** SENSE OF RIGHT AND WRONG?
darb
DID I RUN *DUMB AND DAHMER* BY YOU YET ?
I HAVE A SENSE OF RIGHT AND LEFT...

NICE OUTFIT... AND SODA FOR BREAKFAST, EH? WHERE'S YOUR "I'M A REDNECK" FOAM CAN HOLDER?

MY SHIRT IS IN THE DRYER, I'M NOT A REDNECK.

SURE YOU ARE. YOU'RE A COMMIE-LIBERAL, BUT THAT DOESN'T MEAN YOU'RE NOT A REDNECK. YOU'RE JUST A BLUE STATE REDNECK. YOU'RE A BLUENECK.

I'M NOT A BLUENECK!

...SAID THE SHIRTLESS MAN. YOU LOOK LIKE YOU'RE ON THE SPRINGER SHOW. WHY DON'T YOU JUST FIND YOURSELF A NICE COUSIN AND SETTLE DOWN?

I'M NOT A BLUENECK! AND IF I WERE ON THE SPRINGER SHOW, MY PANTS WOULD BE OFF AND I'D HAVE A LITTLE MICROPHONE ON MY TIE.

darb

NOT EXACTLY HELPING YOUR CAUSE BY KNOWING THAT, BLUENECK.

YEAH, I THOUGHT OF THAT AS I WAS SAYING IT...

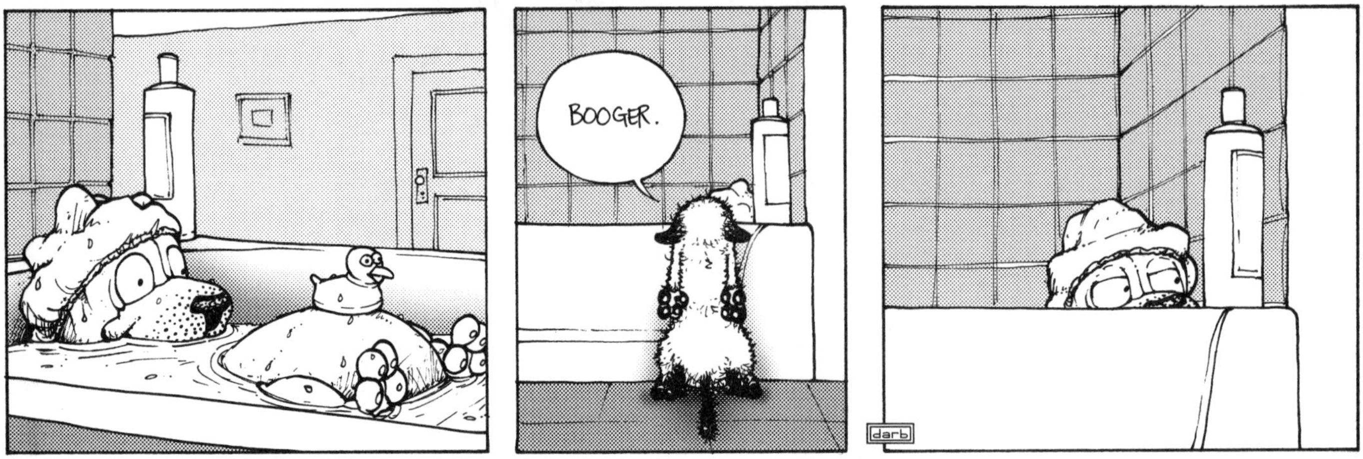
BOOGER.
darb

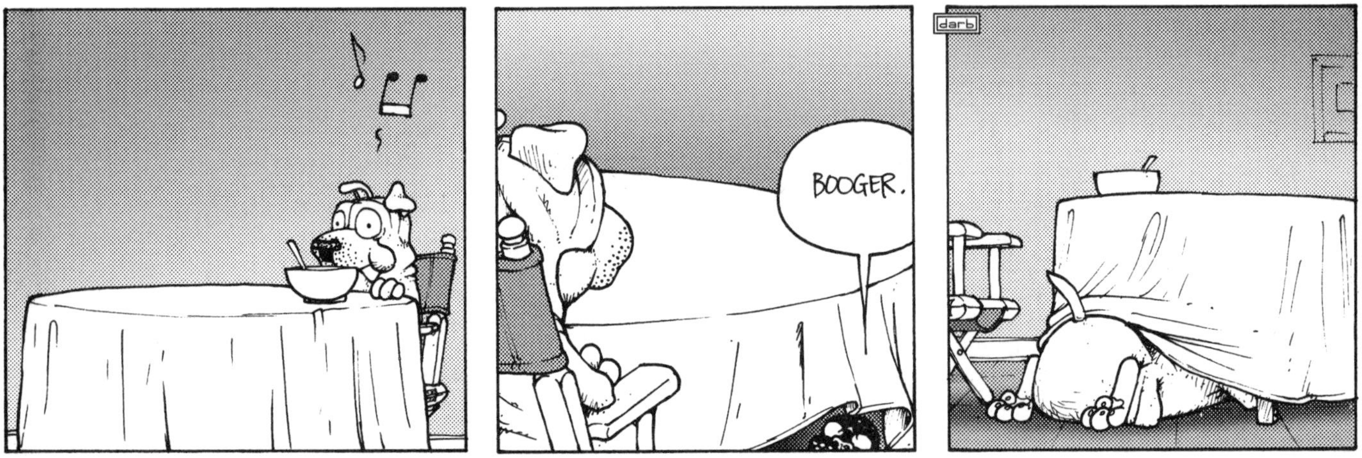
BOOGER.
darb

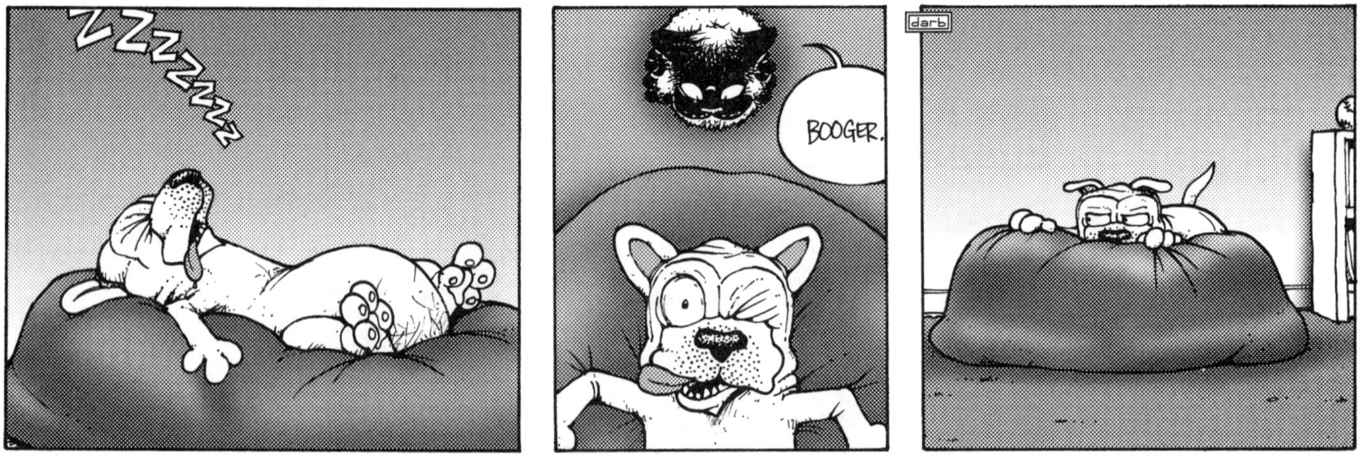
ZZZzzzzz
BOOGER.
darb

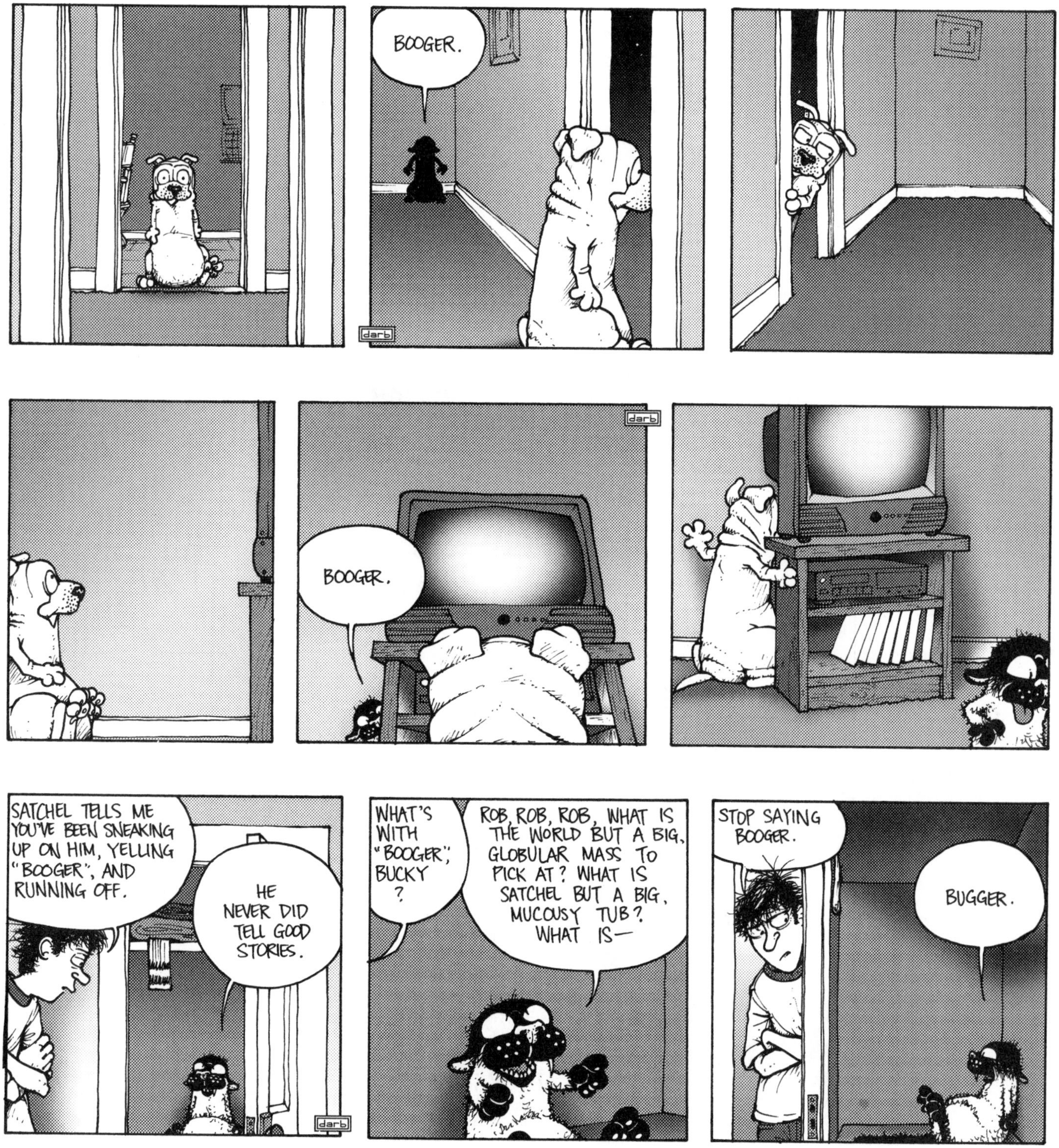
BOOGER.
darb
BOOGER.
SATCHEL TELLS ME YOU'VE BEEN SNEAKING UP ON HIM, YELLING "BOOGER", AND RUNNING OFF.
HE NEVER DID TELL GOOD STORIES.
WHAT'S WITH "BOOGER", BUCKY?
ROB, ROB, ROB, WHAT IS THE WORLD BUT A BIG, GLOBULAR MASS TO PICK AT? WHAT IS SATCHEL BUT A BIG, MUCOUSY TUB? WHAT IS—
STOP SAYING BOOGER.
BUGGER.

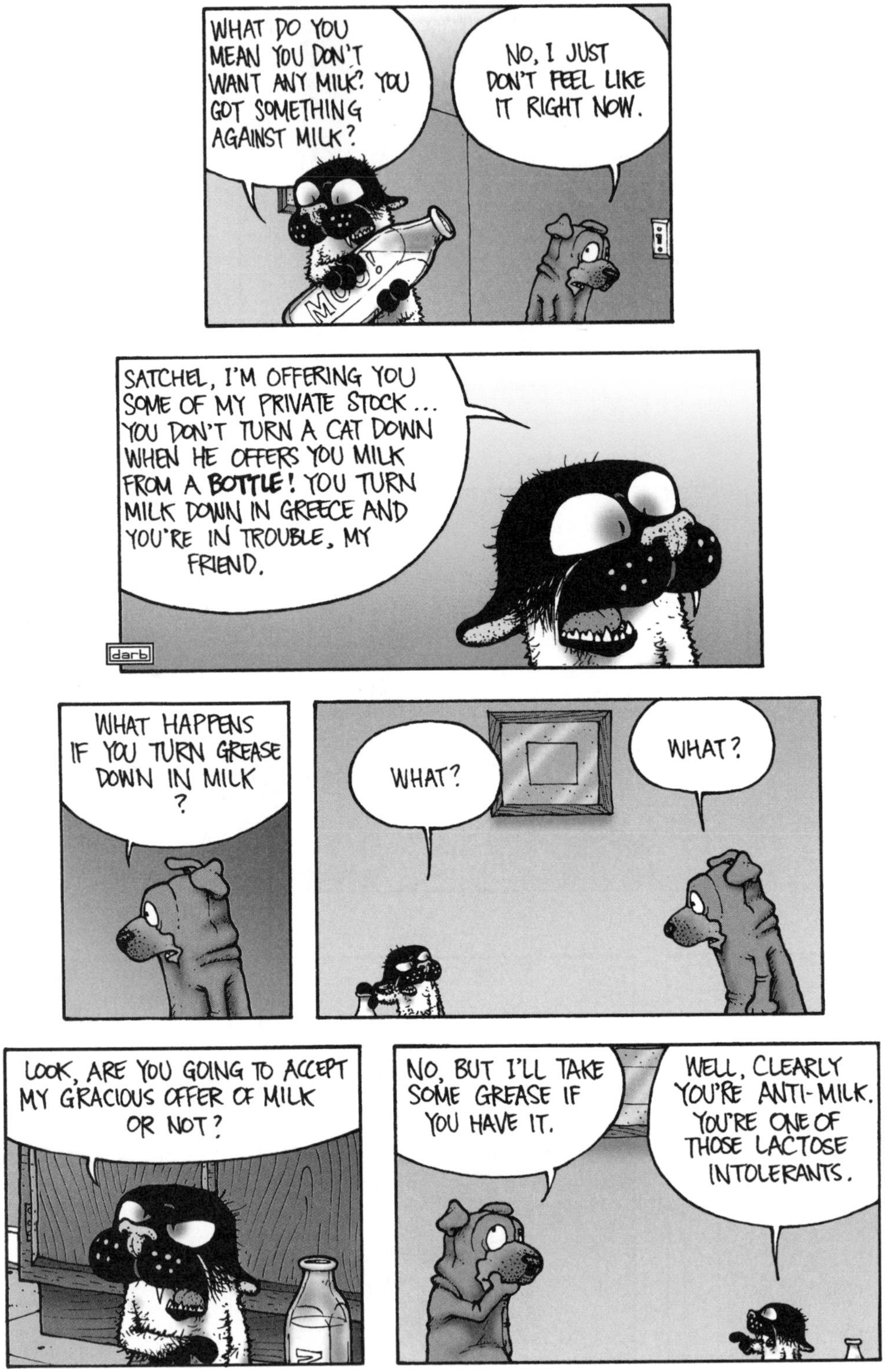
WHAT DO YOU MEAN YOU DON'T WANT ANY MILK? YOU GOT SOMETHING AGAINST MILK?
NO, I JUST DON'T FEEL LIKE IT RIGHT NOW.
MOO!
SATCHEL, I'M OFFERING YOU SOME OF MY PRIVATE STOCK... YOU DON'T TURN A CAT DOWN WHEN HE OFFERS YOU MILK FROM A **BOTTLE**! YOU TURN MILK DOWN IN GREECE AND YOU'RE IN TROUBLE, MY FRIEND.
darb
WHAT HAPPENS IF YOU TURN GREASE DOWN IN MILK ?
WHAT?
WHAT?
LOOK, ARE YOU GOING TO ACCEPT MY GRACIOUS OFFER OF MILK OR NOT?
NO, BUT I'LL TAKE SOME GREASE IF YOU HAVE IT.
WELL, CLEARLY YOU'RE ANTI-MILK. YOU'RE ONE OF THOSE LACTOSE INTOLERANTS.

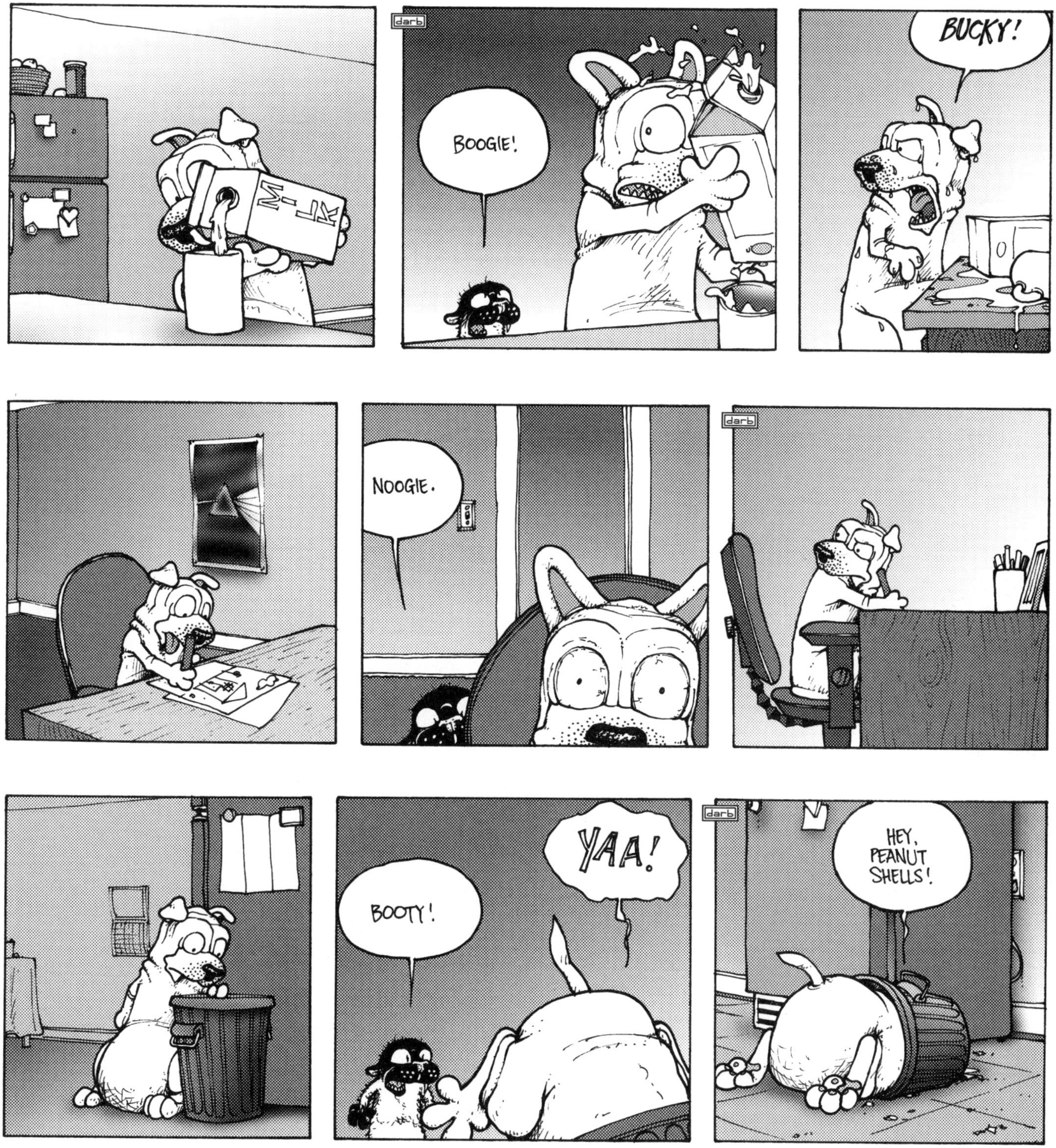
darb
BOOGIE!
BUCKY!
NOOGIE.
darb
BOOTY!
YAA!
darb
HEY, PEANUT SHELLS!

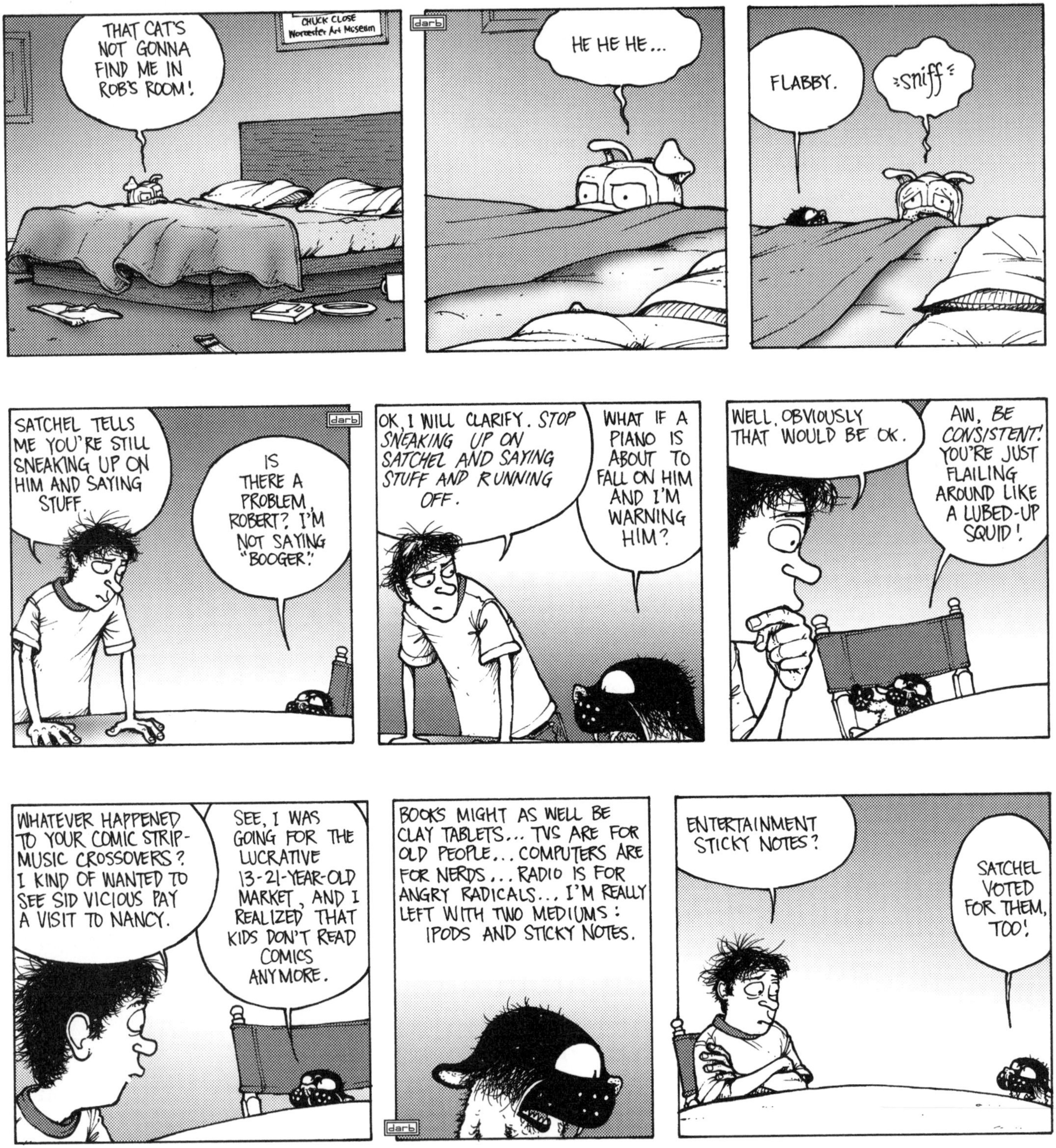

THAT CAT'S NOT GONNA FIND ME IN ROB'S ROOM!
CHUCK CLOSE Worcester Art Museum
HE HE HE...
FLABBY.
sniff
SATCHEL TELLS ME YOU'RE STILL SNEAKING UP ON HIM AND SAYING STUFF.
IS THERE A PROBLEM, ROBERT? I'M NOT SAYING "BOOGER."
OK, I WILL CLARIFY. STOP SNEAKING UP ON SATCHEL AND SAYING STUFF AND RUNNING OFF.
WHAT IF A PIANO IS ABOUT TO FALL ON HIM AND I'M WARNING HIM?
WELL, OBVIOUSLY THAT WOULD BE OK.
AW, BE CONSISTENT! YOU'RE JUST FLAILING AROUND LIKE A LUBED-UP SQUID!
WHATEVER HAPPENED TO YOUR COMIC STRIP-MUSIC CROSSOVERS? I KIND OF WANTED TO SEE SID VICIOUS PAY A VISIT TO NANCY.
SEE, I WAS GOING FOR THE LUCRATIVE 13-21-YEAR-OLD MARKET, AND I REALIZED THAT KIDS DON'T READ COMICS ANYMORE.
BOOKS MIGHT AS WELL BE CLAY TABLETS... TVS ARE FOR OLD PEOPLE... COMPUTERS ARE FOR NERDS... RADIO IS FOR ANGRY RADICALS... I'M REALLY LEFT WITH TWO MEDIUMS: IPODS AND STICKY NOTES.
ENTERTAINMENT STICKY NOTES?
SATCHEL VOTED FOR THEM, TOO!

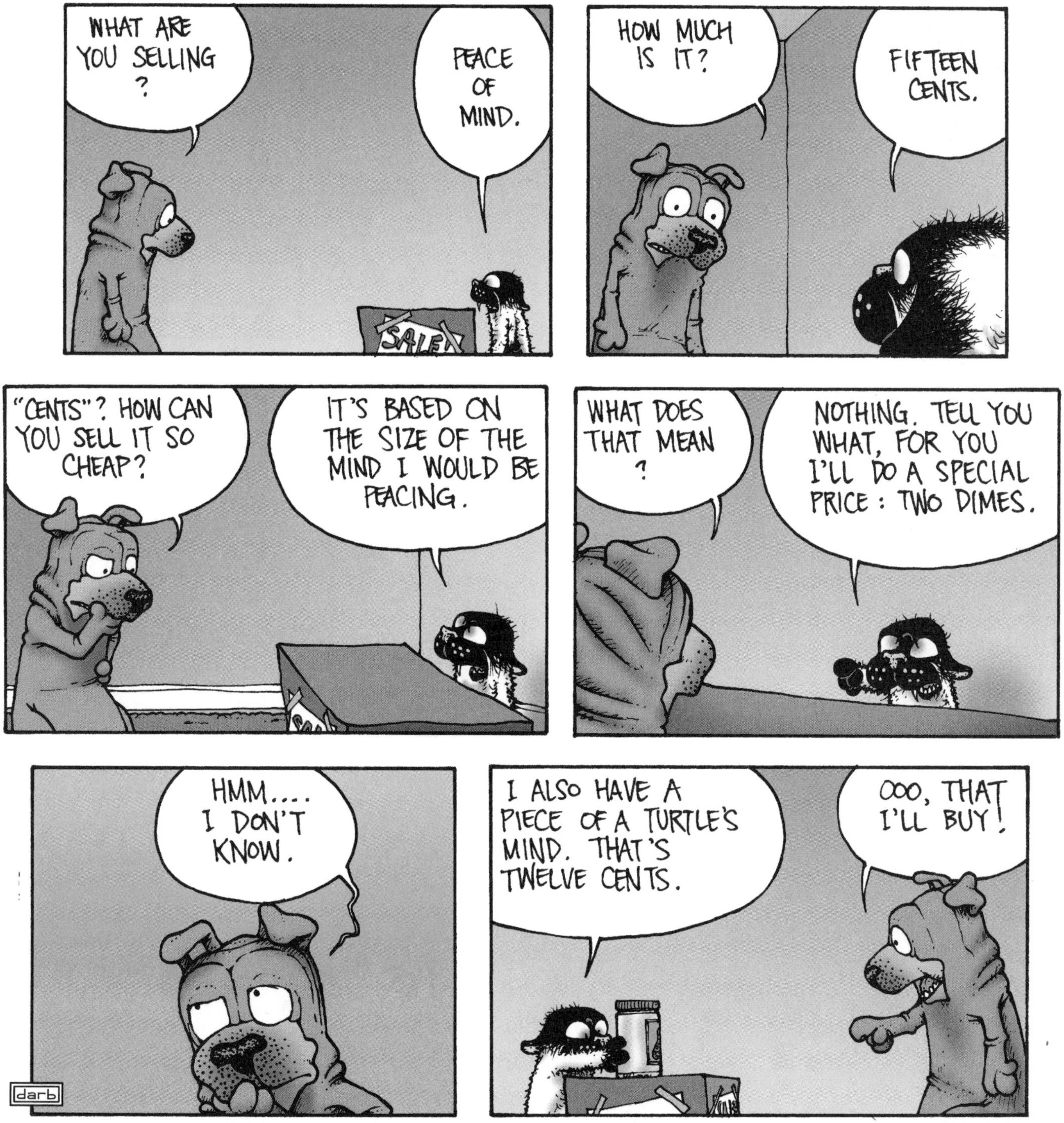
WHAT ARE YOU SELLING ?
PEACE OF MIND.
HOW MUCH IS IT?
FIFTEEN CENTS.
"CENTS"? HOW CAN YOU SELL IT SO CHEAP?
IT'S BASED ON THE SIZE OF THE MIND I WOULD BE PEACING.
WHAT DOES THAT MEAN ?
NOTHING. TELL YOU WHAT, FOR YOU I'LL DO A SPECIAL PRICE: TWO DIMES.
HMM.... I DON'T KNOW.
I ALSO HAVE A PIECE OF A TURTLE'S MIND. THAT'S TWELVE CENTS.
OOO, THAT I'LL BUY!
darb

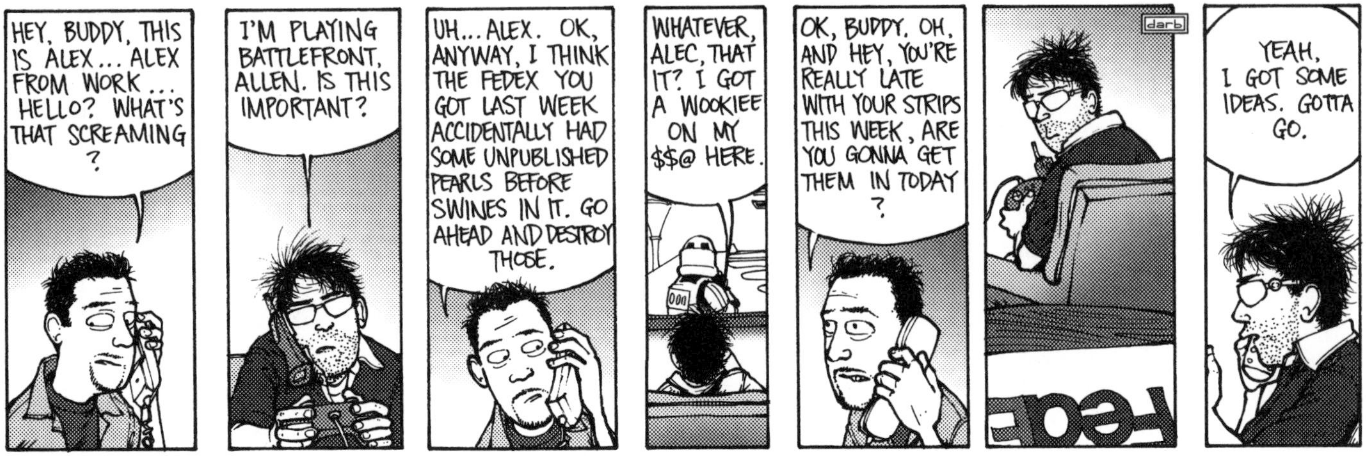
HEY, BUDDY, THIS IS ALEX... ALEX FROM WORK... HELLO? WHAT'S THAT SCREAMING?
I'M PLAYING BATTLEFRONT, ALLEN. IS THIS IMPORTANT?
UH... ALEX. OK, ANYWAY, I THINK THE FEDEX YOU GOT LAST WEEK ACCIDENTALLY HAD SOME UNPUBLISHED PEARLS BEFORE SWINES IN IT. GO AHEAD AND DESTROY THOSE.
WHATEVER, ALEC, THAT IT? I GOT A WOOKIEE ON MY $$@ HERE.
OK, BUDDY. OH, AND HEY, YOU'RE REALLY LATE WITH YOUR STRIPS THIS WEEK, ARE YOU GONNA GET THEM IN TODAY?
darb
YEAH, I GOT SOME IDEAS. GOTTA GO.

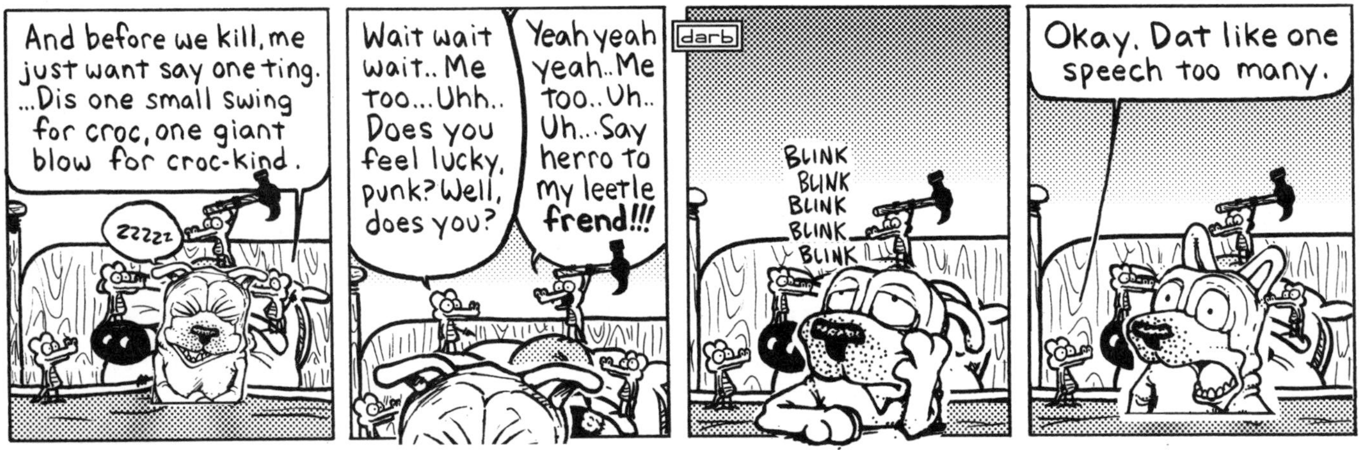
And before we kill, me just want say one ting. ...Dis one small swing for croc, one giant blow for croc-kind.
ZZZZZ
Wait wait wait.. Me too... Uhh.. Does you feel lucky, punk? Well, does you?
Yeah yeah yeah.. Me too.. Uh.. Uh... Say herro to my leetle **frend!!!**
darb
BLINK
BLINK
BLINK
BLINK
BLINK
Okay. Dat like one speech too many.

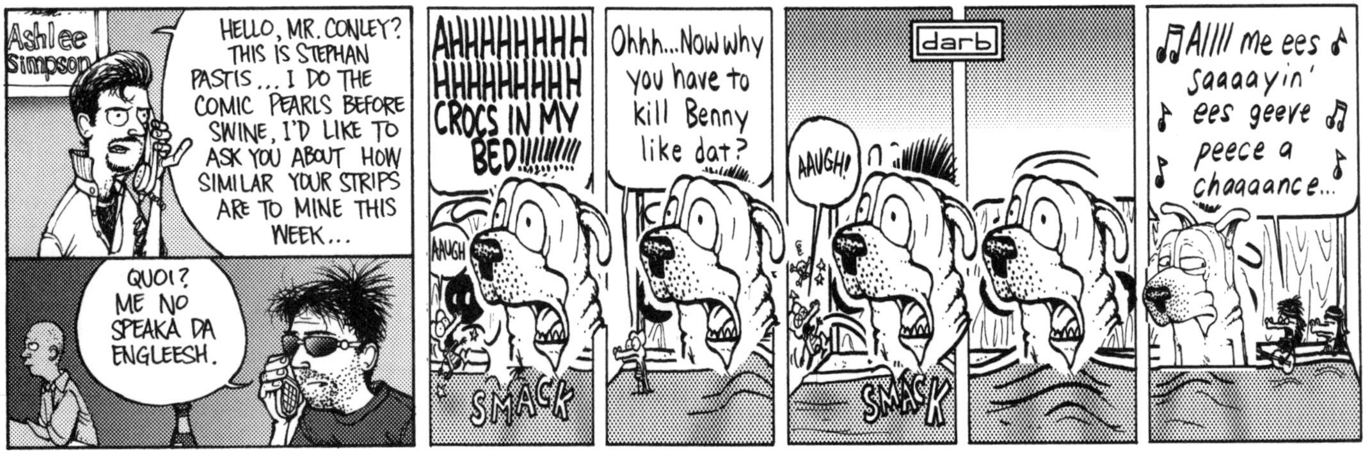
Ashlee Simpson
HELLO, MR. CONLEY? THIS IS STEPHAN PASTIS... I DO THE COMIC PEARLS BEFORE SWINE, I'D LIKE TO ASK YOU ABOUT HOW SIMILAR YOUR STRIPS ARE TO MINE THIS WEEK...
QUOI? ME NO SPEAKA DA ENGLEESH.
AHHHHHHHHHHHHHHHHH CROCS IN MY BED!!!!!!!!
AAUGH
SMACK
Ohhh... Now why you have to kill Benny like dat?
darb
AAUGH!
SMACK
Allll me ees saaaayin' ees geeve peece a chaaaance...

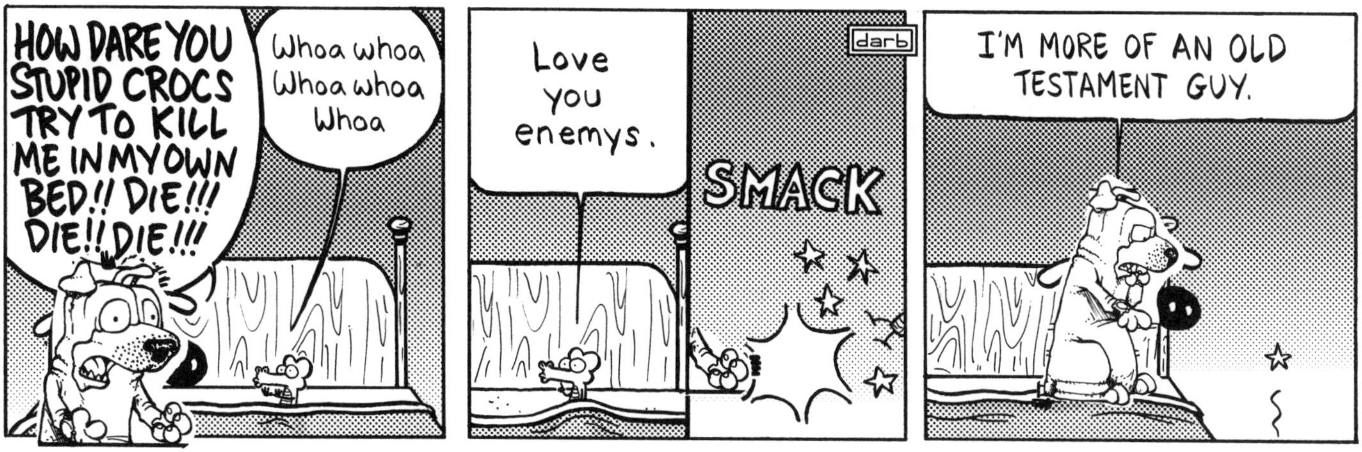
HOW DARE YOU STUPID CROCS TRY TO KILL ME IN MY OWN BED!! DIE!!! DIE!! DIE!!!
Whoa whoa Whoa whoa Whoa
Love you enemys.
darb
SMACK
I'M MORE OF AN OLD TESTAMENT GUY.

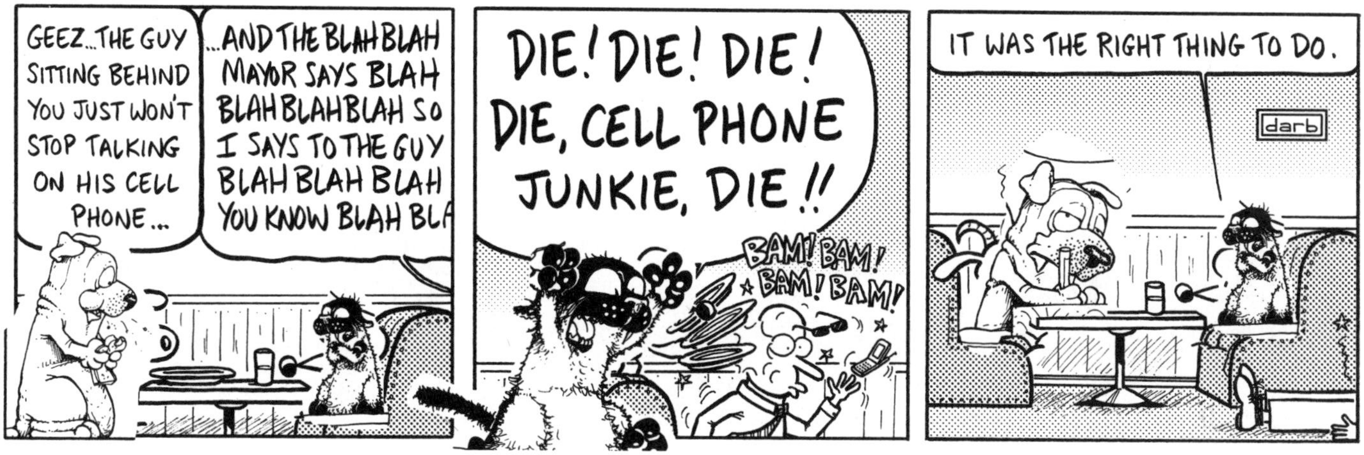
GEEZ...THE GUY SITTING BEHIND YOU JUST WON'T STOP TALKING ON HIS CELL PHONE...
...AND THE BLAH BLAH MAYOR SAYS BLAH BLAH BLAH BLAH SO I SAYS TO THE GUY BLAH BLAH BLAH YOU KNOW BLAH BLA
DIE! DIE! DIE! DIE, CELL PHONE JUNKIE, DIE!!
BAM! BAM! BAM! BAM!
IT WAS THE RIGHT THING TO DO.
darb

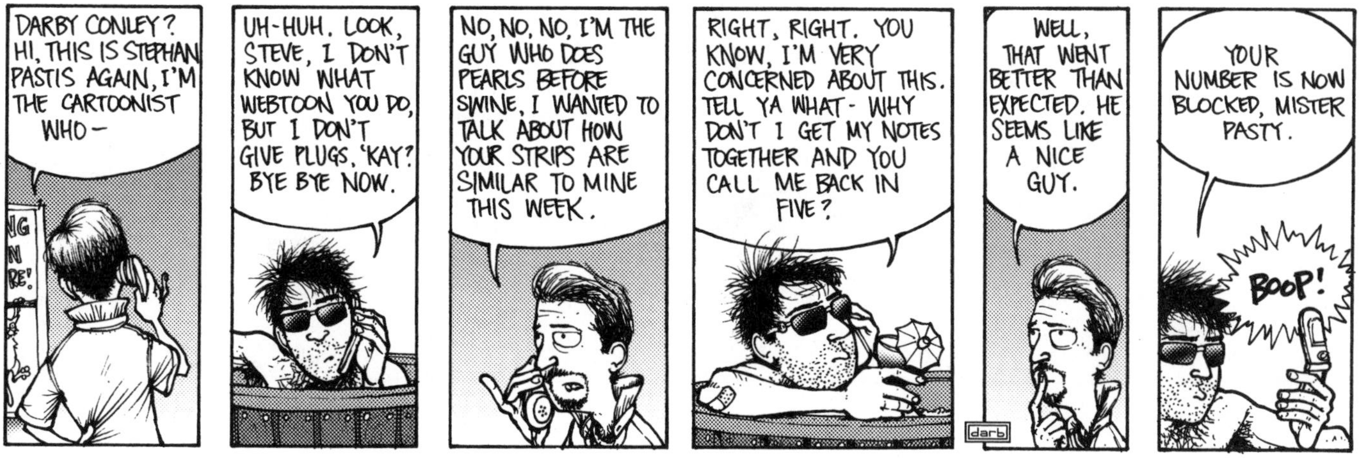
DARBY CONLEY? HI, THIS IS STEPHAN PASTIS AGAIN, I'M THE CARTOONIST WHO–
UH-HUH. LOOK, STEVE, I DON'T KNOW WHAT WEBTOON YOU DO, BUT I DON'T GIVE PLUGS, 'KAY? BYE BYE NOW.
NO, NO, NO, I'M THE GUY WHO DOES PEARLS BEFORE SWINE, I WANTED TO TALK ABOUT HOW YOUR STRIPS ARE SIMILAR TO MINE THIS WEEK.
RIGHT, RIGHT. YOU KNOW, I'M VERY CONCERNED ABOUT THIS. TELL YA WHAT- WHY DON'T I GET MY NOTES TOGETHER AND YOU CALL ME BACK IN FIVE?
darb
WELL, THAT WENT BETTER THAN EXPECTED. HE SEEMS LIKE A NICE GUY.
YOUR NUMBER IS NOW BLOCKED, MISTER PASTY.
BOOP!

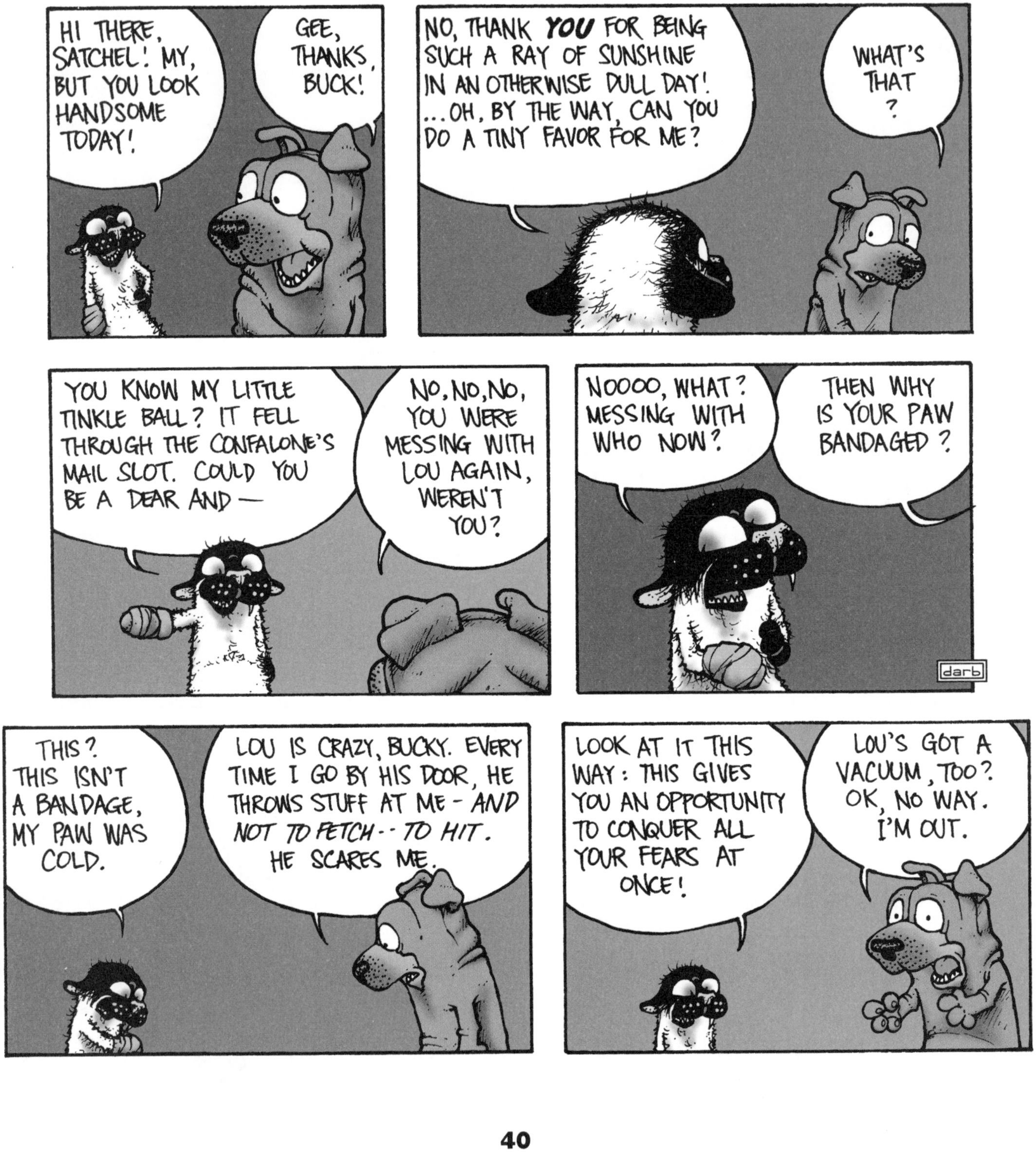

HI THERE, SATCHEL! MY, BUT YOU LOOK HANDSOME TODAY!
GEE, THANKS, BUCK!
NO, THANK **YOU** FOR BEING SUCH A RAY OF SUNSHINE IN AN OTHERWISE DULL DAY! ...OH, BY THE WAY, CAN YOU DO A TINY FAVOR FOR ME?
WHAT'S THAT ?
YOU KNOW MY LITTLE TINKLE BALL? IT FELL THROUGH THE CONFALONE'S MAIL SLOT. COULD YOU BE A DEAR AND—
NO, NO, NO, YOU WERE MESSING WITH LOU AGAIN, WEREN'T YOU?
NOOOO, WHAT? MESSING WITH WHO NOW?
THEN WHY IS YOUR PAW BANDAGED?
darb
THIS? THIS ISN'T A BANDAGE, MY PAW WAS COLD.
LOU IS CRAZY, BUCKY. EVERY TIME I GO BY HIS DOOR, HE THROWS STUFF AT ME - *AND NOT TO FETCH - - TO HIT.* HE SCARES ME.
LOOK AT IT THIS WAY: THIS GIVES YOU AN OPPORTUNITY TO CONQUER ALL YOUR FEARS AT ONCE!
LOU'S GOT A VACUUM, TOO? OK, NO WAY. I'M OUT.

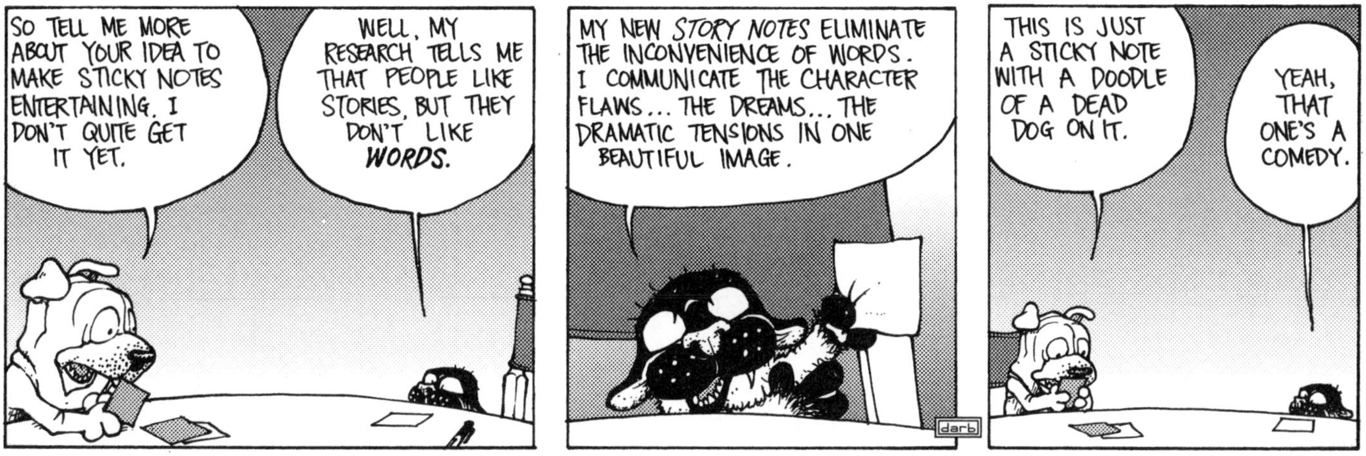
SO TELL ME MORE ABOUT YOUR IDEA TO MAKE STICKY NOTES ENTERTAINING. I DON'T QUITE GET IT YET.
WELL, MY RESEARCH TELLS ME THAT PEOPLE LIKE STORIES, BUT THEY DON'T LIKE WORDS.
MY NEW STORY NOTES ELIMINATE THE INCONVENIENCE OF WORDS. I COMMUNICATE THE CHARACTER FLAWS... THE DREAMS... THE DRAMATIC TENSIONS IN ONE BEAUTIFUL IMAGE.
darb
THIS IS JUST A STICKY NOTE WITH A DOODLE OF A DEAD DOG ON IT.
YEAH, THAT ONE'S A COMEDY.

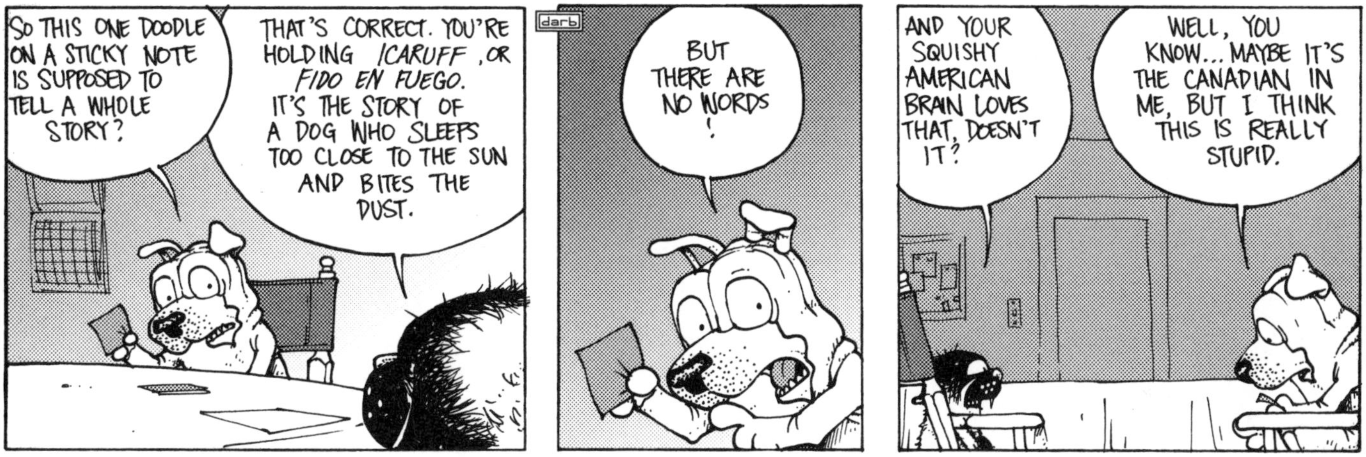
SO THIS ONE DOODLE ON A STICKY NOTE IS SUPPOSED TO TELL A WHOLE STORY?
THAT'S CORRECT. YOU'RE HOLDING ICARUFF, OR FIDO EN FUEGO. IT'S THE STORY OF A DOG WHO SLEEPS TOO CLOSE TO THE SUN AND BITES THE DUST.
darb
BUT THERE ARE NO WORDS!
AND YOUR SQUISHY AMERICAN BRAIN LOVES THAT, DOESN'T IT?
WELL, YOU KNOW... MAYBE IT'S THE CANADIAN IN ME, BUT I THINK THIS IS REALLY STUPID.

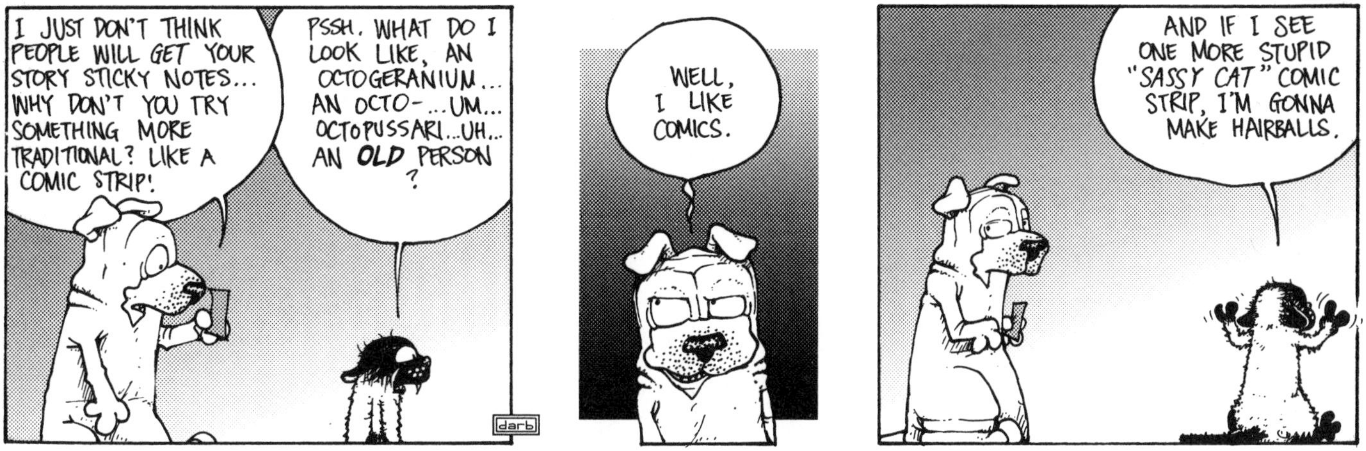
I JUST DON'T THINK PEOPLE WILL GET YOUR STORY STICKY NOTES... WHY DON'T YOU TRY SOMETHING MORE TRADITIONAL? LIKE A COMIC STRIP!
PSSH. WHAT DO I LOOK LIKE, AN OCTOGERANIUM... AN OCTO-...UM... OCTOPUSSARI...UH... AN OLD PERSON?
darb
WELL, I LIKE COMICS.
AND IF I SEE ONE MORE STUPID "SASSY CAT" COMIC STRIP, I'M GONNA MAKE HAIRBALLS.

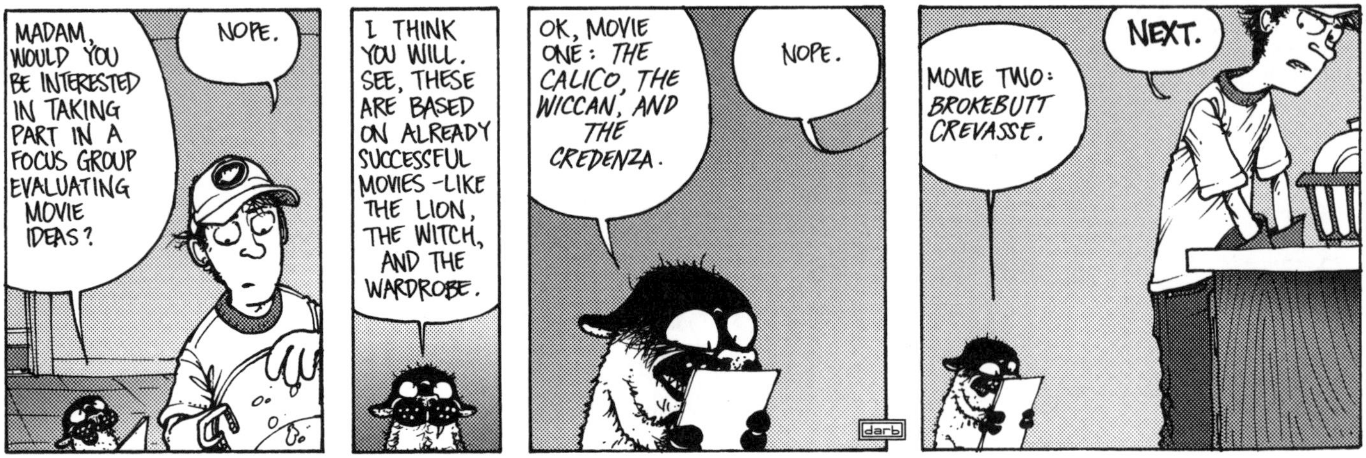
MADAM, WOULD YOU BE INTERESTED IN TAKING PART IN A FOCUS GROUP EVALUATING MOVIE IDEAS?
NOPE.
I THINK YOU WILL. SEE, THESE ARE BASED ON ALREADY SUCCESSFUL MOVIES -LIKE THE LION, THE WITCH, AND THE WARDROBE.
OK, MOVIE ONE: THE CALICO, THE WICCAN, AND THE CREDENZA.
NOPE.
darb
MOVIE TWO: BROKEBUTT CREVASSE.
NEXT.

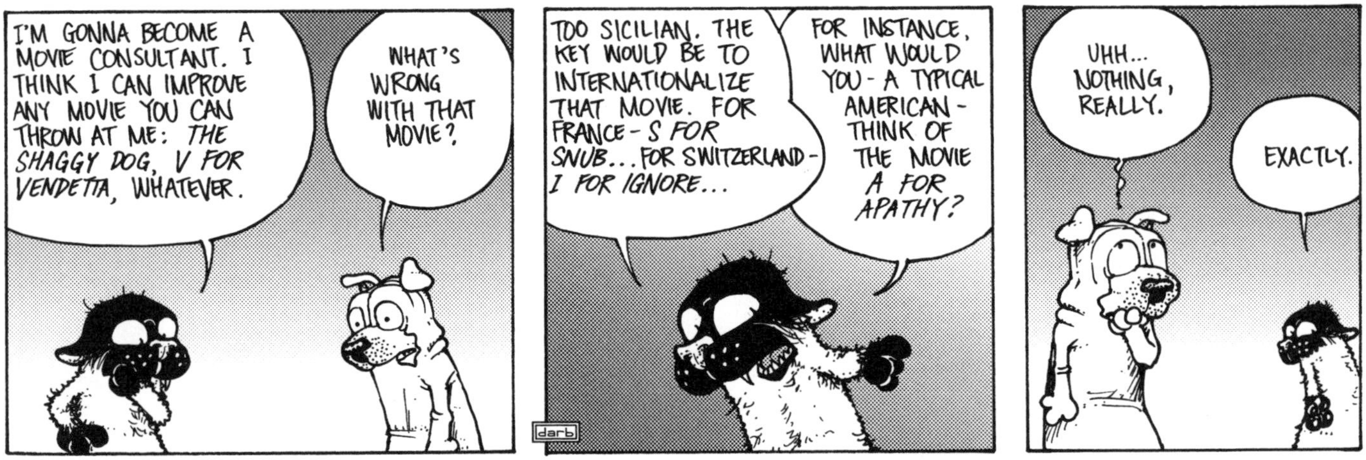
I'M GONNA BECOME A MOVIE CONSULTANT. I THINK I CAN IMPROVE ANY MOVIE YOU CAN THROW AT ME: THE SHAGGY DOG, V FOR VENDETTA, WHATEVER.
WHAT'S WRONG WITH THAT MOVIE?
darb
TOO SICILIAN. THE KEY WOULD BE TO INTERNATIONALIZE THAT MOVIE. FOR FRANCE - S FOR SNUB... FOR SWITZERLAND - I FOR IGNORE...
FOR INSTANCE, WHAT WOULD YOU - A TYPICAL AMERICAN - THINK OF THE MOVIE A FOR APATHY?
UHH... NOTHING, REALLY.
EXACTLY.

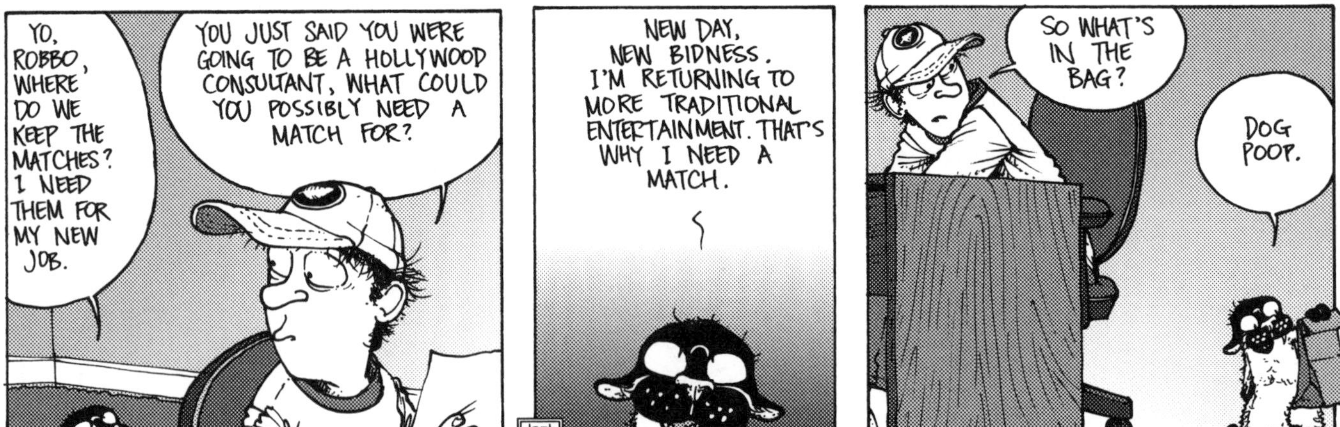
YO, ROBBO, WHERE DO WE KEEP THE MATCHES? I NEED THEM FOR MY NEW JOB.
YOU JUST SAID YOU WERE GOING TO BE A HOLLYWOOD CONSULTANT, WHAT COULD YOU POSSIBLY NEED A MATCH FOR?
darb
NEW DAY, NEW BIDNESS. I'M RETURNING TO MORE TRADITIONAL ENTERTAINMENT. THAT'S WHY I NEED A MATCH.
SO WHAT'S IN THE BAG?
DOG POOP.

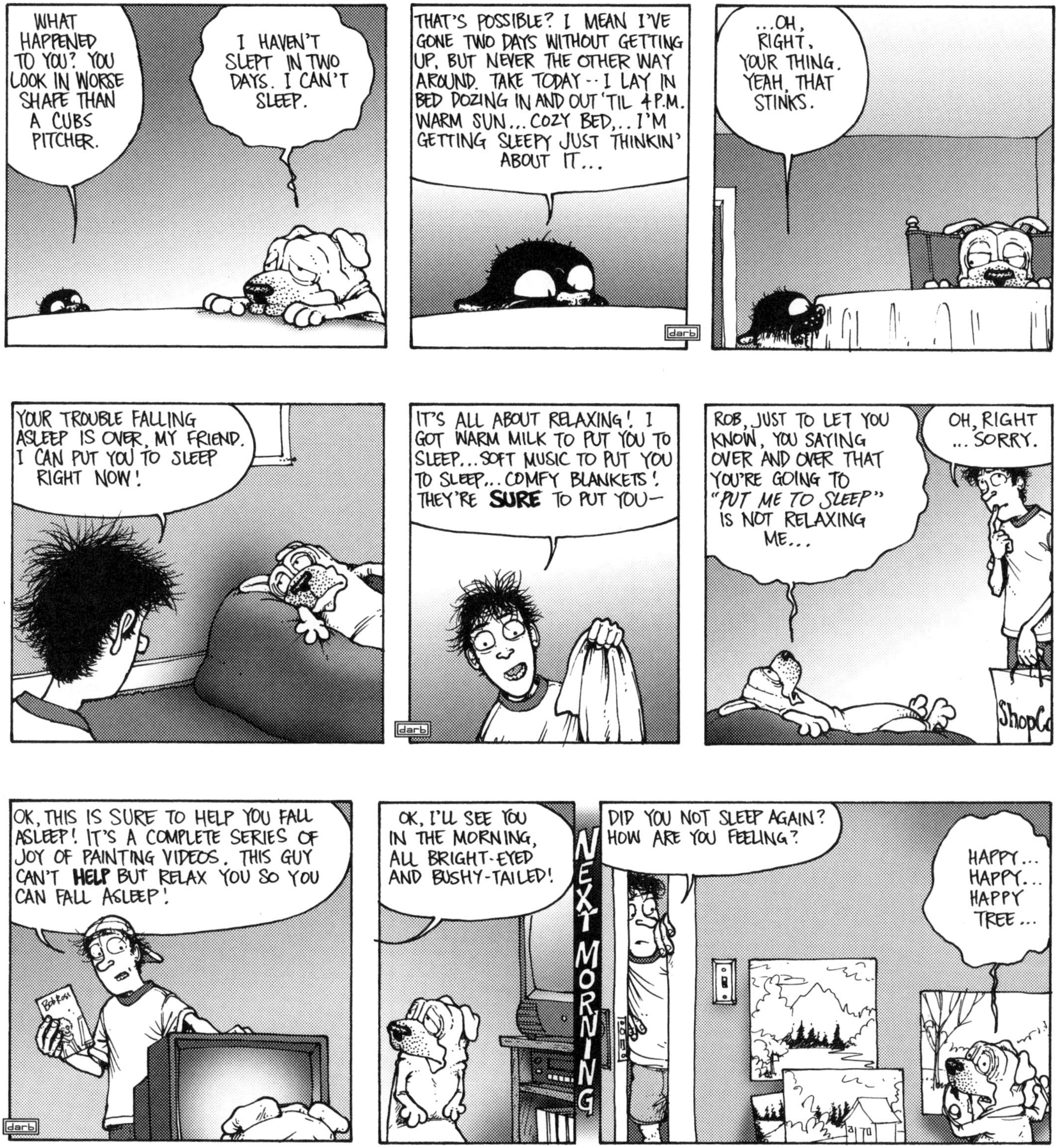
WHAT HAPPENED TO YOU? YOU LOOK IN WORSE SHAPE THAN A CUBS PITCHER.
I HAVEN'T SLEPT IN TWO DAYS. I CAN'T SLEEP.
THAT'S POSSIBLE? I MEAN I'VE GONE TWO DAYS WITHOUT GETTING UP, BUT NEVER THE OTHER WAY AROUND. TAKE TODAY -- I LAY IN BED DOZING IN AND OUT 'TIL 4 P.M. WARM SUN... COZY BED... I'M GETTING SLEEPY JUST THINKIN' ABOUT IT...
darb
...OH, RIGHT. YOUR THING. YEAH, THAT STINKS.
YOUR TROUBLE FALLING ASLEEP IS OVER, MY FRIEND. I CAN PUT YOU TO SLEEP RIGHT NOW!
IT'S ALL ABOUT RELAXING! I GOT WARM MILK TO PUT YOU TO SLEEP... SOFT MUSIC TO PUT YOU TO SLEEP... COMFY BLANKETS! THEY'RE **SURE** TO PUT YOU—
darb
ROB, JUST TO LET YOU KNOW, YOU SAYING OVER AND OVER THAT YOU'RE GOING TO *"PUT ME TO SLEEP"* IS NOT RELAXING ME...
OH, RIGHT ... SORRY.
ShopCo
OK, THIS IS SURE TO HELP YOU FALL ASLEEP! IT'S A COMPLETE SERIES OF JOY OF PAINTING VIDEOS. THIS GUY CAN'T **HELP** BUT RELAX YOU SO YOU CAN FALL ASLEEP!
Bob Ross
darb
OK, I'LL SEE YOU IN THE MORNING, ALL BRIGHT-EYED AND BUSHY-TAILED!
NEXT MORNING
DID YOU NOT SLEEP AGAIN? HOW ARE YOU FEELING?
HAPPY... HAPPY... HAPPY TREE...

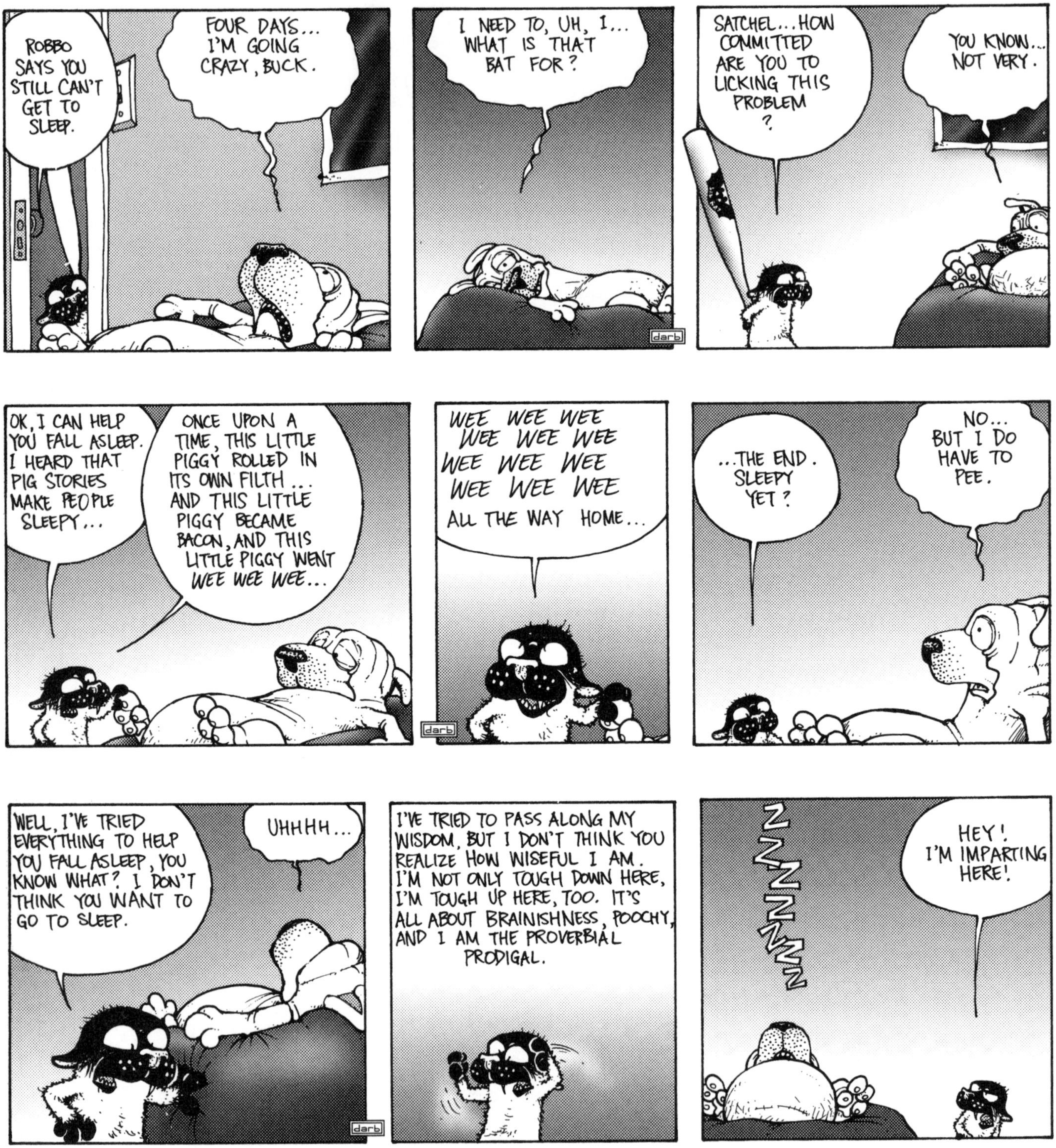
ROBBO SAYS YOU STILL CAN'T GET TO SLEEP.
FOUR DAYS... I'M GOING CRAZY, BUCK.
I NEED TO, UH, I... WHAT IS THAT BAT FOR?
darb
SATCHEL...HOW COMMITTED ARE YOU TO LICKING THIS PROBLEM?
YOU KNOW... NOT VERY.
OK, I CAN HELP YOU FALL ASLEEP. I HEARD THAT PIG STORIES MAKE PEOPLE SLEEPY...
ONCE UPON A TIME, THIS LITTLE PIGGY ROLLED IN ITS OWN FILTH... AND THIS LITTLE PIGGY BECAME BACON, AND THIS LITTLE PIGGY WENT WEE WEE WEE...
darb
WEE WEE WEE WEE WEE WEE WEE WEE WEE WEE WEE WEE ALL THE WAY HOME...
...THE END. SLEEPY YET?
NO... BUT I DO HAVE TO PEE.
WELL, I'VE TRIED EVERYTHING TO HELP YOU FALL ASLEEP, YOU KNOW WHAT? I DON'T THINK YOU WANT TO GO TO SLEEP.
UHHHH...
darb
I'VE TRIED TO PASS ALONG MY WISDOM, BUT I DON'T THINK YOU REALIZE HOW WISEFUL I AM. I'M NOT ONLY TOUGH DOWN HERE, I'M TOUGH UP HERE, TOO. IT'S ALL ABOUT BRAININSHNESS, POOCHY, AND I AM THE PROVERBIAL PRODIGAL.
ZZZZZZZ
HEY! I'M IMPARTING HERE!

HEYYY, MY OBEDIENCE COLLEGE REUNION IS COMIN' UP!

AH, YES. THE GOOD OL' ALMA MUTTER.

YUP!

THE BELOVED COLLIE-AGE.

darb

MM-HM. MM-HM.

DIDN'T YOU GRADUATE MAGNA CUM LABRADOR?

I WISH! THE BORDER COLLIES MESSED UP THE CURVE TOO MUCH TO—

WELL, I'M SURE YOU PRODUCED A SCHOLARLY FECES.

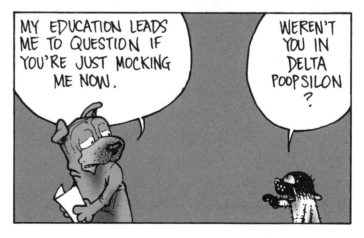

MY EDUCATION LEADS ME TO QUESTION IF YOU'RE JUST MOCKING ME NOW.

WEREN'T YOU IN DELTA POOPSILON?

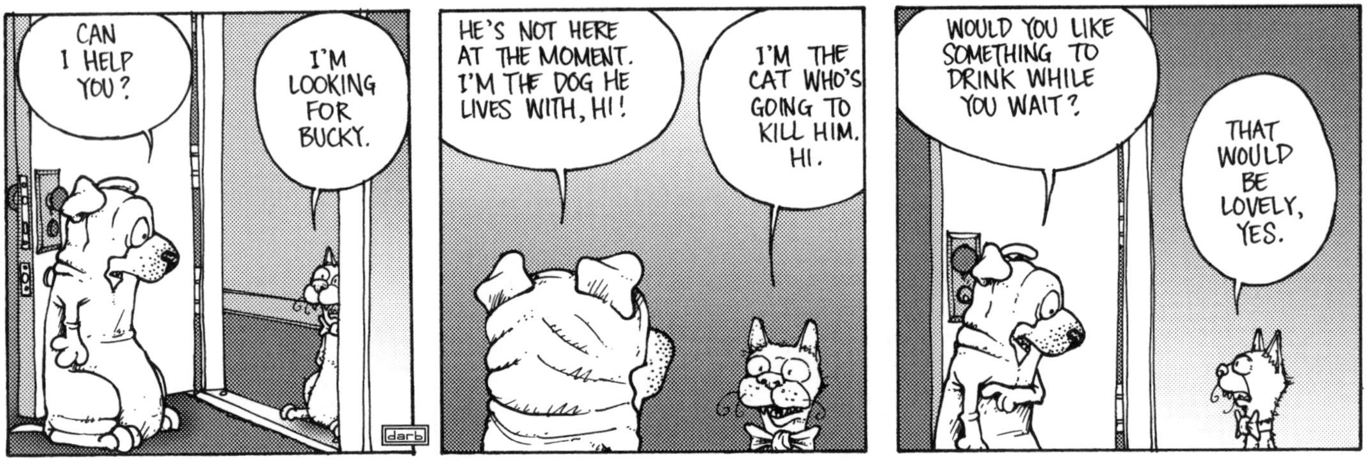
CAN I HELP YOU?
I'M LOOKING FOR BUCKY.
darb
HE'S NOT HERE AT THE MOMENT. I'M THE DOG HE LIVES WITH, HI!
I'M THE CAT WHO'S GOING TO KILL HIM. HI.
WOULD YOU LIKE SOMETHING TO DRINK WHILE YOU WAIT?
THAT WOULD BE LOVELY, YES.

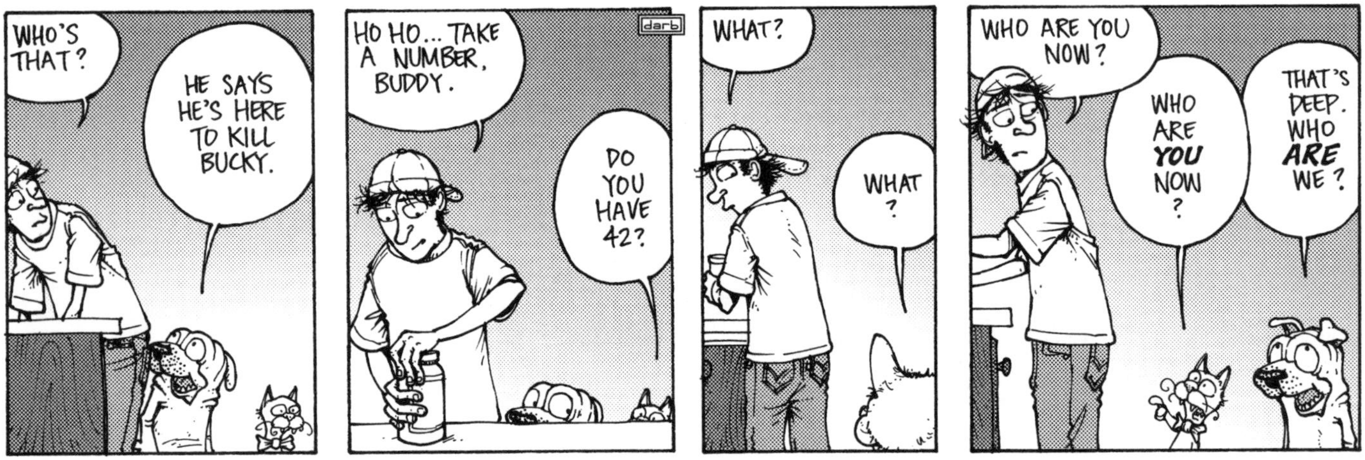
WHO'S THAT?
HE SAYS HE'S HERE TO KILL BUCKY.
darb
HO HO... TAKE A NUMBER, BUDDY.
DO YOU HAVE 42?
WHAT?
WHAT?
WHO ARE YOU NOW?
WHO ARE **YOU** NOW?
THAT'S DEEP. WHO **ARE** WE?

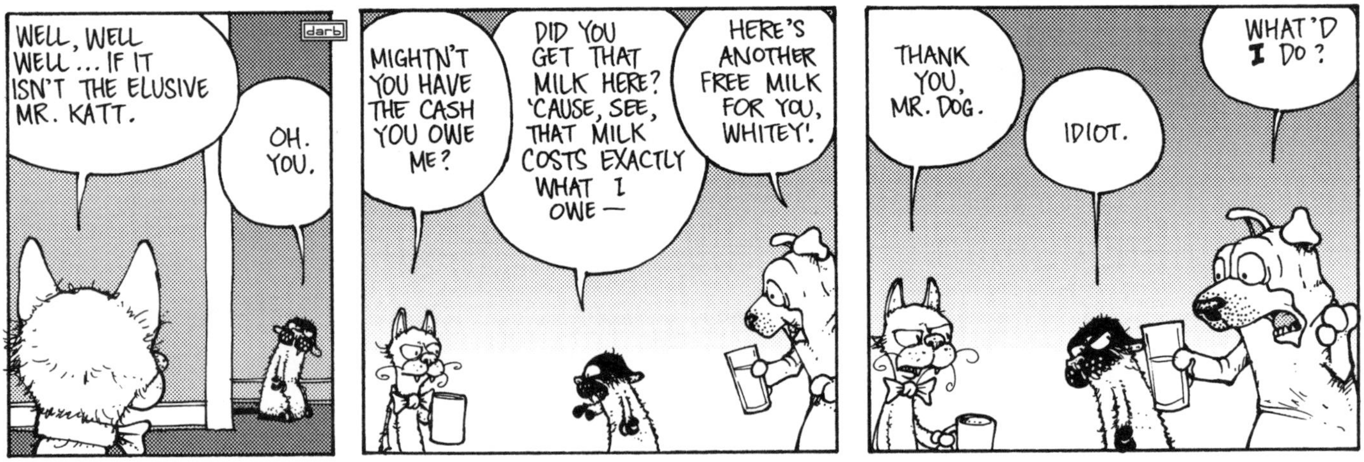
darb
WELL, WELL WELL... IF IT ISN'T THE ELUSIVE MR. KATT.
OH. YOU.
MIGHTN'T YOU HAVE THE CASH YOU OWE ME?
DID YOU GET THAT MILK HERE? 'CAUSE, SEE, THAT MILK COSTS EXACTLY WHAT I OWE—
HERE'S ANOTHER FREE MILK FOR YOU, WHITEY!
THANK YOU, MR. DOG.
IDIOT.
WHAT'D **I** DO?

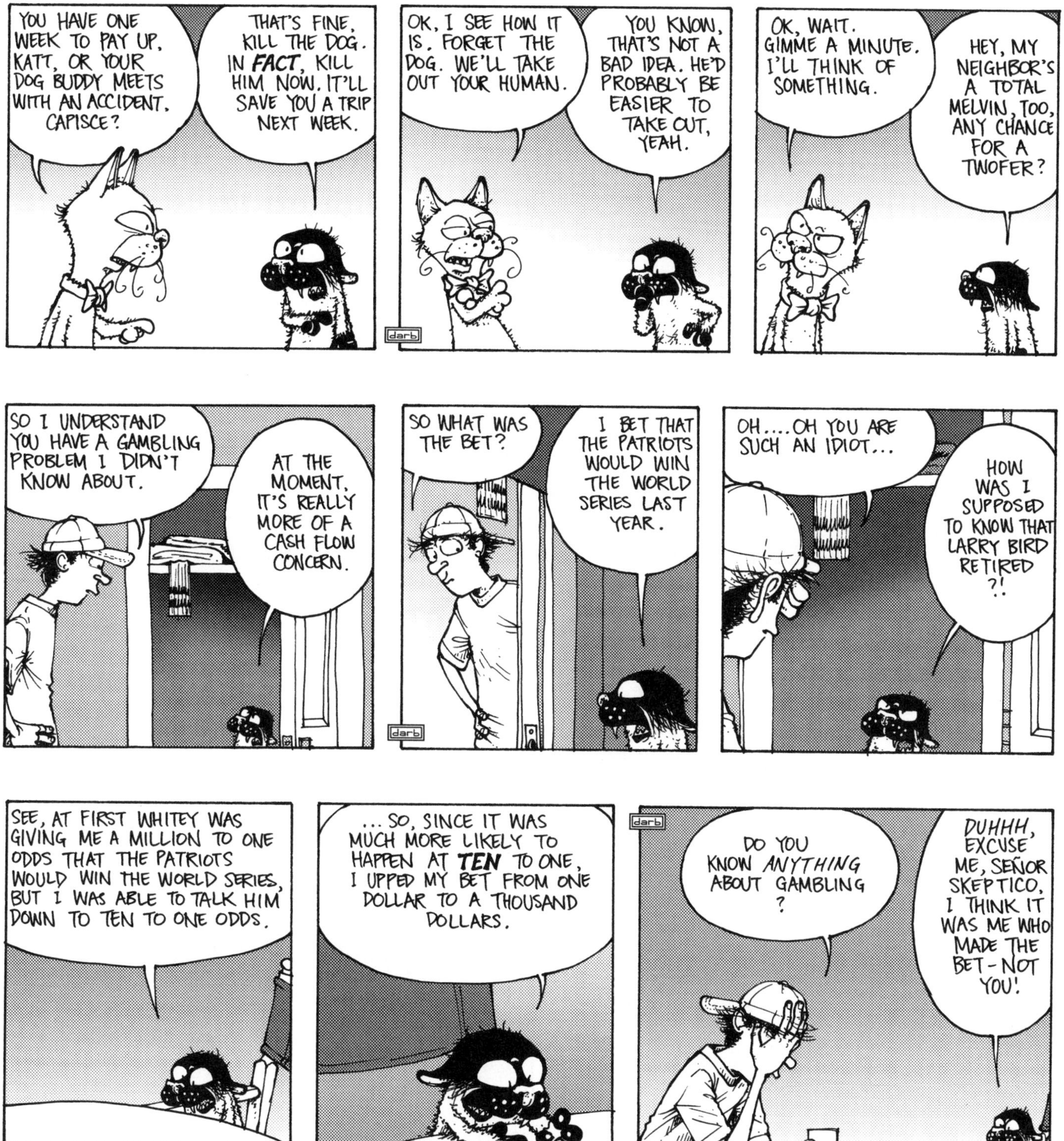
YOU HAVE ONE WEEK TO PAY UP, KATT, OR YOUR DOG BUDDY MEETS WITH AN ACCIDENT. CAPISCE?
THAT'S FINE, KILL THE DOG. IN FACT, KILL HIM NOW. IT'LL SAVE YOU A TRIP NEXT WEEK.
darb
OK, I SEE HOW IT IS. FORGET THE DOG. WE'LL TAKE OUT YOUR HUMAN.
YOU KNOW, THAT'S NOT A BAD IDEA. HE'D PROBABLY BE EASIER TO TAKE OUT, YEAH.
OK, WAIT. GIMME A MINUTE. I'LL THINK OF SOMETHING.
HEY, MY NEIGHBOR'S A TOTAL MELVIN, TOO, ANY CHANCE FOR A TWOFER?
SO I UNDERSTAND YOU HAVE A GAMBLING PROBLEM I DIDN'T KNOW ABOUT.
AT THE MOMENT, IT'S REALLY MORE OF A CASH FLOW CONCERN.
darb
SO WHAT WAS THE BET?
I BET THAT THE PATRIOTS WOULD WIN THE WORLD SERIES LAST YEAR.
OH.... OH YOU ARE SUCH AN IDIOT...
HOW WAS I SUPPOSED TO KNOW THAT LARRY BIRD RETIRED ?!
SEE, AT FIRST WHITEY WAS GIVING ME A MILLION TO ONE ODDS THAT THE PATRIOTS WOULD WIN THE WORLD SERIES, BUT I WAS ABLE TO TALK HIM DOWN TO TEN TO ONE ODDS.
...SO, SINCE IT WAS MUCH MORE LIKELY TO HAPPEN AT TEN TO ONE, I UPPED MY BET FROM ONE DOLLAR TO A THOUSAND DOLLARS.
darb
DO YOU KNOW ANYTHING ABOUT GAMBLING ?
DUHHH, EXCUSE ME, SEÑOR SKEPTICO, I THINK IT WAS ME WHO MADE THE BET - NOT YOU!

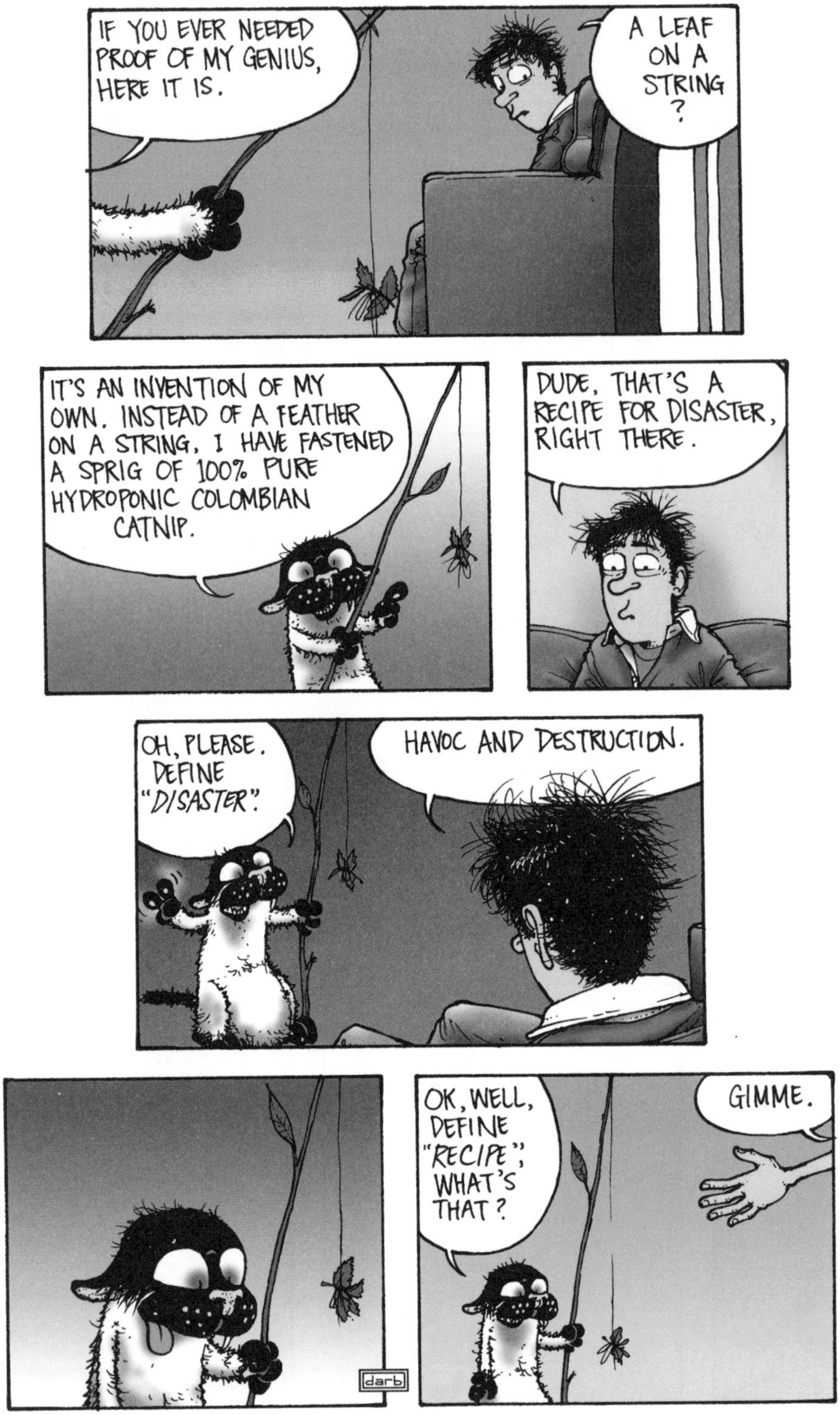
IF YOU EVER NEEDED PROOF OF MY GENIUS, HERE IT IS.
A LEAF ON A STRING ?
IT'S AN INVENTION OF MY OWN. INSTEAD OF A FEATHER ON A STRING, I HAVE FASTENED A SPRIG OF 100% PURE HYDROPONIC COLOMBIAN CATNIP.
DUDE, THAT'S A RECIPE FOR DISASTER, RIGHT THERE.
OH, PLEASE. DEFINE "DISASTER".
HAVOC AND DESTRUCTION.
OK, WELL, DEFINE "RECIPE"; WHAT'S THAT ?
GIMME.
darb

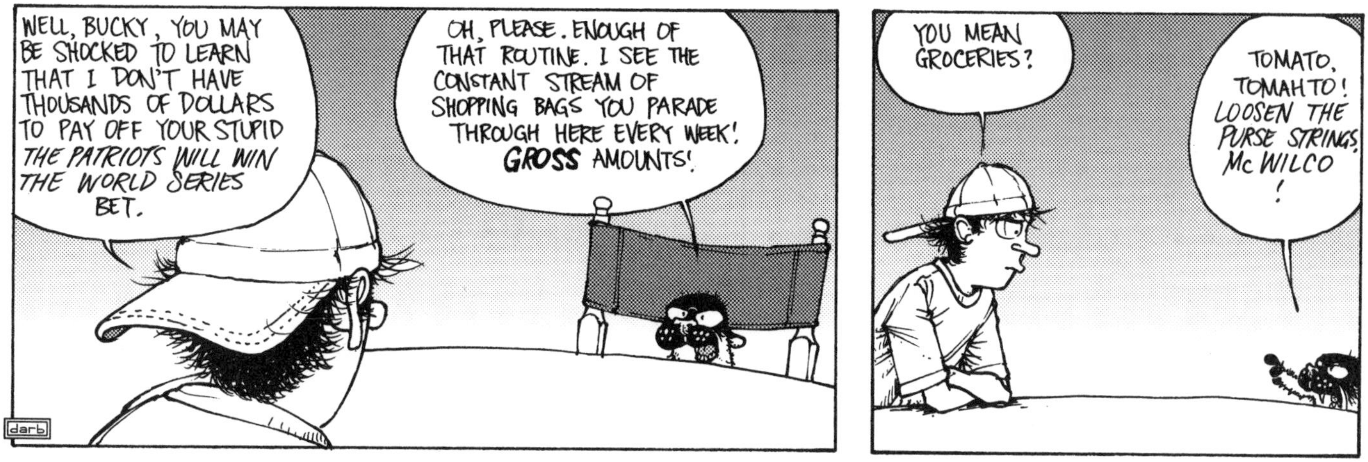
WELL, BUCKY, YOU MAY BE SHOCKED TO LEARN THAT I DON'T HAVE THOUSANDS OF DOLLARS TO PAY OFF YOUR STUPID *THE PATRIOTS WILL WIN THE WORLD SERIES* BET.
OH, PLEASE. ENOUGH OF THAT ROUTINE. I SEE THE CONSTANT STREAM OF SHOPPING BAGS YOU PARADE THROUGH HERE EVERY WEEK! **GROSS** AMOUNTS!
YOU MEAN GROCERIES?
TOMATO, TOMAHTO! *LOOSEN THE PURSE STRINGS,* McWILCO!
darb

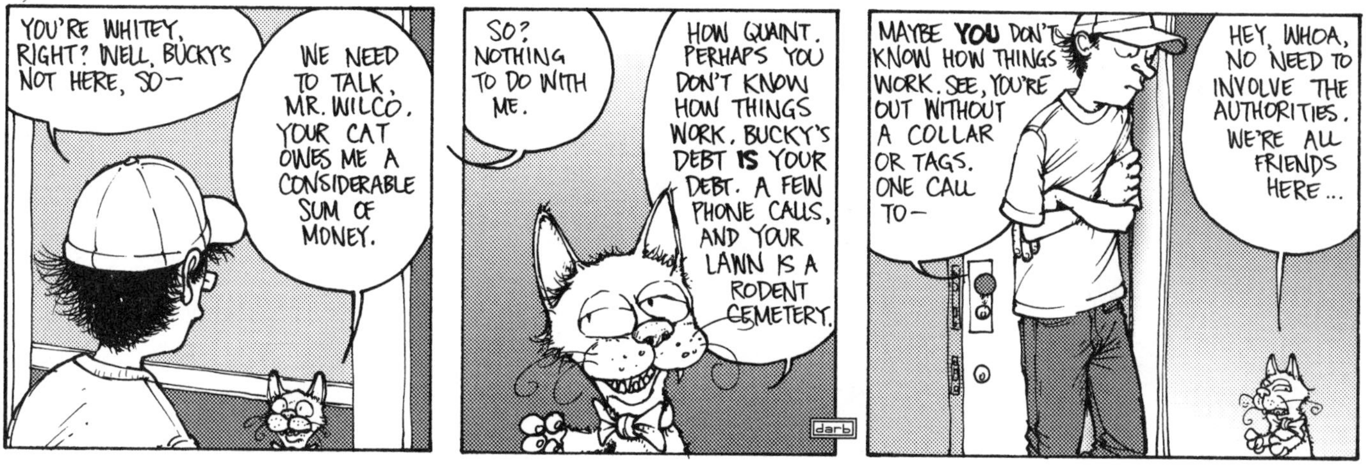
YOU'RE WHITEY, RIGHT? WELL, BUCKY'S NOT HERE, SO—
WE NEED TO TALK, MR. WILCO. YOUR CAT OWES ME A CONSIDERABLE SUM OF MONEY.
SO? NOTHING TO DO WITH ME.
HOW QUAINT. PERHAPS YOU DON'T KNOW HOW THINGS WORK. BUCKY'S DEBT **IS** YOUR DEBT. A FEW PHONE CALLS, AND YOUR LAWN IS A RODENT CEMETERY.
darb
MAYBE **YOU** DON'T KNOW HOW THINGS WORK. SEE, YOU'RE OUT WITHOUT A COLLAR OR TAGS. ONE CALL TO—
HEY, WHOA, NO NEED TO INVOLVE THE AUTHORITIES. WE'RE ALL FRIENDS HERE...

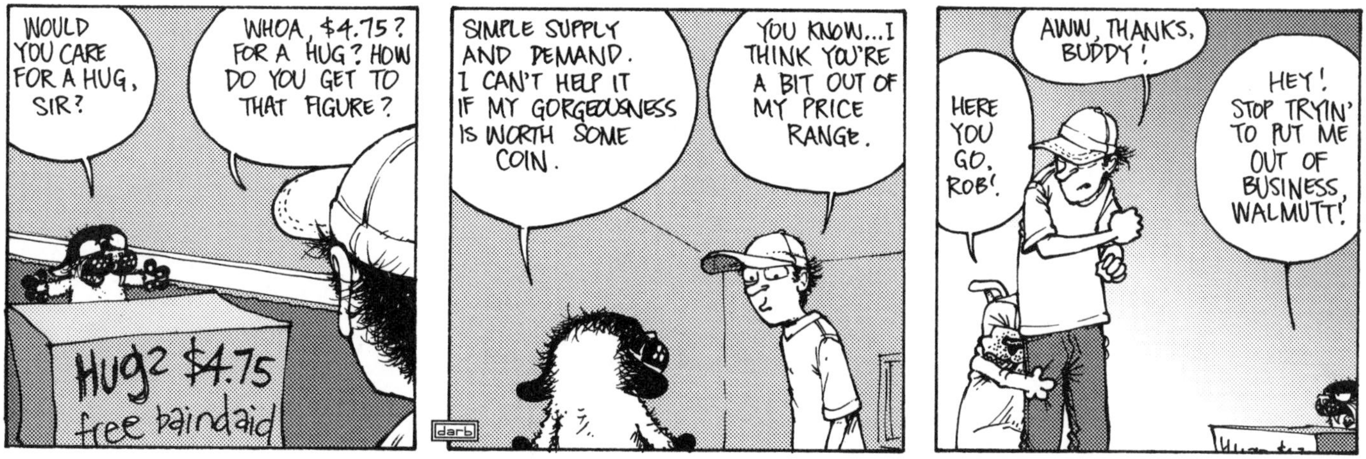
WOULD YOU CARE FOR A HUG, SIR?
WHOA, $4.75? FOR A HUG? HOW DO YOU GET TO THAT FIGURE?
Hugz $4.75
free baindaid
SIMPLE SUPPLY AND DEMAND. I CAN'T HELP IT IF MY GORGEOUSNESS IS WORTH SOME COIN.
YOU KNOW...I THINK YOU'RE A BIT OUT OF MY PRICE RANGE.
darb
AWW, THANKS, BUDDY!
HERE YOU GO, ROB!
HEY! STOP TRYIN' TO PUT ME OUT OF BUSINESS, WALMUTT!

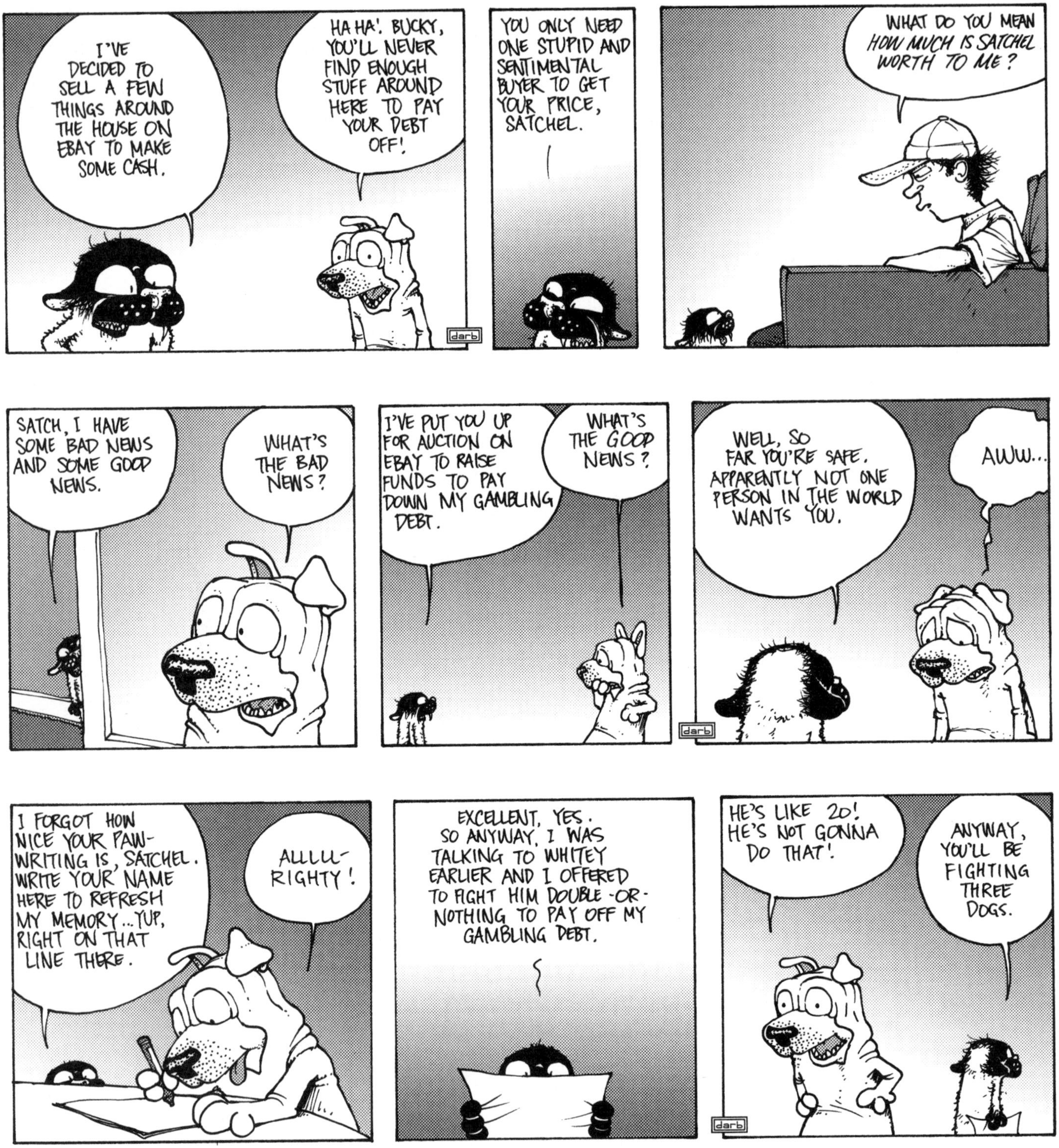
I'VE DECIDED TO SELL A FEW THINGS AROUND THE HOUSE ON EBAY TO MAKE SOME CASH.
HA HA! BUCKY, YOU'LL NEVER FIND ENOUGH STUFF AROUND HERE TO PAY YOUR DEBT OFF!
YOU ONLY NEED ONE STUPID AND SENTIMENTAL BUYER TO GET YOUR PRICE, SATCHEL.
WHAT DO YOU MEAN *HOW MUCH IS SATCHEL WORTH TO ME?*
darb
SATCH, I HAVE SOME BAD NEWS AND SOME GOOD NEWS.
WHAT'S THE BAD NEWS?
I'VE PUT YOU UP FOR AUCTION ON EBAY TO RAISE FUNDS TO PAY DOWN MY GAMBLING DEBT.
WHAT'S THE *GOOD* NEWS?
WELL, SO FAR YOU'RE SAFE. APPARENTLY NOT ONE PERSON IN THE WORLD WANTS YOU.
AWW...
darb
I FORGOT HOW NICE YOUR PAW-WRITING IS, SATCHEL. WRITE YOUR NAME HERE TO REFRESH MY MEMORY...YUP, RIGHT ON THAT LINE THERE.
ALLLL-RIGHTY!
EXCELLENT, YES. SO ANYWAY, I WAS TALKING TO WHITEY EARLIER AND I OFFERED TO FIGHT HIM DOUBLE-OR-NOTHING TO PAY OFF MY GAMBLING DEBT.
HE'S LIKE 20! HE'S NOT GONNA DO THAT!
ANYWAY, YOU'LL BE FIGHTING THREE DOGS.
darb

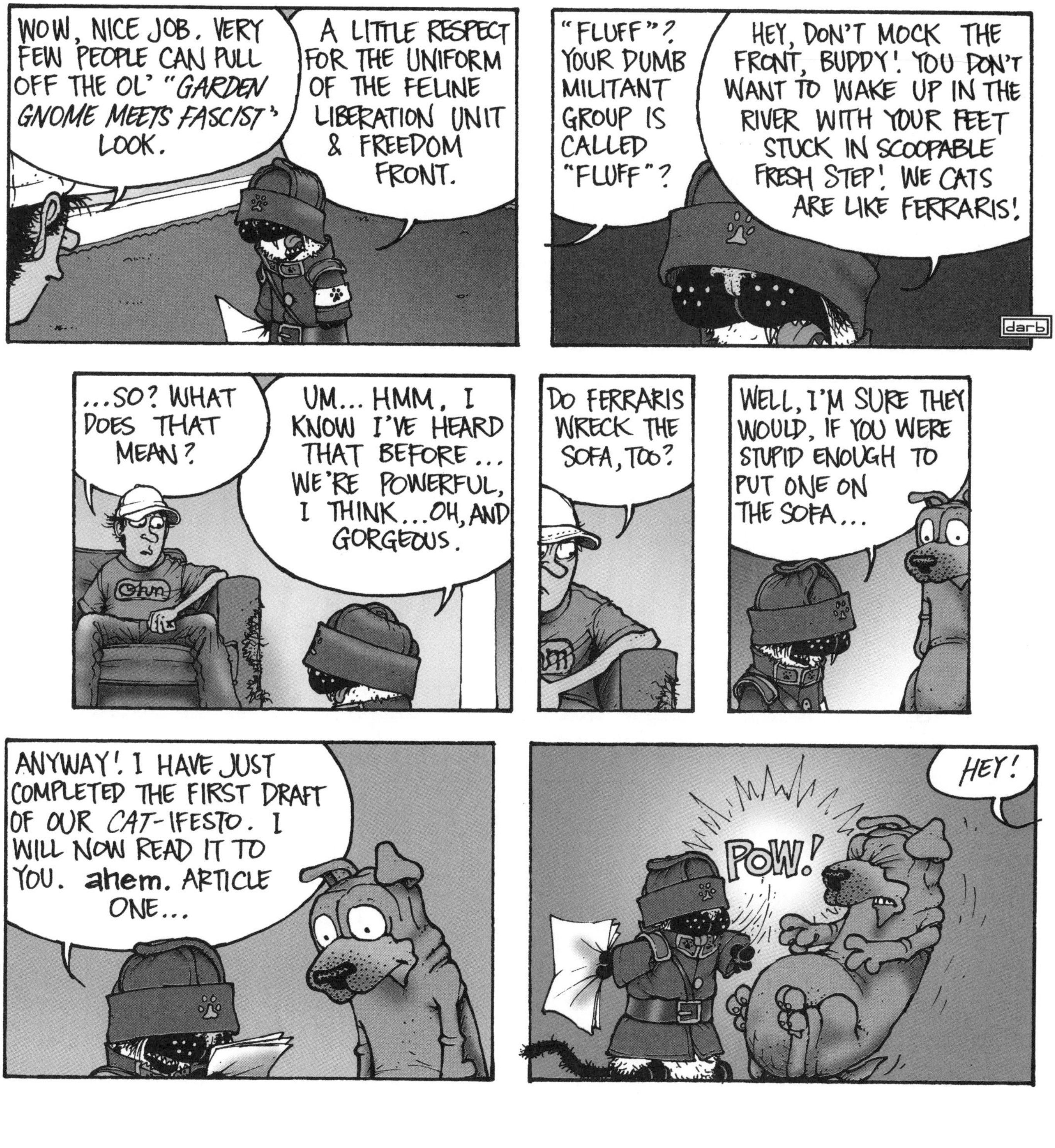
WOW, NICE JOB. VERY FEW PEOPLE CAN PULL OFF THE OL' "GARDEN GNOME MEETS FASCIST" LOOK.
A LITTLE RESPECT FOR THE UNIFORM OF THE FELINE LIBERATION UNIT & FREEDOM FRONT.
"FLUFF"? YOUR DUMB MILITANT GROUP IS CALLED "FLUFF"?
HEY, DON'T MOCK THE FRONT, BUDDY! YOU DON'T WANT TO WAKE UP IN THE RIVER WITH YOUR FEET STUCK IN SCOOPABLE FRESH STEP! WE CATS ARE LIKE FERRARIS!
darb
...SO? WHAT DOES THAT MEAN?
UM... HMM, I KNOW I'VE HEARD THAT BEFORE... WE'RE POWERFUL, I THINK... OH, AND GORGEOUS.
DO FERRARIS WRECK THE SOFA, TOO?
WELL, I'M SURE THEY WOULD, IF YOU WERE STUPID ENOUGH TO PUT ONE ON THE SOFA...
ANYWAY! I HAVE JUST COMPLETED THE FIRST DRAFT OF OUR CAT-IFESTO. I WILL NOW READ IT TO YOU. ahem. ARTICLE ONE...
POW!
HEY!

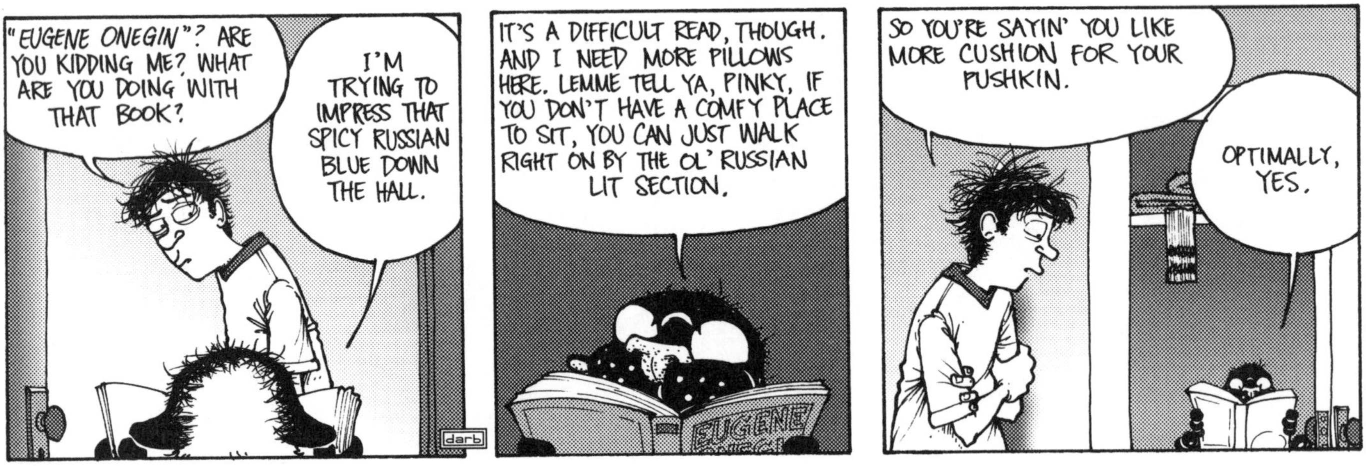
"EUGENE ONEGIN"? ARE YOU KIDDING ME? WHAT ARE YOU DOING WITH THAT BOOK?
I'M TRYING TO IMPRESS THAT SPICY RUSSIAN BLUE DOWN THE HALL.
IT'S A DIFFICULT READ, THOUGH. AND I NEED MORE PILLOWS HERE. LEMME TELL YA, PINKY, IF YOU DON'T HAVE A COMFY PLACE TO SIT, YOU CAN JUST WALK RIGHT ON BY THE OL' RUSSIAN LIT SECTION.
EUGENE
SO YOU'RE SAYIN' YOU LIKE MORE CUSHION FOR YOUR PUSHKIN.
OPTIMALLY, YES.
darb

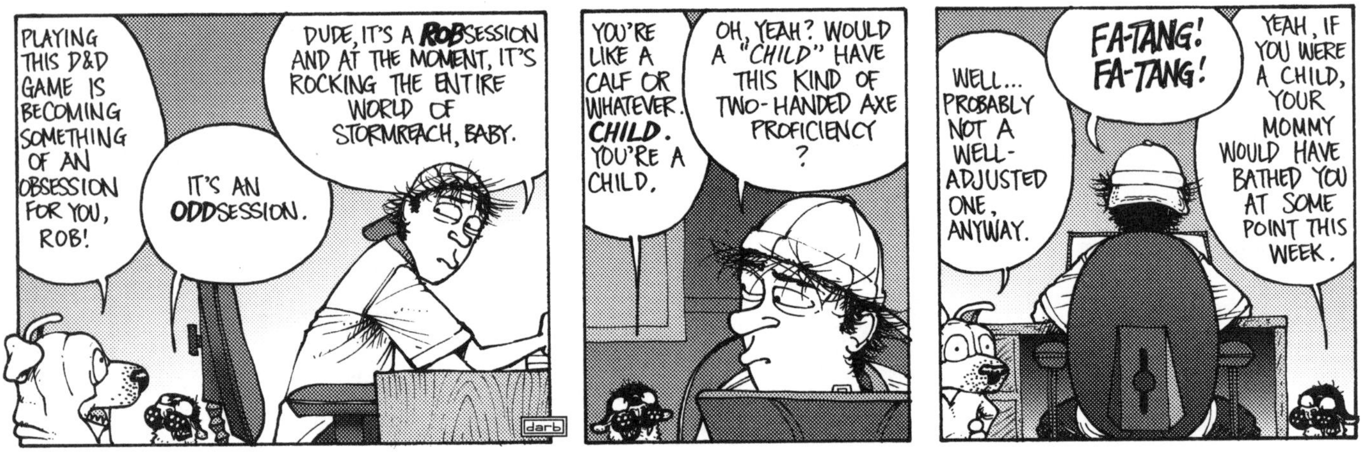
PLAYING THIS D&D GAME IS BECOMING SOMETHING OF AN OBSESSION FOR YOU, ROB!
IT'S AN **ODD**SESSION.
DUDE, IT'S A **ROB**SESSION AND AT THE MOMENT, IT'S ROCKING THE ENTIRE WORLD OF STORMREACH, BABY.
darb
YOU'RE LIKE A CALF OR WHATEVER. **CHILD.** YOU'RE A CHILD.
OH, YEAH? WOULD A "CHILD" HAVE THIS KIND OF TWO-HANDED AXE PROFICIENCY?
WELL... PROBABLY NOT A WELL-ADJUSTED ONE, ANYWAY.
FA-TANG! FA-TANG!
YEAH, IF YOU WERE A CHILD, YOUR MOMMY WOULD HAVE BATHED YOU AT SOME POINT THIS WEEK.

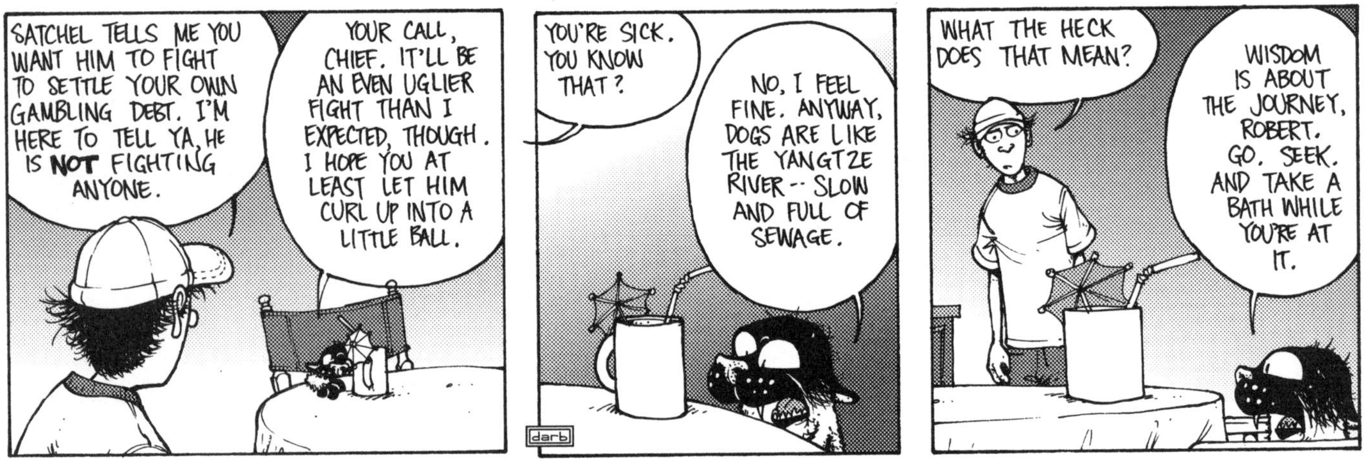
SATCHEL TELLS ME YOU WANT HIM TO FIGHT TO SETTLE YOUR OWN GAMBLING DEBT. I'M HERE TO TELL YA, HE IS **NOT** FIGHTING ANYONE.
YOUR CALL, CHIEF. IT'LL BE AN EVEN UGLIER FIGHT THAN I EXPECTED, THOUGH. I HOPE YOU AT LEAST LET HIM CURL UP INTO A LITTLE BALL.
YOU'RE SICK. YOU KNOW THAT?
NO, I FEEL FINE. ANYWAY, DOGS ARE LIKE THE YANGTZE RIVER -- SLOW AND FULL OF SEWAGE.
darb
WHAT THE HECK DOES THAT MEAN?
WISDOM IS ABOUT THE JOURNEY, ROBERT. GO. SEEK. AND TAKE A BATH WHILE YOU'RE AT IT.

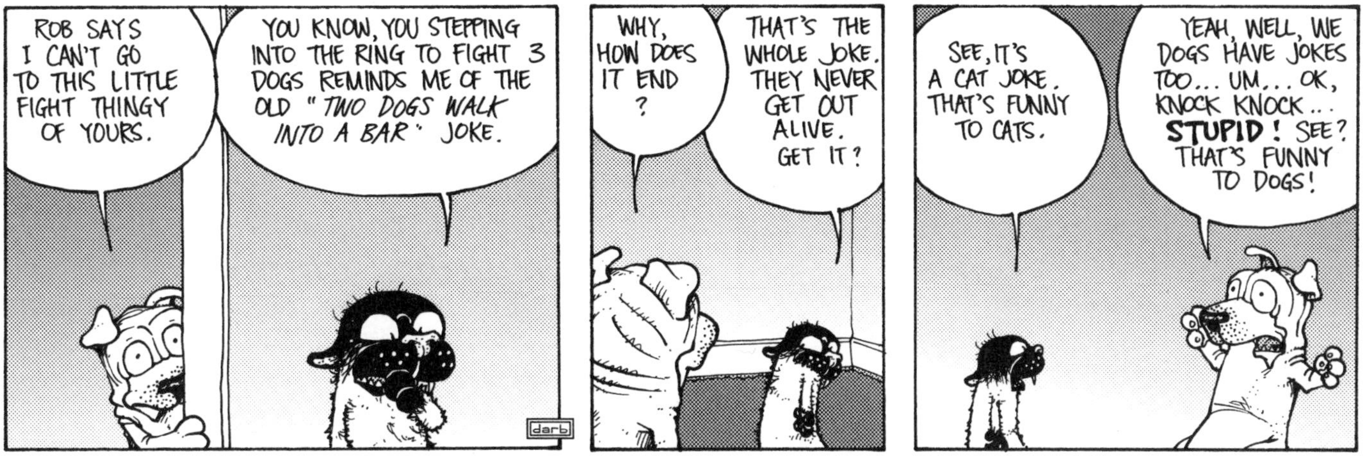
ROB SAYS I CAN'T GO TO THIS LITTLE FIGHT THINGY OF YOURS.
YOU KNOW, YOU STEPPING INTO THE RING TO FIGHT 3 DOGS REMINDS ME OF THE OLD "*TWO DOGS WALK INTO A BAR*" JOKE.
WHY, HOW DOES IT END ?
THAT'S THE WHOLE JOKE. THEY NEVER GET OUT ALIVE. GET IT?
SEE, IT'S A CAT JOKE. THAT'S FUNNY TO CATS.
YEAH, WELL, WE DOGS HAVE JOKES TOO... UM... OK, KNOCK KNOCK... **STUPID!** SEE? THAT'S FUNNY TO DOGS!

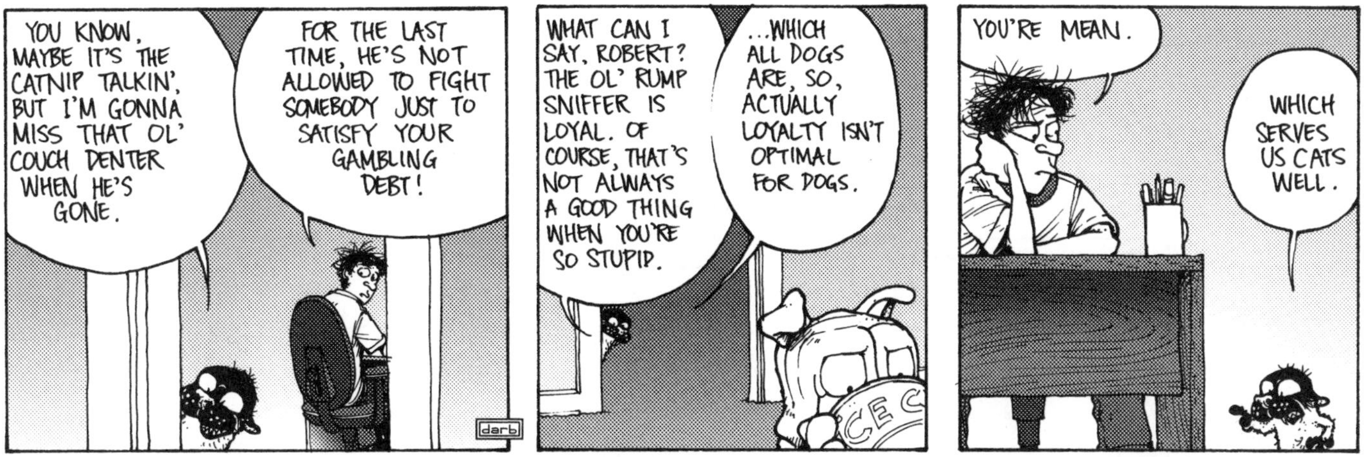
YOU KNOW, MAYBE IT'S THE CATNIP TALKIN', BUT I'M GONNA MISS THAT OL' COUCH DENTER WHEN HE'S GONE.
FOR THE LAST TIME, HE'S NOT ALLOWED TO FIGHT SOMEBODY JUST TO SATISFY YOUR GAMBLING DEBT!
WHAT CAN I SAY, ROBERT? THE OL' RUMP SNIFFER IS LOYAL. OF COURSE, THAT'S NOT ALWAYS A GOOD THING WHEN YOU'RE SO STUPID.
...WHICH ALL DOGS ARE, SO, ACTUALLY LOYALTY ISN'T OPTIMAL FOR DOGS.
YOU'RE MEAN.
WHICH SERVES US CATS WELL.

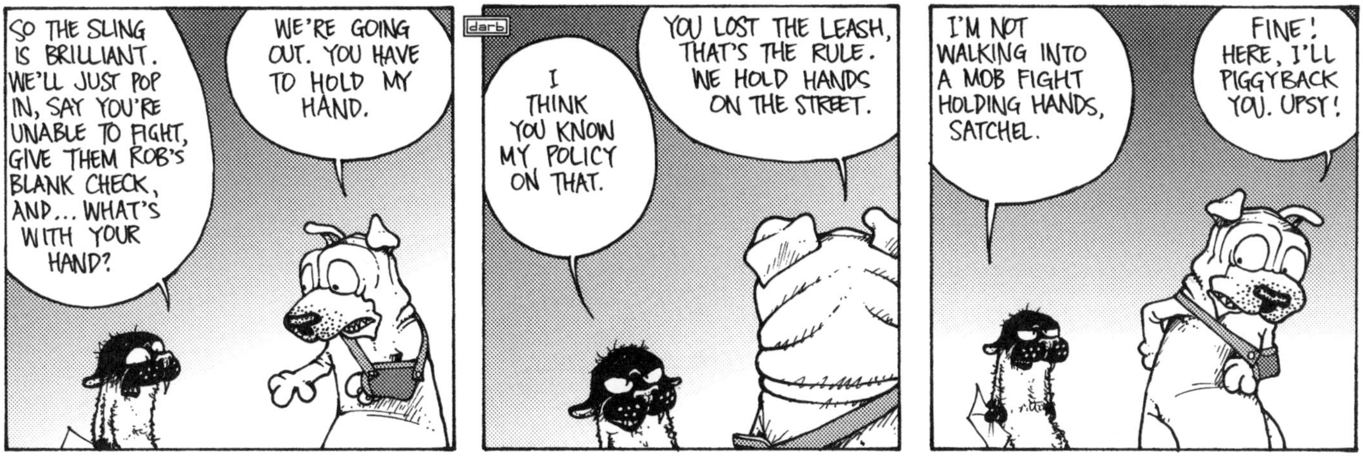
SO THE SLING IS BRILLIANT. WE'LL JUST POP IN, SAY YOU'RE UNABLE TO FIGHT, GIVE THEM ROB'S BLANK CHECK, AND... WHAT'S WITH YOUR HAND?
WE'RE GOING OUT. YOU HAVE TO HOLD MY HAND.
I THINK YOU KNOW MY POLICY ON THAT.
YOU LOST THE LEASH, THAT'S THE RULE. WE HOLD HANDS ON THE STREET.
I'M NOT WALKING INTO A MOB FIGHT HOLDING HANDS, SATCHEL.
FINE! HERE, I'LL PIGGYBACK YOU. UPSY!

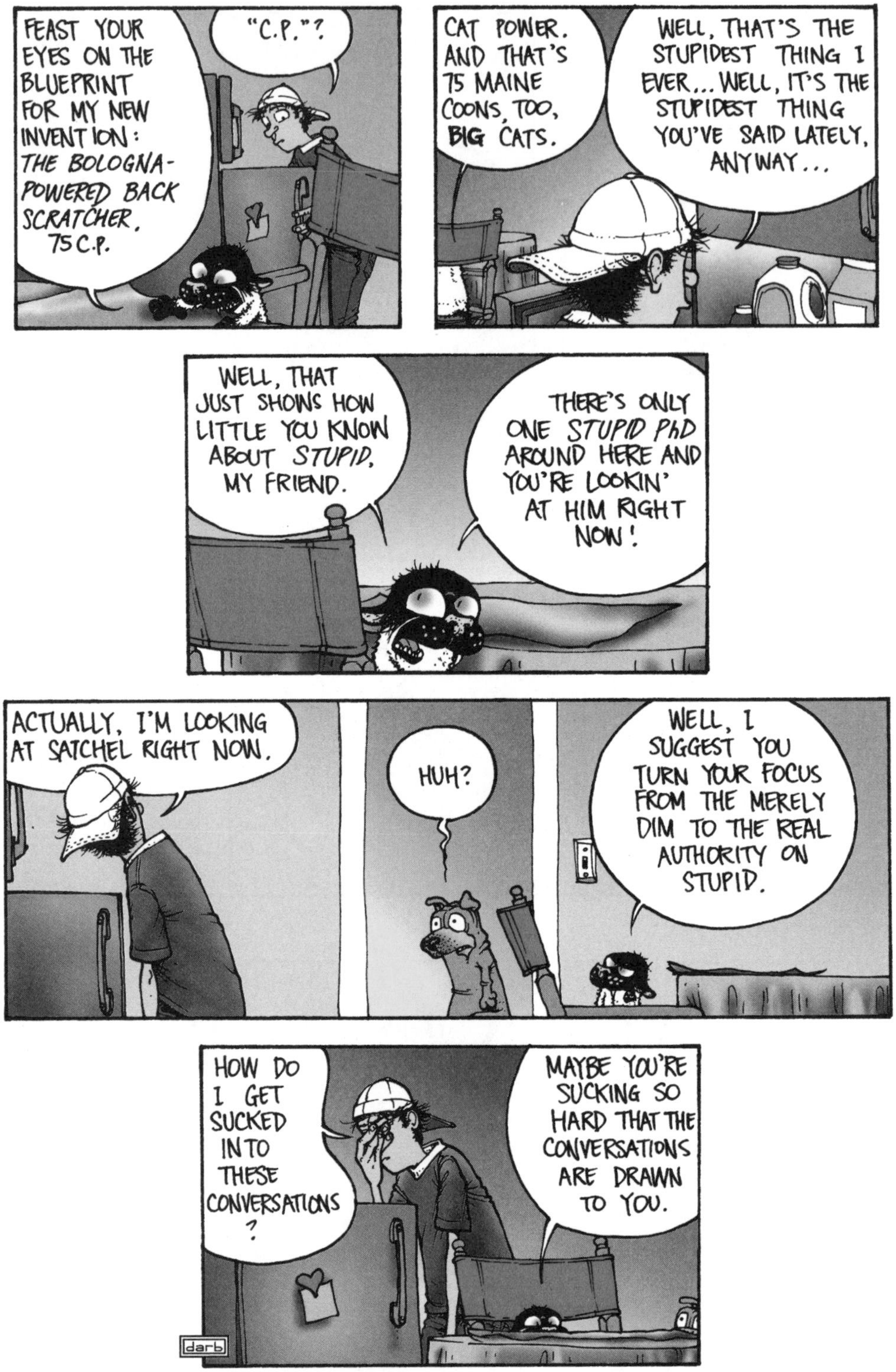

FEAST YOUR EYES ON THE BLUEPRINT FOR MY NEW INVENTION: *THE BOLOGNA-POWERED BACK SCRATCHER.* 75 C.P.
"C.P."?
CAT POWER. AND THAT'S 75 MAINE COONS, TOO, **BIG** CATS.
WELL, THAT'S THE STUPIDEST THING I EVER... WELL, IT'S THE STUPIDEST THING YOU'VE SAID LATELY, ANYWAY...
WELL, THAT JUST SHOWS HOW LITTLE YOU KNOW ABOUT *STUPID*, MY FRIEND.
THERE'S ONLY ONE *STUPID PhD* AROUND HERE AND YOU'RE LOOKIN' AT HIM RIGHT NOW!
ACTUALLY, I'M LOOKING AT SATCHEL RIGHT NOW.
HUH?
WELL, I SUGGEST YOU TURN YOUR FOCUS FROM THE MERELY DIM TO THE REAL AUTHORITY ON STUPID.
HOW DO I GET SUCKED INTO THESE CONVERSATIONS?
MAYBE YOU'RE SUCKING SO HARD THAT THE CONVERSATIONS ARE DRAWN TO YOU.
darb

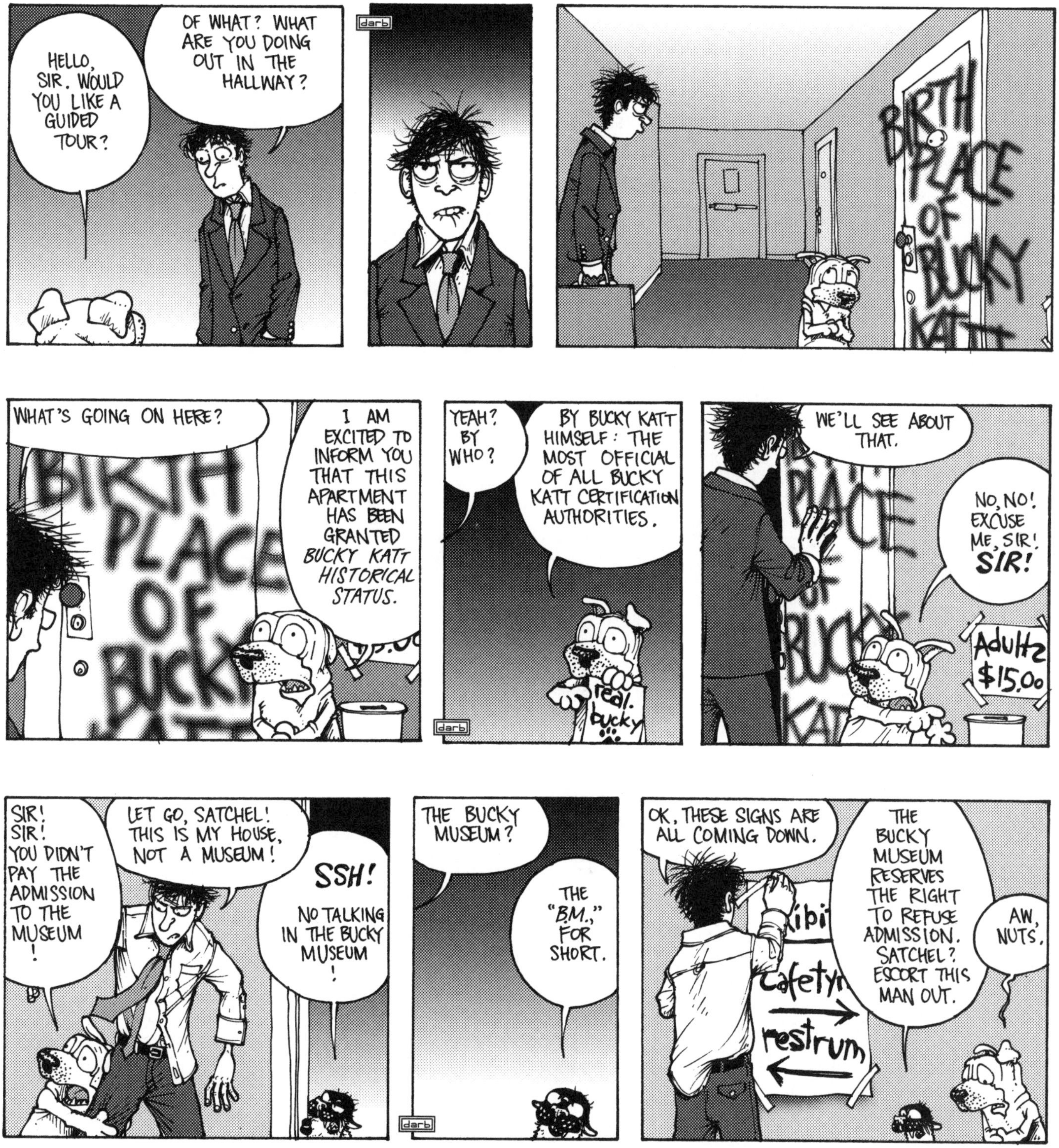
HELLO, SIR. WOULD YOU LIKE A GUIDED TOUR?
OF WHAT? WHAT ARE YOU DOING OUT IN THE HALLWAY?
BIRTH PLACE OF BUCKY KATT
WHAT'S GOING ON HERE?
I AM EXCITED TO INFORM YOU THAT THIS APARTMENT HAS BEEN GRANTED *BUCKY KATT HISTORICAL STATUS.*
YEAH? BY WHO?
BY BUCKY KATT HIMSELF: THE MOST OFFICIAL OF ALL BUCKY KATT CERTIFICATION AUTHORITIES.
real bucky
WE'LL SEE ABOUT THAT.
NO, NO! EXCUSE ME, SIR! **SIR!**
Adultz $15.00
SIR! SIR! YOU DIDN'T PAY THE ADMISSION TO THE MUSEUM!
LET GO, SATCHEL! THIS IS MY HOUSE, NOT A MUSEUM!
SSH!
NO TALKING IN THE BUCKY MUSEUM!
THE BUCKY MUSEUM?
THE "B.M.," FOR SHORT.
OK, THESE SIGNS ARE ALL COMING DOWN.
Cafetyr
restrum
THE BUCKY MUSEUM RESERVES THE RIGHT TO REFUSE ADMISSION. SATCHEL? ESCORT THIS MAN OUT.
AW, NUTS.

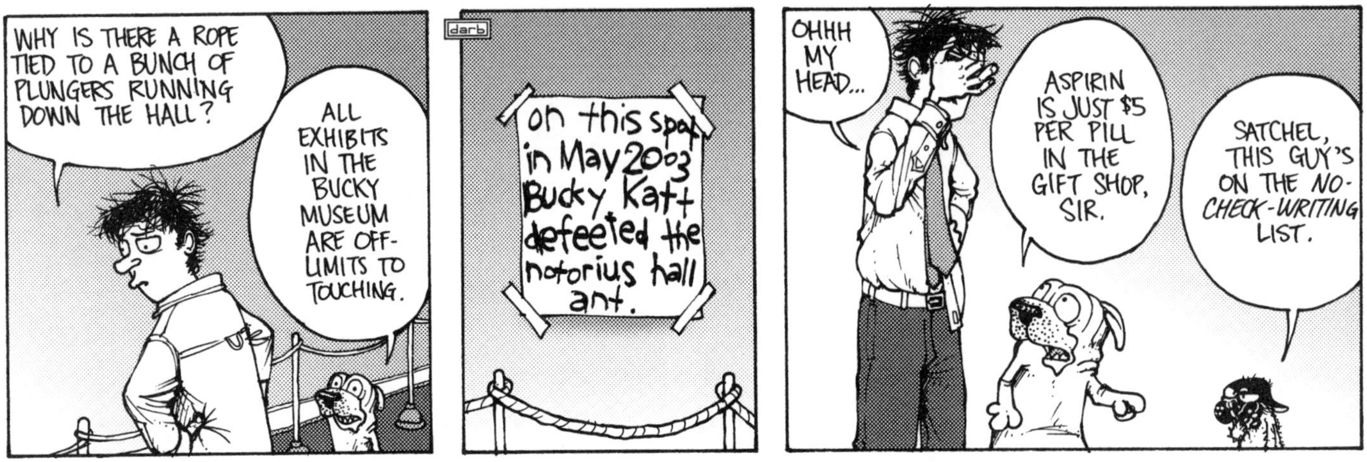
WHY IS THERE A ROPE TIED TO A BUNCH OF PLUNGERS RUNNING DOWN THE HALL?
ALL EXHIBITS IN THE BUCKY MUSEUM ARE OFF-LIMITS TO TOUCHING.
darb
on this spot in May 2003 Bucky Katt defeeted the notorius hall ant.
OHHH MY HEAD...
ASPIRIN IS JUST $5 PER PILL IN THE GIFT SHOP, SIR.
SATCHEL, THIS GUY'S ON THE NO-CHECK-WRITING LIST.

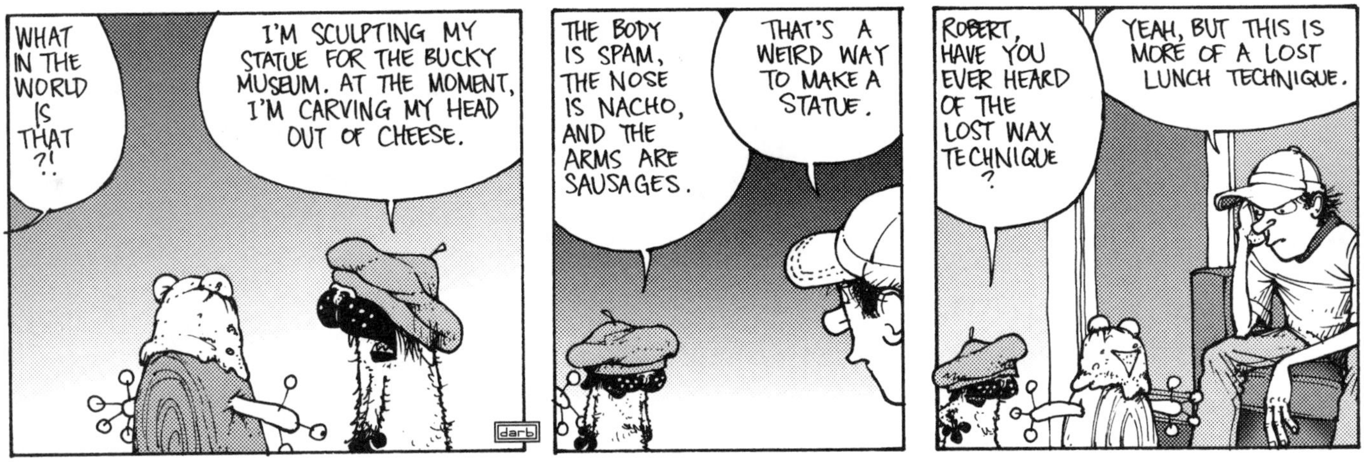
WHAT IN THE WORLD IS THAT?!
I'M SCULPTING MY STATUE FOR THE BUCKY MUSEUM. AT THE MOMENT, I'M CARVING MY HEAD OUT OF CHEESE.
darb
THE BODY IS SPAM, THE NOSE IS NACHO, AND THE ARMS ARE SAUSAGES.
THAT'S A WEIRD WAY TO MAKE A STATUE.
ROBERT, HAVE YOU EVER HEARD OF THE LOST WAX TECHNIQUE?
YEAH, BUT THIS IS MORE OF A LOST LUNCH TECHNIQUE.

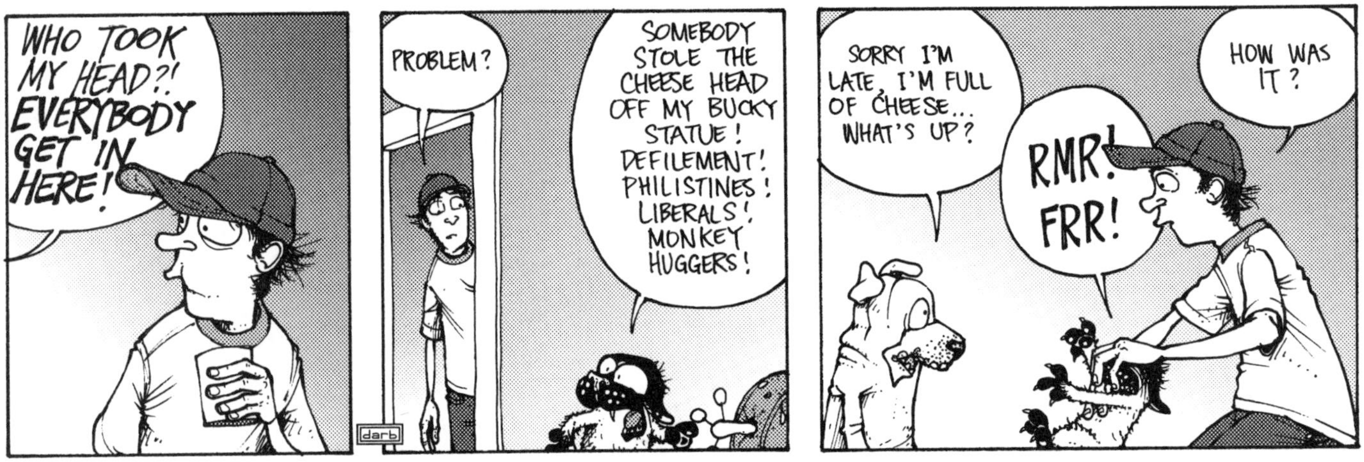
WHO TOOK MY HEAD?! EVERYBODY GET IN HERE!
darb
PROBLEM?
SOMEBODY STOLE THE CHEESE HEAD OFF MY BUCKY STATUE! DEFILEMENT! PHILISTINES! LIBERALS! MONKEY HUGGERS!
SORRY I'M LATE, I'M FULL OF CHEESE... WHAT'S UP?
RMR! FRR!
HOW WAS IT?

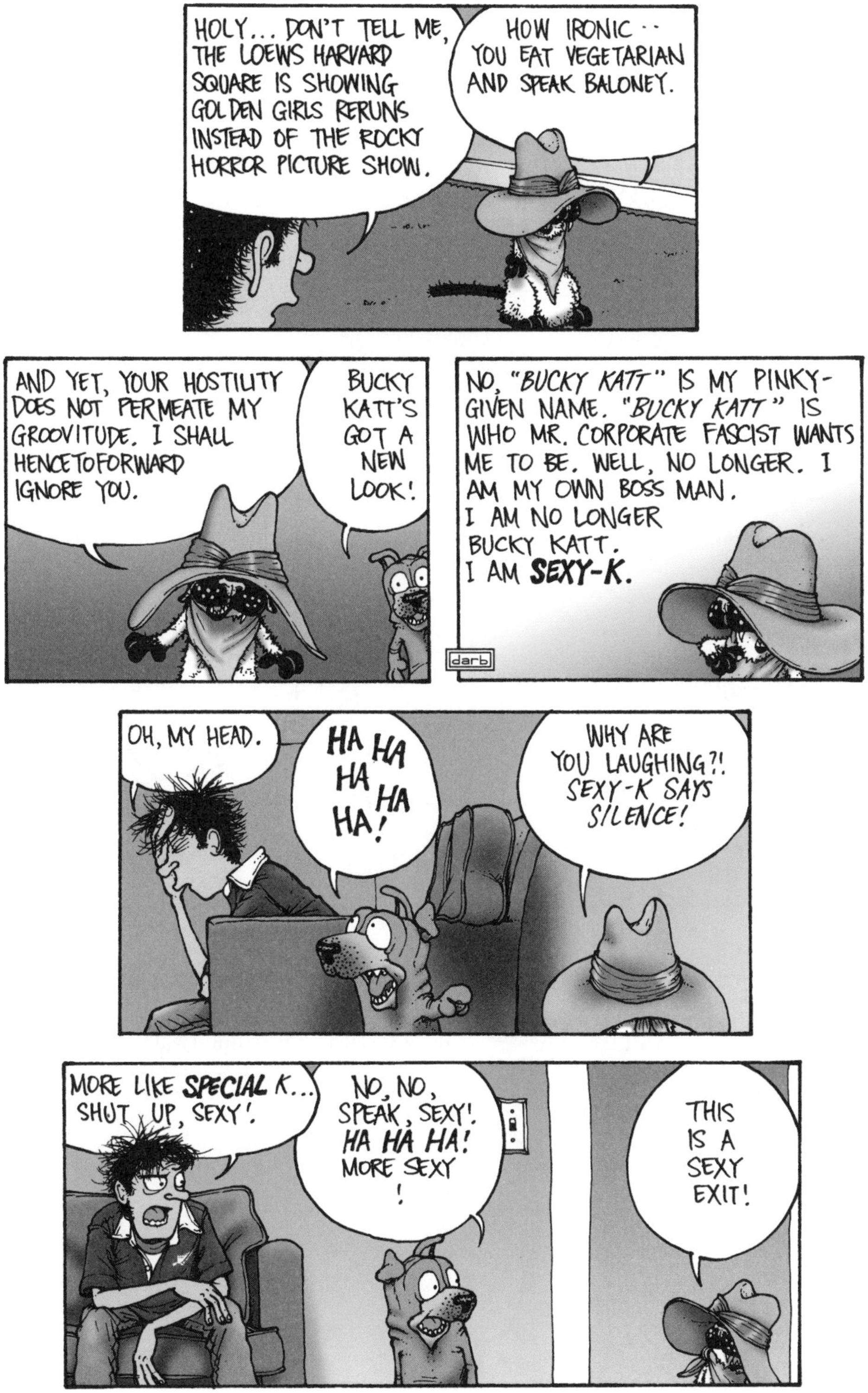
HOLY... DON'T TELL ME, THE LOEWS HARVARD SQUARE IS SHOWING GOLDEN GIRLS RERUNS INSTEAD OF THE ROCKY HORROR PICTURE SHOW.
HOW IRONIC.. YOU EAT VEGETARIAN AND SPEAK BALONEY.
AND YET, YOUR HOSTILITY DOES NOT PERMEATE MY GROOVITUDE. I SHALL HENCETOFORWARD IGNORE YOU.
BUCKY KATT'S GOT A NEW LOOK!
NO, "BUCKY KATT" IS MY PINKY-GIVEN NAME. "BUCKY KATT" IS WHO MR. CORPORATE FASCIST WANTS ME TO BE. WELL, NO LONGER. I AM MY OWN BOSS MAN. I AM NO LONGER BUCKY KATT. I AM SEXY-K.
darb
OH, MY HEAD.
HA HA HA HA HA!
WHY ARE YOU LAUGHING?! SEXY-K SAYS SILENCE!
MORE LIKE SPECIAL K... SHUT UP, SEXY!
NO, NO, SPEAK, SEXY! HA HA HA! MORE SEXY!
THIS IS A SEXY EXIT!

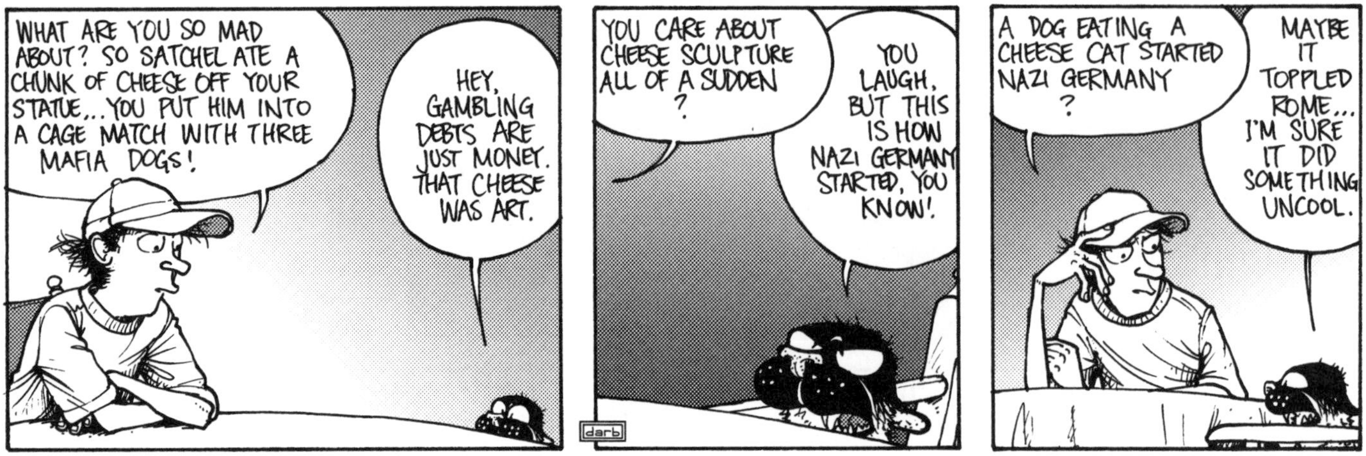
WHAT ARE YOU SO MAD ABOUT? SO SATCHEL ATE A CHUNK OF CHEESE OFF YOUR STATUE... YOU PUT HIM INTO A CAGE MATCH WITH THREE MAFIA DOGS!
HEY, GAMBLING DEBTS ARE JUST MONEY. THAT CHEESE WAS ART.
YOU CARE ABOUT CHEESE SCULPTURE ALL OF A SUDDEN?
YOU LAUGH, BUT THIS IS HOW NAZI GERMANY STARTED, YOU KNOW!
A DOG EATING A CHEESE CAT STARTED NAZI GERMANY?
MAYBE IT TOPPLED ROME... I'M SURE IT DID SOMETHING UNCOOL.
darb

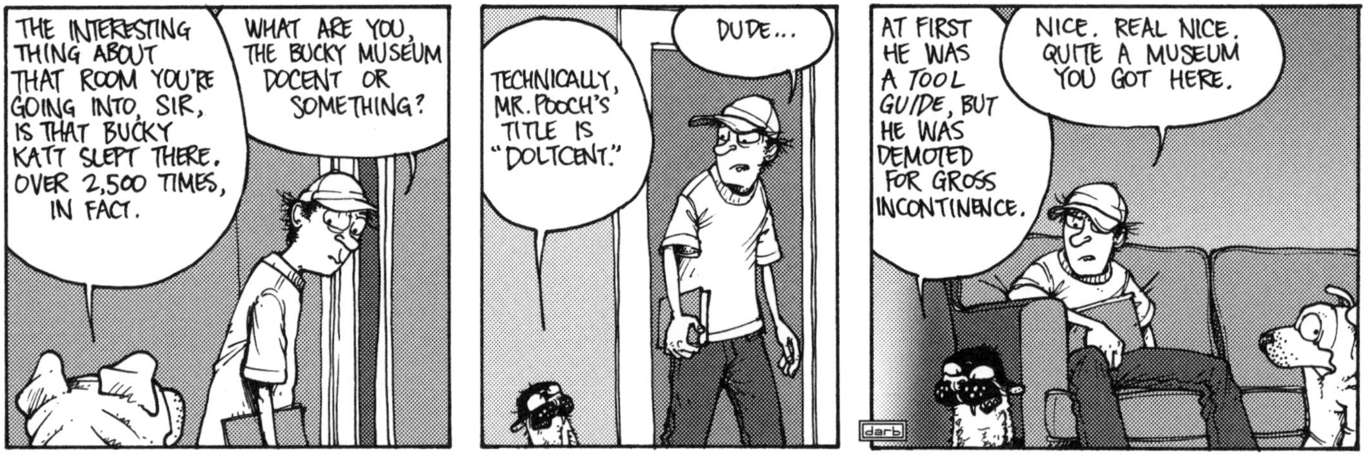
THE INTERESTING THING ABOUT THAT ROOM YOU'RE GOING INTO, SIR, IS THAT BUCKY KATT SLEPT THERE. OVER 2,500 TIMES, IN FACT.
WHAT ARE YOU, THE BUCKY MUSEUM DOCENT OR SOMETHING?
DUDE...
TECHNICALLY, MR. POOCH'S TITLE IS "DOLTCENT."
AT FIRST HE WAS A *TOOL GUIDE*, BUT HE WAS DEMOTED FOR GROSS INCONTINENCE.
NICE. REAL NICE. QUITE A MUSEUM YOU GOT HERE.
darb

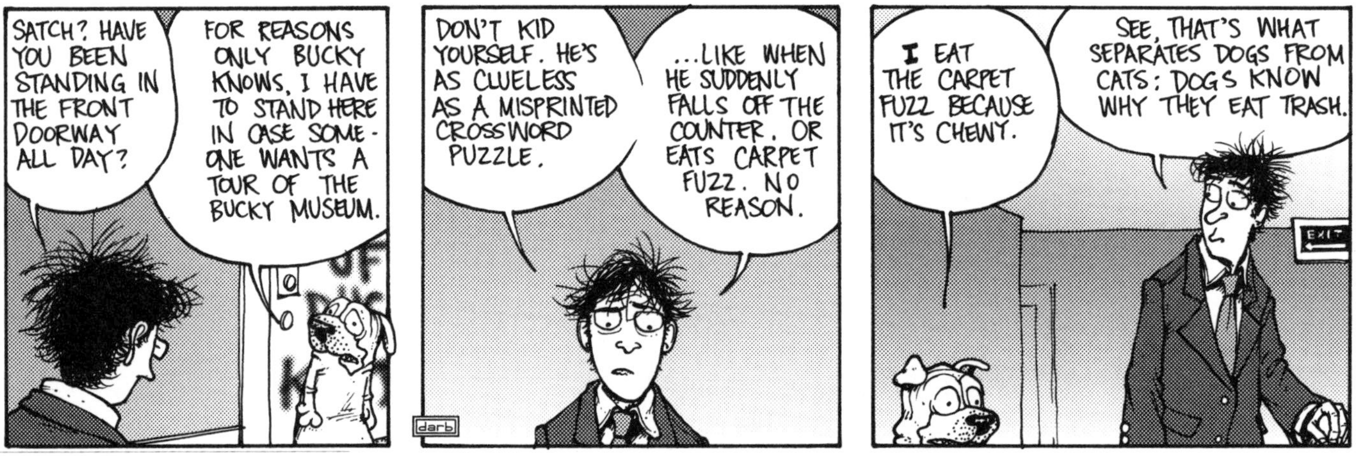
SATCH? HAVE YOU BEEN STANDING IN THE FRONT DOORWAY ALL DAY?
FOR REASONS ONLY BUCKY KNOWS, I HAVE TO STAND HERE IN CASE SOME-ONE WANTS A TOUR OF THE BUCKY MUSEUM.
DON'T KID YOURSELF. HE'S AS CLUELESS AS A MISPRINTED CROSSWORD PUZZLE.
...LIKE WHEN HE SUDDENLY FALLS OFF THE COUNTER. OR EATS CARPET FUZZ. NO REASON.
I EAT THE CARPET FUZZ BECAUSE IT'S CHEWY.
SEE, THAT'S WHAT SEPARATES DOGS FROM CATS: DOGS KNOW WHY THEY EAT TRASH.
EXIT
darb

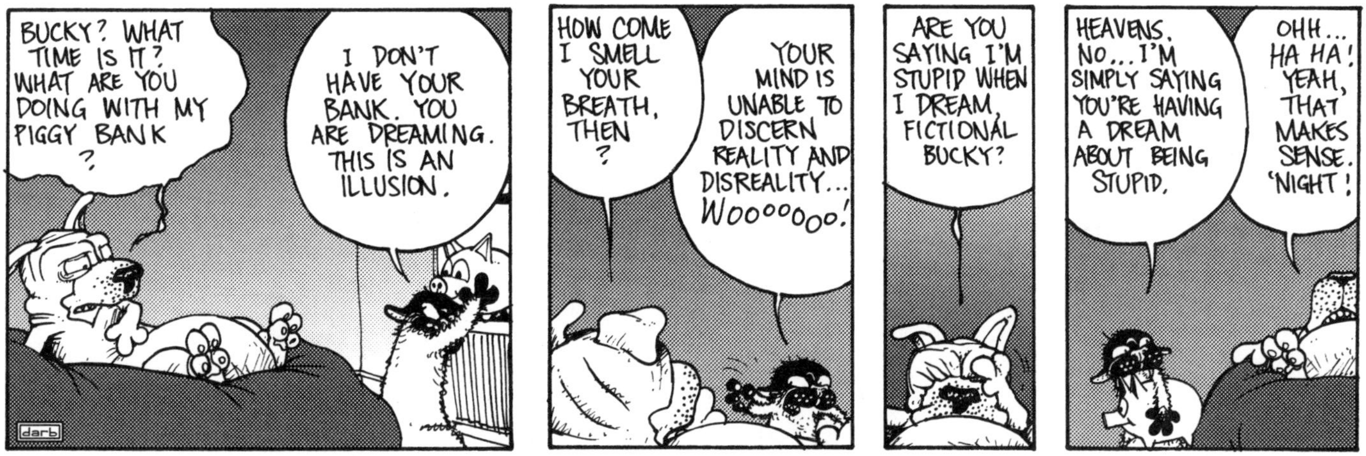
BUCKY? WHAT TIME IS IT? WHAT ARE YOU DOING WITH MY PIGGY BANK?
I DON'T HAVE YOUR BANK. YOU ARE DREAMING. THIS IS AN ILLUSION.
darb
HOW COME I SMELL YOUR BREATH, THEN?
YOUR MIND IS UNABLE TO DISCERN REALITY AND DISREALITY... WOooooo!
ARE YOU SAYING I'M STUPID WHEN I DREAM, FICTIONAL BUCKY?
HEAVENS, NO... I'M SIMPLY SAYING YOU'RE HAVING A DREAM ABOUT BEING STUPID.
OHH... HA HA! YEAH, THAT MAKES SENSE. 'NIGHT!

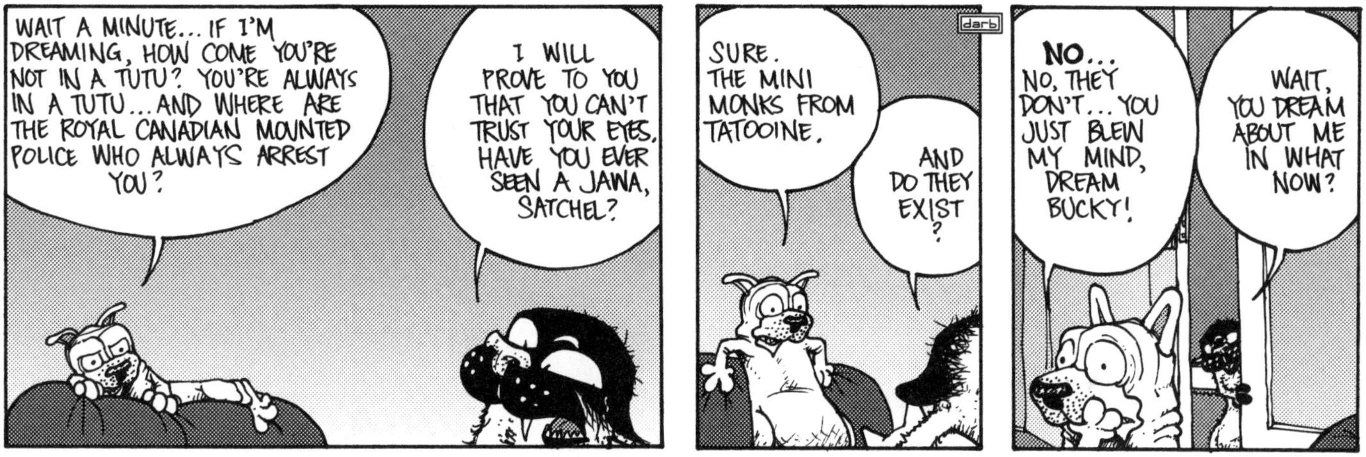
WAIT A MINUTE... IF I'M DREAMING, HOW COME YOU'RE NOT IN A TUTU? YOU'RE ALWAYS IN A TUTU... AND WHERE ARE THE ROYAL CANADIAN MOUNTED POLICE WHO ALWAYS ARREST YOU?
I WILL PROVE TO YOU THAT YOU CAN'T TRUST YOUR EYES. HAVE YOU EVER SEEN A JAWA, SATCHEL?
darb
SURE. THE MINI MONKS FROM TATOOINE.
AND DO THEY EXIST?
NO... NO, THEY DON'T... YOU JUST BLEW MY MIND, DREAM BUCKY!
WAIT, YOU DREAM ABOUT ME IN WHAT NOW?

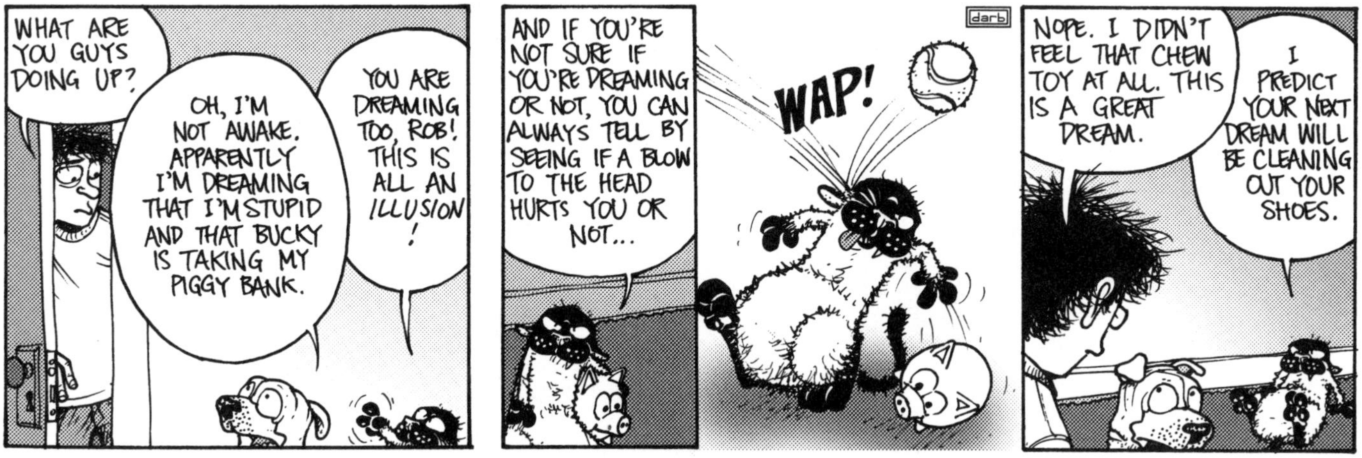
WHAT ARE YOU GUYS DOING UP?
OH, I'M NOT AWAKE. APPARENTLY I'M DREAMING THAT I'M STUPID AND THAT BUCKY IS TAKING MY PIGGY BANK.
YOU ARE DREAMING TOO, ROB! THIS IS ALL AN ILLUSION!
AND IF YOU'RE NOT SURE IF YOU'RE DREAMING OR NOT, YOU CAN ALWAYS TELL BY SEEING IF A BLOW TO THE HEAD HURTS YOU OR NOT...
darb
WAP!
NOPE. I DIDN'T FEEL THAT CHEW TOY AT ALL. THIS IS A GREAT DREAM.
I PREDICT YOUR NEXT DREAM WILL BE CLEANING OUT YOUR SHOES.

WHOA, THERE! PASSING THROUGH THIS DOORWAY COSTS SEVEN DOLLARS.

BUCKY, I ALREADY TOLD YOU THAT YOU CAN'T CHARGE ADMISSION FOR YOUR BUCKY MUSEUM.

NO, NO, NO, THIS IS THE *BUCKY KATT MEMORIAL DOORWAY.* THE SEVEN DOLLARS IS A TOLL.

YOU CAN'T CALL IT THE MEMORIAL DOORWAY UNTIL YOU'RE DEAD.

MAN, THIS HOUSE COULD NOT GET MORE STUPID...

OK, THEN IT'S THE *BUCKY KATT CELEBRATORIAL DOORWAY.* **TEN** DOLLARS.

ROB, CAN YOU HAND ME MY BONE, THERE? I CAN'T AFFORD TO GO OVER THERE AND GET IT.

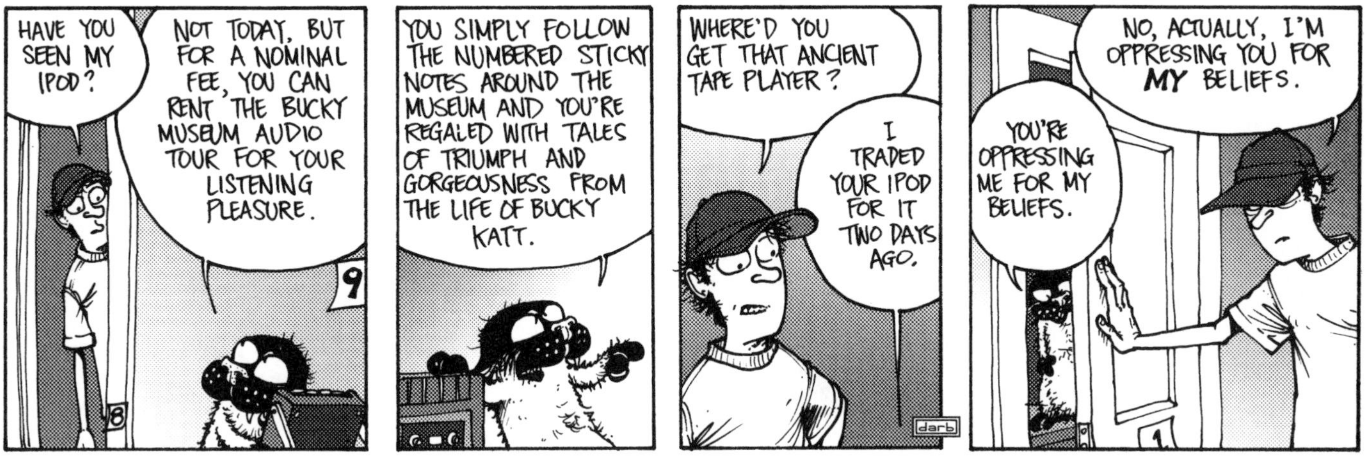
HAVE YOU SEEN MY IPOD?
NOT TODAY, BUT FOR A NOMINAL FEE, YOU CAN RENT THE BUCKY MUSEUM AUDIO TOUR FOR YOUR LISTENING PLEASURE.
YOU SIMPLY FOLLOW THE NUMBERED STICKY NOTES AROUND THE MUSEUM AND YOU'RE REGALED WITH TALES OF TRIUMPH AND GORGEOUSNESS FROM THE LIFE OF BUCKY KATT.
WHERE'D YOU GET THAT ANCIENT TAPE PLAYER?
I TRADED YOUR IPOD FOR IT TWO DAYS AGO.
YOU'RE OPPRESSING ME FOR MY BELIEFS.
NO, ACTUALLY, I'M OPPRESSING YOU FOR **MY** BELIEFS.

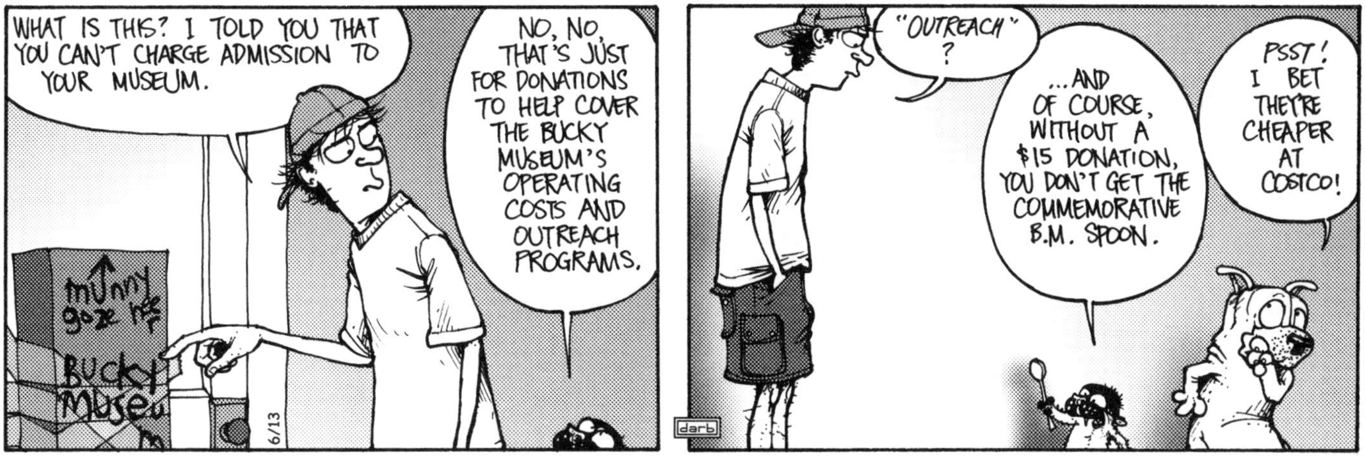
WHAT IS THIS? I TOLD YOU THAT YOU CAN'T CHARGE ADMISSION TO YOUR MUSEUM.
NO, NO, THAT'S JUST FOR DONATIONS TO HELP COVER THE BUCKY MUSEUM'S OPERATING COSTS AND OUTREACH PROGRAMS.
6/13
"OUTREACH"?
...AND OF COURSE, WITHOUT A $15 DONATION, YOU DON'T GET THE COMMEMORATIVE B.M. SPOON.
PSST! I BET THEY'RE CHEAPER AT COSTCO!

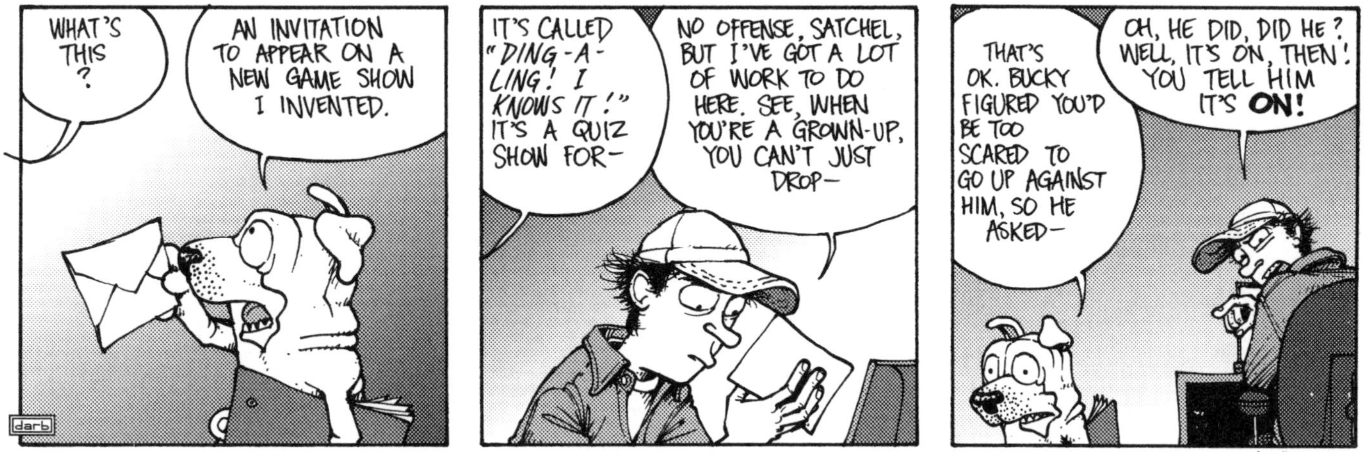
WHAT'S THIS?
AN INVITATION TO APPEAR ON A NEW GAME SHOW I INVENTED.
IT'S CALLED "DING-A-LING! I KNOWS IT!" IT'S A QUIZ SHOW FOR—
NO OFFENSE, SATCHEL, BUT I'VE GOT A LOT OF WORK TO DO HERE. SEE, WHEN YOU'RE A GROWN-UP, YOU CAN'T JUST DROP—
THAT'S OK. BUCKY FIGURED YOU'D BE TOO SCARED TO GO UP AGAINST HIM, SO HE ASKED—
OH, HE DID, DID HE? WELL, IT'S ON, THEN! YOU TELL HIM IT'S **ON!**

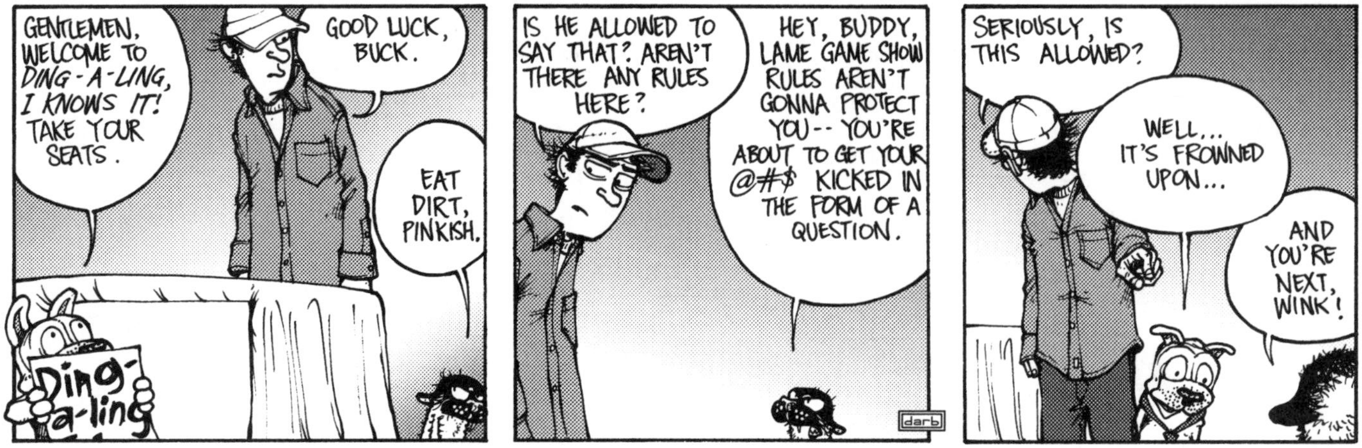
GENTLEMEN, WELCOME TO *DING-A-LING, I KNOWS IT!* TAKE YOUR SEATS.
GOOD LUCK, BUCK.
EAT DIRT, PINKISH.
Ding-a-ling
IS HE ALLOWED TO SAY THAT? AREN'T THERE ANY RULES HERE?
HEY, BUDDY, LAME GAME SHOW RULES AREN'T GONNA PROTECT YOU-- YOU'RE ABOUT TO GET YOUR @#$ KICKED IN THE FORM OF A QUESTION.
darb
SERIOUSLY, IS THIS ALLOWED?
WELL... IT'S FROWNED UPON...
AND YOU'RE NEXT, WINK!

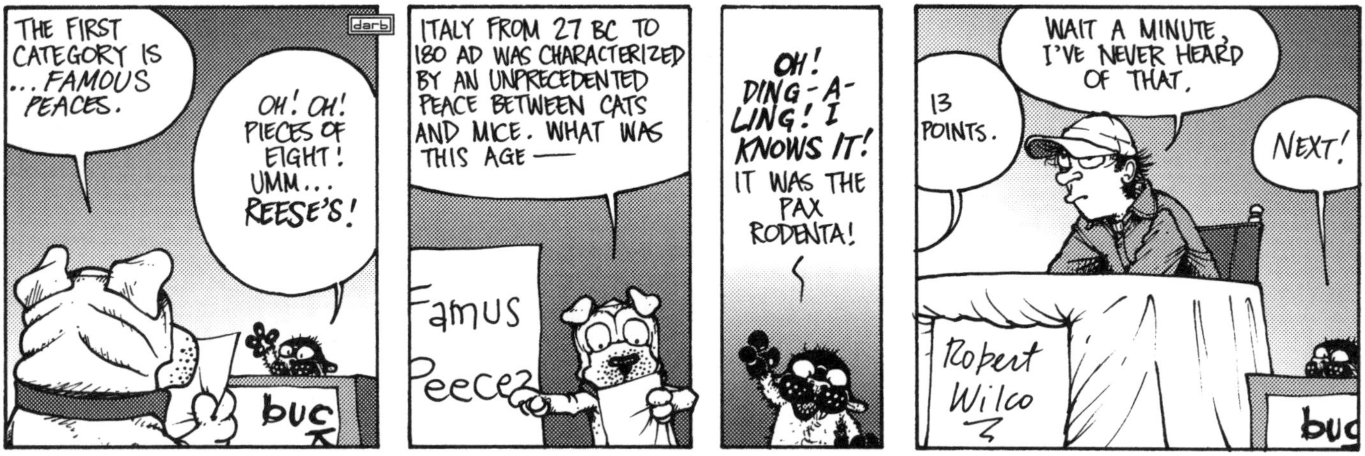
darb
THE FIRST CATEGORY IS ...*FAMOUS PEACES.*
OH! OH! PIECES OF EIGHT! UMM... **REESE'S!**
buc
ITALY FROM 27 BC TO 180 AD WAS CHARACTERIZED BY AN UNPRECEDENTED PEACE BETWEEN CATS AND MICE. WHAT WAS THIS AGE—
Famus Peecez
OH! DING-A-LING! I KNOWS IT! IT WAS THE PAX RODENTA!
WAIT A MINUTE, I'VE NEVER HEARD OF THAT.
13 POINTS.
NEXT!
Robert Wilco
buc

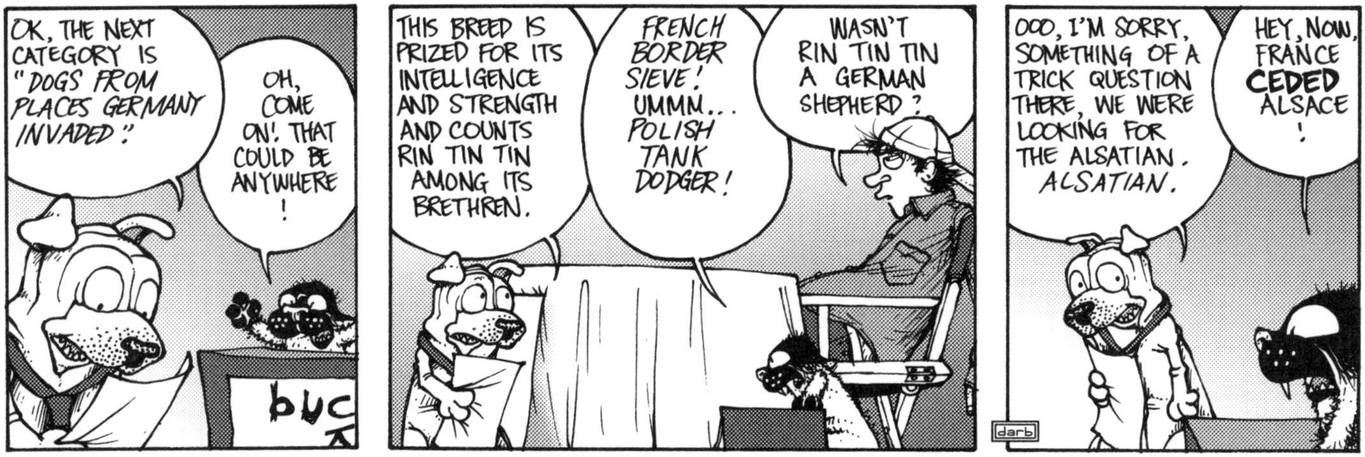
OK, THE NEXT CATEGORY IS "*DOGS FROM PLACES GERMANY INVADED.*"
OH, COME ON! THAT COULD BE ANYWHERE!
buc
THIS BREED IS PRIZED FOR ITS INTELLIGENCE AND STRENGTH AND COUNTS RIN TIN TIN AMONG ITS BRETHREN.
FRENCH BORDER SIEVE! UMMM... *POLISH TANK DODGER!*
WASN'T RIN TIN TIN A GERMAN SHEPHERD?
darb
OOO, I'M SORRY, SOMETHING OF A TRICK QUESTION THERE, WE WERE LOOKING FOR THE ALSATIAN. *ALSATIAN.*
HEY, NOW, FRANCE **CEDED** ALSACE!

OH, WHAT NOW, BUCKY?

"BUCKY KATT" IS WHO CORPORATE MAN WANTS ME TO BE. I'M NOW SEXY B.

DO YOU EVEN KNOW WHAT SEXY MEANS? 'CAUSE IT REALLY DOESN'T APPLY TO YOU.

YOU DON'T HAVE TO KNOW EVERY NUMBER IN THE DICTIOMARY TO KNOW WHAT R-O-X.

ME LISTENS TO TV, IT'S WELL EDOOCATIONISH. AND SEXY IS THE THING TO BE. SPORTS CARS ARE SEXY, PLASMA TVS ARE SEXY. AND NOW SEXY B SETS THE SEXY CURVE. **BOO YAMAHA!**

snap

OK, YOU'RE COPYING SOMEONE FROM TV, BUT HE'S KIDDING WHEN HE ACTS LIKE THAT.

LOOK, SEXY IS AS SEXY B DOES. IT'S A SEXY CIRCLE.

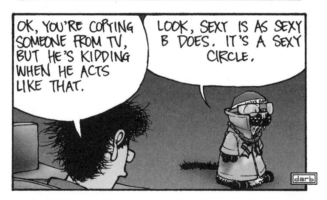

darb

WELL, THAT GUY ON THE NEWS JUST CALLED A CONGRESSIONAL CONFIRMATION HEARING SEXY. ARE YOU SAYING YOU'RE LIKE A CONFIRMATION HEARING?

CABINET OR JUDICIAL?

THERE GOES YOUR SEXY CRED.

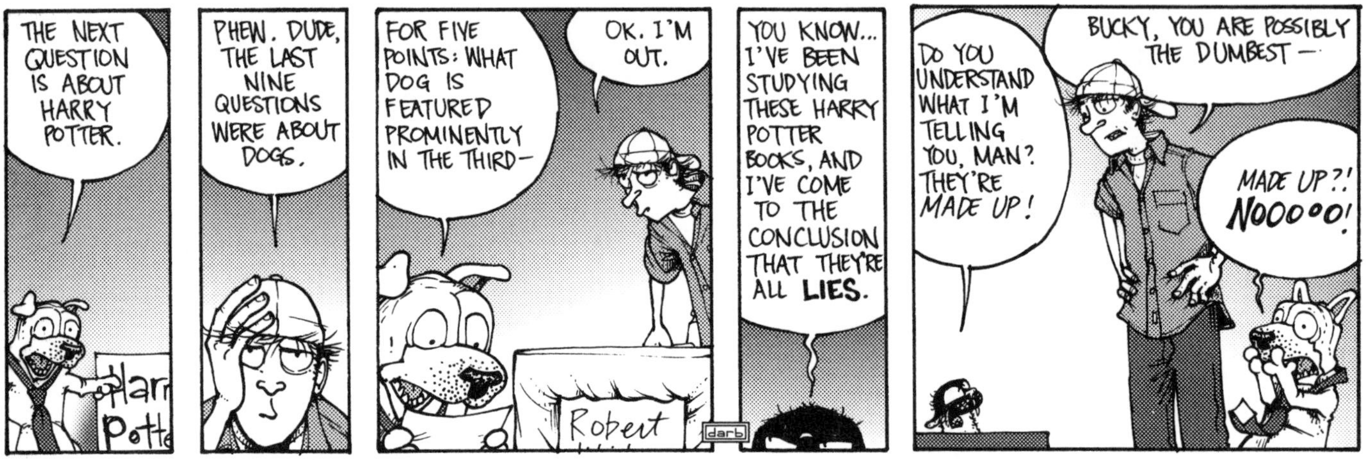
THE NEXT QUESTION IS ABOUT HARRY POTTER.
PHEW. DUDE, THE LAST NINE QUESTIONS WERE ABOUT DOGS.
FOR FIVE POINTS: WHAT DOG IS FEATURED PROMINENTLY IN THE THIRD–
OK. I'M OUT.
Robert
YOU KNOW... I'VE BEEN STUDYING THESE HARRY POTTER BOOKS, AND I'VE COME TO THE CONCLUSION THAT THEY'RE ALL **LIES**.
DO YOU UNDERSTAND WHAT I'M TELLING YOU, MAN? THEY'RE *MADE UP*!
BUCKY, YOU ARE POSSIBLY THE DUMBEST –
MADE UP?! NOOOOO!

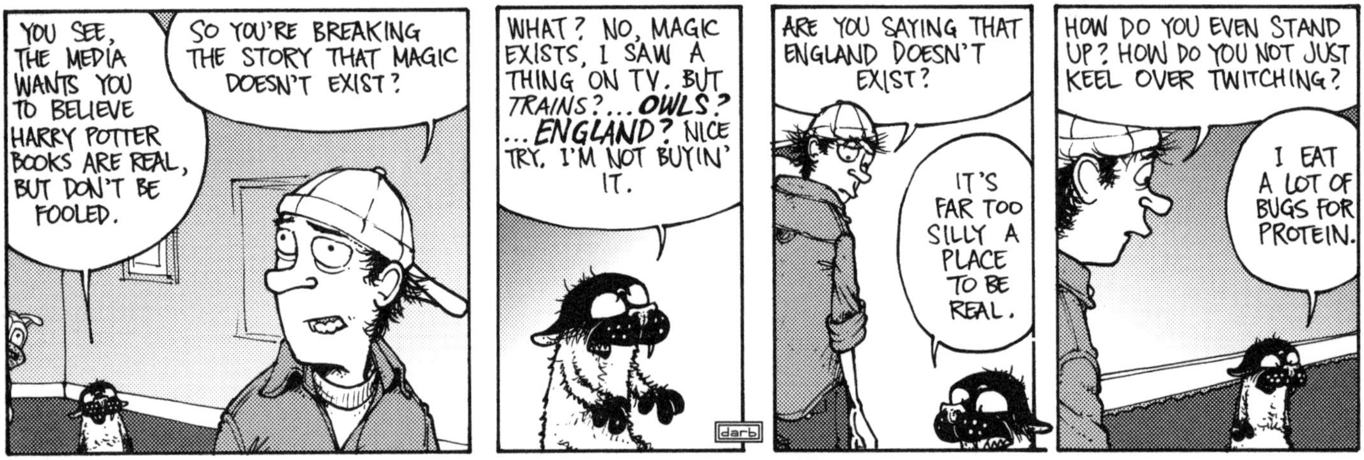
YOU SEE, THE MEDIA WANTS YOU TO BELIEVE HARRY POTTER BOOKS ARE REAL, BUT DON'T BE FOOLED.
SO YOU'RE BREAKING THE STORY THAT MAGIC DOESN'T EXIST?
WHAT? NO, MAGIC EXISTS, I SAW A THING ON TV. BUT *TRAINS?... **OWLS?*** ...***ENGLAND?*** NICE TRY. I'M NOT BUYIN' IT.
ARE YOU SAYING THAT ENGLAND DOESN'T EXIST?
IT'S FAR TOO SILLY A PLACE TO BE REAL.
HOW DO YOU EVEN STAND UP? HOW DO YOU NOT JUST KEEL OVER TWITCHING?
I EAT A LOT OF BUGS FOR PROTEIN.

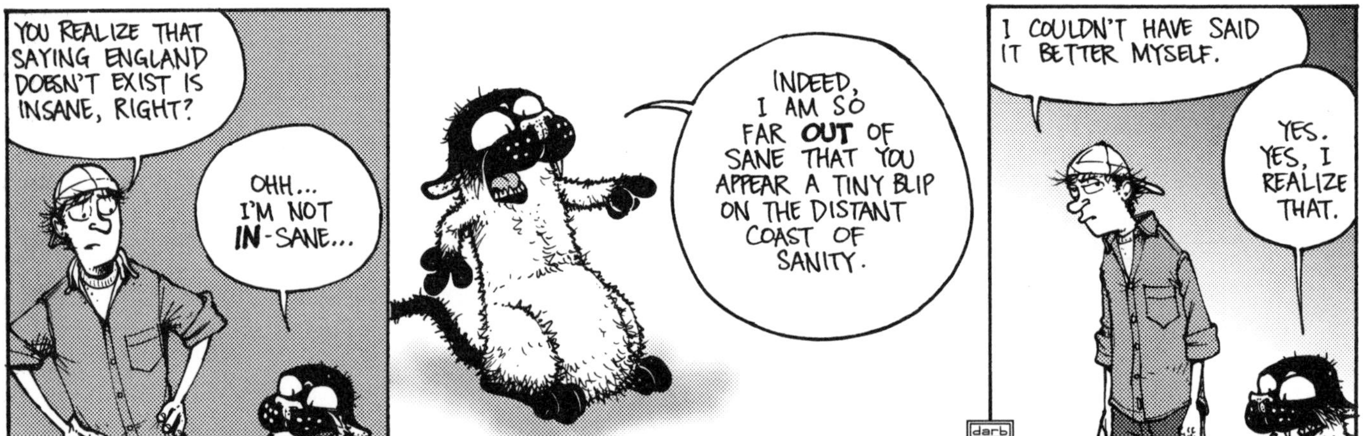
YOU REALIZE THAT SAYING ENGLAND DOESN'T EXIST IS INSANE, RIGHT?
OHH... I'M NOT **IN**-SANE...
INDEED, I AM SO FAR **OUT** OF SANE THAT YOU APPEAR A TINY BLIP ON THE DISTANT COAST OF SANITY.
I COULDN'T HAVE SAID IT BETTER MYSELF.
YES. YES, I REALIZE THAT.

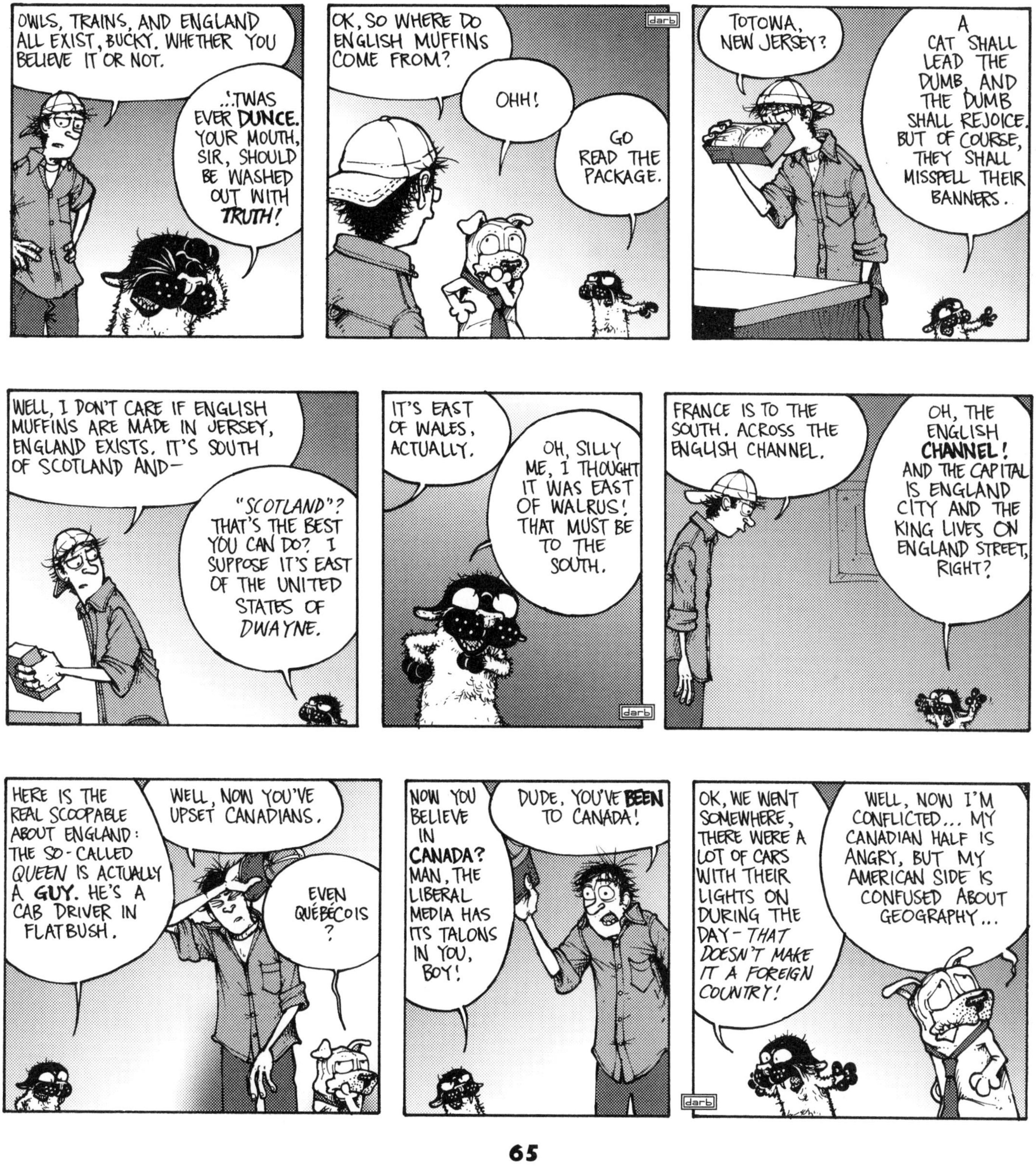
OWLS, TRAINS, AND ENGLAND ALL EXIST, BUCKY. WHETHER YOU BELIEVE IT OR NOT.
..'TWAS EVER **DUNCE.** YOUR MOUTH, SIR, SHOULD BE WASHED OUT WITH ***TRUTH!***
OK, SO WHERE DO ENGLISH MUFFINS COME FROM?
OHH!
GO READ THE PACKAGE.
TOTOWA, NEW JERSEY?
A CAT SHALL LEAD THE DUMB, AND THE DUMB SHALL REJOICE. BUT OF COURSE, THEY SHALL MISSPELL THEIR BANNERS.
WELL, I DON'T CARE IF ENGLISH MUFFINS ARE MADE IN JERSEY, ENGLAND EXISTS. IT'S SOUTH OF SCOTLAND AND—
"SCOTLAND"? THAT'S THE BEST YOU CAN DO? I SUPPOSE IT'S EAST OF THE UNITED STATES OF *DWAYNE.*
IT'S EAST OF WALES, ACTUALLY.
OH, SILLY ME, I THOUGHT IT WAS EAST OF WALRUS! THAT MUST BE TO THE SOUTH.
FRANCE IS TO THE SOUTH. ACROSS THE ENGLISH CHANNEL.
OH, THE ENGLISH **CHANNEL!** AND THE CAPITAL IS ENGLAND CITY AND THE KING LIVES ON ENGLAND STREET, RIGHT?
HERE IS THE REAL SCOOPABLE ABOUT ENGLAND: THE SO-CALLED *QUEEN* IS ACTUALLY A **GUY.** HE'S A CAB DRIVER IN FLATBUSH.
WELL, NOW YOU'VE UPSET CANADIANS.
EVEN QUÉBÉCOIS?
NOW YOU BELIEVE IN **CANADA?** MAN, THE LIBERAL MEDIA HAS ITS TALONS IN YOU, BOY!
DUDE, YOU'VE **BEEN** TO CANADA!
OK, WE WENT SOMEWHERE, THERE WERE A LOT OF CARS WITH THEIR LIGHTS ON DURING THE DAY—*THAT DOESN'T MAKE IT A FOREIGN COUNTRY!*
WELL, NOW I'M CONFLICTED... MY CANADIAN HALF IS ANGRY, BUT MY AMERICAN SIDE IS CONFUSED ABOUT GEOGRAPHY...

AH! DOG! YOU ARE ON HAND TO WITNESS THE DEPLOYMENT OF MY NEW INVENTION, THE TWEETER TRAPPER!

DO WHAT NOW?

I HAVE FASTENED — AT GREAT PERSONAL EXPENSE — A RAT TOY TO THIS NOOSE. RATBIRDS, SEEING THIS, WILL SWOOP DOWN FOR A QUICK—

I DON'T THINK THERE'S SUCH A THING AS A RATBIRD. NOW, AN *OWL* MIGHT EAT IT.

OH, I'M SURE I'VE HEARD OF A RATBIRD... SEE, THAT MEANS THEY FEED ON RATS...

SO WHAT'S A *CATBIRD*?

OH, HO HO! **SNAP**!

SHUT UP! BIRDS CAN'T EAT CATS! IT'S UNNATURAL! AND "OWLS" ARE A MYTH! LIKE ABDOMINAL SNOWMEN... OR SOUTHERN DEMOCRATS.

THE FOOD CHAIN GOES: FISH, COWS, MONKEYS AND HUMANS SPLIT OFF HERE, BIRDS, DOGS, AND CATS AT THE TOP. LIONS! TIGERS! SIAMESE!

WHAT ABOUT TONY TIGER? HE EATS CEREAL.

CLEARLY, HE SUFFERED SOME KITTENHOOD TRAUMA TO — **OOP!** A TUG ON THE TRAPPER!

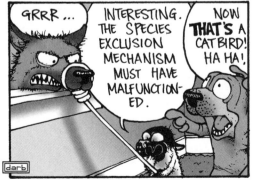

GRRR...

INTERESTING. THE SPECIES EXCLUSION MECHANISM MUST HAVE MALFUNCTIONED.

NOW **THAT'S** A CATBIRD! HA HA!

darb

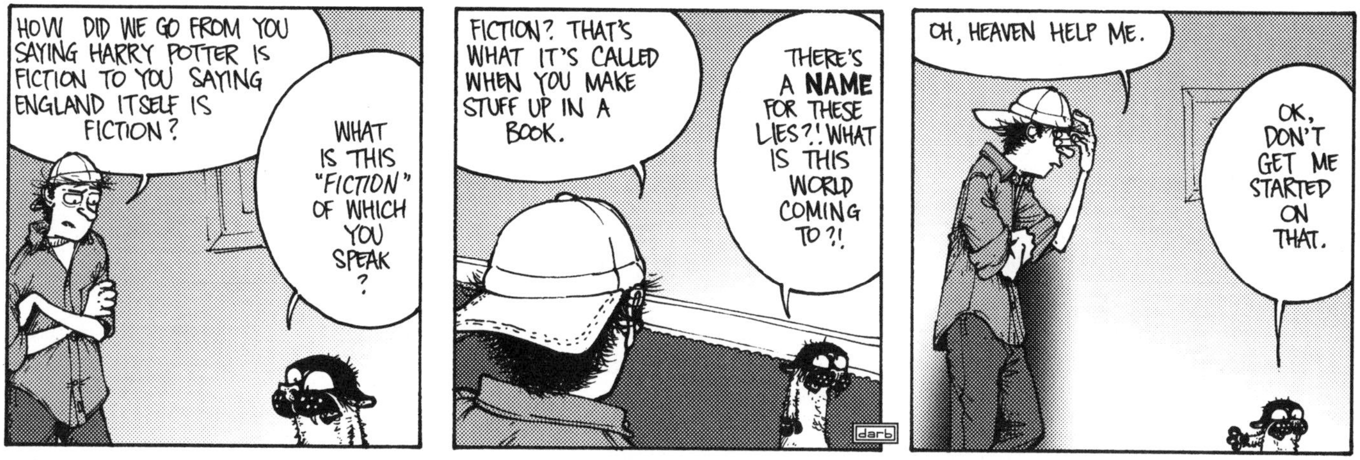
HOW DID WE GO FROM YOU SAYING HARRY POTTER IS FICTION TO YOU SAYING ENGLAND ITSELF IS FICTION?
WHAT IS THIS "FICTION" OF WHICH YOU SPEAK?
FICTION? THAT'S WHAT IT'S CALLED WHEN YOU MAKE STUFF UP IN A BOOK.
THERE'S A **NAME** FOR THESE LIES?! WHAT IS THIS WORLD COMING TO?!
darb
OH, HEAVEN HELP ME.
OK, DON'T GET ME STARTED ON THAT.

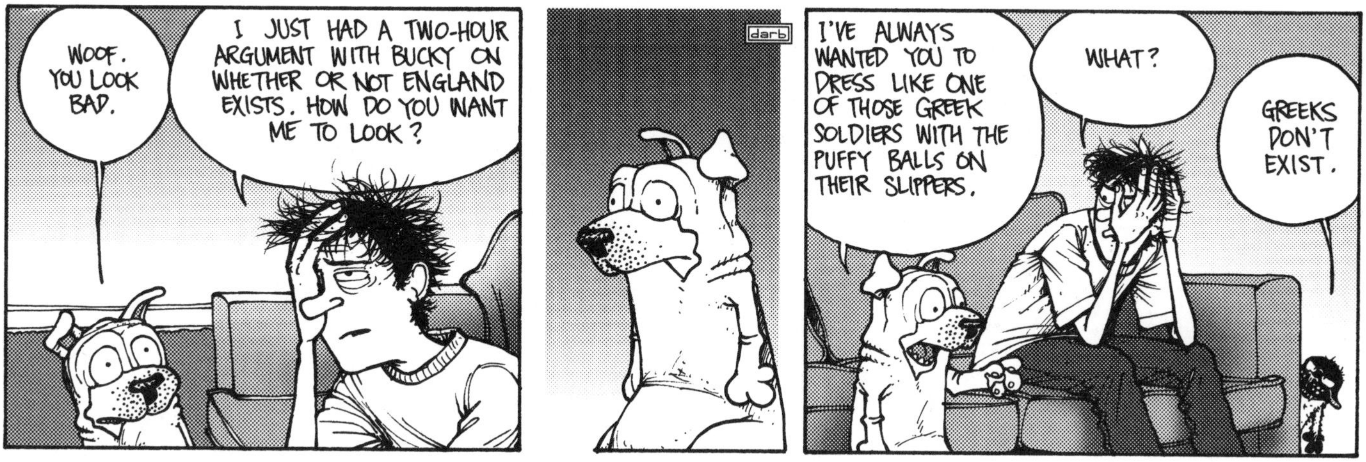
WOOF. YOU LOOK BAD.
I JUST HAD A TWO-HOUR ARGUMENT WITH BUCKY ON WHETHER OR NOT ENGLAND EXISTS. HOW DO YOU WANT ME TO LOOK?
darb
I'VE ALWAYS WANTED YOU TO DRESS LIKE ONE OF THOSE GREEK SOLDIERS WITH THE PUFFY BALLS ON THEIR SLIPPERS.
WHAT?
GREEKS DON'T EXIST.

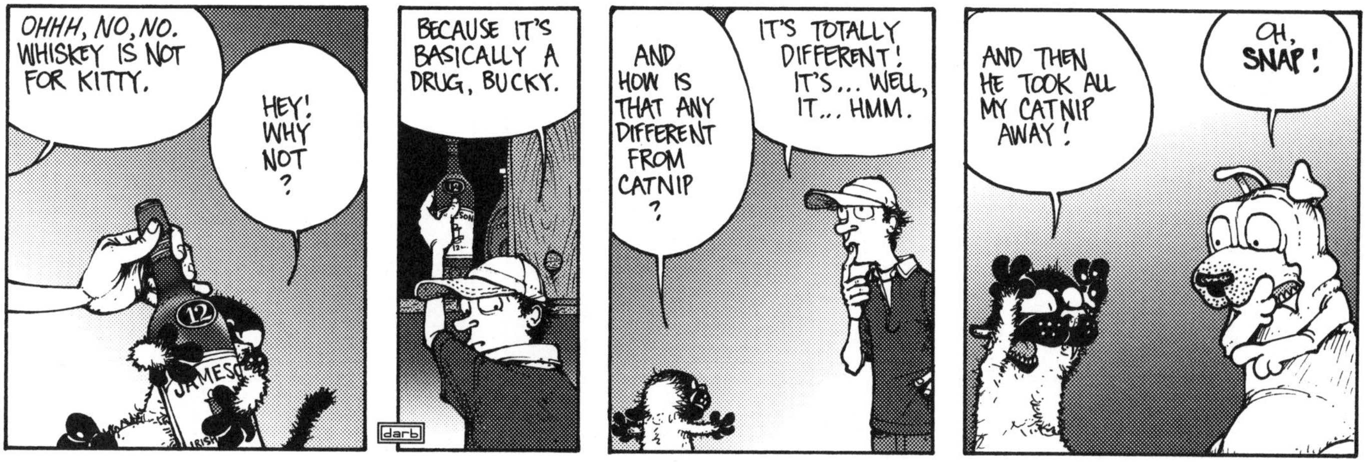
OHHH, NO, NO. WHISKEY IS NOT FOR KITTY.
HEY! WHY NOT?
BECAUSE IT'S BASICALLY A DRUG, BUCKY.
darb
AND HOW IS THAT ANY DIFFERENT FROM CATNIP?
IT'S TOTALLY DIFFERENT! IT'S... WELL, IT... HMM.
AND THEN HE TOOK ALL MY CATNIP AWAY!
OH, **SNAP**!

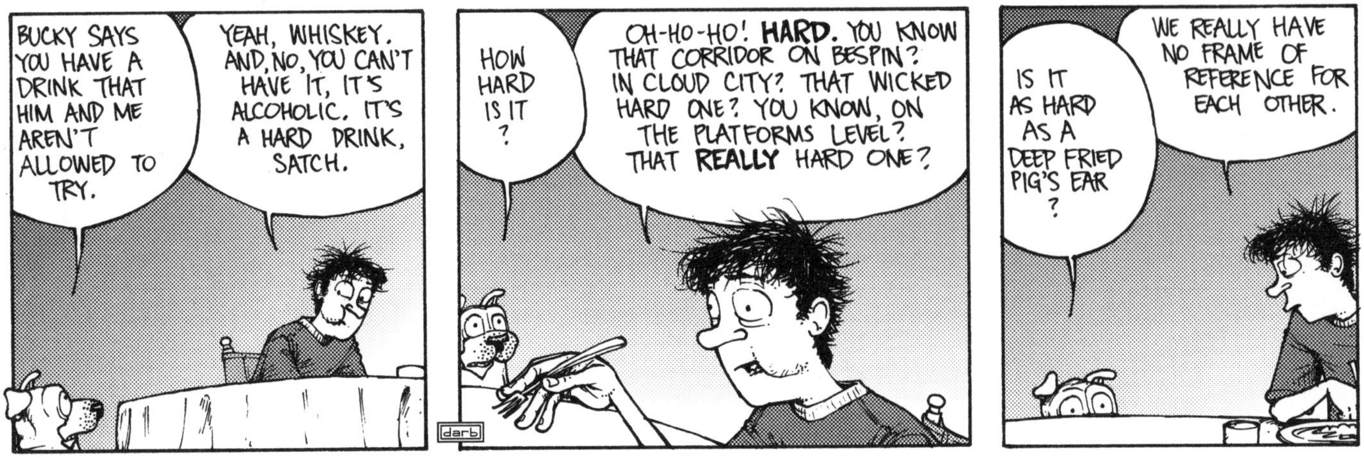
BUCKY SAYS YOU HAVE A DRINK THAT HIM AND ME AREN'T ALLOWED TO TRY.
YEAH, WHISKEY. AND, NO, YOU CAN'T HAVE IT, IT'S ALCOHOLIC. IT'S A HARD DRINK, SATCH.
HOW HARD IS IT ?
OH-HO-HO! **HARD.** YOU KNOW THAT CORRIDOR ON BESPIN? IN CLOUD CITY? THAT WICKED HARD ONE? YOU KNOW, ON THE PLATFORMS LEVEL? THAT **REALLY** HARD ONE?
darb
IS IT AS HARD AS A DEEP FRIED PIG'S EAR ?
WE REALLY HAVE NO FRAME OF REFERENCE FOR EACH OTHER.

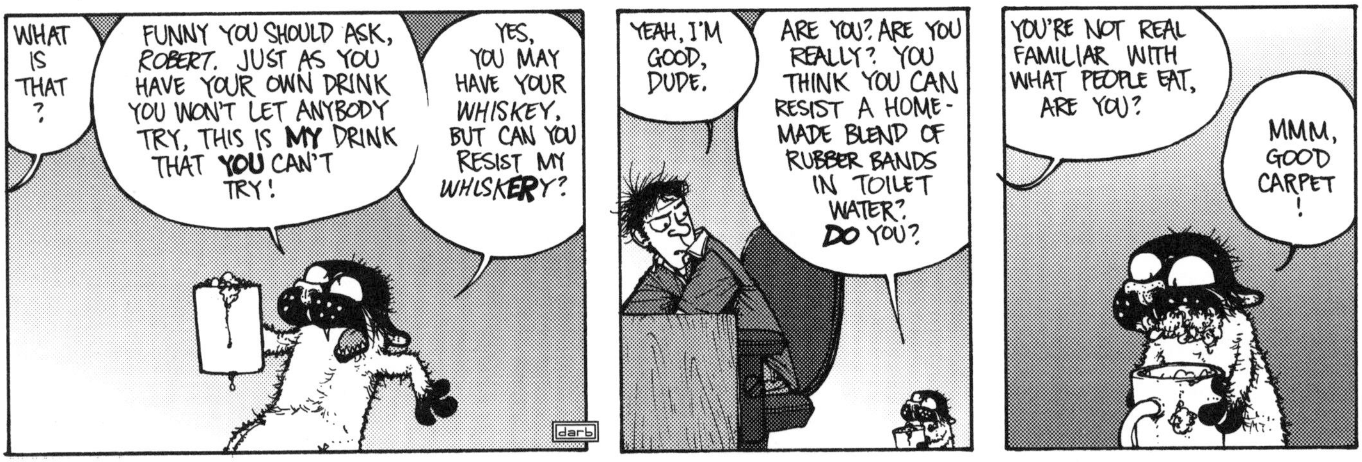
WHAT IS THAT ?
FUNNY YOU SHOULD ASK, *ROBERT.* JUST AS YOU HAVE YOUR OWN DRINK YOU WON'T LET ANYBODY TRY, THIS IS **MY** DRINK THAT **YOU** CAN'T TRY!
YES, YOU MAY HAVE YOUR *WHISKEY,* BUT CAN YOU RESIST MY *WHISK**ER**Y?*
darb
YEAH, I'M GOOD, DUDE.
ARE YOU? ARE YOU REALLY? YOU THINK YOU CAN RESIST A HOME-MADE BLEND OF RUBBER BANDS IN TOILET WATER? **DO** YOU?
YOU'RE NOT REAL FAMILIAR WITH WHAT PEOPLE EAT, ARE YOU?
MMM, GOOD CARPET !

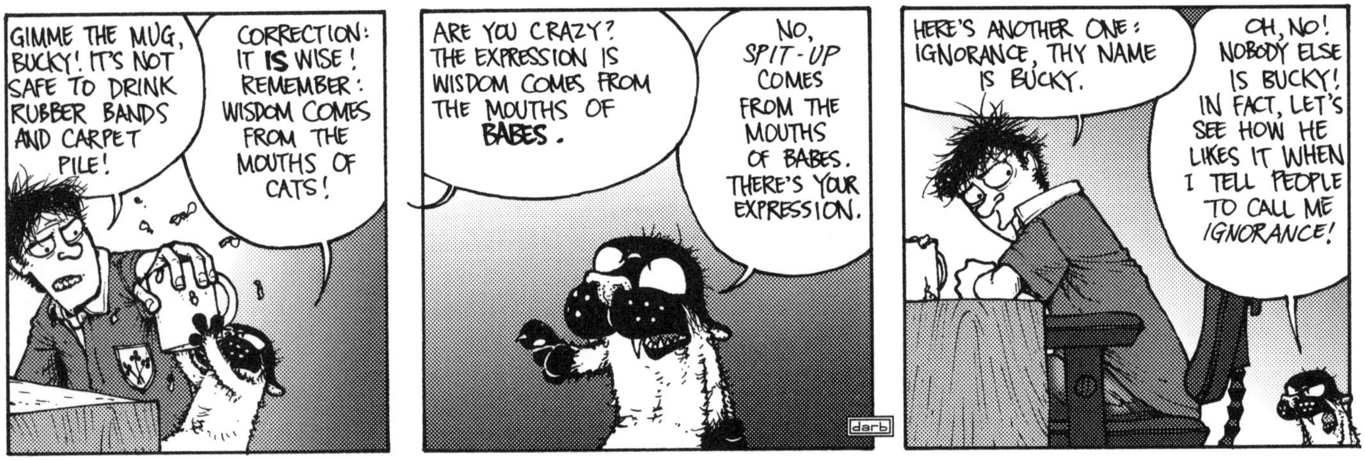
GIMME THE MUG, BUCKY! IT'S NOT SAFE TO DRINK RUBBER BANDS AND CARPET PILE!
CORRECTION: IT **IS** WISE! REMEMBER: WISDOM COMES FROM THE MOUTHS OF CATS!
ARE YOU CRAZY? THE EXPRESSION IS WISDOM COMES FROM THE MOUTHS OF **BABES.**
NO, *SPIT-UP* COMES FROM THE MOUTHS OF BABES. THERE'S YOUR EXPRESSION.
darb
HERE'S ANOTHER ONE: IGNORANCE, THY NAME IS BUCKY.
OH, NO! NOBODY ELSE IS BUCKY! IN FACT, LET'S SEE HOW HE LIKES IT WHEN I TELL PEOPLE TO CALL ME *IGNORANCE!*

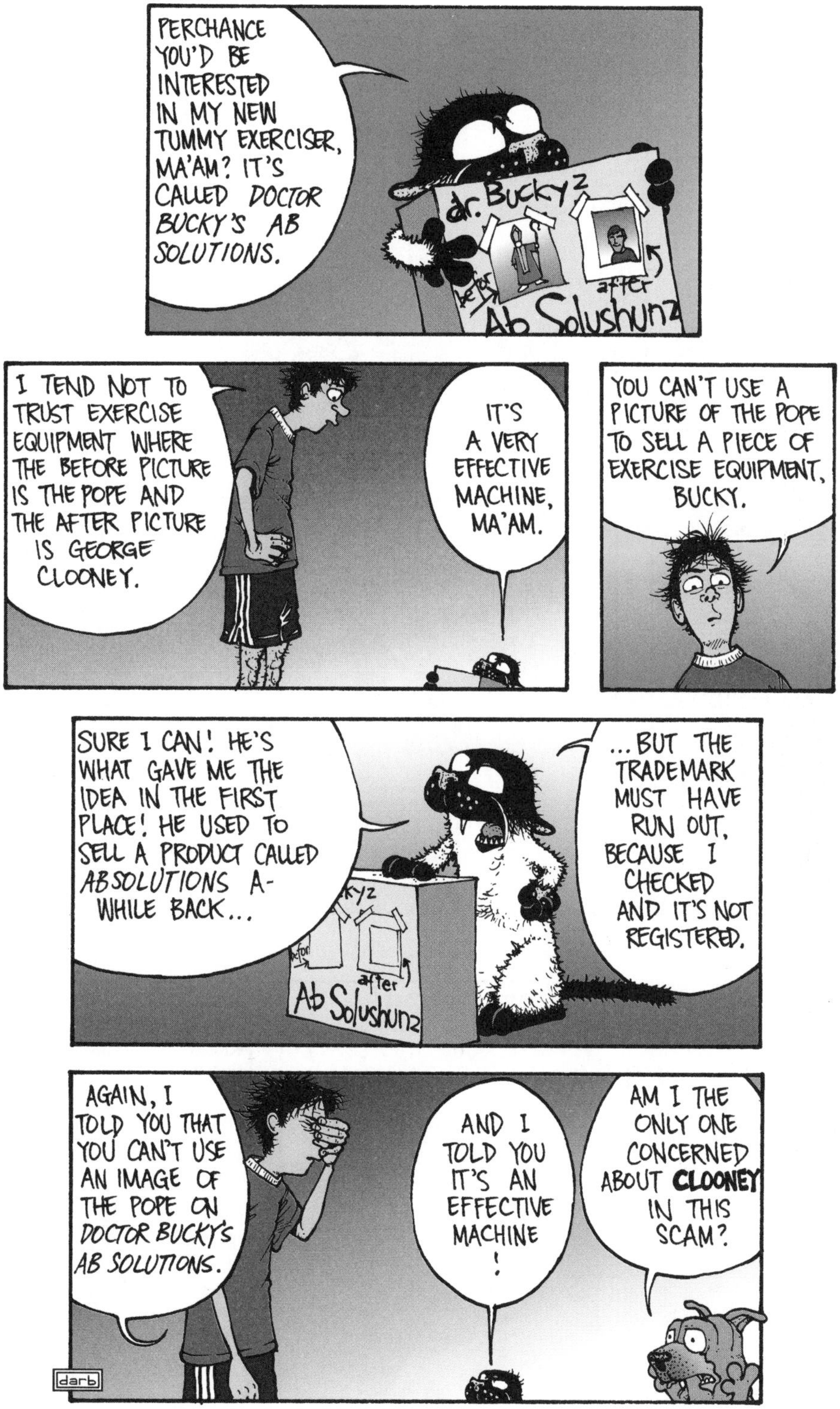
PERCHANCE YOU'D BE INTERESTED IN MY NEW TUMMY EXERCISER, MA'AM? IT'S CALLED DOCTOR BUCKY'S AB SOLUTIONS.
dr. Bucky'z
befor
after
Ab Solushunz
I TEND NOT TO TRUST EXERCISE EQUIPMENT WHERE THE BEFORE PICTURE IS THE POPE AND THE AFTER PICTURE IS GEORGE CLOONEY.
IT'S A VERY EFFECTIVE MACHINE, MA'AM.
YOU CAN'T USE A PICTURE OF THE POPE TO SELL A PIECE OF EXERCISE EQUIPMENT, BUCKY.
SURE I CAN! HE'S WHAT GAVE ME THE IDEA IN THE FIRST PLACE! HE USED TO SELL A PRODUCT CALLED ABSOLUTIONS A-WHILE BACK...
...BUT THE TRADEMARK MUST HAVE RUN OUT, BECAUSE I CHECKED AND IT'S NOT REGISTERED.
after
Ab Solushunz
AGAIN, I TOLD YOU THAT YOU CAN'T USE AN IMAGE OF THE POPE ON DOCTOR BUCKY'S AB SOLUTIONS.
AND I TOLD YOU IT'S AN EFFECTIVE MACHINE!
AM I THE ONLY ONE CONCERNED ABOUT CLOONEY IN THIS SCAM?
darb

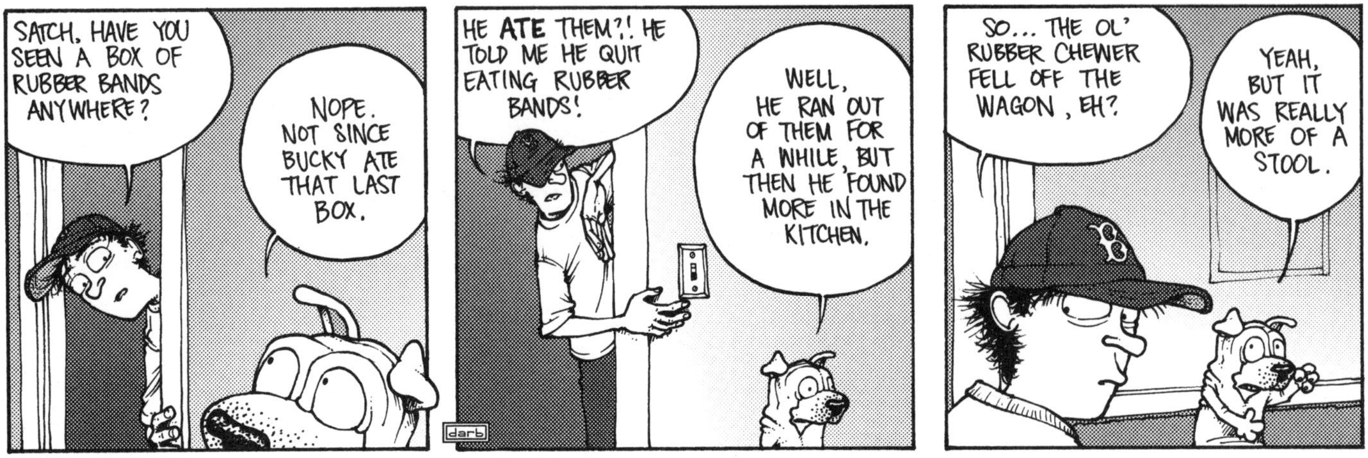
SATCH, HAVE YOU SEEN A BOX OF RUBBER BANDS ANYWHERE?
NOPE. NOT SINCE BUCKY ATE THAT LAST BOX.
darb
HE **ATE** THEM?! HE TOLD ME HE QUIT EATING RUBBER BANDS!
WELL, HE RAN OUT OF THEM FOR A WHILE, BUT THEN HE FOUND MORE IN THE KITCHEN.
SO... THE OL' RUBBER CHEWER FELL OFF THE WAGON, EH?
YEAH, BUT IT WAS REALLY MORE OF A STOOL.

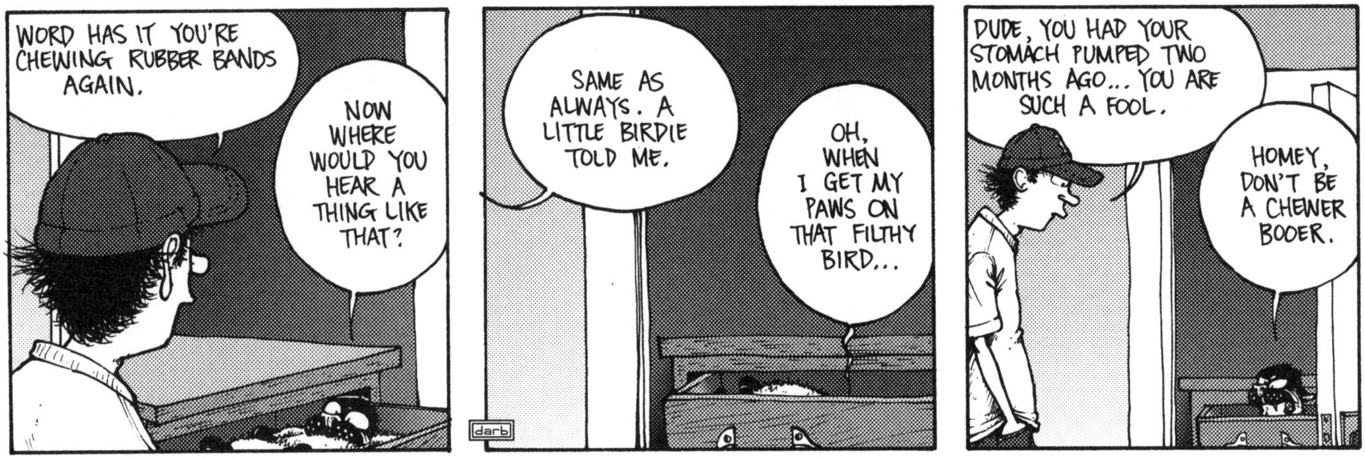
WORD HAS IT YOU'RE CHEWING RUBBER BANDS AGAIN.
NOW WHERE WOULD YOU HEAR A THING LIKE THAT?
darb
SAME AS ALWAYS. A LITTLE BIRDIE TOLD ME.
OH, WHEN I GET MY PAWS ON THAT FILTHY BIRD...
DUDE, YOU HAD YOUR STOMACH PUMPED TWO MONTHS AGO... YOU ARE SUCH A FOOL.
HOMEY, DON'T BE A CHEWER BOOER.

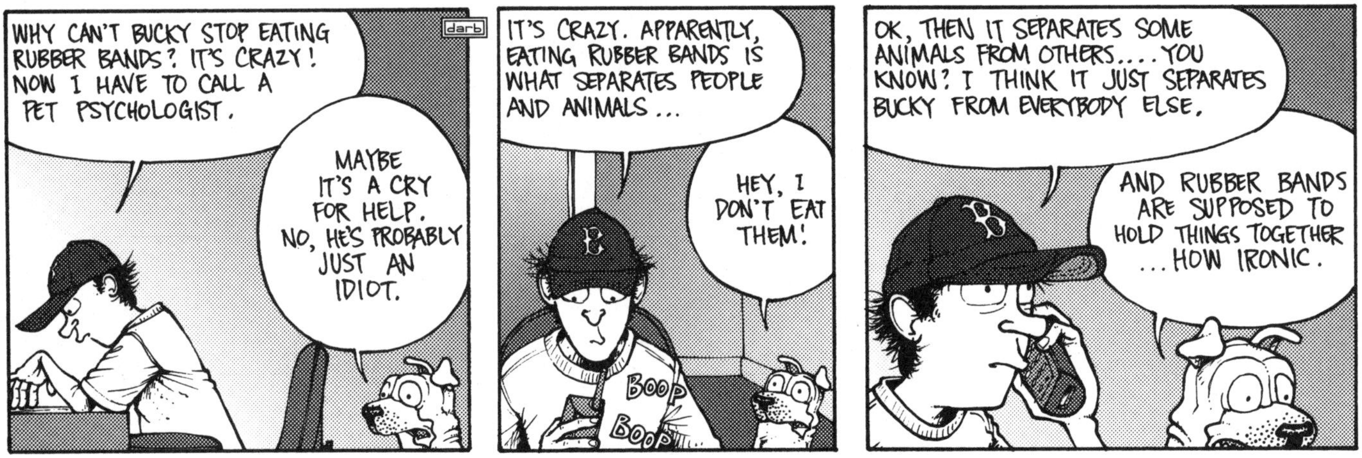
darb
WHY CAN'T BUCKY STOP EATING RUBBER BANDS? IT'S CRAZY! NOW I HAVE TO CALL A PET PSYCHOLOGIST.
MAYBE IT'S A CRY FOR HELP. NO, HE'S PROBABLY JUST AN IDIOT.
IT'S CRAZY. APPARENTLY, EATING RUBBER BANDS IS WHAT SEPARATES PEOPLE AND ANIMALS...
HEY, I DON'T EAT THEM!
BOOP
BOOP
OK, THEN IT SEPARATES SOME ANIMALS FROM OTHERS.... YOU KNOW? I THINK IT JUST SEPARATES BUCKY FROM EVERYBODY ELSE.
AND RUBBER BANDS ARE SUPPOSED TO HOLD THINGS TOGETHER ...HOW IRONIC.

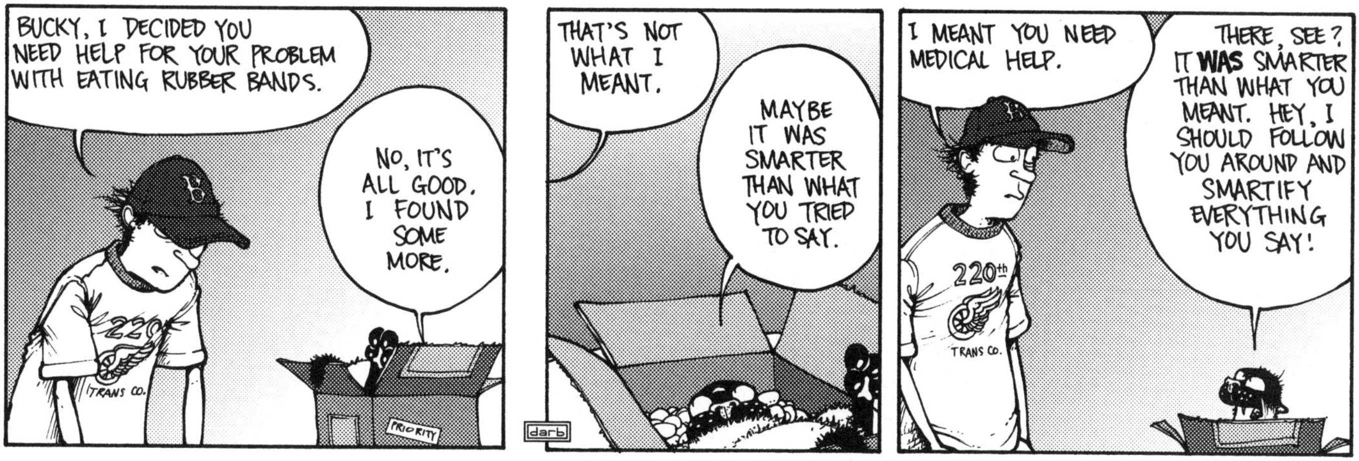
BUCKY, I DECIDED YOU NEED HELP FOR YOUR PROBLEM WITH EATING RUBBER BANDS.
NO, IT'S ALL GOOD. I FOUND SOME MORE.
PRIORITY
THAT'S NOT WHAT I MEANT.
MAYBE IT WAS SMARTER THAN WHAT YOU TRIED TO SAY.
I MEANT YOU NEED MEDICAL HELP.
THERE, SEE? IT **WAS** SMARTER THAN WHAT YOU MEANT. HEY, I SHOULD FOLLOW YOU AROUND AND SMARTIFY EVERYTHING YOU SAY!

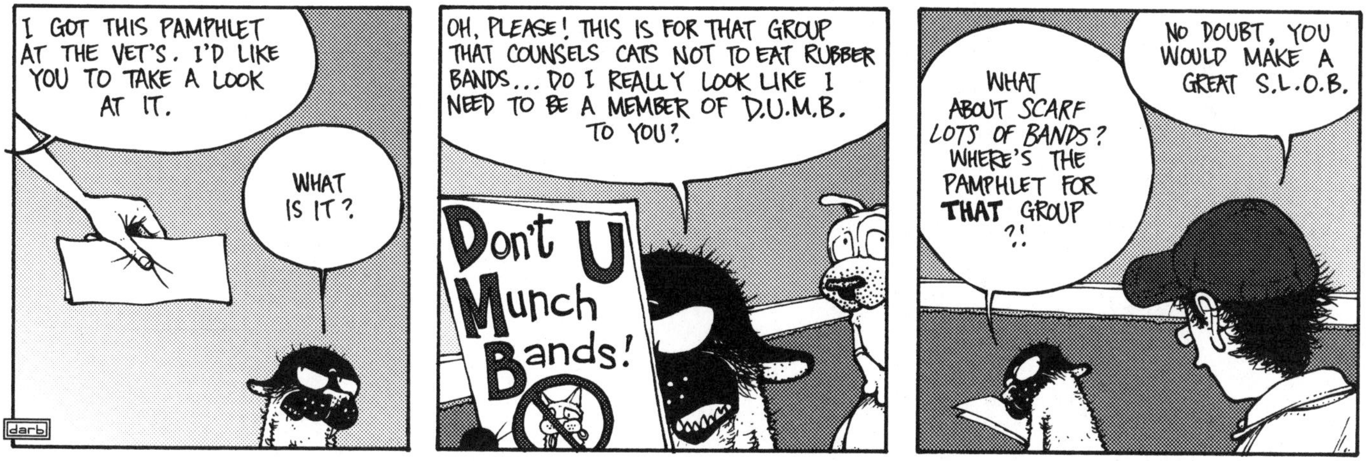
I GOT THIS PAMPHLET AT THE VET'S. I'D LIKE YOU TO TAKE A LOOK AT IT.
WHAT IS IT?
OH, PLEASE! THIS IS FOR THAT GROUP THAT COUNSELS CATS NOT TO EAT RUBBER BANDS... DO I REALLY LOOK LIKE I NEED TO BE A MEMBER OF D.U.M.B. TO YOU?
Don't U Munch Bands!
WHAT ABOUT *SCARF LOTS OF BANDS?* WHERE'S THE PAMPHLET FOR **THAT** GROUP ?!
NO DOUBT, YOU WOULD MAKE A GREAT S.L.O.B.

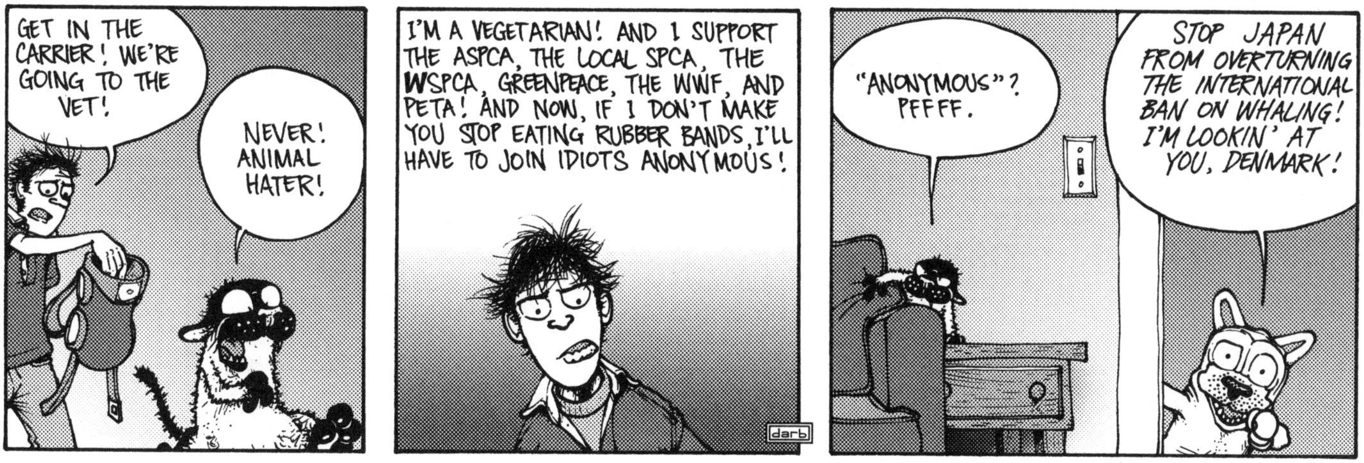
GET IN THE CARRIER! WE'RE GOING TO THE VET!
NEVER! ANIMAL HATER!
I'M A VEGETARIAN! AND I SUPPORT THE ASPCA, THE LOCAL SPCA, THE WSPCA, GREENPEACE, THE WWF, AND PETA! AND NOW, IF I DON'T MAKE YOU STOP EATING RUBBER BANDS, I'LL HAVE TO JOIN IDIOTS ANONYMOUS!
"ANONYMOUS"? PFFFF.
STOP JAPAN FROM OVERTURNING THE INTERNATIONAL BAN ON WHALING! I'M LOOKIN' AT YOU, DENMARK!

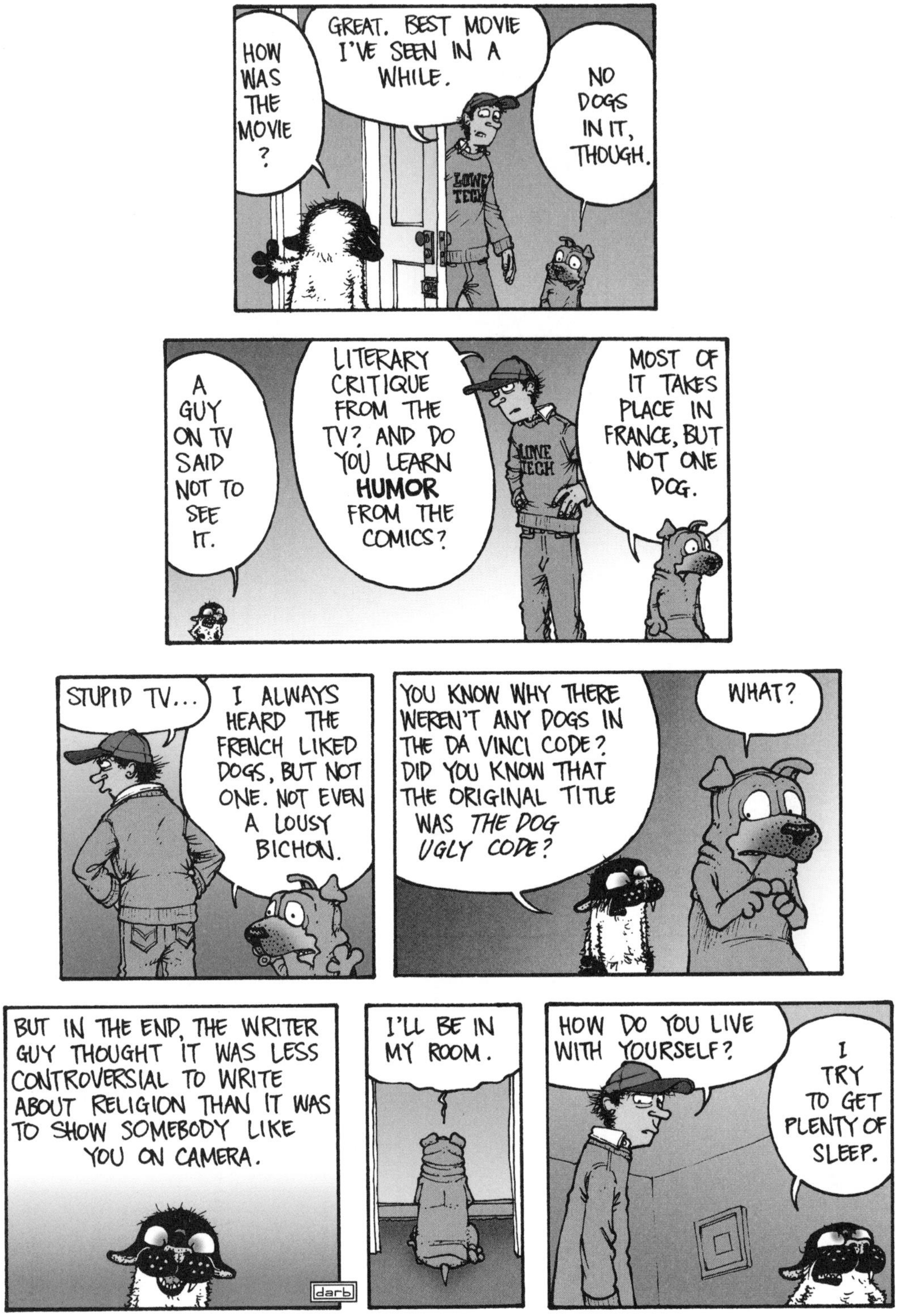
HOW WAS THE MOVIE ?
GREAT. BEST MOVIE I'VE SEEN IN A WHILE.
NO DOGS IN IT, THOUGH.
LOWE TECH
A GUY ON TV SAID NOT TO SEE IT.
LITERARY CRITIQUE FROM THE TV? AND DO YOU LEARN **HUMOR** FROM THE COMICS?
MOST OF IT TAKES PLACE IN FRANCE, BUT NOT ONE DOG.
LOWE TECH
STUPID TV...
I ALWAYS HEARD THE FRENCH LIKED DOGS, BUT NOT ONE. NOT EVEN A LOUSY BICHON.
YOU KNOW WHY THERE WEREN'T ANY DOGS IN THE DA VINCI CODE? DID YOU KNOW THAT THE ORIGINAL TITLE WAS *THE DOG UGLY CODE?*
WHAT?
BUT IN THE END, THE WRITER GUY THOUGHT IT WAS LESS CONTROVERSIAL TO WRITE ABOUT RELIGION THAN IT WAS TO SHOW SOMEBODY LIKE YOU ON CAMERA.
darb
I'LL BE IN MY ROOM.
HOW DO YOU LIVE WITH YOURSELF?
I TRY TO GET PLENTY OF SLEEP.

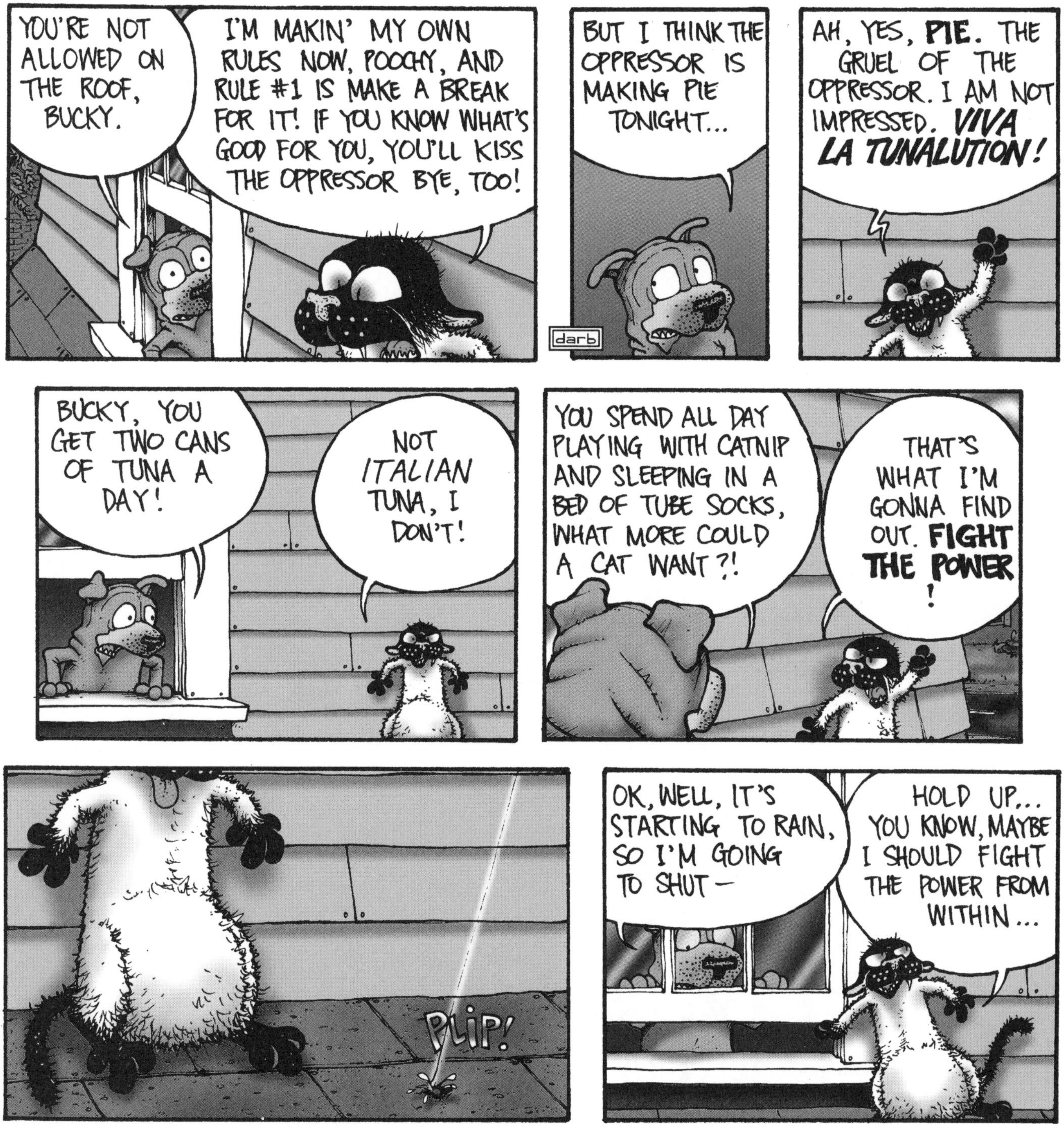
YOU'RE NOT ALLOWED ON THE ROOF, BUCKY.
I'M MAKIN' MY OWN RULES NOW, POOCHY, AND RULE #1 IS MAKE A BREAK FOR IT! IF YOU KNOW WHAT'S GOOD FOR YOU, YOU'LL KISS THE OPPRESSOR BYE, TOO!
BUT I THINK THE OPPRESSOR IS MAKING PIE TONIGHT...
darb
AH, YES, **PIE**. THE GRUEL OF THE OPPRESSOR. I AM NOT IMPRESSED. ***VIVA LA TUNALUTION!***
BUCKY, YOU GET TWO CANS OF TUNA A DAY!
NOT *ITALIAN* TUNA, I DON'T!
YOU SPEND ALL DAY PLAYING WITH CATNIP AND SLEEPING IN A BED OF TUBE SOCKS, WHAT MORE COULD A CAT WANT?!
THAT'S WHAT I'M GONNA FIND OUT. **FIGHT THE POWER!**
PLIP!
OK, WELL, IT'S STARTING TO RAIN, SO I'M GOING TO SHUT—
HOLD UP... YOU KNOW, MAYBE I SHOULD FIGHT THE POWER FROM WITHIN...

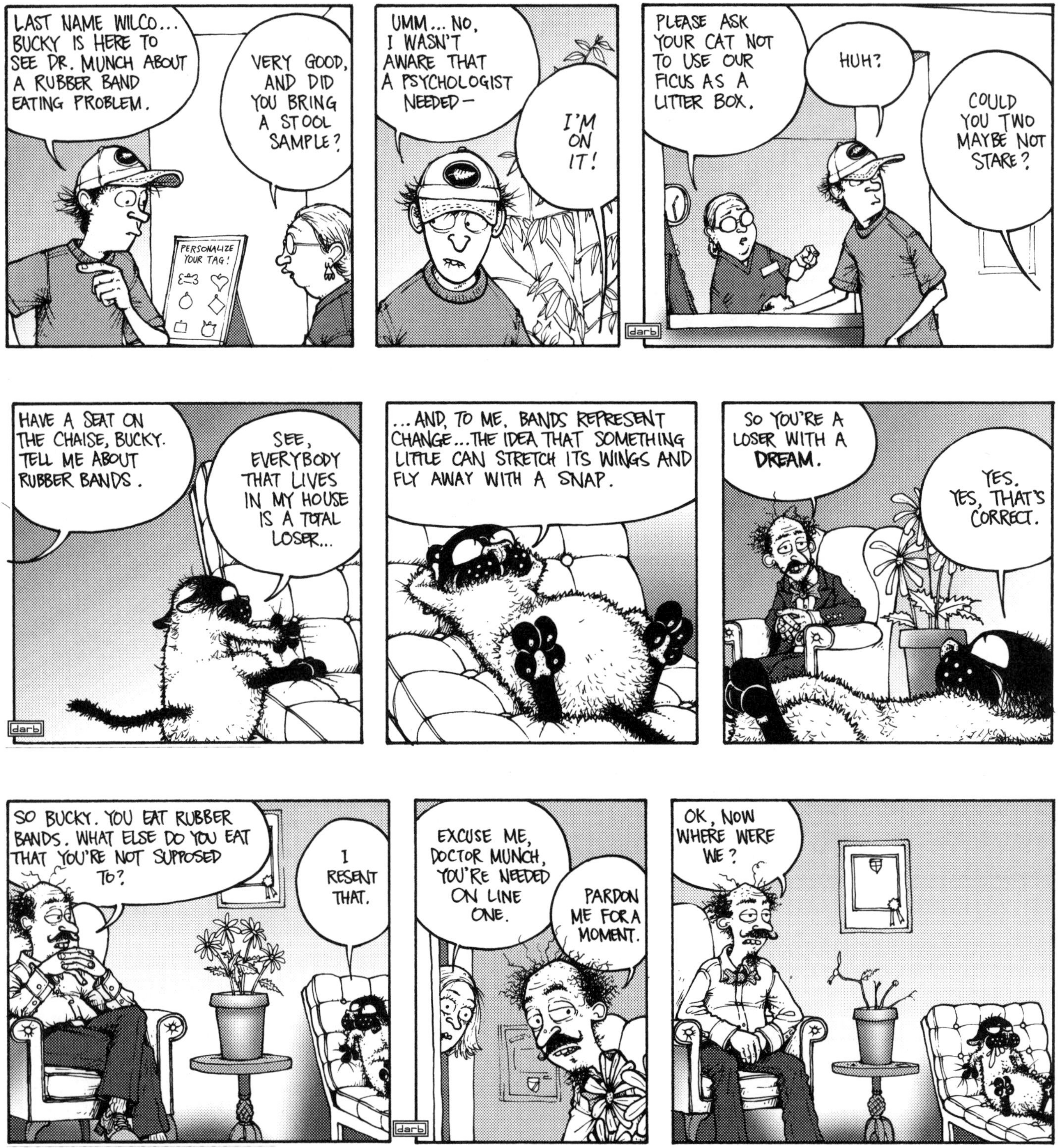
LAST NAME WILCO... BUCKY IS HERE TO SEE DR. MUNCH ABOUT A RUBBER BAND EATING PROBLEM.
VERY GOOD, AND DID YOU BRING A STOOL SAMPLE?
PERSONALIZE YOUR TAG!
UMM... NO, I WASN'T AWARE THAT A PSYCHOLOGIST NEEDED—
I'M ON IT!
PLEASE ASK YOUR CAT NOT TO USE OUR FICUS AS A LITTER BOX.
HUH?
COULD YOU TWO MAYBE NOT STARE?
darb
HAVE A SEAT ON THE CHAISE, BUCKY. TELL ME ABOUT RUBBER BANDS.
SEE, EVERYBODY THAT LIVES IN MY HOUSE IS A TOTAL LOSER...
darb
...AND, TO ME, BANDS REPRESENT CHANGE...THE IDEA THAT SOMETHING LITTLE CAN STRETCH ITS WINGS AND FLY AWAY WITH A SNAP.
SO YOU'RE A LOSER WITH A **DREAM**.
YES. YES, THAT'S CORRECT.
SO BUCKY. YOU EAT RUBBER BANDS. WHAT ELSE DO YOU EAT THAT YOU'RE NOT SUPPOSED TO?
I RESENT THAT.
EXCUSE ME, DOCTOR MUNCH, YOU'RE NEEDED ON LINE ONE.
PARDON ME FOR A MOMENT.
darb
OK, NOW WHERE WERE WE?

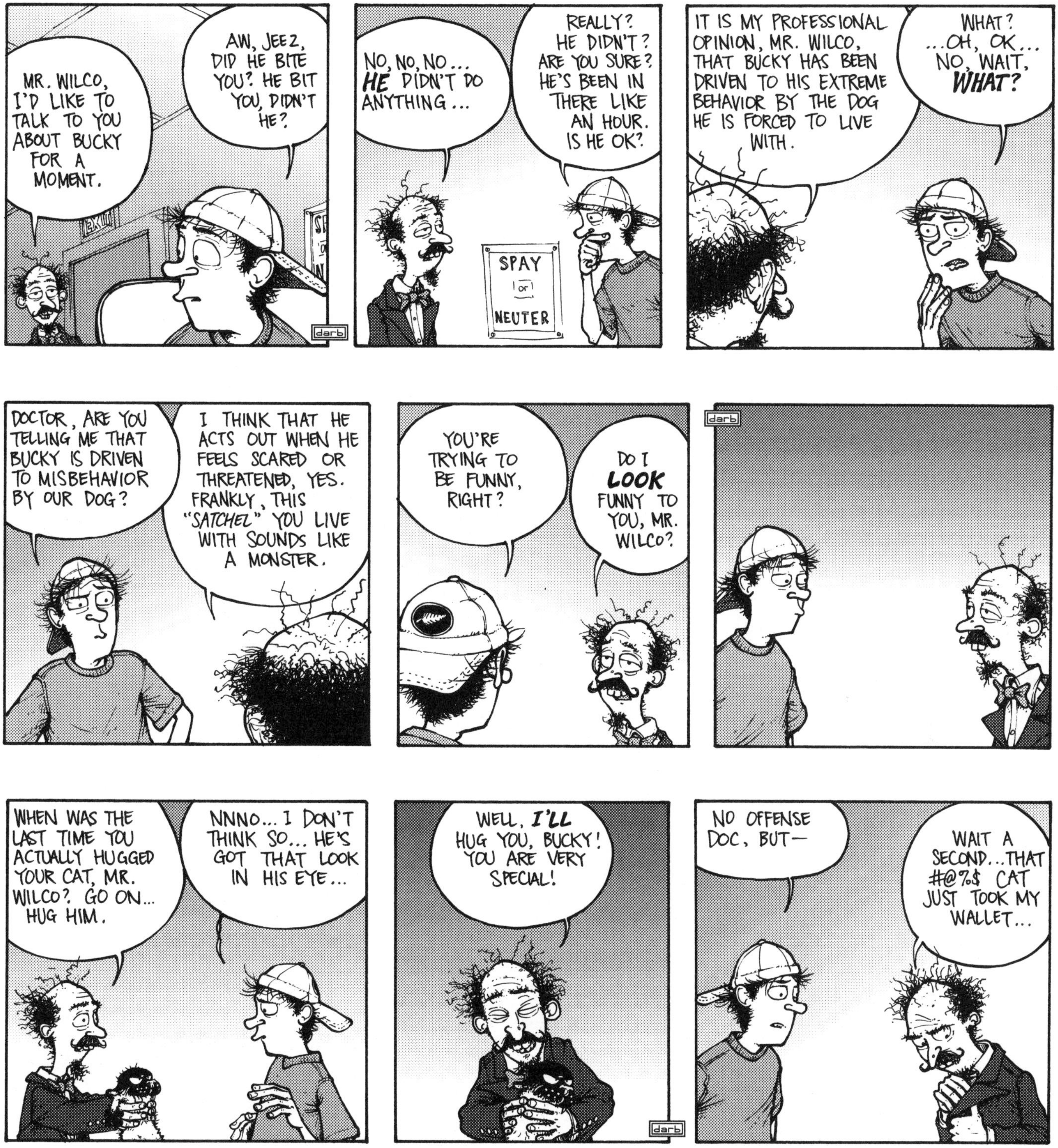
MR. WILCO, I'D LIKE TO TALK TO YOU ABOUT BUCKY FOR A MOMENT.
AW, JEEZ, DID HE BITE YOU? HE BIT YOU, DIDN'T HE?
EXIT
NO, NO, NO... **HE** DIDN'T DO ANYTHING...
REALLY? HE DIDN'T? ARE YOU SURE? HE'S BEEN IN THERE LIKE AN HOUR. IS HE OK?
SPAY
or
NEUTER
IT IS MY PROFESSIONAL OPINION, MR. WILCO, THAT BUCKY HAS BEEN DRIVEN TO HIS EXTREME BEHAVIOR BY THE DOG HE IS FORCED TO LIVE WITH.
WHAT? ...OH, OK... NO, WAIT, ***WHAT?***
DOCTOR, ARE YOU TELLING ME THAT BUCKY IS DRIVEN TO MISBEHAVIOR BY OUR DOG?
I THINK THAT HE ACTS OUT WHEN HE FEELS SCARED OR THREATENED, YES. FRANKLY, THIS "*SATCHEL*" YOU LIVE WITH SOUNDS LIKE A MONSTER.
YOU'RE TRYING TO BE FUNNY, RIGHT?
DO I **LOOK** FUNNY TO YOU, MR. WILCO?
WHEN WAS THE LAST TIME YOU ACTUALLY HUGGED YOUR CAT, MR. WILCO? GO ON... HUG HIM.
NNNO... I DON'T THINK SO... HE'S GOT THAT LOOK IN HIS EYE...
WELL, ***I'LL*** HUG YOU, BUCKY! YOU ARE VERY SPECIAL!
NO OFFENSE DOC, BUT—
WAIT A SECOND... THAT #@%$ CAT JUST TOOK MY WALLET...

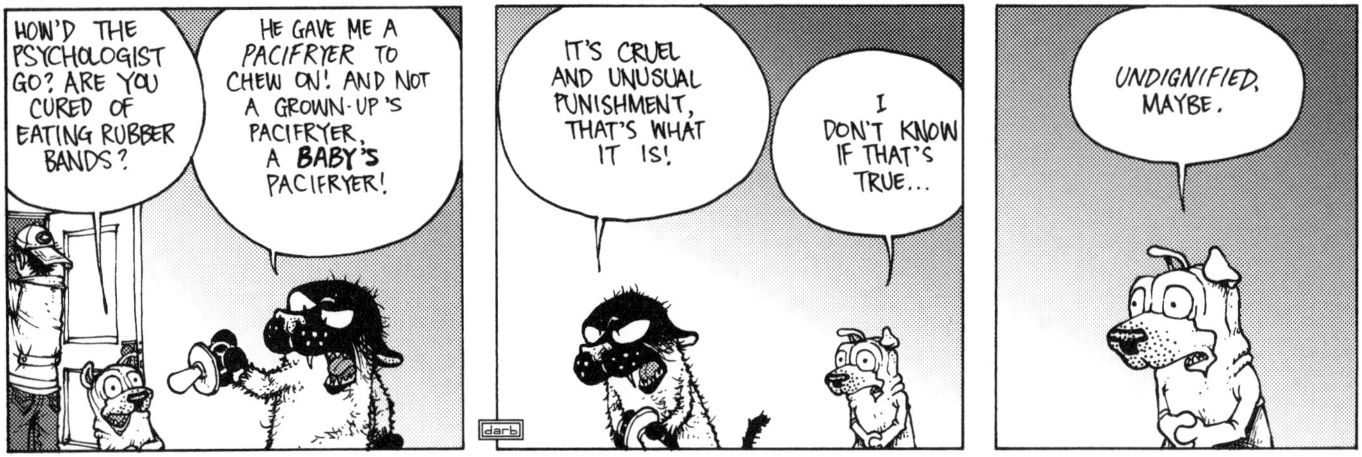
HOW'D THE PSYCHOLOGIST GO? ARE YOU CURED OF EATING RUBBER BANDS?
HE GAVE ME A *PACIFRYER* TO CHEW ON! AND NOT A GROWN-UP'S PACIFRYER, A **BABY'S** PACIFRYER!
darb
IT'S CRUEL AND UNUSUAL PUNISHMENT, THAT'S WHAT IT IS!
I DON'T KNOW IF THAT'S TRUE...
UNDIGNIFIED, MAYBE.

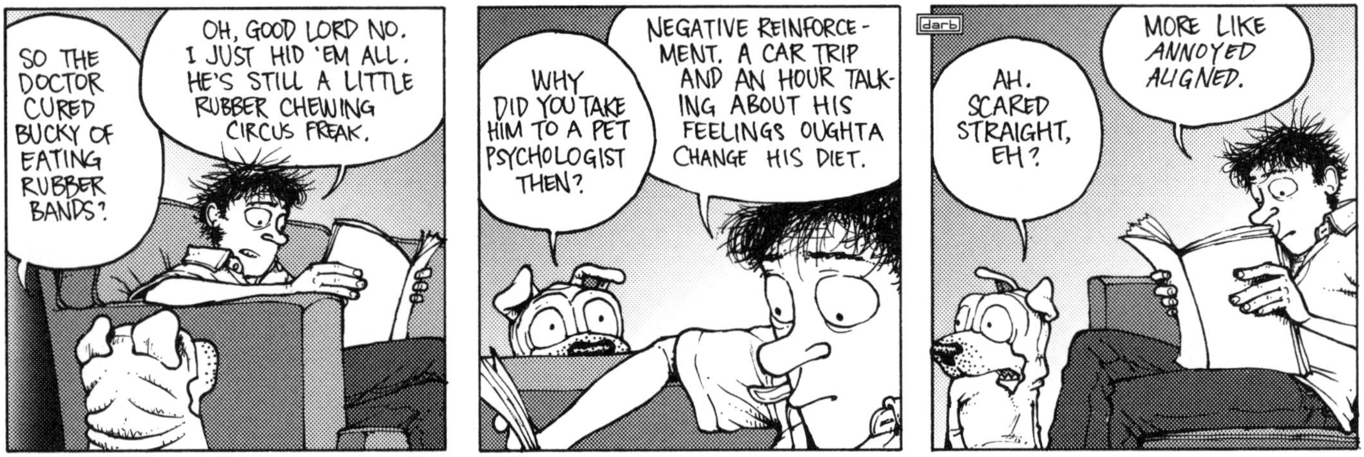
SO THE DOCTOR CURED BUCKY OF EATING RUBBER BANDS?
OH, GOOD LORD NO. I JUST HID 'EM ALL. HE'S STILL A LITTLE RUBBER CHEWING CIRCUS FREAK.
WHY DID YOU TAKE HIM TO A PET PSYCHOLOGIST THEN?
NEGATIVE REINFORCEMENT. A CAR TRIP AND AN HOUR TALKING ABOUT HIS FEELINGS OUGHTA CHANGE HIS DIET.
darb
AH. SCARED STRAIGHT, EH?
MORE LIKE *ANNOYED ALIGNED*.

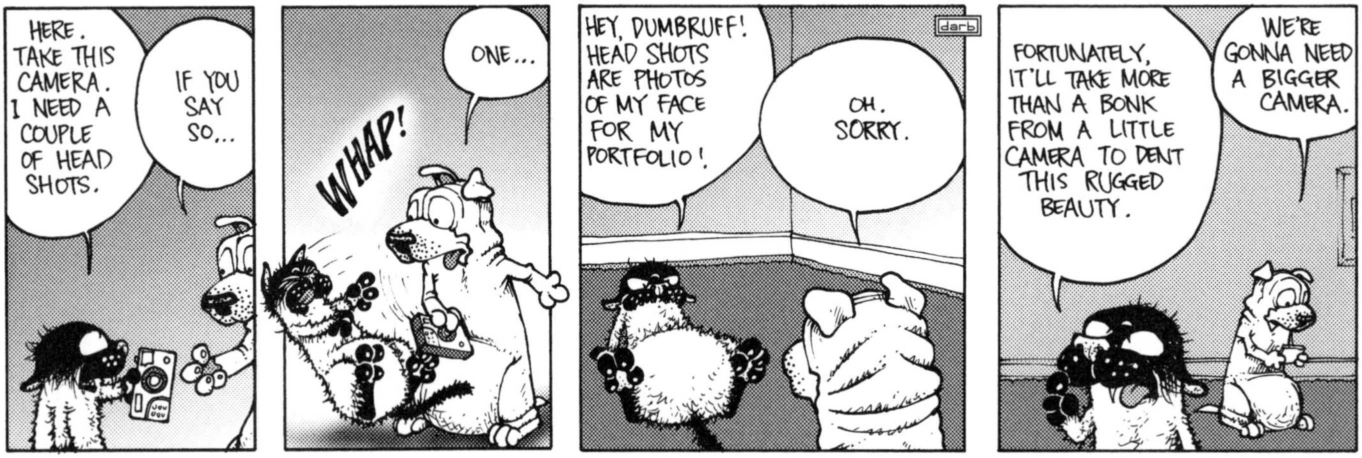
HERE. TAKE THIS CAMERA. I NEED A COUPLE OF HEAD SHOTS.
IF YOU SAY SO...
ONE...
WHAP!
HEY, DUMBRUFF! HEAD SHOTS ARE PHOTOS OF MY FACE FOR MY PORTFOLIO!
OH. SORRY.
darb
FORTUNATELY, IT'LL TAKE MORE THAN A BONK FROM A LITTLE CAMERA TO DENT THIS RUGGED BEAUTY.
WE'RE GONNA NEED A BIGGER CAMERA.

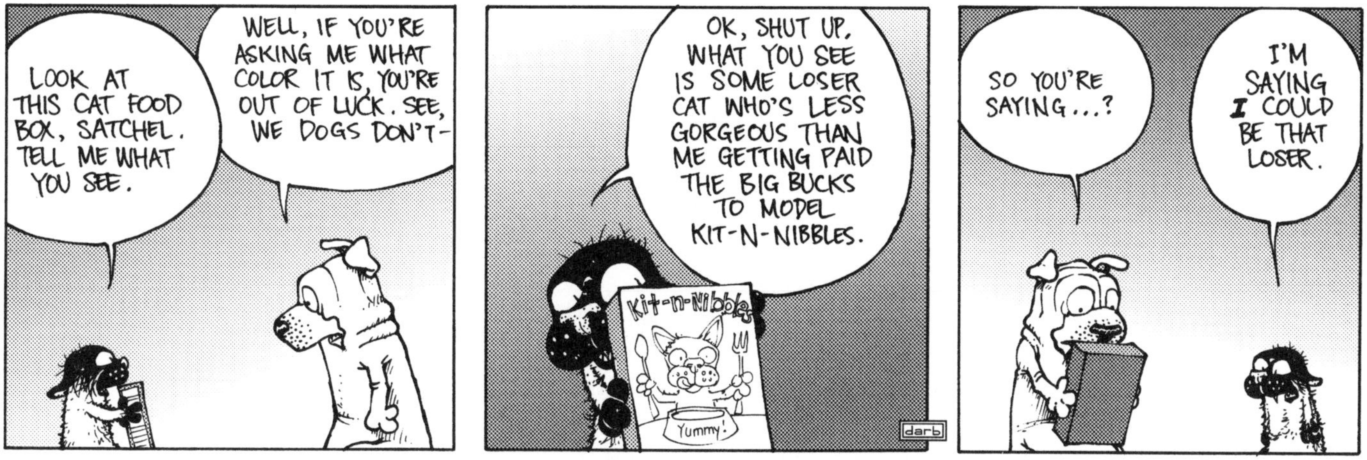
LOOK AT THIS CAT FOOD BOX, SATCHEL. TELL ME WHAT YOU SEE.
WELL, IF YOU'RE ASKING ME WHAT COLOR IT IS, YOU'RE OUT OF LUCK. SEE, WE DOGS DON'T-
OK, SHUT UP. WHAT YOU SEE IS SOME LOSER CAT WHO'S LESS GORGEOUS THAN ME GETTING PAID THE BIG BUCKS TO MODEL KIT-N-NIBBLES.
Kit-n-Nibbles
Yummy!
darb
SO YOU'RE SAYING...?
I'M SAYING *I* COULD BE THAT LOSER.

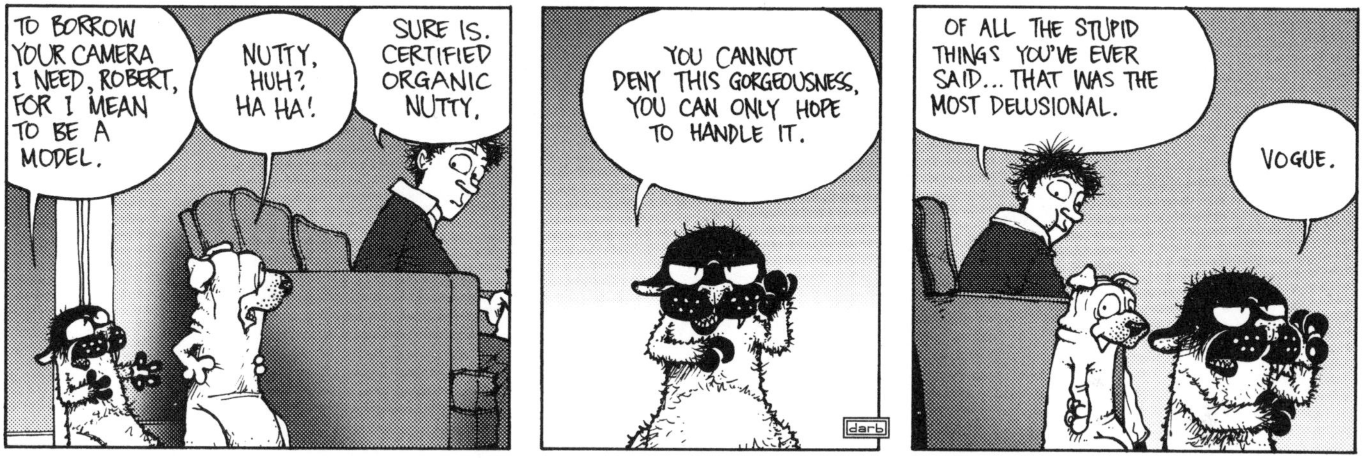
TO BORROW YOUR CAMERA I NEED, ROBERT, FOR I MEAN TO BE A MODEL.
NUTTY, HUH? HA HA!
SURE IS. CERTIFIED ORGANIC NUTTY.
YOU CANNOT DENY THIS GORGEOUSNESS, YOU CAN ONLY HOPE TO HANDLE IT.
darb
OF ALL THE STUPID THINGS YOU'VE EVER SAID... THAT WAS THE MOST DELUSIONAL.
VOGUE.

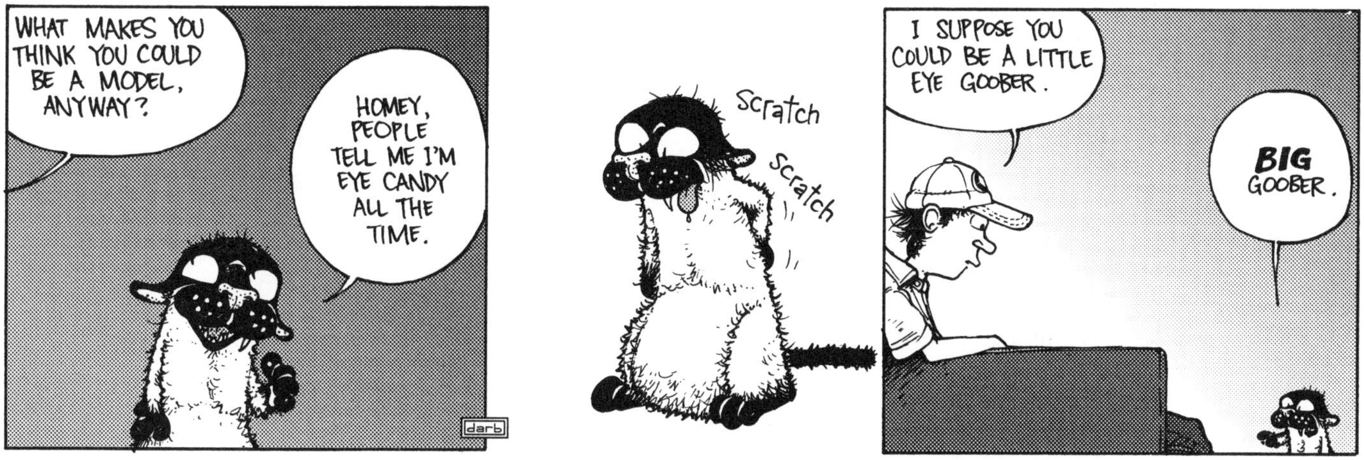
WHAT MAKES YOU THINK YOU COULD BE A MODEL, ANYWAY?
HOMEY, PEOPLE TELL ME I'M EYE CANDY ALL THE TIME.
darb
Scratch
Scratch
I SUPPOSE YOU COULD BE A LITTLE EYE GOOBER.
BIG GOOBER.

JACKSON HOLE

OH, I GET IT. IT'S MONA LASSIE OR SOMETHING, RIGHT?
WHAT?! THIS IS SPAWN OF SATAN AVEC WIG!
YOU SAID I WAS FAT ELVIS!

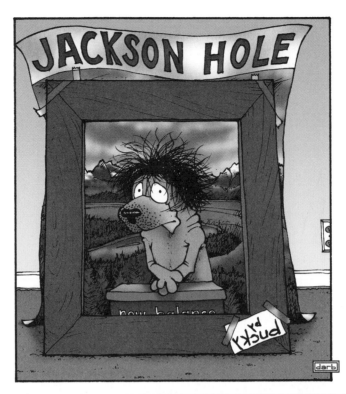

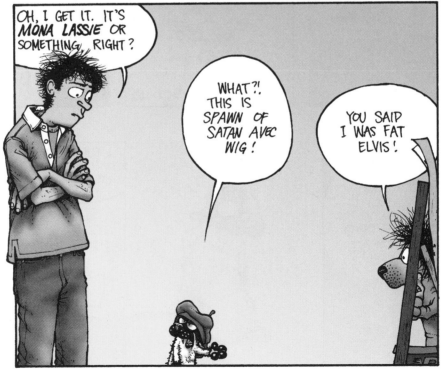

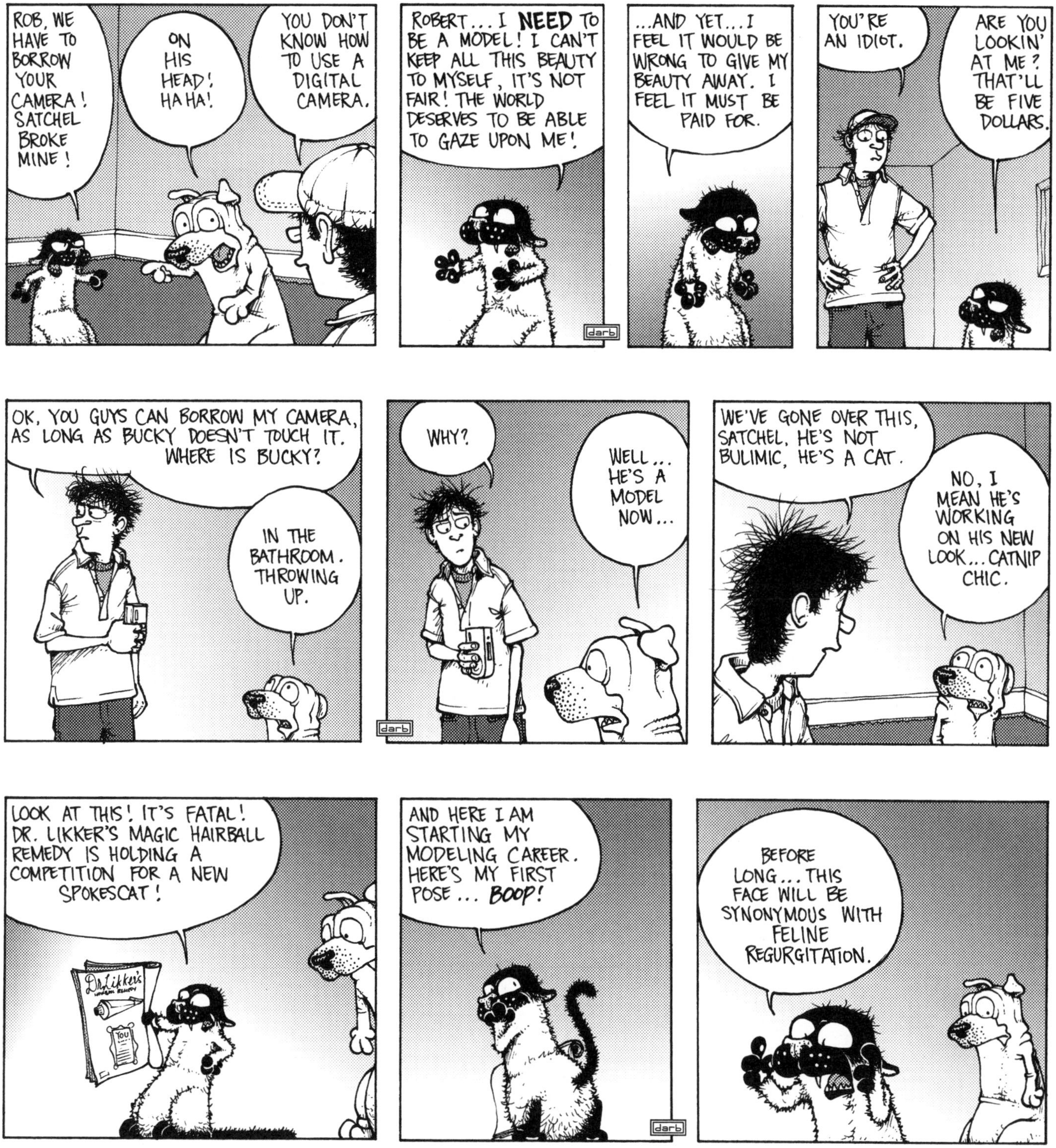
ROB, WE HAVE TO BORROW YOUR CAMERA! SATCHEL BROKE MINE!
ON HIS HEAD! HA HA!
YOU DON'T KNOW HOW TO USE A DIGITAL CAMERA.
ROBERT... I **NEED** TO BE A MODEL! I CAN'T KEEP ALL THIS BEAUTY TO MYSELF, IT'S NOT FAIR! THE WORLD DESERVES TO BE ABLE TO GAZE UPON ME!
darb
...AND YET... I FEEL IT WOULD BE WRONG TO GIVE MY BEAUTY AWAY. I FEEL IT MUST BE PAID FOR.
YOU'RE AN IDIOT.
ARE YOU LOOKIN' AT ME? THAT'LL BE FIVE DOLLARS.
OK, YOU GUYS CAN BORROW MY CAMERA, AS LONG AS BUCKY DOESN'T TOUCH IT. WHERE IS BUCKY?
IN THE BATHROOM. THROWING UP.
darb
WHY?
WELL... HE'S A MODEL NOW...
WE'VE GONE OVER THIS, SATCHEL. HE'S NOT BULIMIC, HE'S A CAT.
NO, I MEAN HE'S WORKING ON HIS NEW LOOK... CATNIP CHIC.
LOOK AT THIS! IT'S FATAL! DR. LIKKER'S MAGIC HAIRBALL REMEDY IS HOLDING A COMPETITION FOR A NEW SPOKESCAT!
Dr. Likker's
You
AND HERE I AM STARTING MY MODELING CAREER. HERE'S MY FIRST POSE... ***BOOP!***
darb
BEFORE LONG... THIS FACE WILL BE SYNONYMOUS WITH FELINE REGURGITATION.

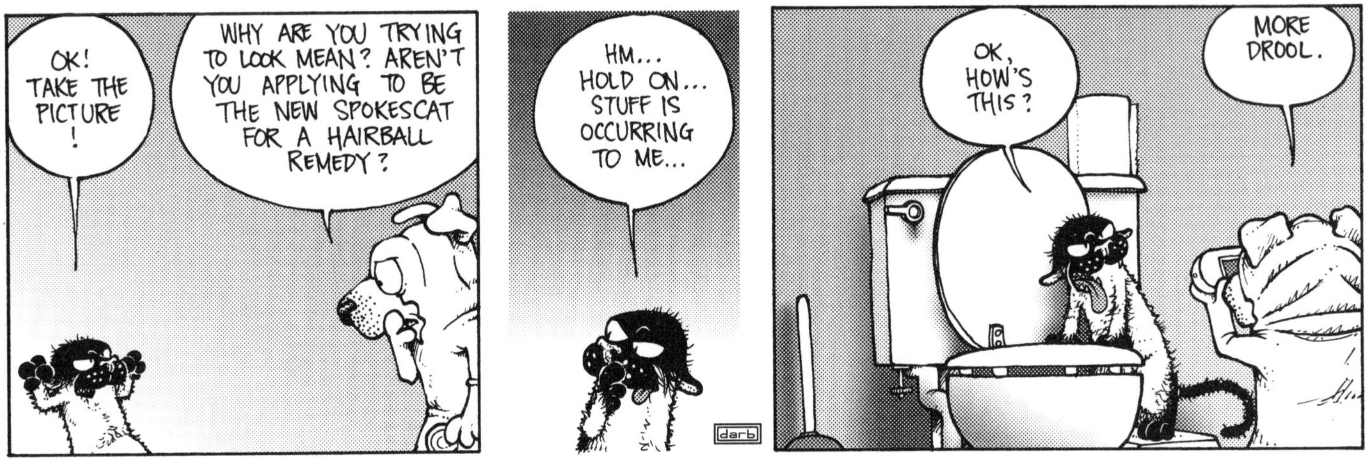
OK! TAKE THE PICTURE!
WHY ARE YOU TRYING TO LOOK MEAN? AREN'T YOU APPLYING TO BE THE NEW SPOKESCAT FOR A HAIRBALL REMEDY?
HM... HOLD ON... STUFF IS OCCURRING TO ME...
darb
OK, HOW'S THIS?
MORE DROOL.

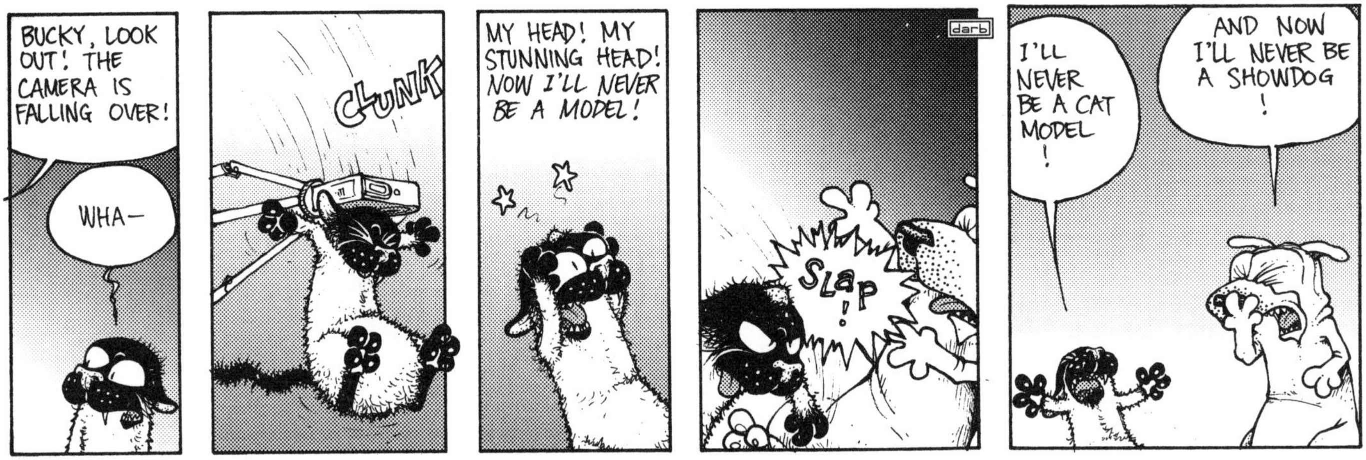
BUCKY, LOOK OUT! THE CAMERA IS FALLING OVER!
WHA—
CLUNK
MY HEAD! MY STUNNING HEAD! *NOW I'LL NEVER BE A MODEL!*
darb
SLAP!
I'LL NEVER BE A CAT MODEL!
AND NOW I'LL NEVER BE A SHOWDOG!

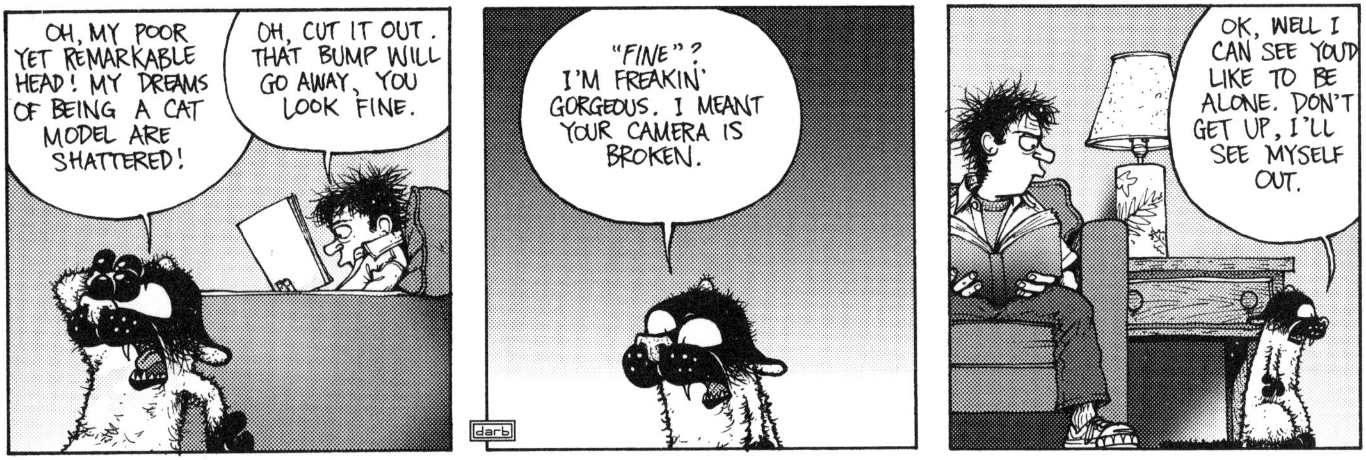
OH, MY POOR YET REMARKABLE HEAD! MY DREAMS OF BEING A CAT MODEL ARE SHATTERED!
OH, CUT IT OUT. THAT BUMP WILL GO AWAY, YOU LOOK FINE.
darb
"FINE"? I'M FREAKIN' GORGEOUS. I MEANT YOUR CAMERA IS BROKEN.
OK, WELL I CAN SEE YOU'D LIKE TO BE ALONE. DON'T GET UP, I'LL SEE MYSELF OUT.

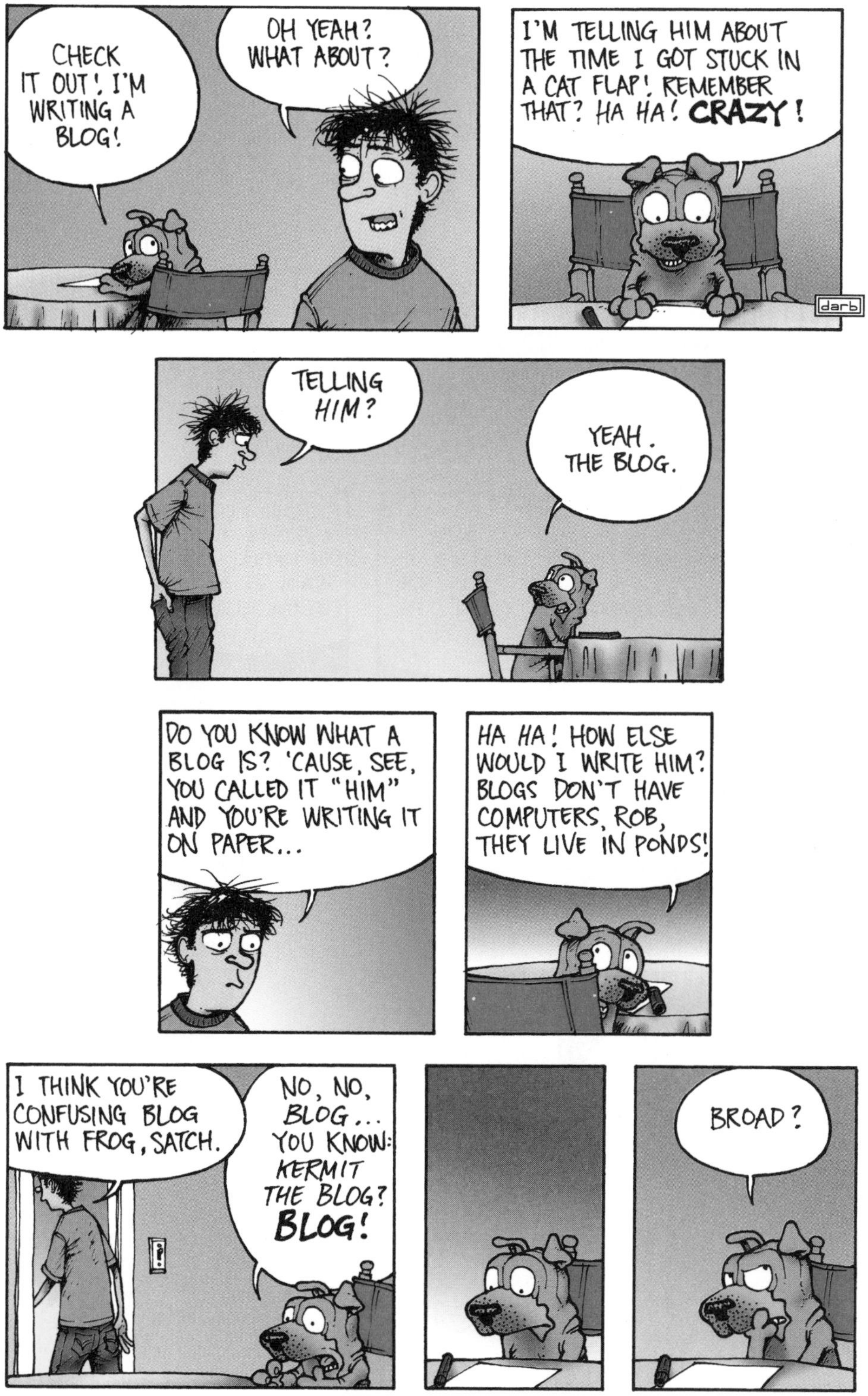
CHECK IT OUT! I'M WRITING A BLOG!
OH YEAH? WHAT ABOUT?
I'M TELLING HIM ABOUT THE TIME I GOT STUCK IN A CAT FLAP! REMEMBER THAT? HA HA! CRAZY!
darb
TELLING HIM?
YEAH. THE BLOG.
DO YOU KNOW WHAT A BLOG IS? 'CAUSE, SEE, YOU CALLED IT "HIM" AND YOU'RE WRITING IT ON PAPER...
HA HA! HOW ELSE WOULD I WRITE HIM? BLOGS DON'T HAVE COMPUTERS, ROB, THEY LIVE IN PONDS!
I THINK YOU'RE CONFUSING BLOG WITH FROG, SATCH.
NO, NO, BLOG... YOU KNOW: KERMIT THE BLOG? BLOG!
BROAD?

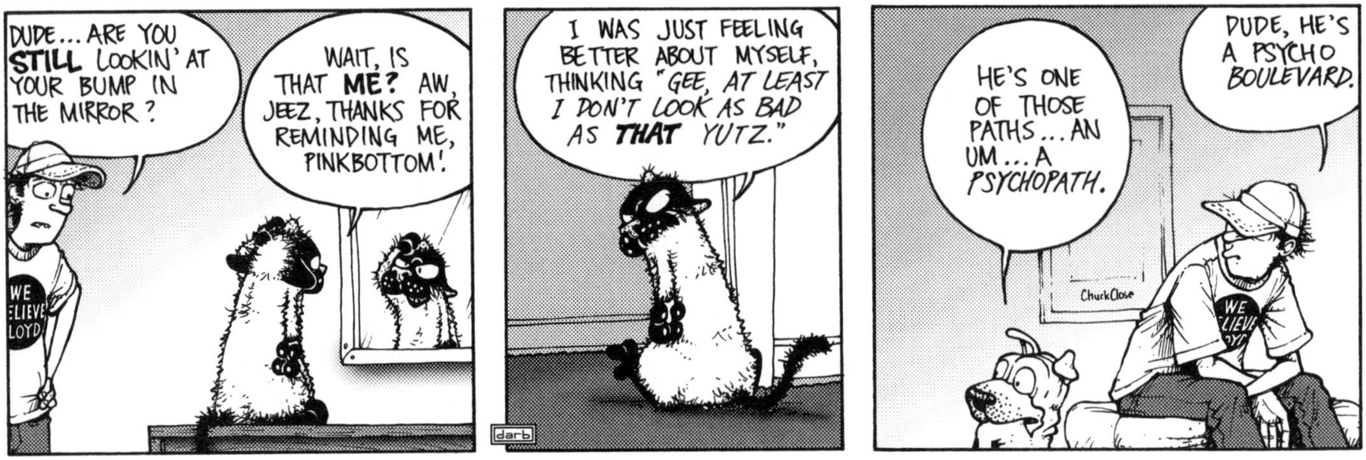
DUDE... ARE YOU **STILL** LOOKIN' AT YOUR BUMP IN THE MIRROR?
WAIT, IS THAT **ME?** AW, JEEZ, THANKS FOR REMINDING ME, PINKBOTTOM!
I WAS JUST FEELING BETTER ABOUT MYSELF, THINKING *"GEE, AT LEAST I DON'T LOOK AS BAD AS **THAT** YUTZ."*
HE'S ONE OF THOSE PATHS... AN UM... A *PSYCHOPATH.*
DUDE, HE'S A PSYCHO *BOULEVARD.*

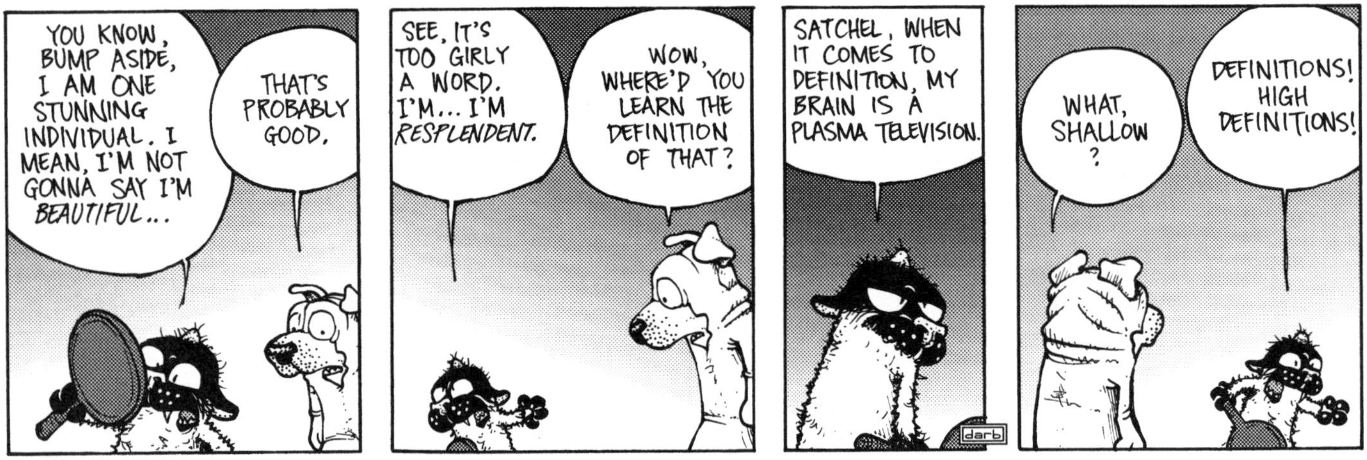
YOU KNOW, BUMP ASIDE, I AM ONE STUNNING INDIVIDUAL. I MEAN, I'M NOT GONNA SAY I'M *BEAUTIFUL...*
THAT'S PROBABLY GOOD.
SEE, IT'S TOO GIRLY A WORD. I'M... I'M *RESPLENDENT.*
WOW, WHERE'D YOU LEARN THE DEFINITION OF THAT?
SATCHEL, WHEN IT COMES TO DEFINITION, MY BRAIN IS A PLASMA TELEVISION.
WHAT, SHALLOW?
DEFINITIONS! HIGH DEFINITIONS!

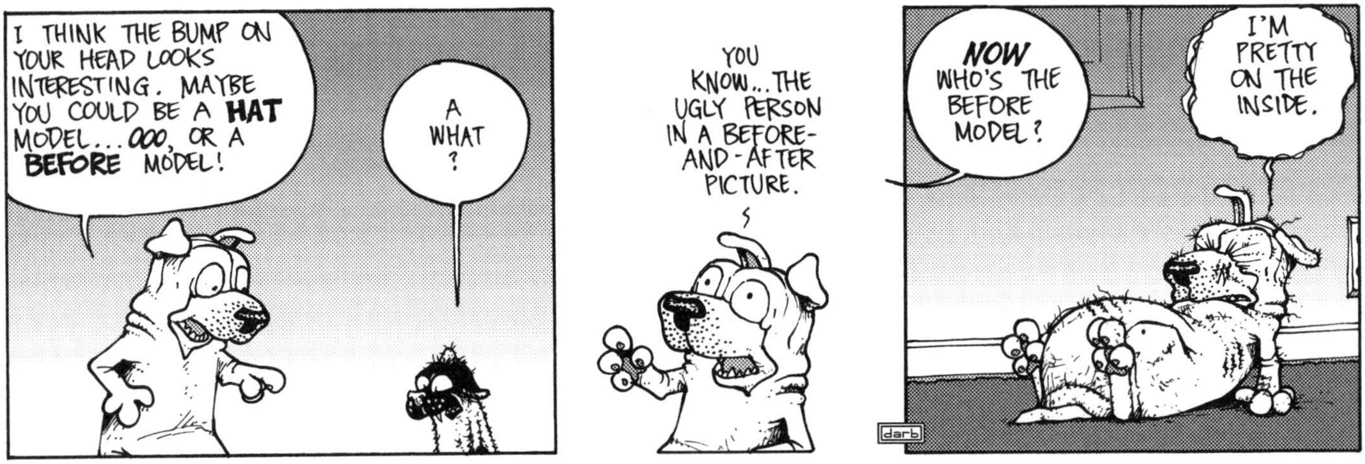
I THINK THE BUMP ON YOUR HEAD LOOKS INTERESTING. MAYBE YOU COULD BE A **HAT** MODEL... OOO, OR A **BEFORE** MODEL!
A WHAT?
YOU KNOW... THE UGLY PERSON IN A BEFORE-AND-AFTER PICTURE.
NOW WHO'S THE BEFORE MODEL?
I'M PRETTY ON THE INSIDE.

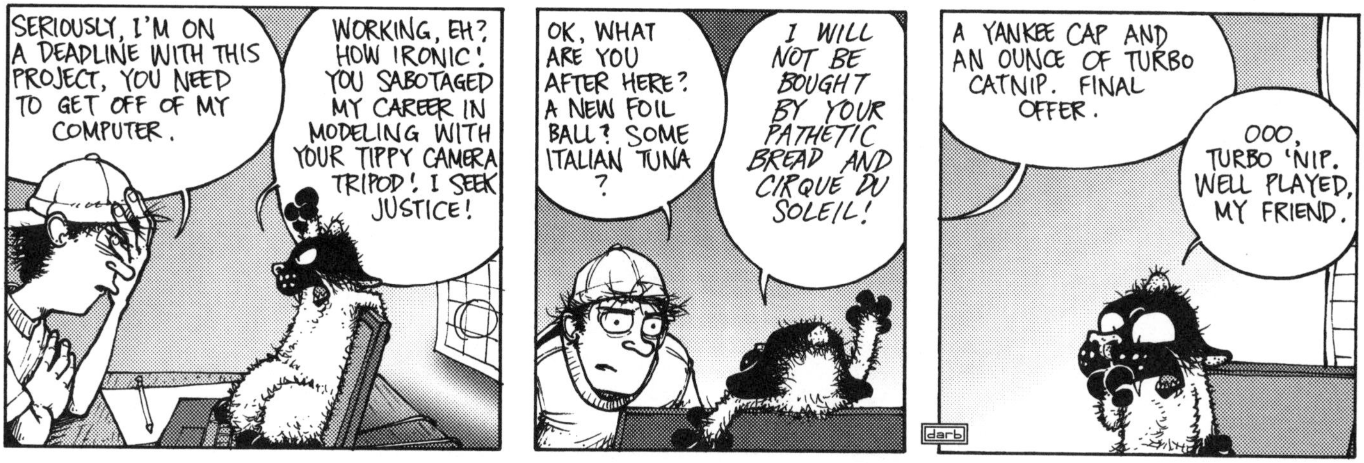
SERIOUSLY, I'M ON A DEADLINE WITH THIS PROJECT, YOU NEED TO GET OFF OF MY COMPUTER.
WORKING, EH? HOW IRONIC! YOU SABOTAGED MY CAREER IN MODELING WITH YOUR TIPPY CAMERA TRIPOD! I SEEK JUSTICE!
OK, WHAT ARE YOU AFTER HERE? A NEW FOIL BALL? SOME ITALIAN TUNA ?
I WILL NOT BE BOUGHT BY YOUR PATHETIC BREAD AND CIRQUE DU SOLEIL!
A YANKEE CAP AND AN OUNCE OF TURBO CATNIP. FINAL OFFER.
OOO, TURBO 'NIP. WELL PLAYED, MY FRIEND.
darb

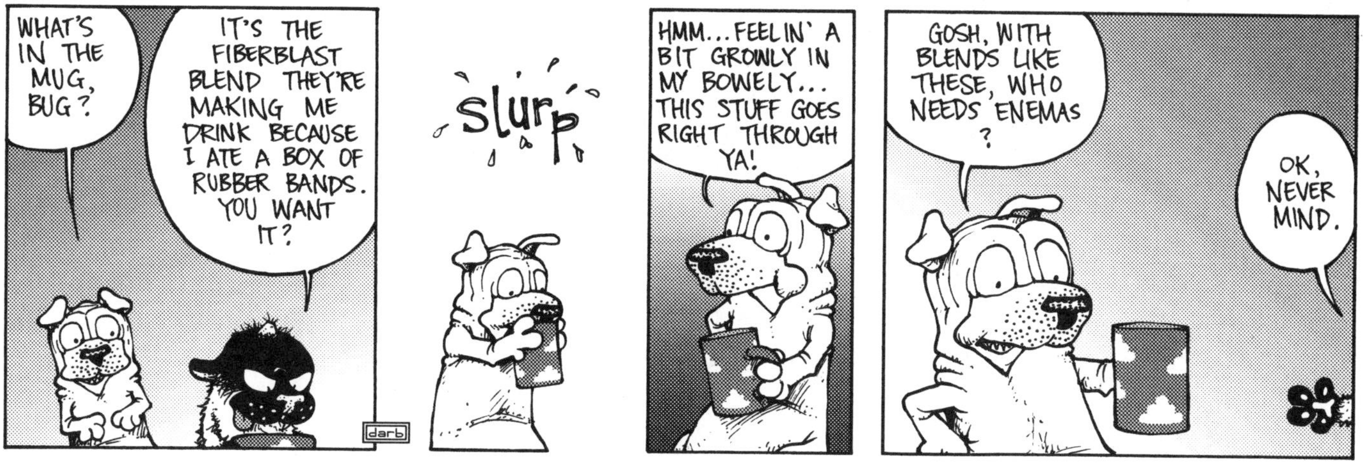
WHAT'S IN THE MUG, BUG?
IT'S THE FIBERBLAST BLEND THEY'RE MAKING ME DRINK BECAUSE I ATE A BOX OF RUBBER BANDS. YOU WANT IT?
darb
slurp
HMM...FEELIN' A BIT GROWLY IN MY BOWELY... THIS STUFF GOES RIGHT THROUGH YA!
GOSH, WITH BLENDS LIKE THESE, WHO NEEDS ENEMAS ?
OK, NEVER MIND.

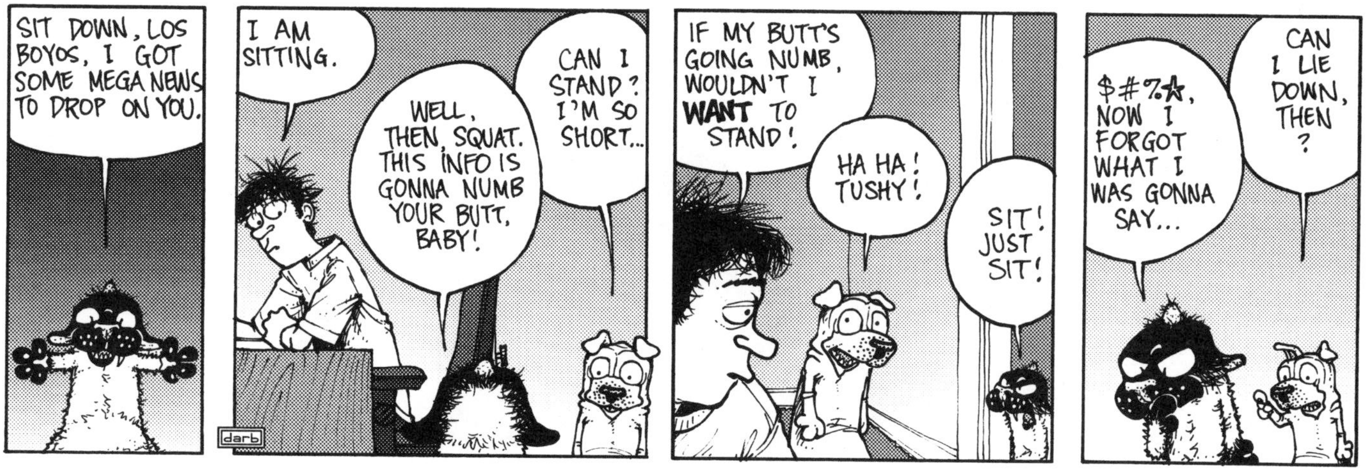
SIT DOWN, LOS BOYOS, I GOT SOME MEGA NEWS TO DROP ON YOU.
I AM SITTING.
WELL, THEN, SQUAT. THIS INFO IS GONNA NUMB YOUR BUTT, BABY!
CAN I STAND? I'M SO SHORT...
darb
IF MY BUTT'S GOING NUMB, WOULDN'T I **WANT** TO STAND!
HA HA! TUSHY!
SIT! JUST SIT!
$#%☆, NOW I FORGOT WHAT I WAS GONNA SAY...
CAN I LIE DOWN, THEN ?

HEY, BUCK. MIND IF I STAND HERE?
WHOA, BACK OFF, THERE, VELCRO.
NO, NO, YOU HAVE TO STAND THERE FOR THE JOKE!
WHAT JOKE, YOU IDIOT? GET OFF ME!
darb
OH, WAIT!
IT'S INSIDE OUT!
I'm With STUPID

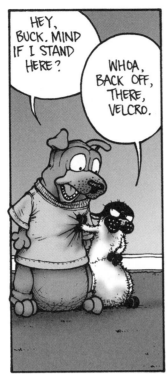

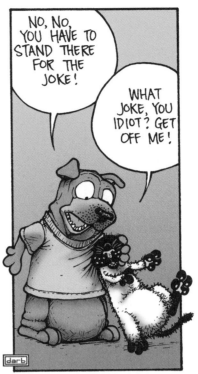

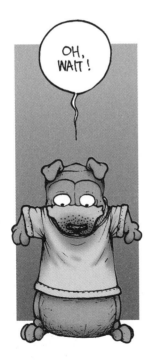

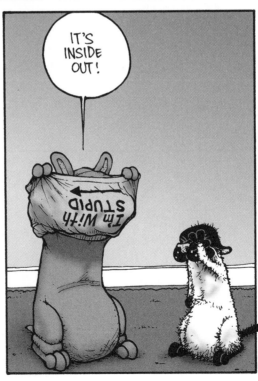

Panel 1:
SO WHAT IS THIS BIG NEWS YOU WERE GONNA TELL US?

OK- WHAT'S THE BEST THING NEXT TO BEING A MODEL?

OH! I KNOW! THE CAMERA!

Panel 2:
NEXT TO *BEING* A MODEL, NOT THE THING NEXT TO THE MODEL HIMSELF!

AH. HMM.

Panel 3:
I AM GOING TO HOLD A CONTEST TO WIN A DAY WITH... WAIT FOR IT... WITH **ME!** FORMER NEARLY SUPER-MODEL BUCKY KATT!

Panel 4:
"WIN"?

OH, AND YOU TWO AREN'T ELIGIBLE.

Panel 5:
A CONTEST TO WIN A DAY WITH YOU? YOU'VE GOT TO BE JOKING.

I ASSURE YOU, I'VE NEVER BEEN LESS FUNNY.

Panel 6:
YOU JUST WORRY ABOUT THE INCONSOLABLE LOSERS THROWING THEMSELVES AGAINST THE DOOR TRYING DESPERATELY TO BE IN MY PRESENCE. I'LL TAKE CARE OF THE REST.

Panel 7:
IS IT JUST ME, OR IS IT DELUSIONAL IN HERE?

NO, I FEEL IT, TOO.

Panel 8:
SO YOU THINK LOTS OF PEOPLE ARE GOING TO ENTER A CONTEST TO WIN A DAY WITH YOU? BASED ON WHAT?

I SENSE THE DEMAND. I READ PEOPLE LIKE BOOKS.

Panel 9:
DUDE, I'VE SEEN YOU READING BOOKS. YOU NEVER FINISH THEM AND YOU ALWAYS MISUNDERSTAND THEM.

THAT'S SLANDER, THAT IS. AND NOT THE GOOD KIND.

Panel 10:
YOU THOUGHT *GREEN EGGS AND HAM* WAS AN ARTICLE ON THE CHERNOBYL DISASTER... IT'S A CHILDREN'S STORY!

IT WAS WRITTEN BY A DOCTOR, ROBERT!

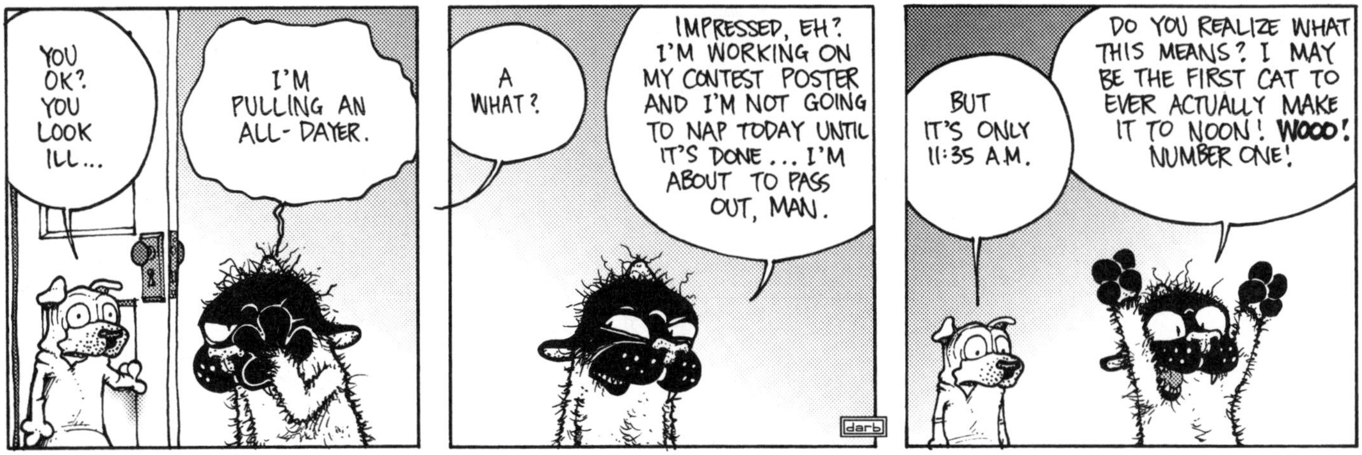
YOU OK? YOU LOOK ILL...
I'M PULLING AN ALL-DAYER.
A WHAT?
IMPRESSED, EH? I'M WORKING ON MY CONTEST POSTER AND I'M NOT GOING TO NAP TODAY UNTIL IT'S DONE... I'M ABOUT TO PASS OUT, MAN.
BUT IT'S ONLY 11:35 A.M.
DO YOU REALIZE WHAT THIS MEANS? I MAY BE THE FIRST CAT TO EVER ACTUALLY MAKE IT TO NOON! WOOO! NUMBER ONE!
darb

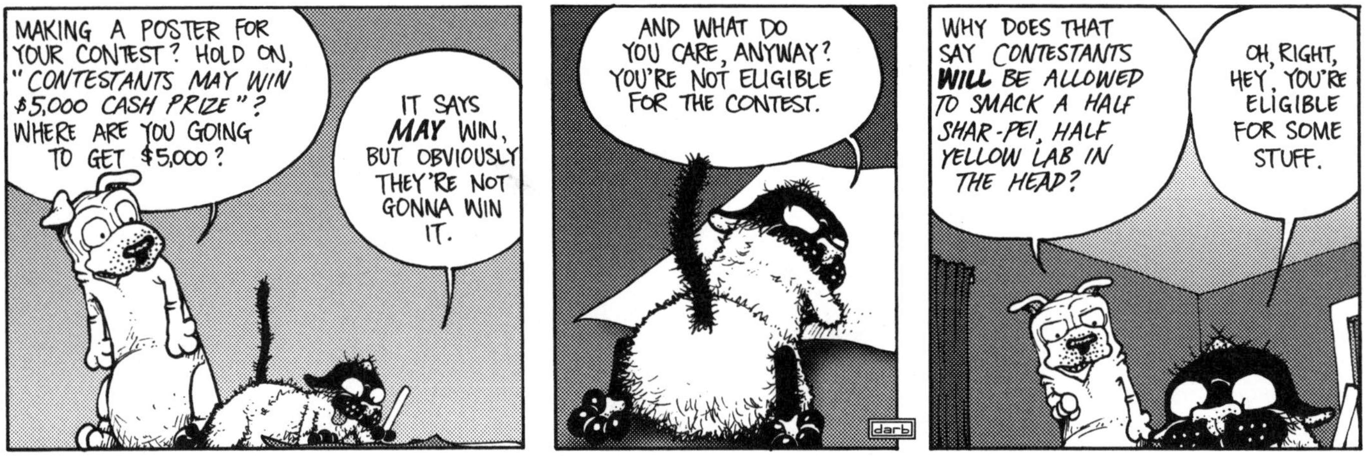
MAKING A POSTER FOR YOUR CONTEST? HOLD ON, "CONTESTANTS MAY WIN $5,000 CASH PRIZE"? WHERE ARE YOU GOING TO GET $5,000?
IT SAYS MAY WIN, BUT OBVIOUSLY THEY'RE NOT GONNA WIN IT.
AND WHAT DO YOU CARE, ANYWAY? YOU'RE NOT ELIGIBLE FOR THE CONTEST.
WHY DOES THAT SAY CONTESTANTS WILL BE ALLOWED TO SMACK A HALF SHAR-PEI, HALF YELLOW LAB IN THE HEAD?
OH, RIGHT, HEY, YOU'RE ELIGIBLE FOR SOME STUFF.
darb

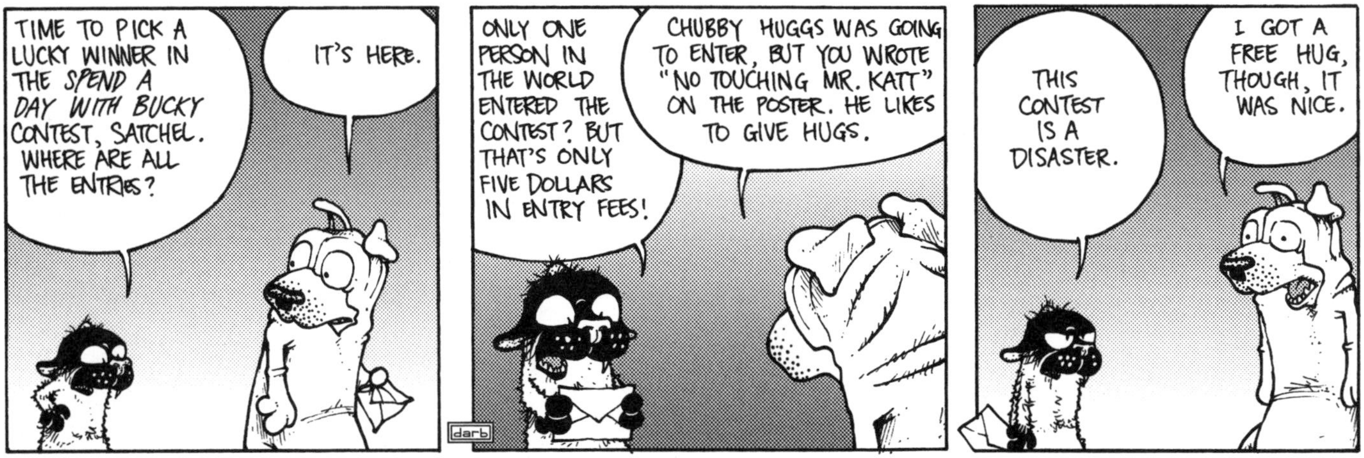
TIME TO PICK A LUCKY WINNER IN THE SPEND A DAY WITH BUCKY CONTEST, SATCHEL. WHERE ARE ALL THE ENTRIES?
IT'S HERE.
ONLY ONE PERSON IN THE WORLD ENTERED THE CONTEST? BUT THAT'S ONLY FIVE DOLLARS IN ENTRY FEES!
CHUBBY HUGGS WAS GOING TO ENTER, BUT YOU WROTE "NO TOUCHING MR. KATT" ON THE POSTER. HE LIKES TO GIVE HUGS.
THIS CONTEST IS A DISASTER.
I GOT A FREE HUG, THOUGH, IT WAS NICE.
darb

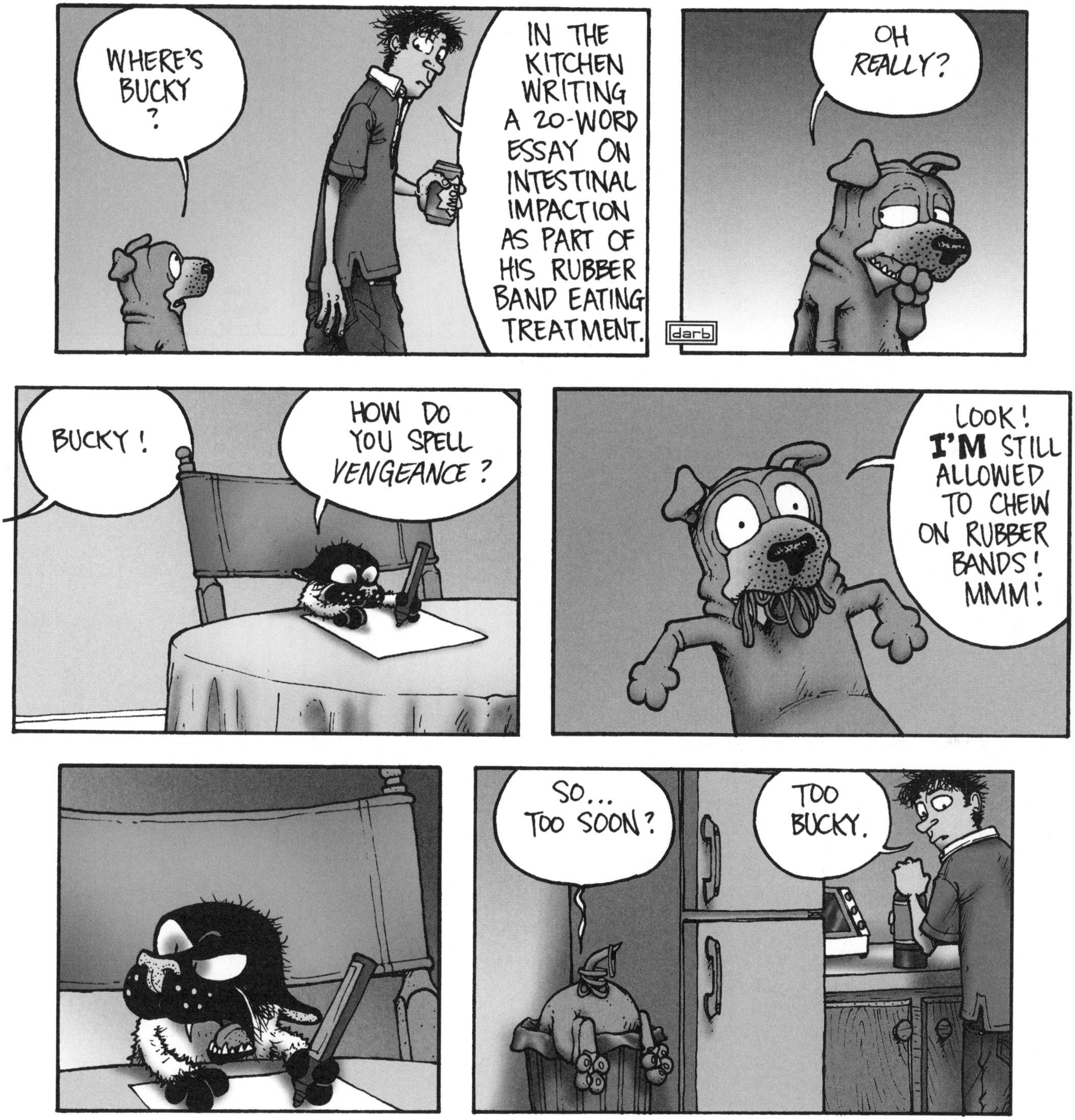
WHERE'S BUCKY ?
IN THE KITCHEN WRITING A 20-WORD ESSAY ON INTESTINAL IMPACTION AS PART OF HIS RUBBER BAND EATING TREATMENT.
darb
OH *REALLY*?
BUCKY !
HOW DO YOU SPELL *VENGEANCE* ?
LOOK! **I'M** STILL ALLOWED TO CHEW ON RUBBER BANDS! MMM!
SO... TOO SOON?
TOO BUCKY.

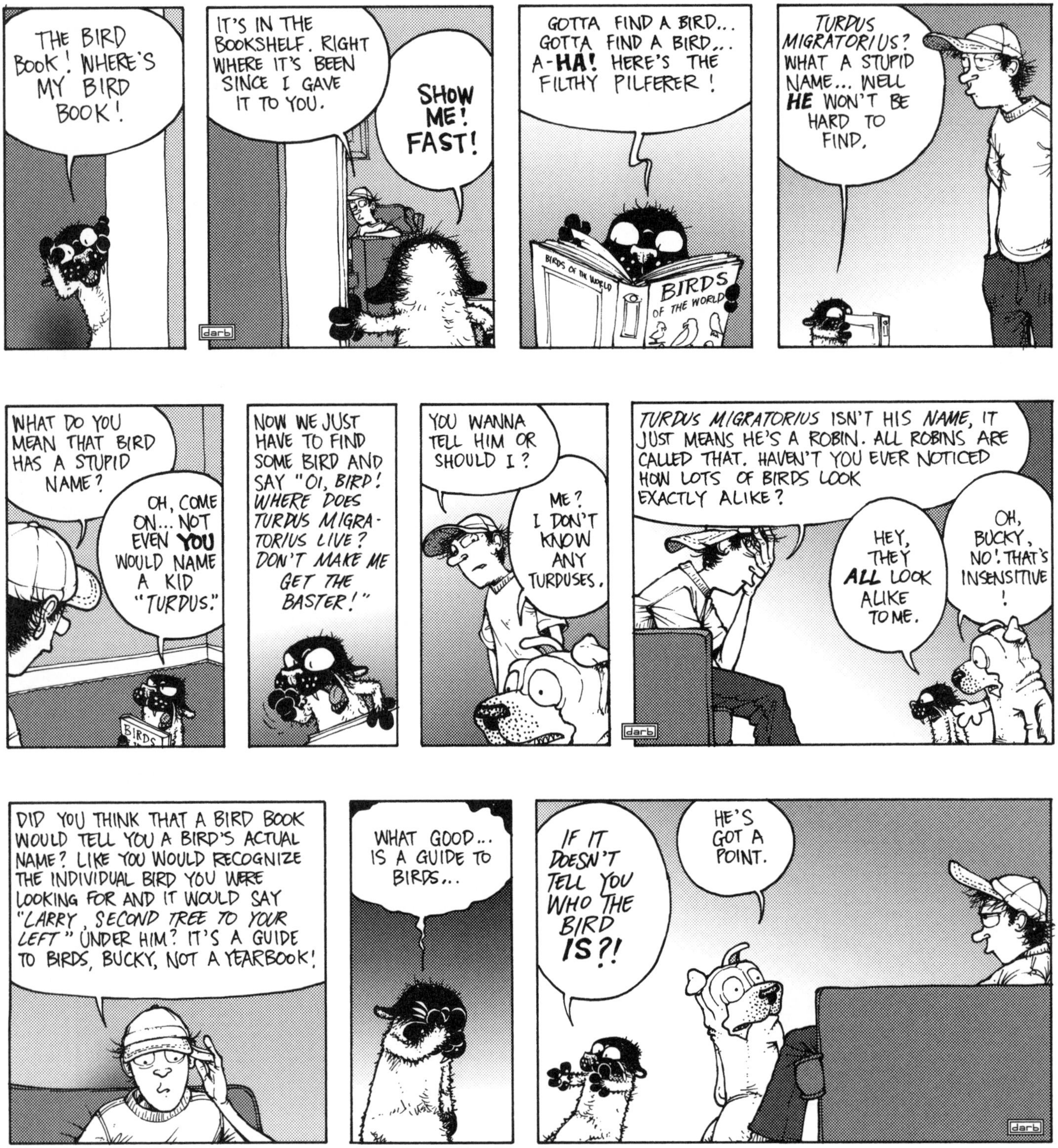
THE BIRD BOOK! WHERE'S MY BIRD BOOK!
IT'S IN THE BOOKSHELF. RIGHT WHERE IT'S BEEN SINCE I GAVE IT TO YOU.
SHOW ME! FAST!
GOTTA FIND A BIRD... GOTTA FIND A BIRD... A-HA! HERE'S THE FILTHY PILFERER!
BIRDS OF THE WORLD
BIRDS OF THE WORLD
TURDUS MIGRATORIUS? WHAT A STUPID NAME... WELL HE WON'T BE HARD TO FIND.
WHAT DO YOU MEAN THAT BIRD HAS A STUPID NAME?
OH, COME ON... NOT EVEN YOU WOULD NAME A KID "TURDUS."
BIRDS
NOW WE JUST HAVE TO FIND SOME BIRD AND SAY "OI, BIRD! WHERE DOES TURDUS MIGRA-TORIUS LIVE? DON'T MAKE ME GET THE BASTER!"
YOU WANNA TELL HIM OR SHOULD I?
ME? I DON'T KNOW ANY TURDUSES.
TURDUS MIGRATORIUS ISN'T HIS NAME, IT JUST MEANS HE'S A ROBIN. ALL ROBINS ARE CALLED THAT. HAVEN'T YOU EVER NOTICED HOW LOTS OF BIRDS LOOK EXACTLY ALIKE?
HEY, THEY ALL LOOK ALIKE TO ME.
OH, BUCKY, NO! THAT'S INSENSITIVE!
DID YOU THINK THAT A BIRD BOOK WOULD TELL YOU A BIRD'S ACTUAL NAME? LIKE YOU WOULD RECOGNIZE THE INDIVIDUAL BIRD YOU WERE LOOKING FOR AND IT WOULD SAY "LARRY, SECOND TREE TO YOUR LEFT" UNDER HIM? IT'S A GUIDE TO BIRDS, BUCKY, NOT A YEARBOOK!
WHAT GOOD... IS A GUIDE TO BIRDS...
IF IT DOESN'T TELL YOU WHO THE BIRD IS?!
HE'S GOT A POINT.

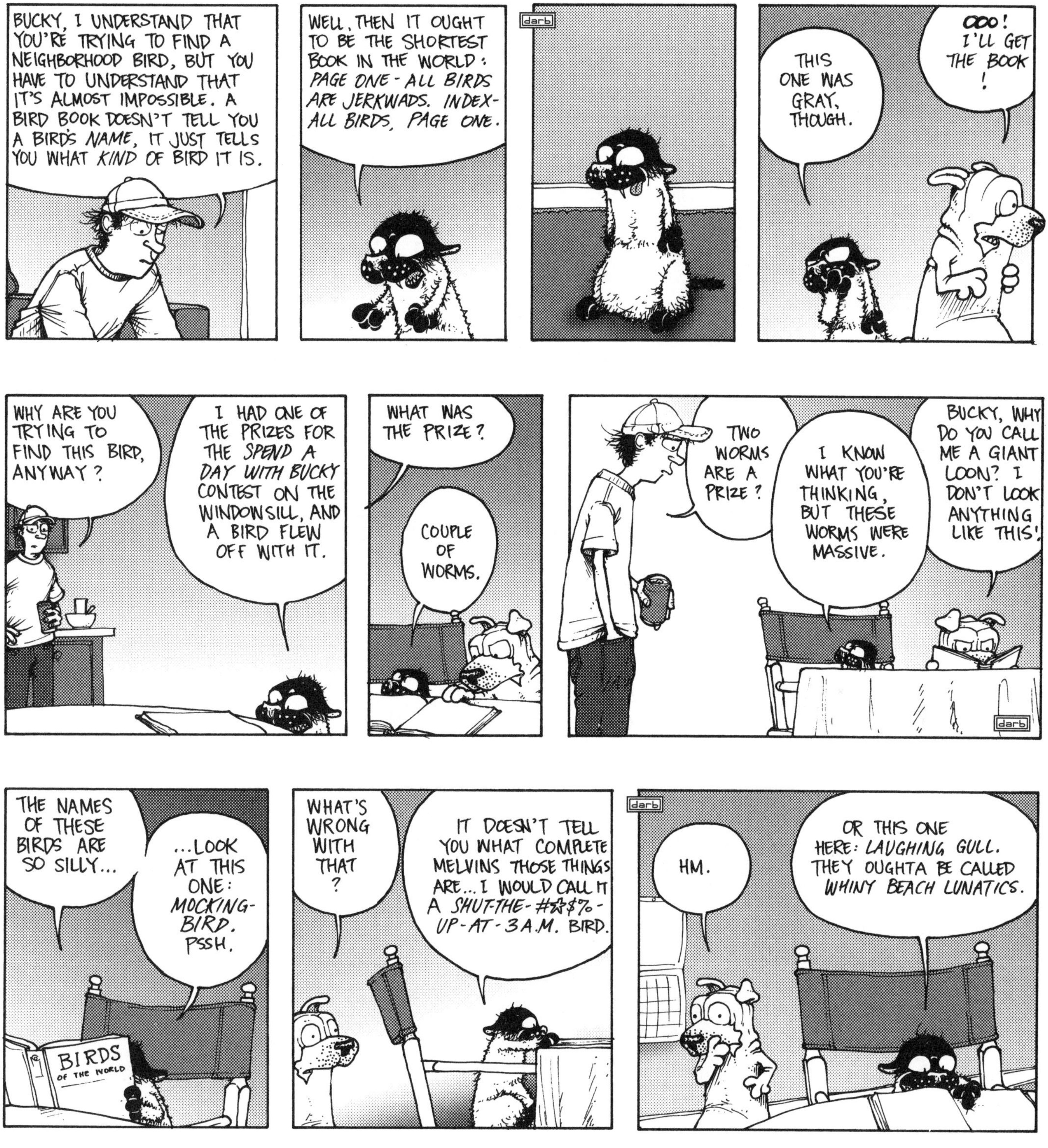
BUCKY, I UNDERSTAND THAT YOU'RE TRYING TO FIND A NEIGHBORHOOD BIRD, BUT YOU HAVE TO UNDERSTAND THAT IT'S ALMOST IMPOSSIBLE. A BIRD BOOK DOESN'T TELL YOU A BIRD'S *NAME*, IT JUST TELLS YOU WHAT *KIND* OF BIRD IT IS.
WELL, THEN IT OUGHT TO BE THE SHORTEST BOOK IN THE WORLD: *PAGE ONE - ALL BIRDS ARE JERKWADS. INDEX - ALL BIRDS, PAGE ONE.*
darb
THIS ONE WAS GRAY, THOUGH.
OOO! I'LL GET THE *BOOK*!
WHY ARE YOU TRYING TO FIND THIS BIRD, ANYWAY?
I HAD ONE OF THE PRIZES FOR THE *SPEND A DAY WITH BUCKY* CONTEST ON THE WINDOWSILL, AND A BIRD FLEW OFF WITH IT.
WHAT WAS THE PRIZE?
COUPLE OF WORMS.
TWO WORMS ARE A PRIZE?
I KNOW WHAT YOU'RE THINKING, BUT THESE WORMS WERE MASSIVE.
BUCKY, WHY DO YOU CALL ME A GIANT LOON? I DON'T LOOK ANYTHING LIKE THIS!
darb
THE NAMES OF THESE BIRDS ARE SO SILLY...
...LOOK AT THIS ONE: *MOCKINGBIRD*. PSSH.
BIRDS OF THE WORLD
WHAT'S WRONG WITH THAT?
IT DOESN'T TELL YOU WHAT COMPLETE MELVINS THOSE THINGS ARE... I WOULD CALL IT A *SHUT-THE-#☆$%-UP-AT-3 A.M.* BIRD.
darb
HM.
OR THIS ONE HERE: *LAUGHING GULL.* THEY OUGHTA BE CALLED *WHINY BEACH LUNATICS.*

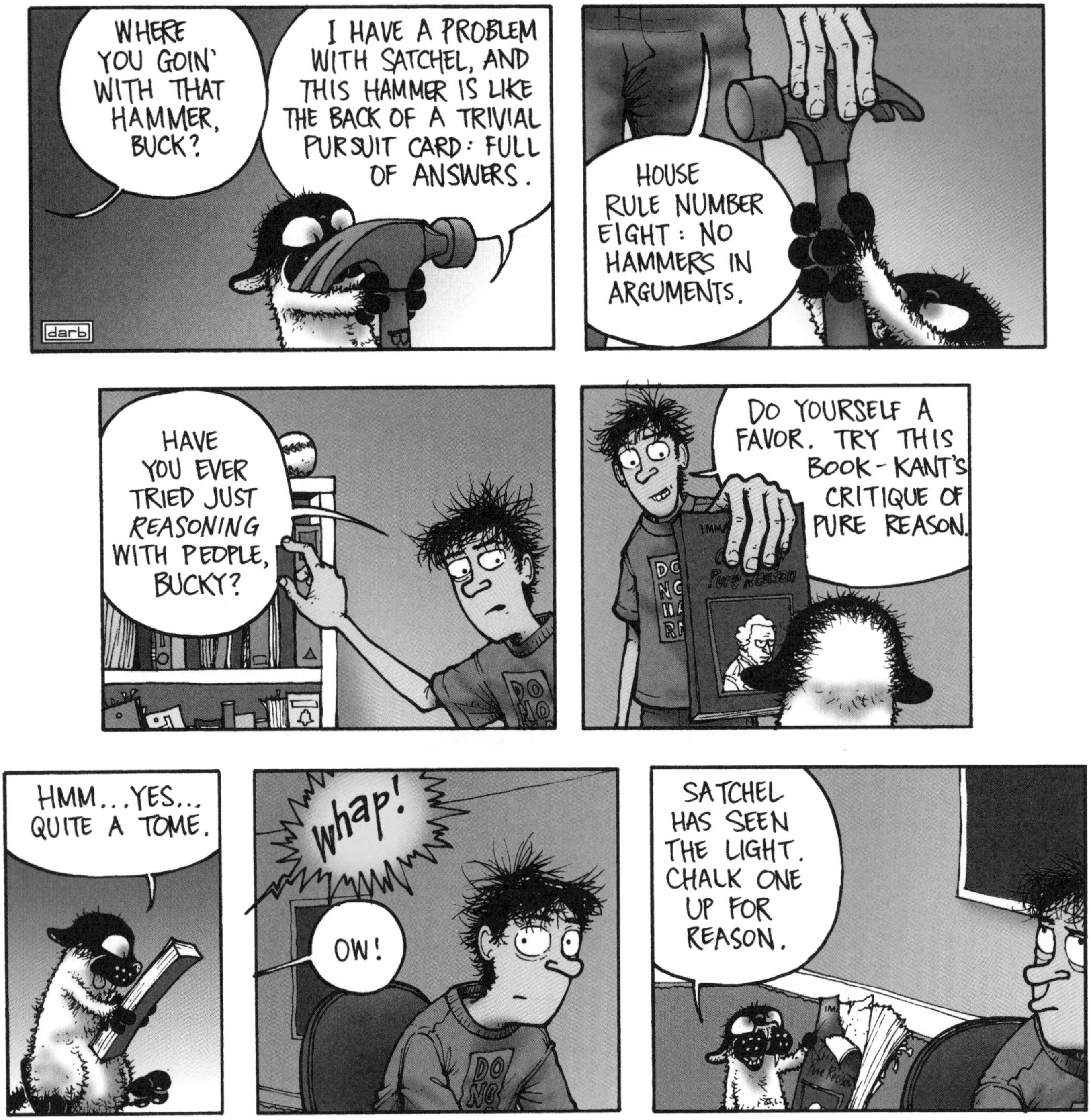
WHERE YOU GOIN' WITH THAT HAMMER, BUCK?
I HAVE A PROBLEM WITH SATCHEL, AND THIS HAMMER IS LIKE THE BACK OF A TRIVIAL PURSUIT CARD: FULL OF ANSWERS.
darb
HOUSE RULE NUMBER EIGHT: NO HAMMERS IN ARGUMENTS.
HAVE YOU EVER TRIED JUST *REASONING* WITH PEOPLE, BUCKY?
DO YOURSELF A FAVOR. TRY THIS BOOK - KANT'S CRITIQUE OF PURE REASON.
Pure Reason
HMM...YES... QUITE A TOME.
whap!
OW!
SATCHEL HAS SEEN THE LIGHT. CHALK ONE UP FOR REASON.

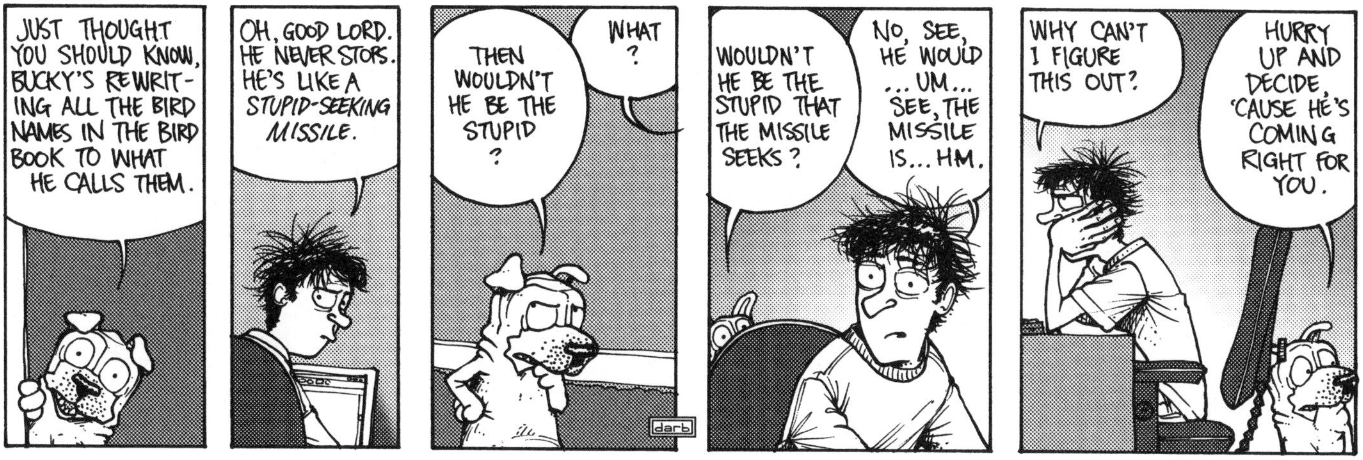
JUST THOUGHT YOU SHOULD KNOW, BUCKY'S REWRITING ALL THE BIRD NAMES IN THE BIRD BOOK TO WHAT HE CALLS THEM.
OH, GOOD LORD. HE NEVER STOPS. HE'S LIKE A *STUPID-SEEKING MISSILE.*
THEN WOULDN'T HE BE THE STUPID ?
WHAT ?
WOULDN'T HE BE THE STUPID THAT THE MISSILE SEEKS ?
NO, SEE, HE WOULD ... UM... SEE, THE MISSILE IS... HM.
WHY CAN'T I FIGURE THIS OUT?
HURRY UP AND DECIDE, 'CAUSE HE'S COMING RIGHT FOR YOU.

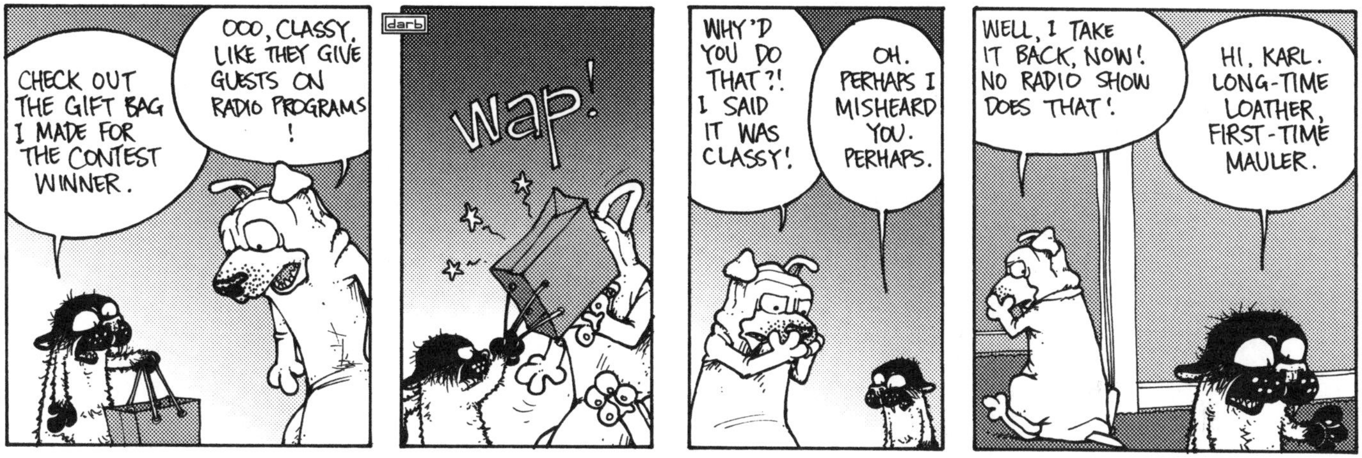
CHECK OUT THE GIFT BAG I MADE FOR THE CONTEST WINNER.
OOO, CLASSY. LIKE THEY GIVE GUESTS ON RADIO PROGRAMS !
WAP!
WHY'D YOU DO THAT?! I SAID IT WAS CLASSY!
OH. PERHAPS I MISHEARD YOU. PERHAPS.
WELL, I TAKE IT BACK, NOW! NO RADIO SHOW DOES THAT!
HI, KARL. LONG-TIME LOATHER, FIRST-TIME MAULER.

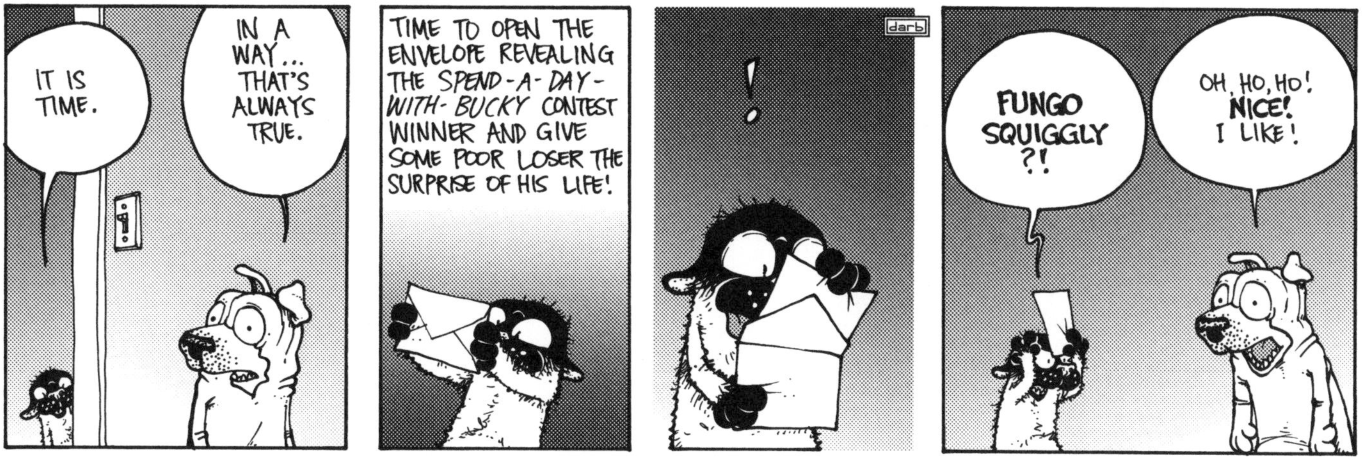
IT IS TIME.
IN A WAY... THAT'S ALWAYS TRUE.
TIME TO OPEN THE ENVELOPE REVEALING THE *SPEND-A-DAY-WITH-BUCKY* CONTEST WINNER AND GIVE SOME POOR LOSER THE SURPRISE OF HIS LIFE!
!
FUNGO SQUIGGLY ?!
OH, HO, HO! **NICE!** I LIKE!

Panel 1:
LOOK! I'M PUTTING A BOW ONTO FUNGO'S GIFT BAG!

WHAT?! I'M NOT GIVING A GIFT BAG TO FUNGO, YOU TRAITOR! MUCH LESS ONE WITH A BOW!

Panel 2:
BUT HE WON YOUR CONTEST! YOU SAID CONTEST WINNERS TRADITIONALLY GET GIFT BAGS. BESIDES...IT'S PRETTY.

Panel 3:
LISTEN, YOU DEMON SPAWN OF BENEDICT ARNOLD AND MARTHA STEWART, *NO GIFT BAG!*

BUT... YOU SAID IT WAS TRADITION!

Panel 4:
GIVE IT HERE!

NO! THE GIFT BAG IS SACRED! THE GIFT BAG IS SACRED!

Panel 5:
I HAVE A MULTI-PHASED PLAN TO GET OUT OF SPENDING A DAY WITH THE FERRET.

BUT HE WON THE CONTEST. YOU HAVE TO SPEND THE DAY WITH HIM.

Panel 6:
SO IT WOULD APPEAR -- BUT HERE, LET'S SEE IF YOU STILL SAY THAT AFTER READING THE OFFICIAL RULES ON THE POSTER I MADE.

"THE ONLY RULE IS THAT THE LUCKY WINNER SPEND A FULL 24 HOURS WITH BUCKY KATT."

Panel 7:
SEEMS PRETTY AIRTIGHT.

OK, PHASE TWO: HOW WOULD YOU LIKE TO CHANGE YOUR NAME TO BUCKY KATT?

Panel 8:
STILL AT IT?

YUP. FIXING THIS BIRD GUIDE SO THAT THE NAMES OF THE BIRDS IN IT REFLECT THEIR CHARACTER MORE ACCURATELY.

Panel 9:
FOR EXAMPLE: AS IT WAS A ROBIN WHO STOLE MY WORMS, I HAVE CHANGED THEIR NAME FROM *TURDUS MIGRATORIUS* TO *TURDUS PILFERUS.*

Panel 10:
BLUE JAYS ARE NOW *BLUEISH MODIFIED COMMAS*, MALE CHICKADEES ARE NOW *DUDE-A-DEES*, AND PELICANS LOOK SO STUPID, I JUST RENAMED THEM DODOS.

Panel 11:
I THINK THERE WAS A DODO BIRD ALREADY. IT WAS SO SLOW IT DIED OUT, THOUGH. IT ... ARE YOU CRYING?

THAT'S A BEAUTIFUL STORY.

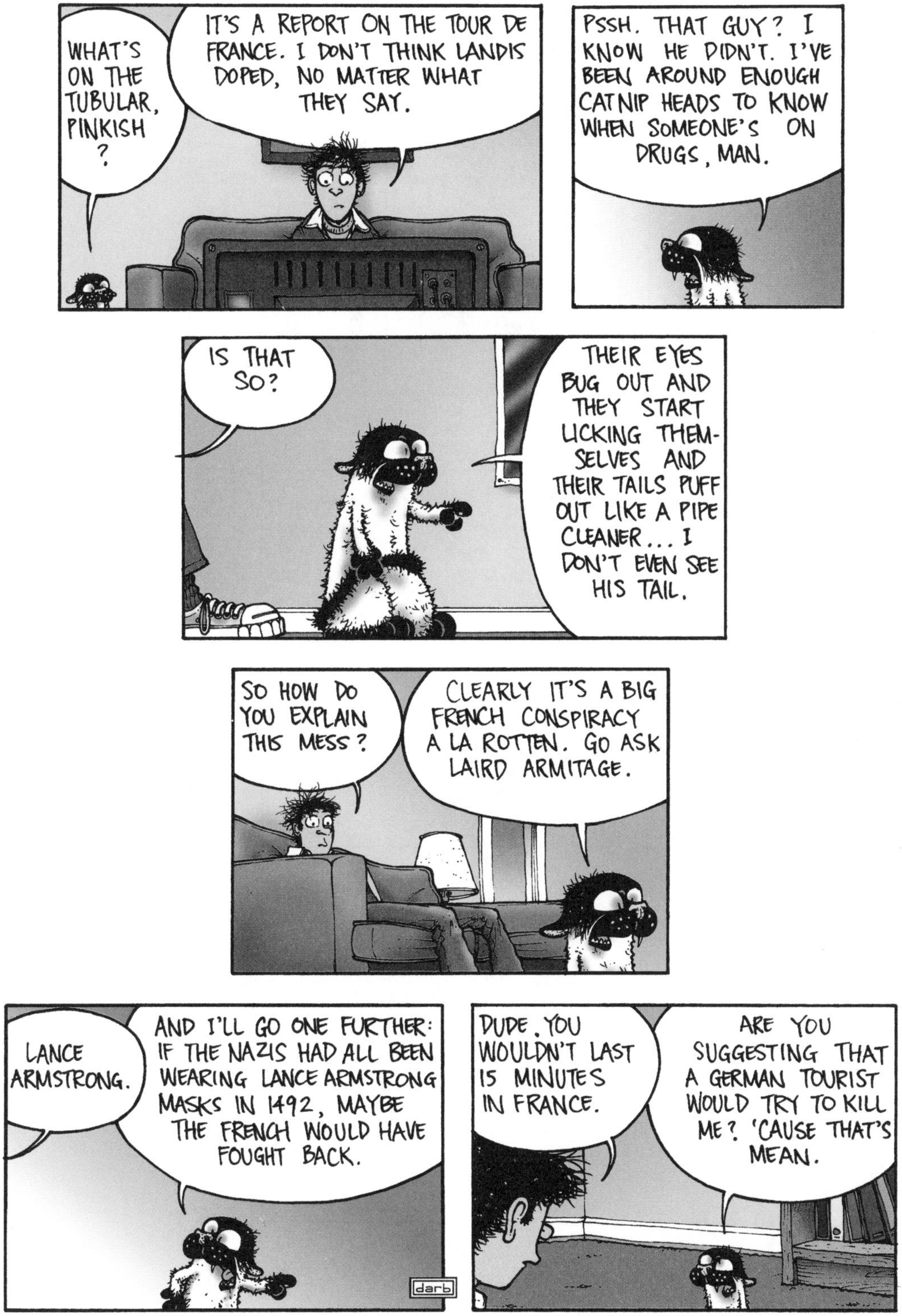
WHAT'S ON THE TUBULAR, PINKISH ?
IT'S A REPORT ON THE TOUR DE FRANCE. I DON'T THINK LANDIS DOPED, NO MATTER WHAT THEY SAY.
PSSH. THAT GUY? I KNOW HE DIDN'T. I'VE BEEN AROUND ENOUGH CATNIP HEADS TO KNOW WHEN SOMEONE'S ON DRUGS, MAN.
IS THAT SO?
THEIR EYES BUG OUT AND THEY START LICKING THEM-SELVES AND THEIR TAILS PUFF OUT LIKE A PIPE CLEANER... I DON'T EVEN SEE HIS TAIL.
SO HOW DO YOU EXPLAIN THIS MESS?
CLEARLY IT'S A BIG FRENCH CONSPIRACY A LA ROTTEN. GO ASK LAIRD ARMITAGE.
LANCE ARMSTRONG.
AND I'LL GO ONE FURTHER: IF THE NAZIS HAD ALL BEEN WEARING LANCE ARMSTRONG MASKS IN 1492, MAYBE THE FRENCH WOULD HAVE FOUGHT BACK.
darb
DUDE, YOU WOULDN'T LAST 15 MINUTES IN FRANCE.
ARE YOU SUGGESTING THAT A GERMAN TOURIST WOULD TRY TO KILL ME? 'CAUSE THAT'S MEAN.

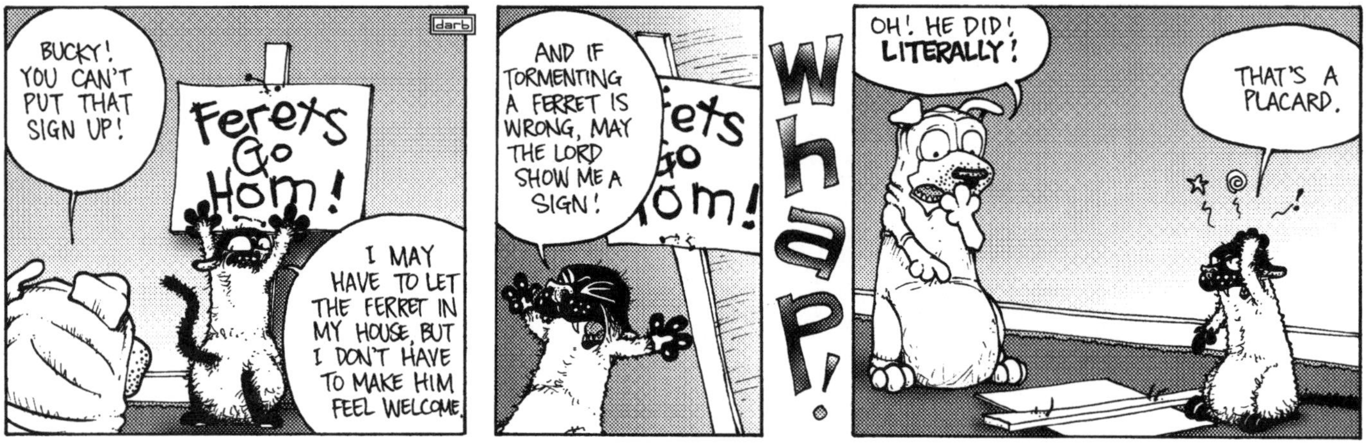
darb
BUCKY! YOU CAN'T PUT THAT SIGN UP!
Ferets Go Hom!
I MAY HAVE TO LET THE FERRET IN MY HOUSE, BUT I DON'T HAVE TO MAKE HIM FEEL WELCOME.
AND IF TORMENTING A FERRET IS WRONG, MAY THE LORD SHOW ME A SIGN!
WHAP!
OH! HE DID! **LITERALLY**!
THAT'S A PLACARD.

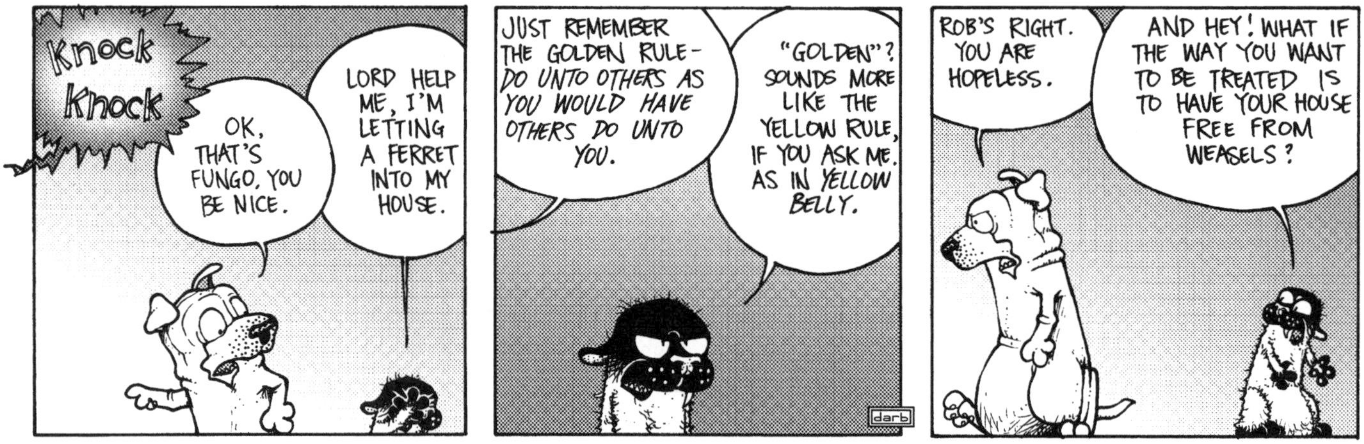
Knock Knock
OK, THAT'S FUNGO, YOU BE NICE.
LORD HELP ME, I'M LETTING A FERRET INTO MY HOUSE.
JUST REMEMBER THE GOLDEN RULE- *DO UNTO OTHERS AS YOU WOULD HAVE OTHERS DO UNTO YOU.*
"GOLDEN"? SOUNDS MORE LIKE THE YELLOW RULE, IF YOU ASK ME. AS IN *YELLOW BELLY.*
darb
ROB'S RIGHT. YOU ARE HOPELESS.
AND HEY! WHAT IF THE WAY YOU WANT TO BE TREATED IS TO HAVE YOUR HOUSE FREE FROM WEASELS?

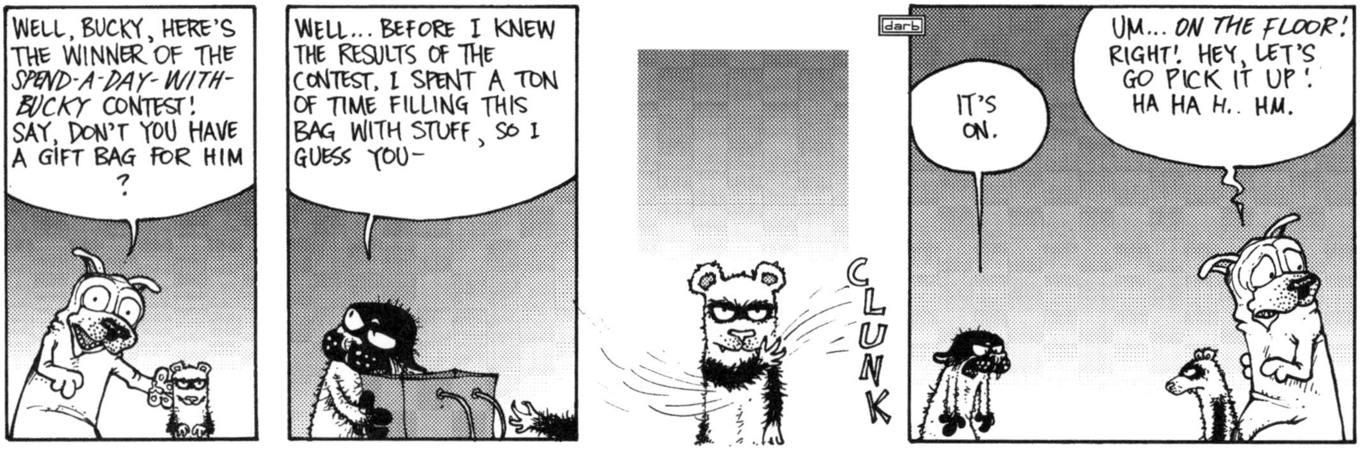
WELL, BUCKY, HERE'S THE WINNER OF THE *SPEND-A-DAY-WITH-BUCKY* CONTEST! SAY, DON'T YOU HAVE A GIFT BAG FOR HIM?
WELL... BEFORE I KNEW THE RESULTS OF THE CONTEST, I SPENT A TON OF TIME FILLING THIS BAG WITH STUFF, SO I GUESS YOU-
CLUNK
darb
IT'S ON.
UM... *ON THE FLOOR!* RIGHT! HEY, LET'S GO PICK IT UP! HA HA H.. HM.

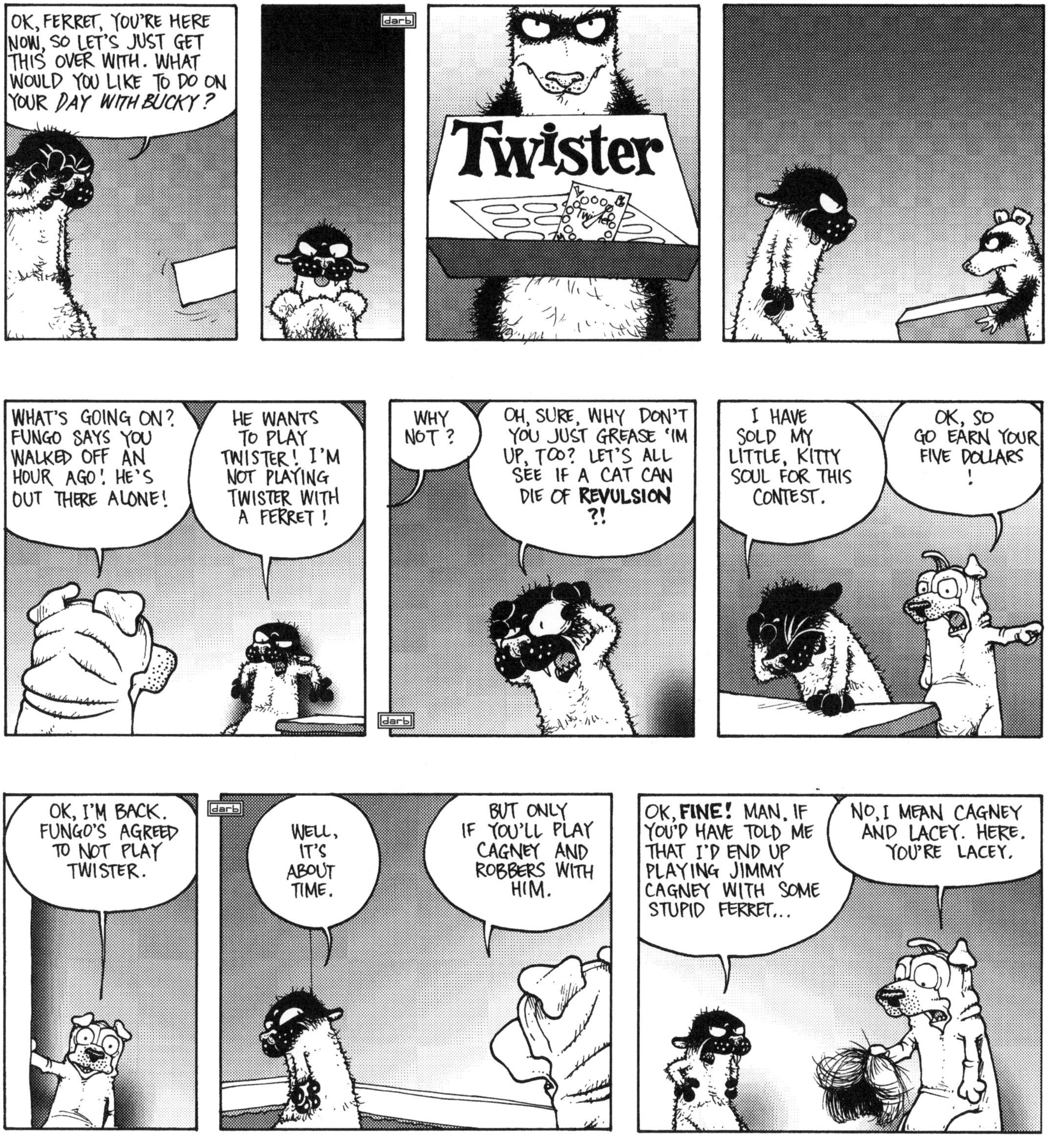
OK, FERRET, YOU'RE HERE NOW, SO LET'S JUST GET THIS OVER WITH. WHAT WOULD YOU LIKE TO DO ON YOUR DAY WITH BUCKY?
darb
Twister
WHAT'S GOING ON? FUNGO SAYS YOU WALKED OFF AN HOUR AGO! HE'S OUT THERE ALONE!
HE WANTS TO PLAY TWISTER! I'M NOT PLAYING TWISTER WITH A FERRET!
WHY NOT?
OH, SURE, WHY DON'T YOU JUST GREASE 'IM UP, TOO? LET'S ALL SEE IF A CAT CAN DIE OF REVULSION?!
darb
I HAVE SOLD MY LITTLE, KITTY SOUL FOR THIS CONTEST.
OK, SO GO EARN YOUR FIVE DOLLARS!
OK, I'M BACK. FUNGO'S AGREED TO NOT PLAY TWISTER.
darb
WELL, IT'S ABOUT TIME.
BUT ONLY IF YOU'LL PLAY CAGNEY AND ROBBERS WITH HIM.
OK, FINE! MAN. IF YOU'D HAVE TOLD ME THAT I'D END UP PLAYING JIMMY CAGNEY WITH SOME STUPID FERRET...
NO, I MEAN CAGNEY AND LACEY. HERE. YOU'RE LACEY.

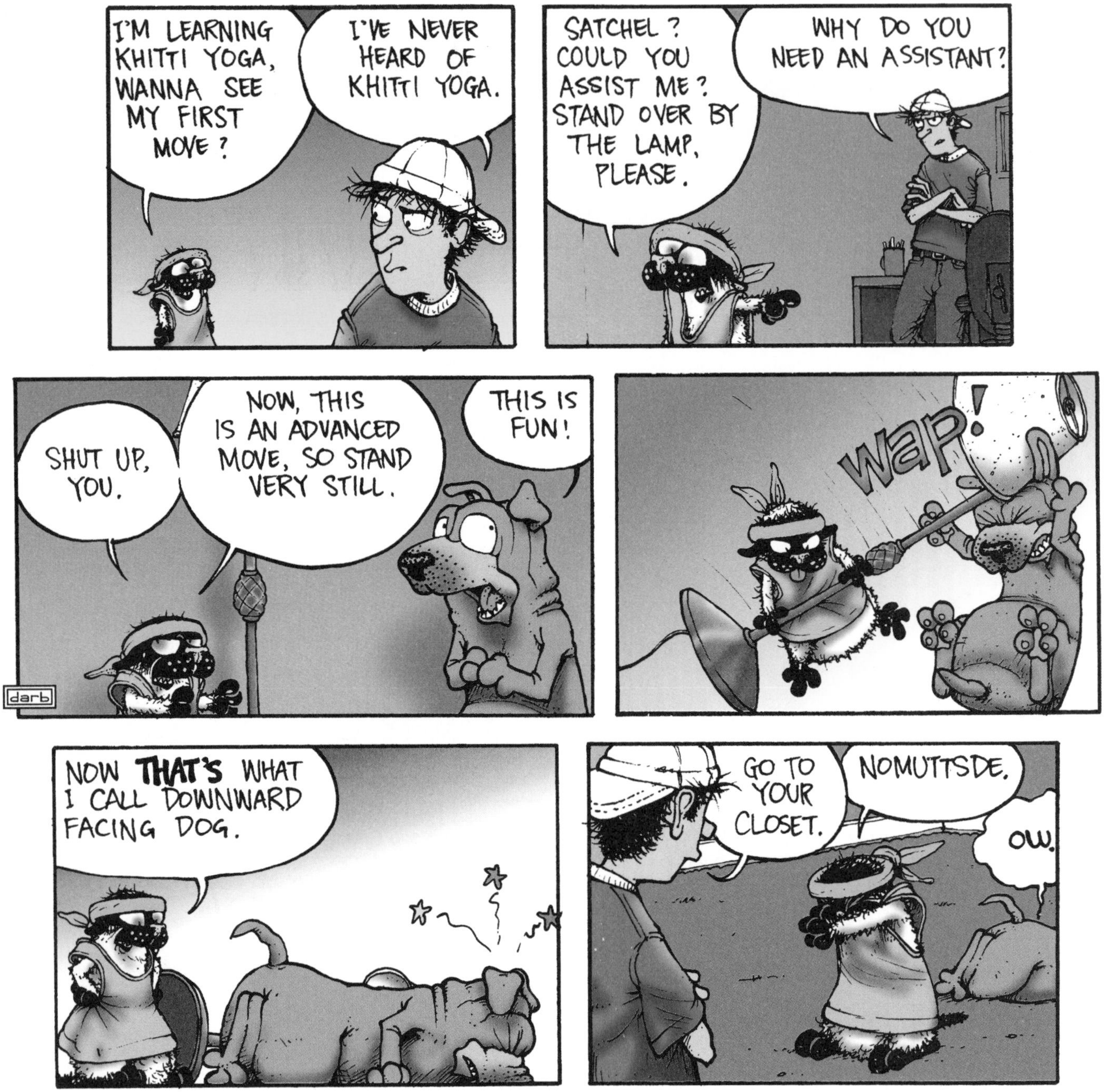
I'M LEARNING KHITTI YOGA, WANNA SEE MY FIRST MOVE?
I'VE NEVER HEARD OF KHITTI YOGA.
SATCHEL? COULD YOU ASSIST ME? STAND OVER BY THE LAMP, PLEASE.
WHY DO YOU NEED AN ASSISTANT?
SHUT UP, YOU.
NOW, THIS IS AN ADVANCED MOVE, SO STAND VERY STILL.
THIS IS FUN!
darb
WAP!
NOW THAT'S WHAT I CALL DOWNWARD FACING DOG.
GO TO YOUR CLOSET.
NOMUTTSDE.
OW.

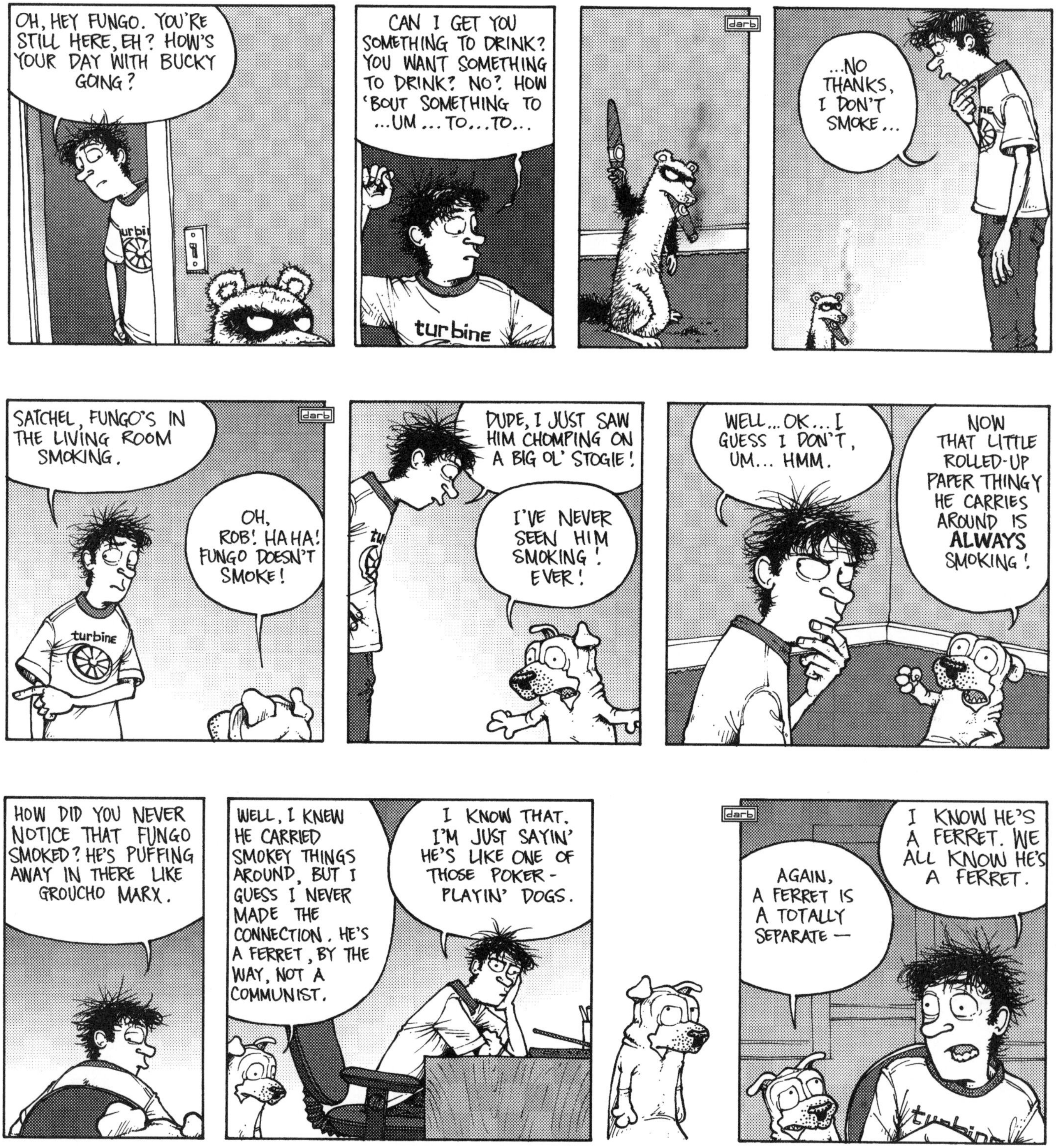
OH, HEY FUNGO. YOU'RE STILL HERE, EH? HOW'S YOUR DAY WITH BUCKY GOING?
CAN I GET YOU SOMETHING TO DRINK? YOU WANT SOMETHING TO DRINK? NO? HOW 'BOUT SOMETHING TO ...UM ... TO... TO...
darb
...NO THANKS, I DON'T SMOKE...
turbine
SATCHEL, FUNGO'S IN THE LIVING ROOM SMOKING.
darb
OH, ROB! HAHA! FUNGO DOESN'T SMOKE!
DUDE, I JUST SAW HIM CHOMPING ON A BIG OL' STOGIE!
I'VE NEVER SEEN HIM SMOKING! EVER!
WELL... OK... I GUESS I DON'T, UM... HMM.
NOW THAT LITTLE ROLLED-UP PAPER THINGY HE CARRIES AROUND IS **ALWAYS** SMOKING!
HOW DID YOU NEVER NOTICE THAT FUNGO SMOKED? HE'S PUFFING AWAY IN THERE LIKE GROUCHO MARX.
WELL, I KNEW HE CARRIED SMOKEY THINGS AROUND, BUT I GUESS I NEVER MADE THE CONNECTION. HE'S A FERRET, BY THE WAY, NOT A COMMUNIST.
I KNOW THAT. I'M JUST SAYIN' HE'S LIKE ONE OF THOSE POKER-PLAYIN' DOGS.
darb
AGAIN, A FERRET IS A TOTALLY SEPARATE —
I KNOW HE'S A FERRET. WE ALL KNOW HE'S A FERRET.

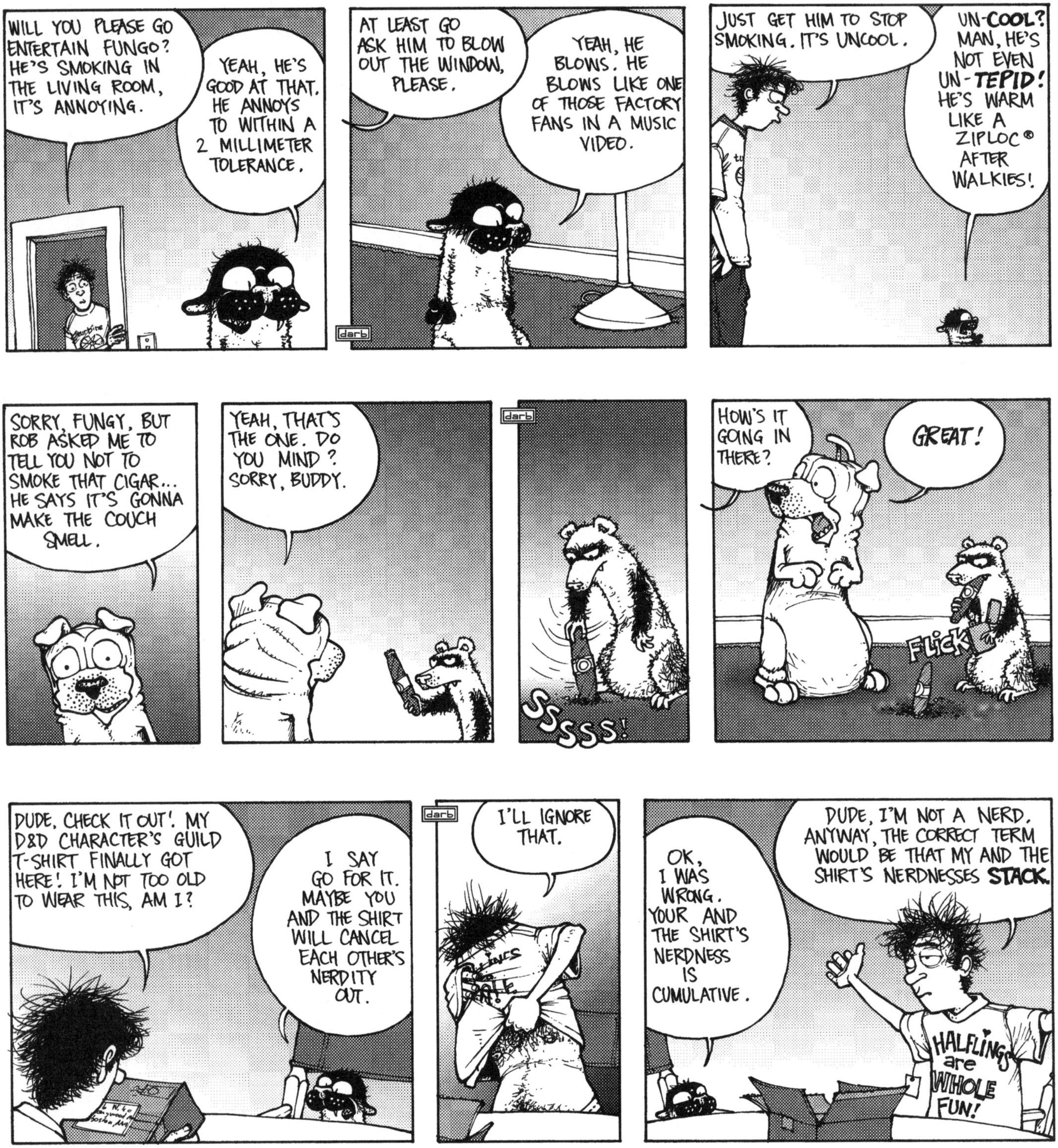
WILL YOU PLEASE GO ENTERTAIN FUNGO? HE'S SMOKING IN THE LIVING ROOM, IT'S ANNOYING.
YEAH, HE'S GOOD AT THAT. HE ANNOYS TO WITHIN A 2 MILLIMETER TOLERANCE.
AT LEAST GO ASK HIM TO BLOW OUT THE WINDOW, PLEASE.
YEAH, HE BLOWS. HE BLOWS LIKE ONE OF THOSE FACTORY FANS IN A MUSIC VIDEO.
JUST GET HIM TO STOP SMOKING. IT'S UNCOOL.
UN-COOL? MAN, HE'S NOT EVEN UN-TEPID! HE'S WARM LIKE A ZIPLOC® AFTER WALKIES!
SORRY, FUNGY, BUT ROB ASKED ME TO TELL YOU NOT TO SMOKE THAT CIGAR... HE SAYS IT'S GONNA MAKE THE COUCH SMELL.
YEAH, THAT'S THE ONE. DO YOU MIND? SORRY, BUDDY.
SSSSS!
HOW'S IT GOING IN THERE?
GREAT!
FLICK
DUDE, CHECK IT OUT! MY D&D CHARACTER'S GUILD T-SHIRT FINALLY GOT HERE! I'M NOT TOO OLD TO WEAR THIS, AM I?
I SAY GO FOR IT. MAYBE YOU AND THE SHIRT WILL CANCEL EACH OTHER'S NERDITY OUT.
I'LL IGNORE THAT.
OK, I WAS WRONG. YOUR AND THE SHIRT'S NERDNESS IS CUMULATIVE.
DUDE, I'M NOT A NERD. ANYWAY, THE CORRECT TERM WOULD BE THAT MY AND THE SHIRT'S NERDNESSES STACK.
HALFLINGS are WHOLE FUN!

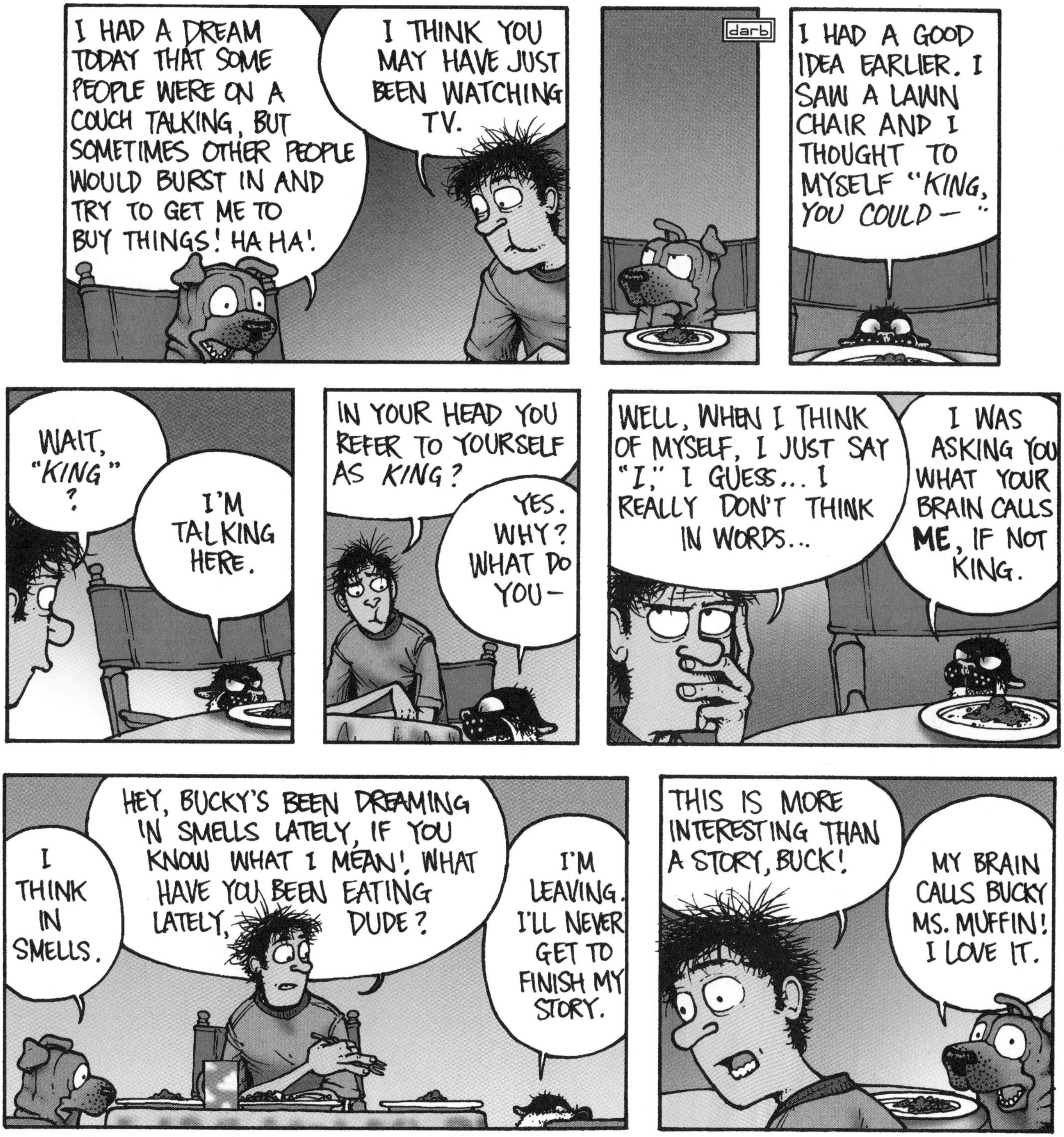
I HAD A DREAM TODAY THAT SOME PEOPLE WERE ON A COUCH TALKING, BUT SOMETIMES OTHER PEOPLE WOULD BURST IN AND TRY TO GET ME TO BUY THINGS! HA HA!
I THINK YOU MAY HAVE JUST BEEN WATCHING TV.
darb
I HAD A GOOD IDEA EARLIER. I SAW A LAWN CHAIR AND I THOUGHT TO MYSELF "KING, YOU COULD—"
WAIT, "KING"?
I'M TALKING HERE.
IN YOUR HEAD YOU REFER TO YOURSELF AS KING?
YES. WHY? WHAT DO YOU—
WELL, WHEN I THINK OF MYSELF, I JUST SAY "I," I GUESS... I REALLY DON'T THINK IN WORDS...
I WAS ASKING YOU WHAT YOUR BRAIN CALLS ME, IF NOT KING.
I THINK IN SMELLS.
HEY, BUCKY'S BEEN DREAMING IN SMELLS LATELY, IF YOU KNOW WHAT I MEAN! WHAT HAVE YOU BEEN EATING LATELY, DUDE?
I'M LEAVING. I'LL NEVER GET TO FINISH MY STORY.
THIS IS MORE INTERESTING THAN A STORY, BUCK!
MY BRAIN CALLS BUCKY MS. MUFFIN! I LOVE IT.

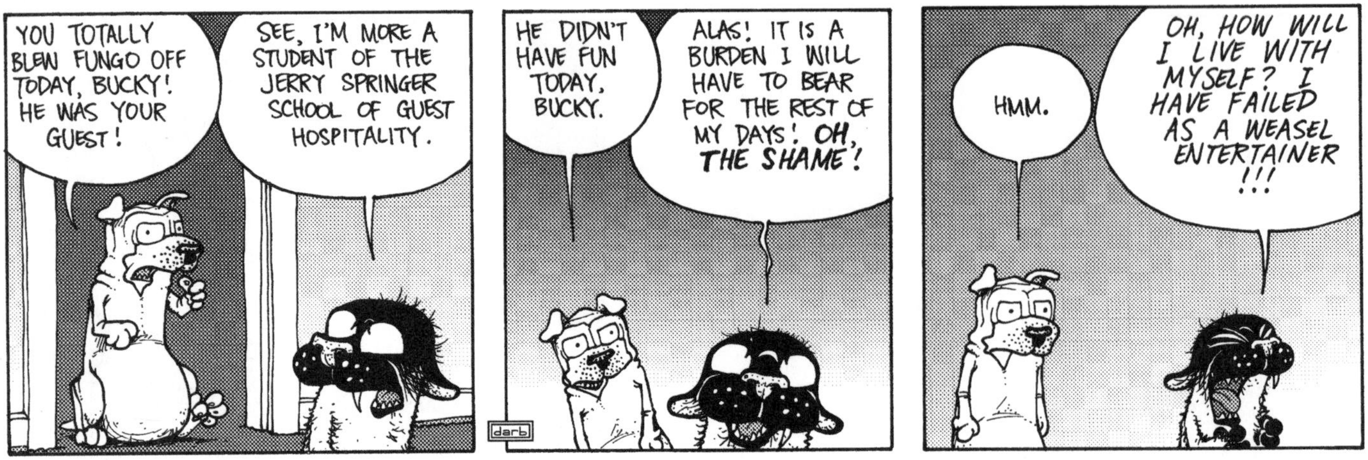
YOU TOTALLY BLEW FUNGO OFF TODAY, BUCKY! HE WAS YOUR GUEST!
SEE, I'M MORE A STUDENT OF THE JERRY SPRINGER SCHOOL OF GUEST HOSPITALITY.
HE DIDN'T HAVE FUN TODAY, BUCKY.
ALAS! IT IS A BURDEN I WILL HAVE TO BEAR FOR THE REST OF MY DAYS! OH, THE SHAME!
HMM.
OH, HOW WILL I LIVE WITH MYSELF? I HAVE FAILED AS A WEASEL ENTERTAINER!!!

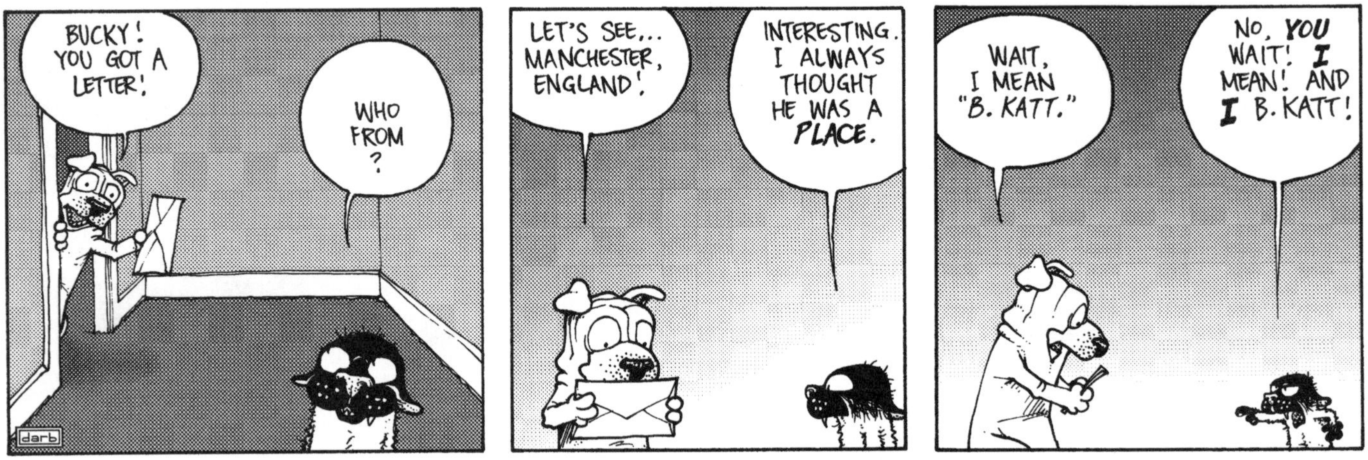
BUCKY! YOU GOT A LETTER!
WHO FROM?
LET'S SEE... MANCHESTER, ENGLAND!
INTERESTING. I ALWAYS THOUGHT HE WAS A PLACE.
WAIT, I MEAN "B. KATT."
NO, YOU WAIT! I MEAN! AND I B. KATT!

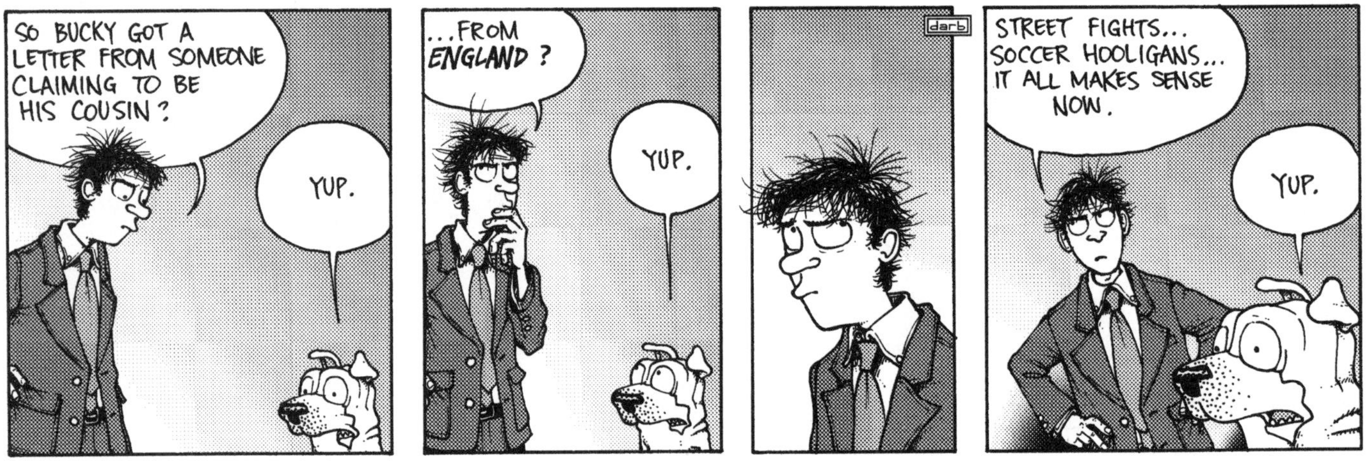
SO BUCKY GOT A LETTER FROM SOMEONE CLAIMING TO BE HIS COUSIN?
YUP.
...FROM ENGLAND?
YUP.
STREET FIGHTS... SOCCER HOOLIGANS... IT ALL MAKES SENSE NOW.
YUP.

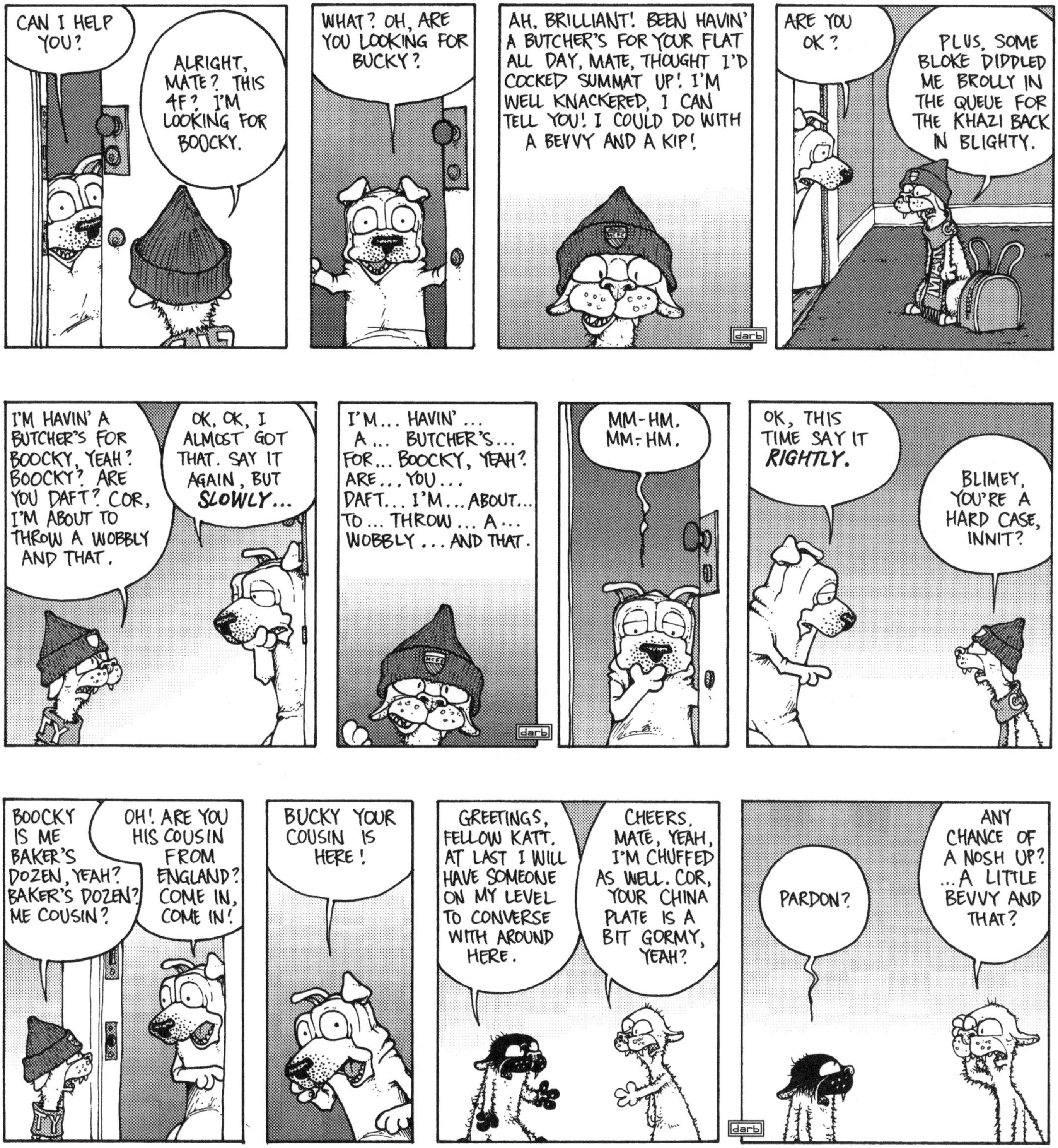
CAN I HELP YOU?
ALRIGHT, MATE? THIS 4F? I'M LOOKING FOR BOOCKY.
WHAT? OH, ARE YOU LOOKING FOR BUCKY?
AH, BRILLIANT! BEEN HAVIN' A BUTCHER'S FOR YOUR FLAT ALL DAY, MATE, THOUGHT I'D COCKED SUMMAT UP! I'M WELL KNACKERED, I CAN TELL YOU! I COULD DO WITH A BEVVY AND A KIP!
darb
ARE YOU OK?
PLUS, SOME BLOKE DIDDLED ME BROLLY IN THE QUEUE FOR THE KHAZI BACK IN BLIGHTY.
I'M HAVIN' A BUTCHER'S FOR BOOCKY, YEAH? BOOCKY? ARE YOU DAFT? COR, I'M ABOUT TO THROW A WOBBLY AND THAT.
OK, OK, I ALMOST GOT THAT. SAY IT AGAIN, BUT SLOWLY...
I'M... HAVIN'... A... BUTCHER'S... FOR... BOOCKY, YEAH? ARE... YOU... DAFT... I'M... ABOUT... TO... THROW... A... WOBBLY... AND THAT.
darb
MM-HM. MM-HM.
OK, THIS TIME SAY IT RIGHTLY.
BLIMEY, YOU'RE A HARD CASE, INNIT?
BOOCKY IS ME BAKER'S DOZEN, YEAH? BAKER'S DOZEN? ME COUSIN?
OH! ARE YOU HIS COUSIN FROM ENGLAND? COME IN, COME IN!
BUCKY YOUR COUSIN IS HERE!
GREETINGS, FELLOW KATT. AT LAST I WILL HAVE SOMEONE ON MY LEVEL TO CONVERSE WITH AROUND HERE.
CHEERS, MATE, YEAH, I'M CHUFFED AS WELL. COR, YOUR CHINA PLATE IS A BIT GORMY, YEAH?
darb
PARDON?
ANY CHANCE OF A NOSH UP? ...A LITTLE BEVVY AND THAT?

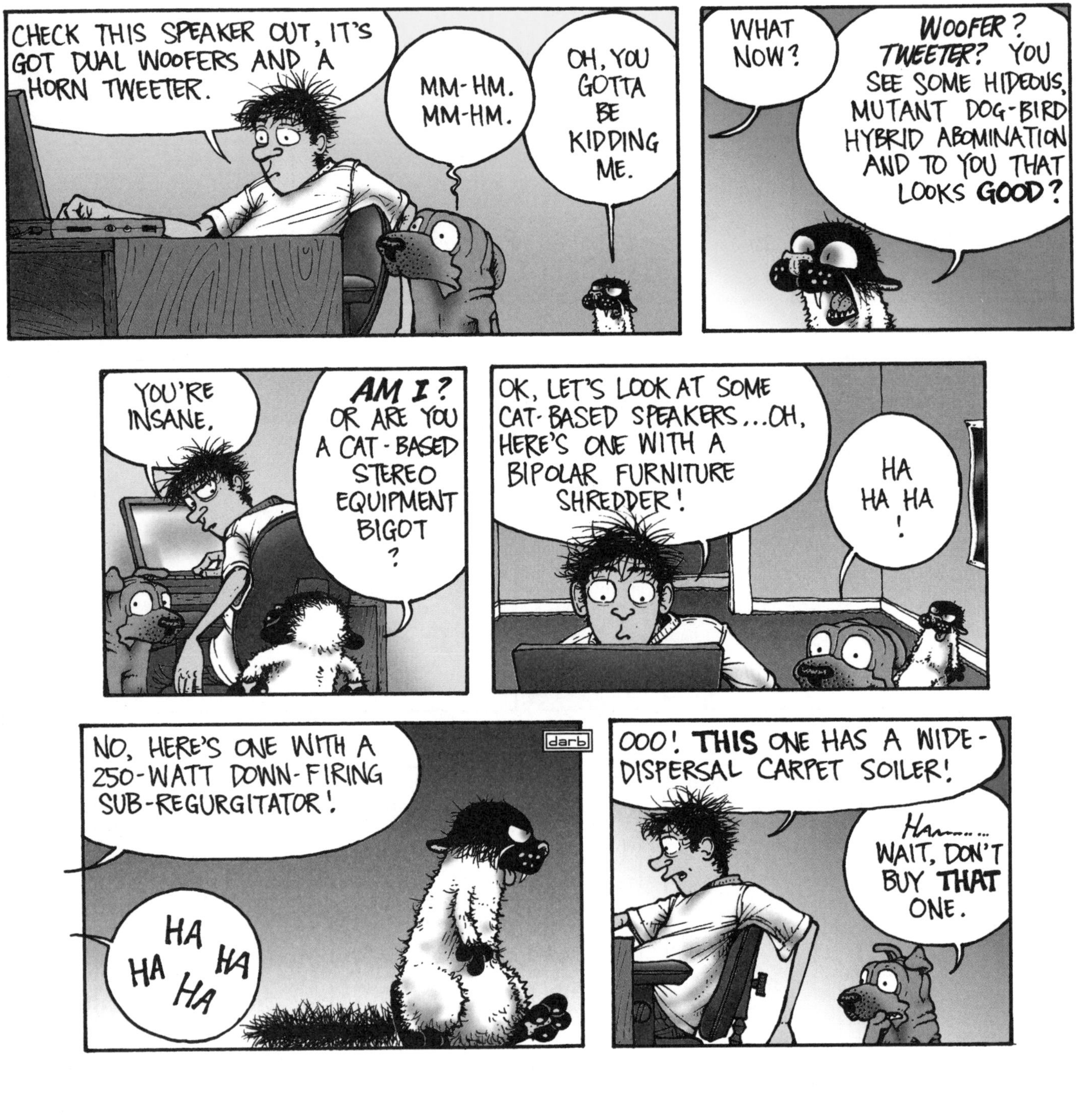

CHECK THIS SPEAKER OUT, IT'S GOT DUAL WOOFERS AND A HORN TWEETER.
MM-HM. MM-HM.
OH, YOU GOTTA BE KIDDING ME.
WHAT NOW?
WOOFER? TWEETER? YOU SEE SOME HIDEOUS, MUTANT DOG-BIRD HYBRID ABOMINATION AND TO YOU THAT LOOKS **GOOD**?
YOU'RE INSANE.
AM I? OR ARE YOU A CAT-BASED STEREO EQUIPMENT BIGOT?
OK, LET'S LOOK AT SOME CAT-BASED SPEAKERS...OH, HERE'S ONE WITH A BIPOLAR FURNITURE SHREDDER!
HA HA HA!
NO, HERE'S ONE WITH A 250-WATT DOWN-FIRING SUB-REGURGITATOR!
HA HA HA HA
darb
OOO! **THIS** ONE HAS A WIDE-DISPERSAL CARPET SOILER!
HA...... WAIT, DON'T BUY **THAT** ONE.

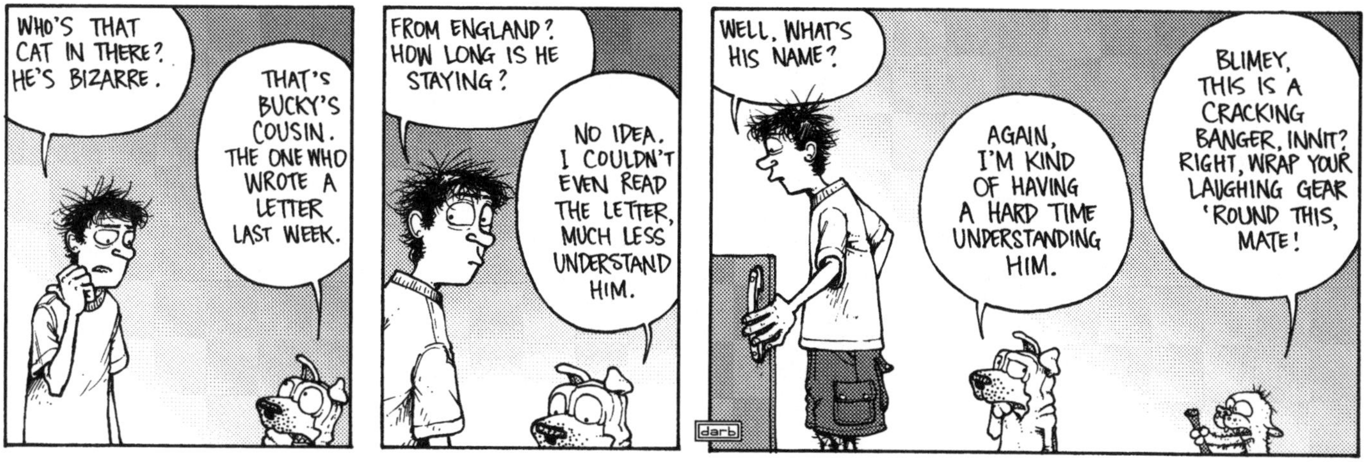
WHO'S THAT CAT IN THERE? HE'S BIZARRE.
THAT'S BUCKY'S COUSIN. THE ONE WHO WROTE A LETTER LAST WEEK.
FROM ENGLAND? HOW LONG IS HE STAYING?
NO IDEA. I COULDN'T EVEN READ THE LETTER, MUCH LESS UNDERSTAND HIM.
WELL, WHAT'S HIS NAME?
AGAIN, I'M KIND OF HAVING A HARD TIME UNDERSTANDING HIM.
BLIMEY, THIS IS A CRACKING BANGER, INNIT? RIGHT, WRAP YOUR LAUGHING GEAR 'ROUND THIS, MATE!
darb

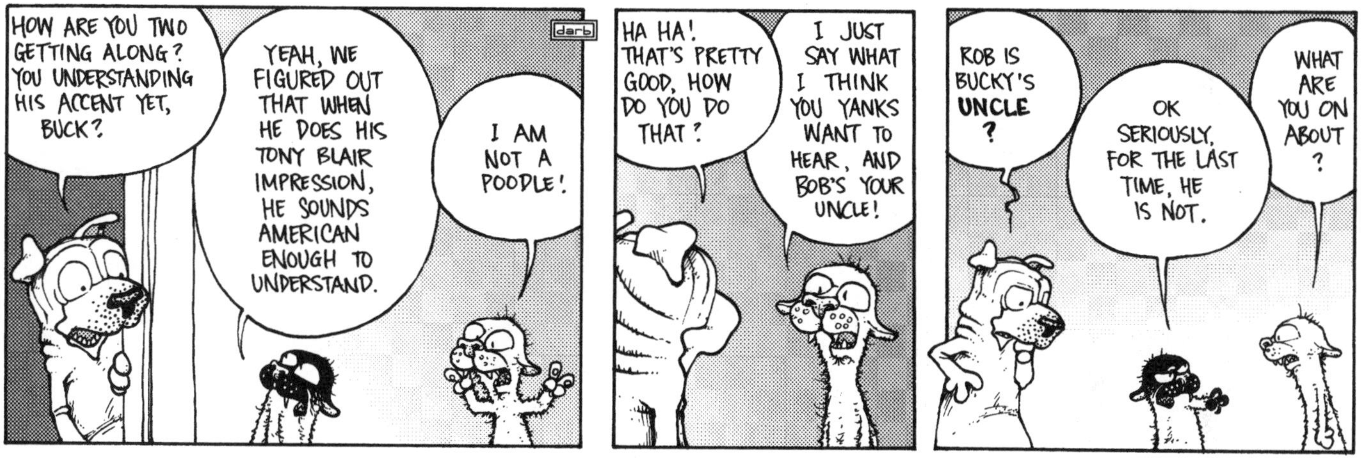
darb
HOW ARE YOU TWO GETTING ALONG? YOU UNDERSTANDING HIS ACCENT YET, BUCK?
YEAH, WE FIGURED OUT THAT WHEN HE DOES HIS TONY BLAIR IMPRESSION, HE SOUNDS AMERICAN ENOUGH TO UNDERSTAND.
I AM NOT A POODLE!
HA HA! THAT'S PRETTY GOOD, HOW DO YOU DO THAT?
I JUST SAY WHAT I THINK YOU YANKS WANT TO HEAR, AND BOB'S YOUR UNCLE!
ROB IS BUCKY'S **UNCLE** ?
OK SERIOUSLY, FOR THE LAST TIME, HE IS NOT.
WHAT ARE YOU ON ABOUT?

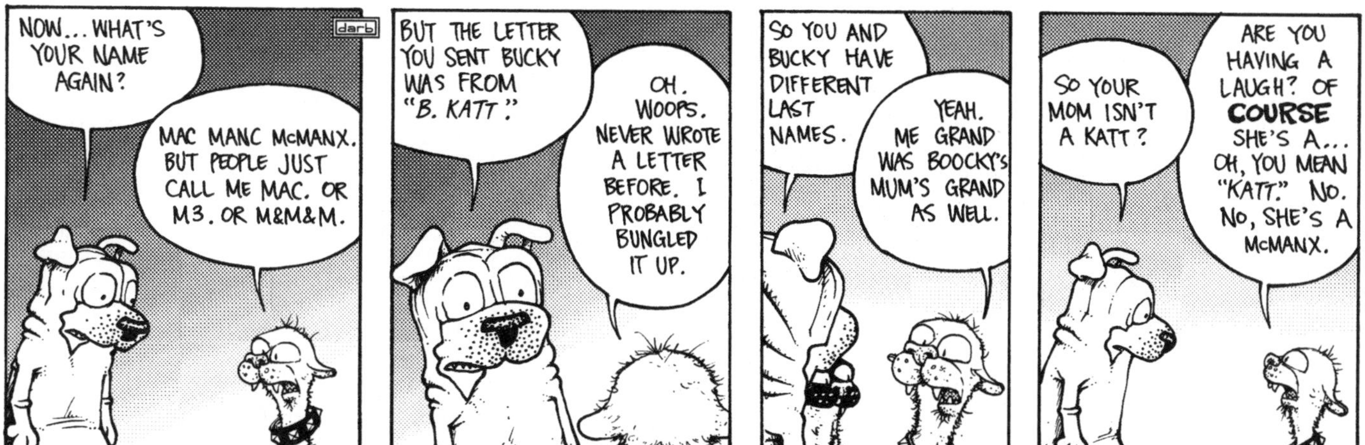
darb
NOW... WHAT'S YOUR NAME AGAIN?
MAC MANC McMANX. BUT PEOPLE JUST CALL ME MAC. OR M3. OR M&M&M.
BUT THE LETTER YOU SENT BUCKY WAS FROM "B. KATT."
OH. WOOPS. NEVER WROTE A LETTER BEFORE. I PROBABLY BUNGLED IT UP.
SO YOU AND BUCKY HAVE DIFFERENT LAST NAMES.
YEAH. ME GRAND WAS BOOCKY'S MUM'S GRAND AS WELL.
SO YOUR MOM ISN'T A KATT?
ARE YOU HAVING A LAUGH? OF **COURSE** SHE'S A... OH, YOU MEAN "KATT." NO. NO, SHE'S A McMANX.

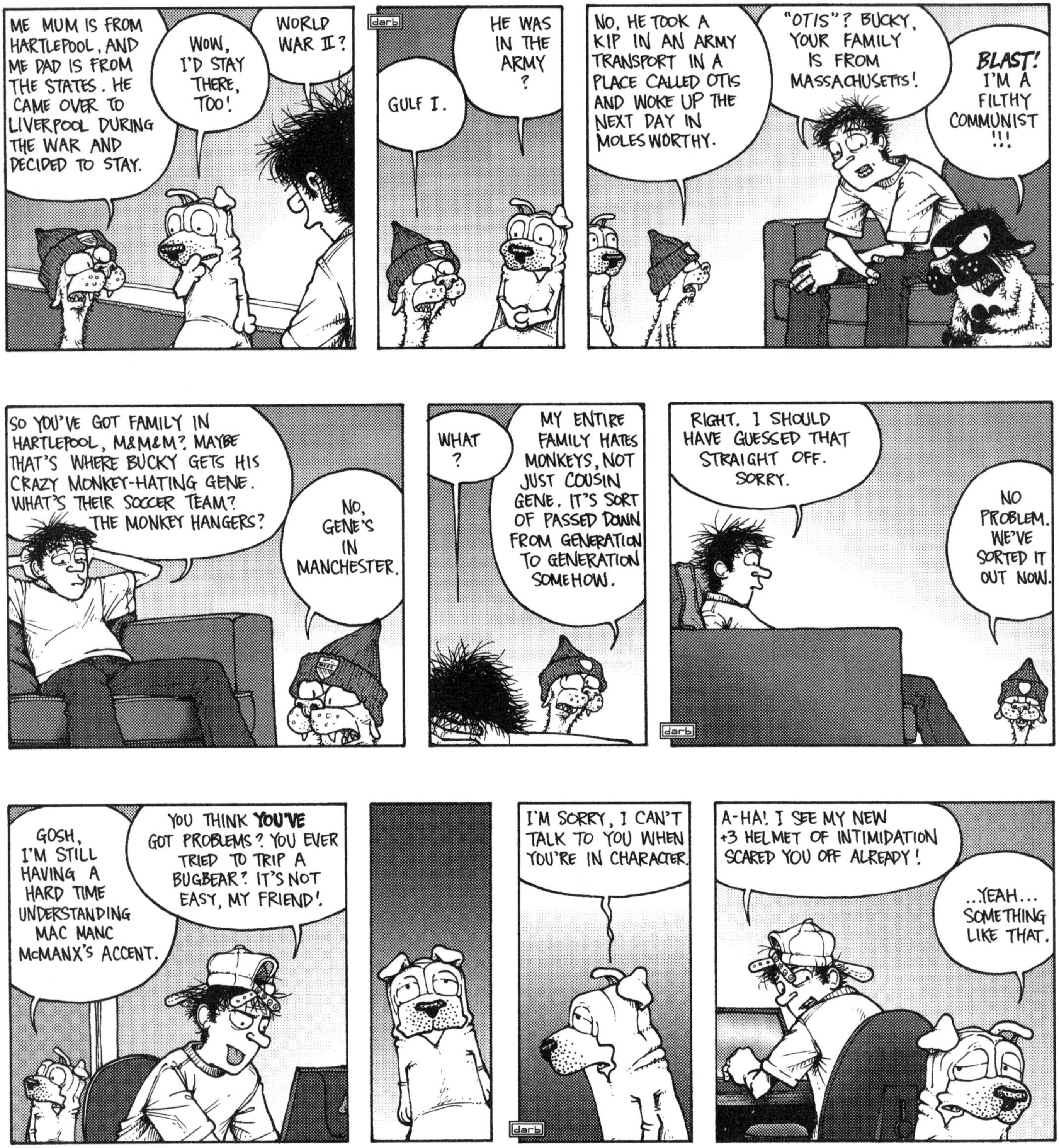
ME MUM IS FROM HARTLEPOOL, AND ME DAD IS FROM THE STATES. HE CAME OVER TO LIVERPOOL DURING THE WAR AND DECIDED TO STAY.
WOW, I'D STAY THERE, TOO!
WORLD WAR II?
darb
HE WAS IN THE ARMY?
GULF I.
NO, HE TOOK A KIP IN AN ARMY TRANSPORT IN A PLACE CALLED OTIS AND WOKE UP THE NEXT DAY IN MOLESWORTHY.
"OTIS"? BUCKY, YOUR FAMILY IS FROM MASSACHUSETTS!
BLAST! I'M A FILTHY COMMUNIST!!!
SO YOU'VE GOT FAMILY IN HARTLEPOOL, M&M&M? MAYBE THAT'S WHERE BUCKY GETS HIS CRAZY MONKEY-HATING GENE. WHAT'S THEIR SOCCER TEAM? THE MONKEY HANGERS?
NO, GENE'S IN MANCHESTER.
WHAT?
MY ENTIRE FAMILY HATES MONKEYS, NOT JUST COUSIN GENE. IT'S SORT OF PASSED DOWN FROM GENERATION TO GENERATION SOMEHOW.
darb
RIGHT. I SHOULD HAVE GUESSED THAT STRAIGHT OFF. SORRY.
NO PROBLEM. WE'VE SORTED IT OUT NOW.
GOSH, I'M STILL HAVING A HARD TIME UNDERSTANDING MAC MANC McMANX'S ACCENT.
YOU THINK YOU'VE GOT PROBLEMS? YOU EVER TRIED TO TRIP A BUGBEAR? IT'S NOT EASY, MY FRIEND!
darb
I'M SORRY, I CAN'T TALK TO YOU WHEN YOU'RE IN CHARACTER.
A-HA! I SEE MY NEW +3 HELMET OF INTIMIDATION SCARED YOU OFF ALREADY!
...YEAH... SOMETHING LIKE THAT.

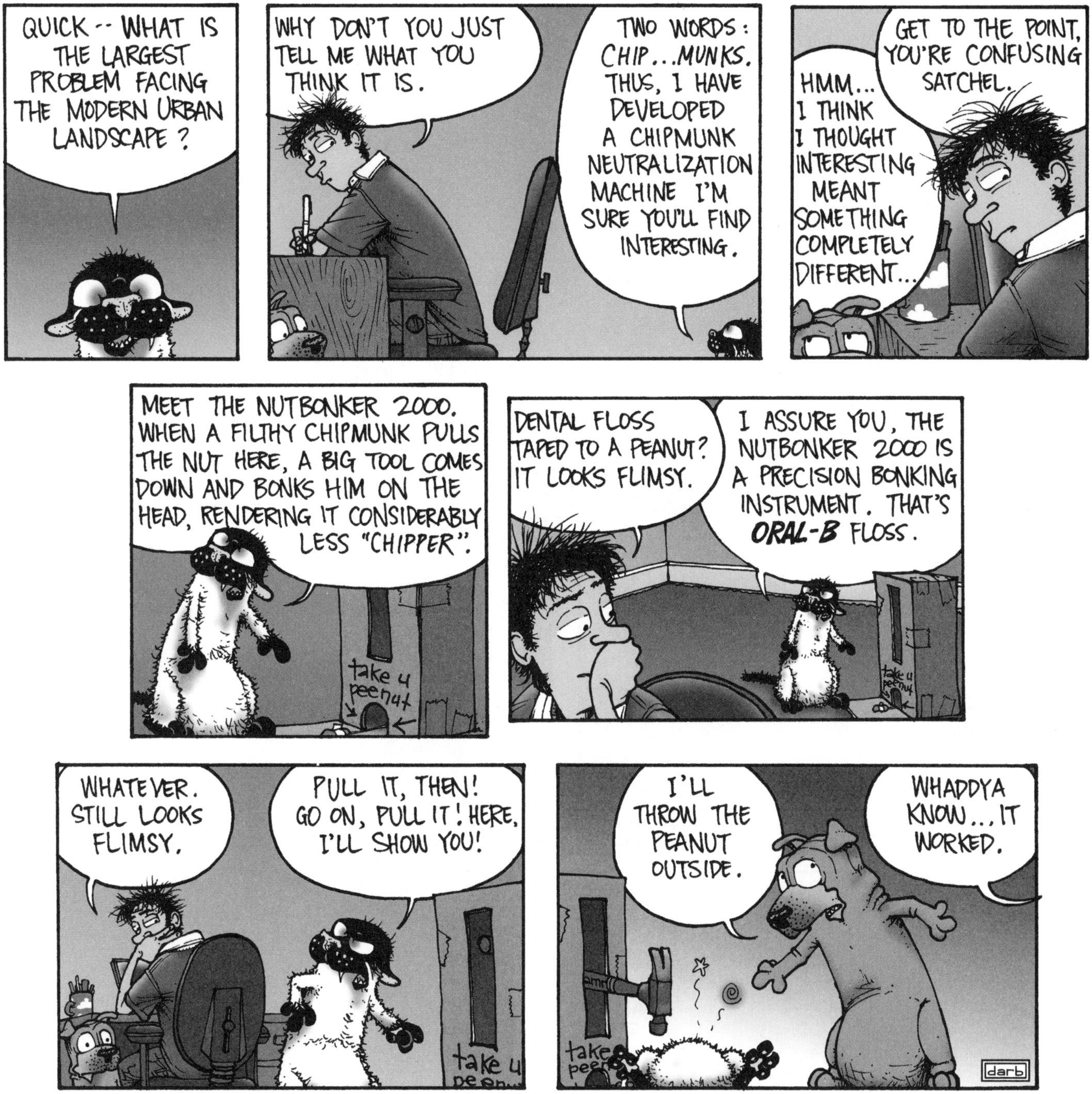
QUICK -- WHAT IS THE LARGEST PROBLEM FACING THE MODERN URBAN LANDSCAPE?
WHY DON'T YOU JUST TELL ME WHAT YOU THINK IT IS.
TWO WORDS: CHIP...MUNKS. THUS, I HAVE DEVELOPED A CHIPMUNK NEUTRALIZATION MACHINE I'M SURE YOU'LL FIND INTERESTING.
GET TO THE POINT, YOU'RE CONFUSING SATCHEL.
HMM... I THINK I THOUGHT INTERESTING MEANT SOMETHING COMPLETELY DIFFERENT...
MEET THE NUTBONKER 2000. WHEN A FILTHY CHIPMUNK PULLS THE NUT HERE, A BIG TOOL COMES DOWN AND BONKS HIM ON THE HEAD, RENDERING IT CONSIDERABLY LESS "CHIPPER".
take u peenut
DENTAL FLOSS TAPED TO A PEANUT? IT LOOKS FLIMSY.
I ASSURE YOU, THE NUTBONKER 2000 IS A PRECISION BONKING INSTRUMENT. THAT'S ORAL-B FLOSS.
WHATEVER. STILL LOOKS FLIMSY.
PULL IT, THEN! GO ON, PULL IT! HERE, I'LL SHOW YOU!
I'LL THROW THE PEANUT OUTSIDE.
WHADDYA KNOW... IT WORKED.
darb

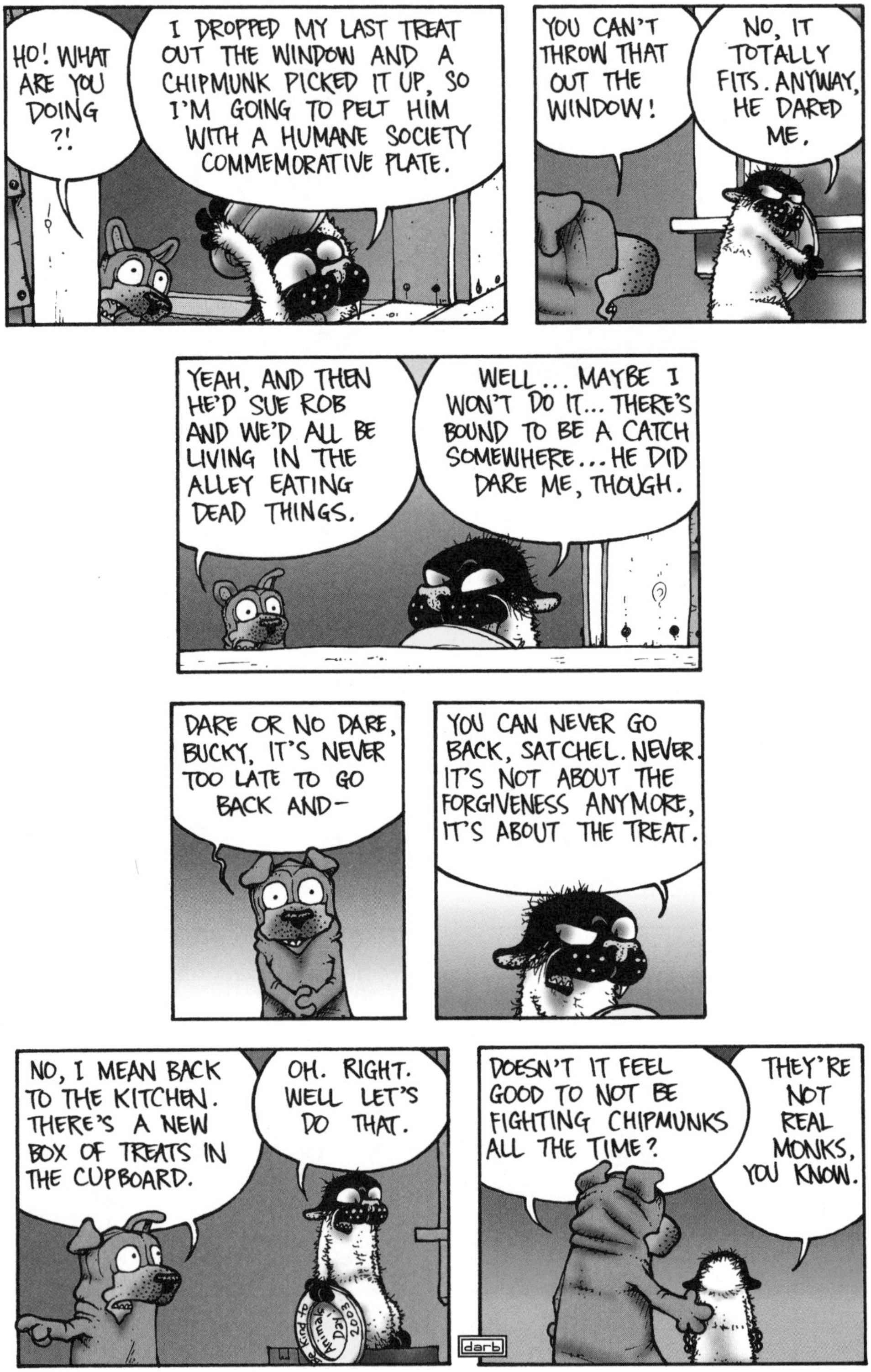
HO! WHAT ARE YOU DOING ?!
I DROPPED MY LAST TREAT OUT THE WINDOW AND A CHIPMUNK PICKED IT UP, SO I'M GOING TO PELT HIM WITH A HUMANE SOCIETY COMMEMORATIVE PLATE.
YOU CAN'T THROW THAT OUT THE WINDOW!
NO, IT TOTALLY FITS. ANYWAY, HE DARED ME.
YEAH, AND THEN HE'D SUE ROB AND WE'D ALL BE LIVING IN THE ALLEY EATING DEAD THINGS.
WELL... MAYBE I WON'T DO IT... THERE'S BOUND TO BE A CATCH SOMEWHERE... HE DID DARE ME, THOUGH.
DARE OR NO DARE, BUCKY, IT'S NEVER TOO LATE TO GO BACK AND–
YOU CAN NEVER GO BACK, SATCHEL. NEVER. IT'S NOT ABOUT THE FORGIVENESS ANYMORE, IT'S ABOUT THE TREAT.
NO, I MEAN BACK TO THE KITCHEN. THERE'S A NEW BOX OF TREATS IN THE CUPBOARD.
OH. RIGHT. WELL LET'S DO THAT.
DOESN'T IT FEEL GOOD TO NOT BE FIGHTING CHIPMUNKS ALL THE TIME?
THEY'RE NOT REAL MONKS, YOU KNOW.

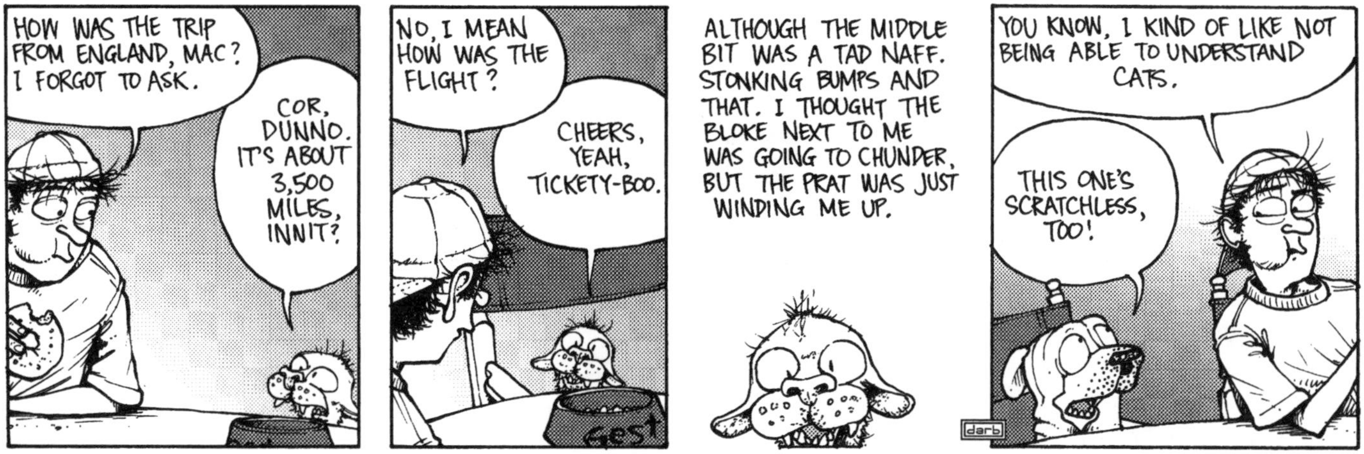
HOW WAS THE TRIP FROM ENGLAND, MAC? I FORGOT TO ASK.
COR, DUNNO. IT'S ABOUT 3,500 MILES, INNIT?
NO, I MEAN HOW WAS THE FLIGHT?
CHEERS, YEAH, TICKETY-BOO.
ALTHOUGH THE MIDDLE BIT WAS A TAD NAFF. STONKING BUMPS AND THAT. I THOUGHT THE BLOKE NEXT TO ME WAS GOING TO CHUNDER, BUT THE PRAT WAS JUST WINDING ME UP.
YOU KNOW, I KIND OF LIKE NOT BEING ABLE TO UNDERSTAND CATS.
THIS ONE'S SCRATCHLESS, TOO!
darb

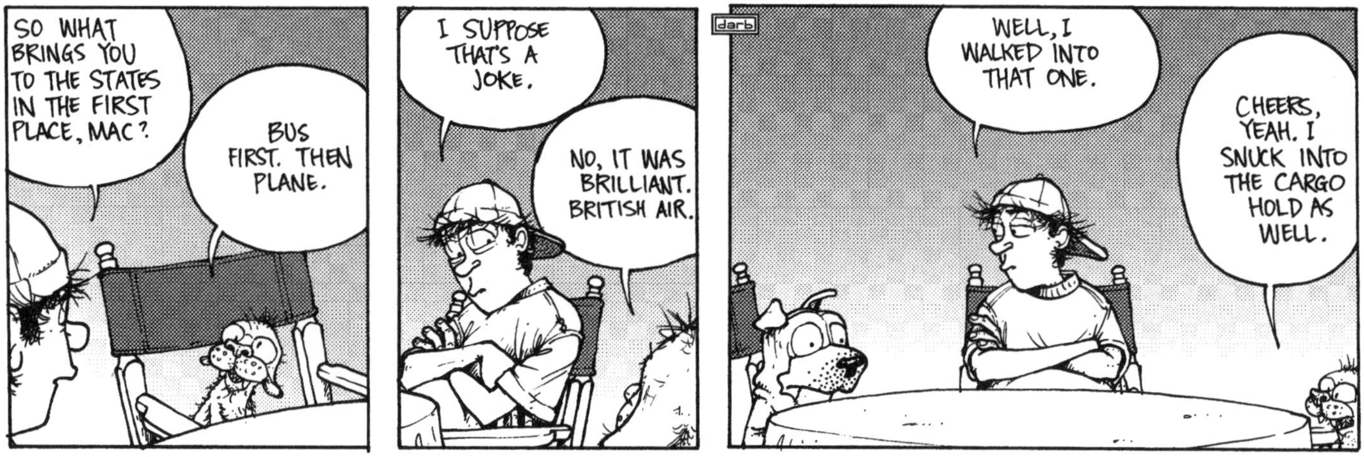
SO WHAT BRINGS YOU TO THE STATES IN THE FIRST PLACE, MAC?
BUS FIRST. THEN PLANE.
I SUPPOSE THAT'S A JOKE.
NO, IT WAS BRILLIANT. BRITISH AIR.
darb
WELL, I WALKED INTO THAT ONE.
CHEERS, YEAH. I SNUCK INTO THE CARGO HOLD AS WELL.

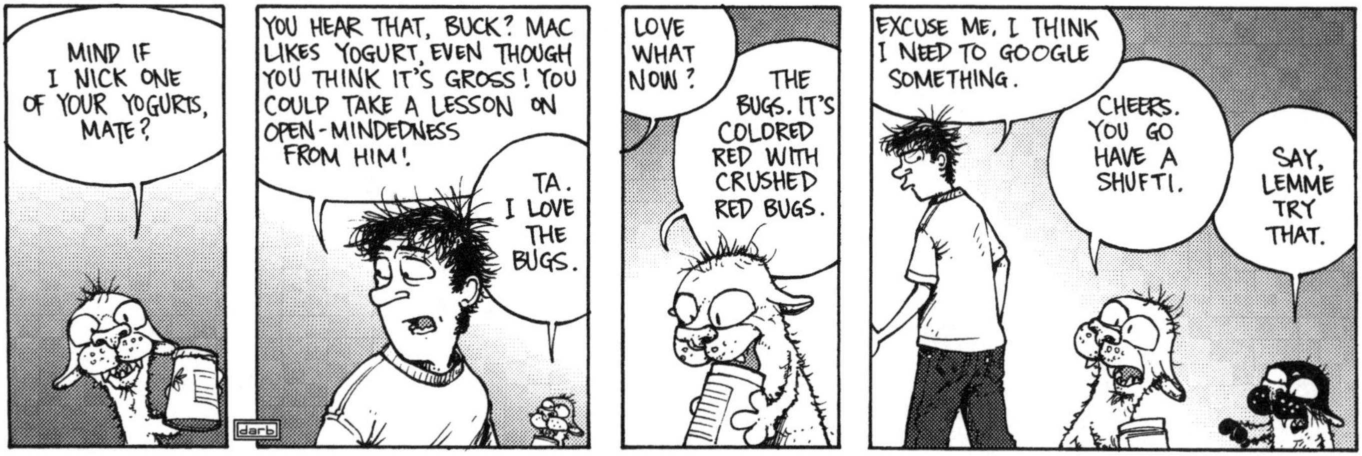
MIND IF I NICK ONE OF YOUR YOGURTS, MATE?
darb
YOU HEAR THAT, BUCK? MAC LIKES YOGURT, EVEN THOUGH YOU THINK IT'S GROSS! YOU COULD TAKE A LESSON ON OPEN-MINDEDNESS FROM HIM!
TA. I LOVE THE BUGS.
LOVE WHAT NOW?
THE BUGS. IT'S COLORED RED WITH CRUSHED RED BUGS.
EXCUSE ME. I THINK I NEED TO GOOGLE SOMETHING.
CHEERS. YOU GO HAVE A SHUFTI.
SAY, LEMME TRY THAT.

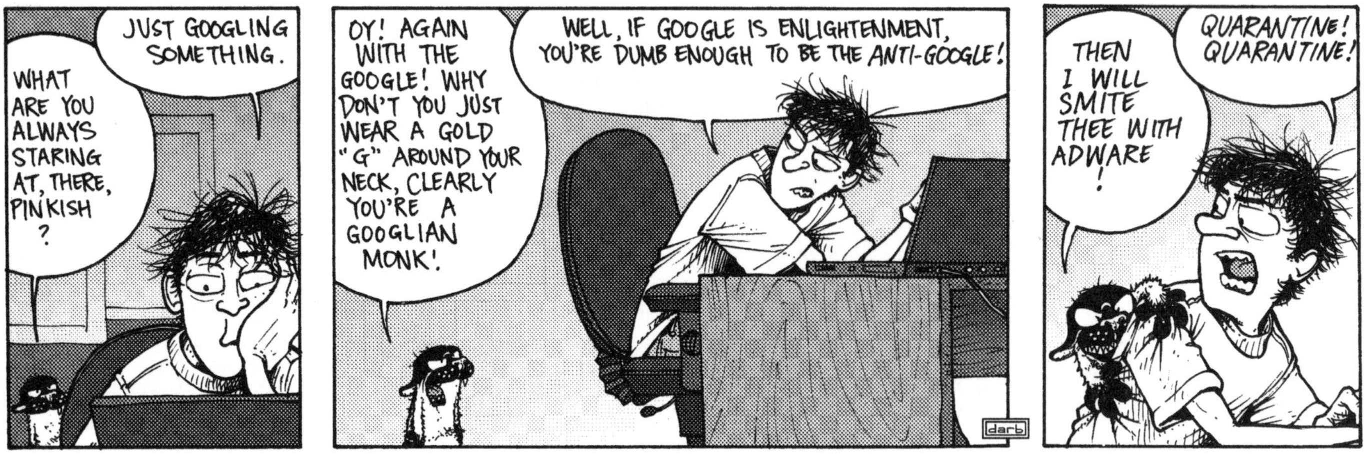
WHAT ARE YOU ALWAYS STARING AT, THERE, PINKISH?
JUST GOOGLING SOMETHING.
OY! AGAIN WITH THE GOOGLE! WHY DON'T YOU JUST WEAR A GOLD "G" AROUND YOUR NECK, CLEARLY YOU'RE A GOOGLIAN MONK!
WELL, IF GOOGLE IS ENLIGHTENMENT, YOU'RE DUMB ENOUGH TO BE THE ANTI-GOOGLE!
THEN I WILL SMITE THEE WITH ADWARE!
QUARANTINE! QUARANTINE!

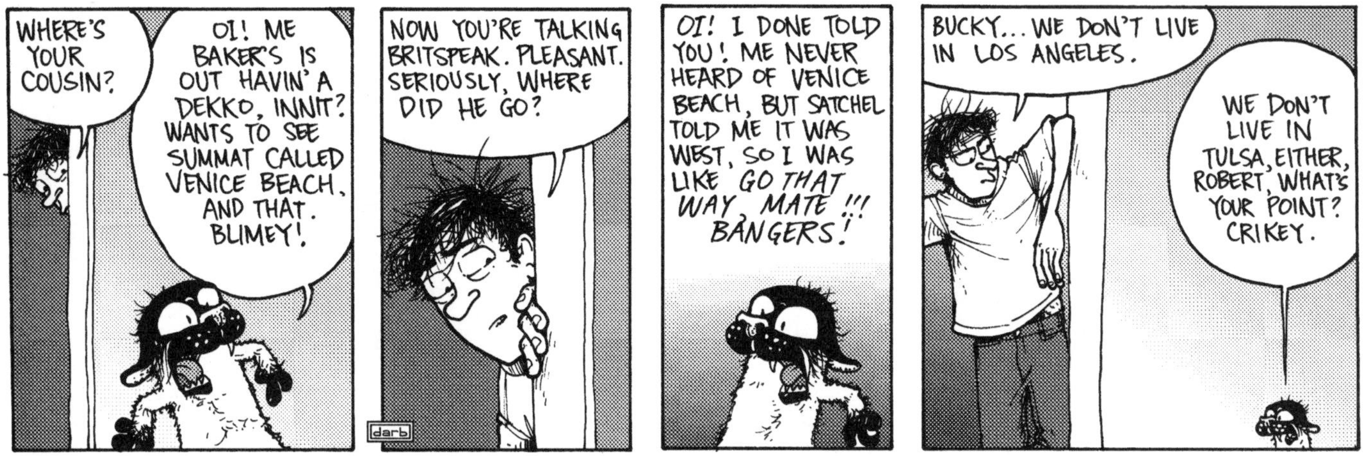
WHERE'S YOUR COUSIN?
OI! ME BAKER'S IS OUT HAVIN' A DEKKO, INNIT? WANTS TO SEE SUMMAT CALLED VENICE BEACH, AND THAT. BLIMEY!
NOW YOU'RE TALKING BRITSPEAK. PLEASANT. SERIOUSLY, WHERE DID HE GO?
OI! I DONE TOLD YOU! ME NEVER HEARD OF VENICE BEACH, BUT SATCHEL TOLD ME IT WAS WEST, SO I WAS LIKE GO THAT WAY, MATE!!! BANGERS!
BUCKY... WE DON'T LIVE IN LOS ANGELES.
WE DON'T LIVE IN TULSA, EITHER, ROBERT, WHAT'S YOUR POINT? CRIKEY.

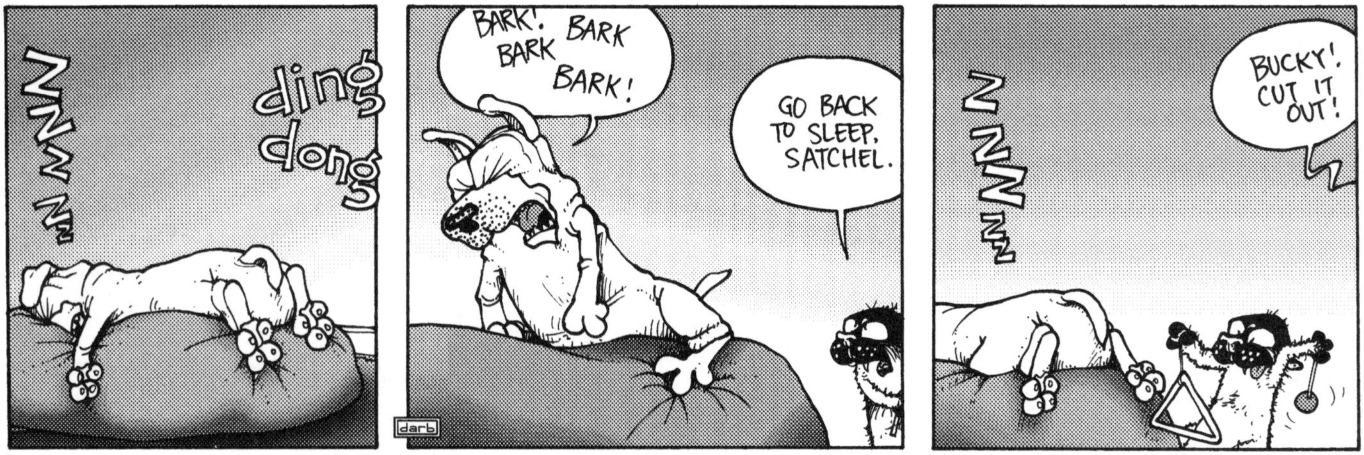
ZZZ
ding dong
BARK! BARK BARK BARK!
GO BACK TO SLEEP, SATCHEL.
ZZZ
BUCKY! CUT IT OUT!

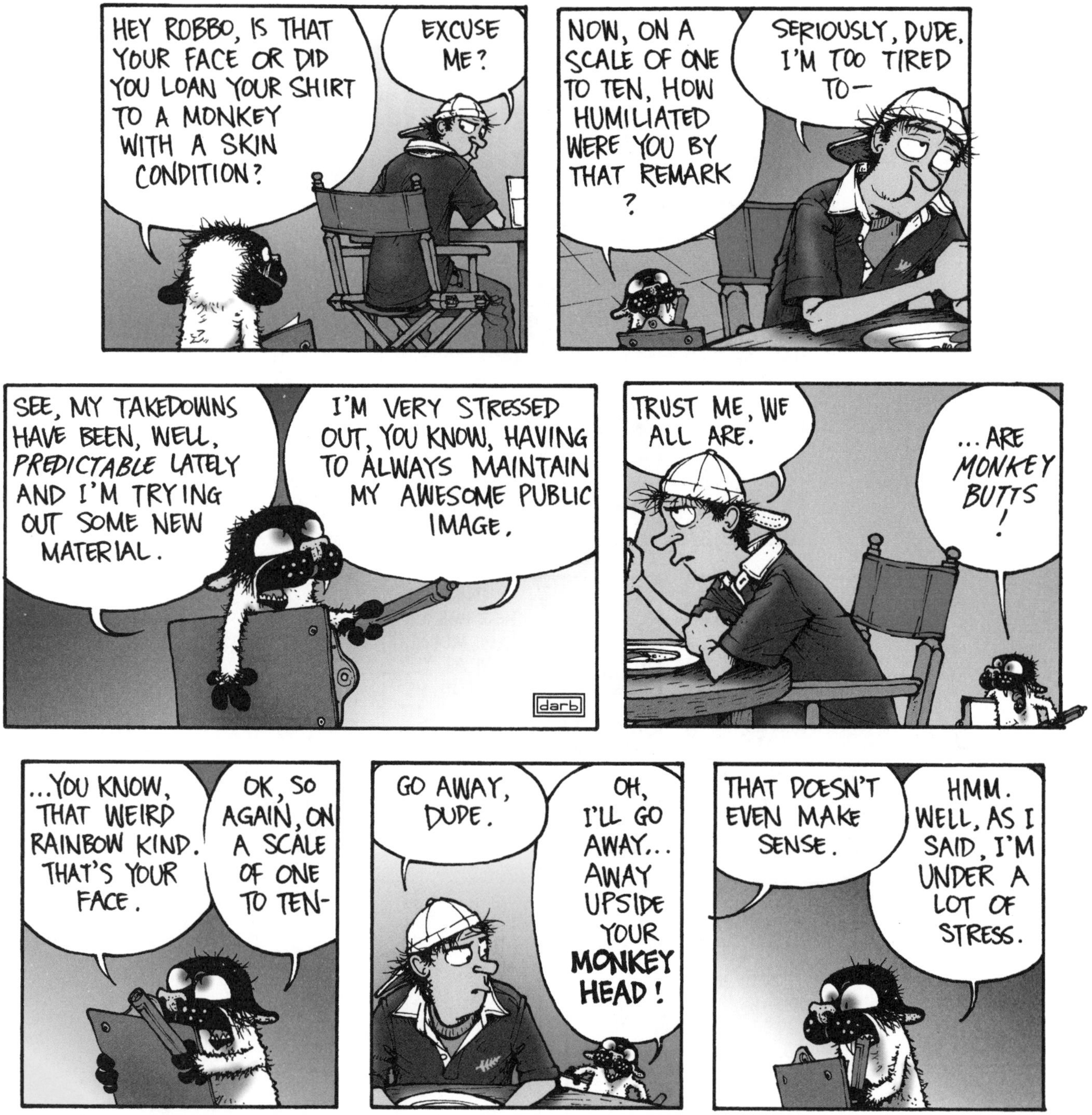
HEY ROBBO, IS THAT YOUR FACE OR DID YOU LOAN YOUR SHIRT TO A MONKEY WITH A SKIN CONDITION?
EXCUSE ME?
NOW, ON A SCALE OF ONE TO TEN, HOW HUMILIATED WERE YOU BY THAT REMARK?
SERIOUSLY, DUDE, I'M TOO TIRED TO—
SEE, MY TAKEDOWNS HAVE BEEN, WELL, *PREDICTABLE* LATELY AND I'M TRYING OUT SOME NEW MATERIAL.
I'M VERY STRESSED OUT, YOU KNOW, HAVING TO ALWAYS MAINTAIN MY AWESOME PUBLIC IMAGE.
darb
TRUST ME, WE ALL ARE.
...ARE *MONKEY BUTTS*!
...YOU KNOW, THAT WEIRD RAINBOW KIND. THAT'S YOUR FACE.
OK, SO AGAIN, ON A SCALE OF ONE TO TEN-
GO AWAY, DUDE.
OH, I'LL GO AWAY... AWAY UPSIDE YOUR **MONKEY HEAD**!
THAT DOESN'T EVEN MAKE SENSE.
HMM. WELL, AS I SAID, I'M UNDER A LOT OF STRESS.

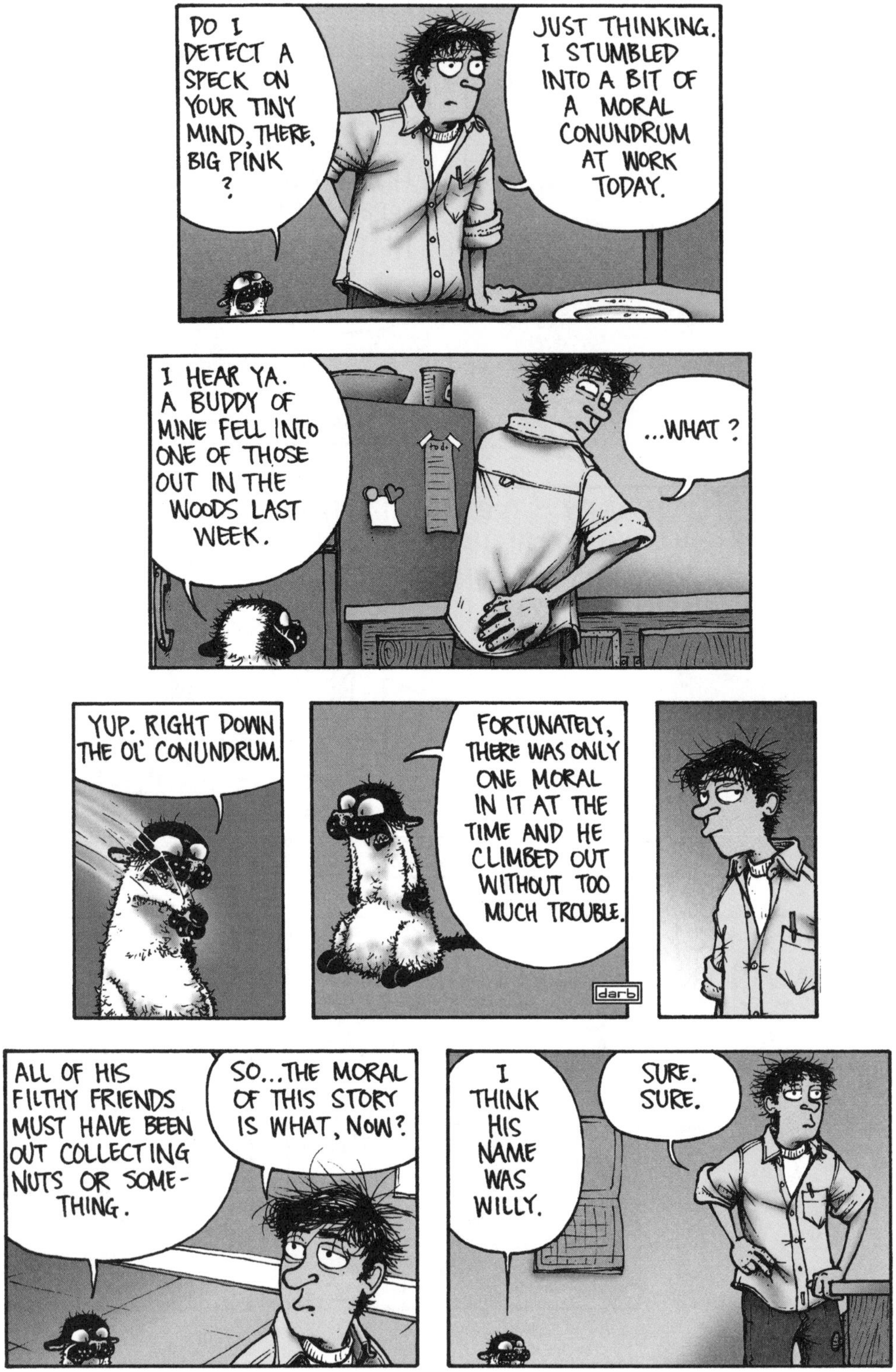
DO I DETECT A SPECK ON YOUR TINY MIND, THERE, BIG PINK ?
JUST THINKING. I STUMBLED INTO A BIT OF A MORAL CONUNDRUM AT WORK TODAY.
I HEAR YA. A BUDDY OF MINE FELL INTO ONE OF THOSE OUT IN THE WOODS LAST WEEK.
...WHAT ?
YUP. RIGHT DOWN THE OL' CONUNDRUM.
FORTUNATELY, THERE WAS ONLY ONE MORAL IN IT AT THE TIME AND HE CLIMBED OUT WITHOUT TOO MUCH TROUBLE.
darb
ALL OF HIS FILTHY FRIENDS MUST HAVE BEEN OUT COLLECTING NUTS OR SOME-THING.
SO...THE MORAL OF THIS STORY IS WHAT, NOW?
I THINK HIS NAME WAS WILLY.
SURE. SURE.

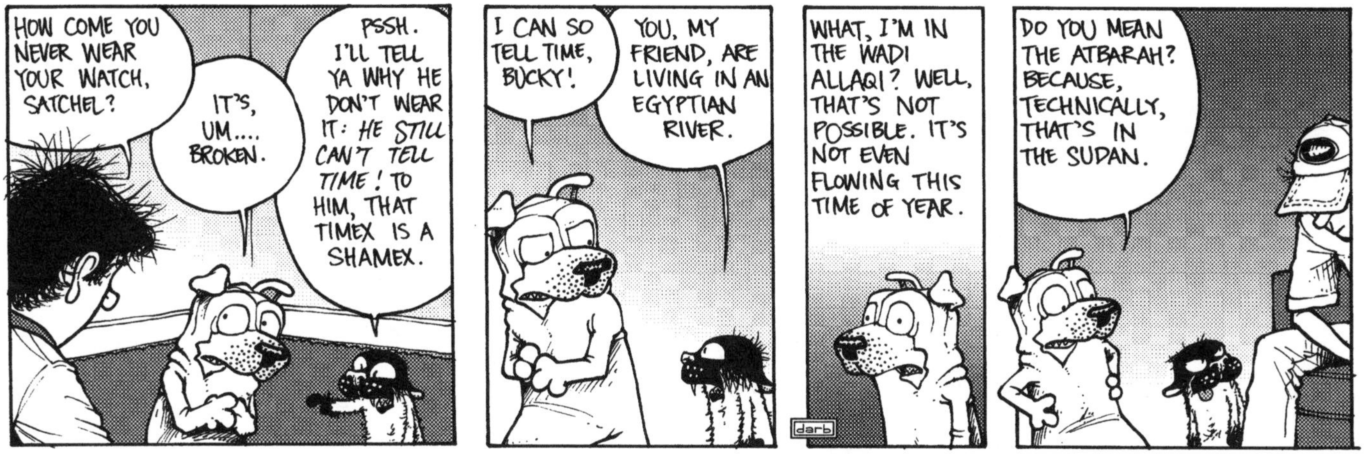
HOW COME YOU NEVER WEAR YOUR WATCH, SATCHEL?
IT'S, UM.... BROKEN.
PSSH. I'LL TELL YA WHY HE DON'T WEAR IT: HE STILL CAN'T TELL TIME! TO HIM, THAT TIMEX IS A SHAMEX.
I CAN SO TELL TIME, BUCKY!
YOU, MY FRIEND, ARE LIVING IN AN EGYPTIAN RIVER.
darb
WHAT, I'M IN THE WADI ALLAQI? WELL, THAT'S NOT POSSIBLE. IT'S NOT EVEN FLOWING THIS TIME OF YEAR.
DO YOU MEAN THE ATBARAH? BECAUSE, TECHNICALLY, THAT'S IN THE SUDAN.

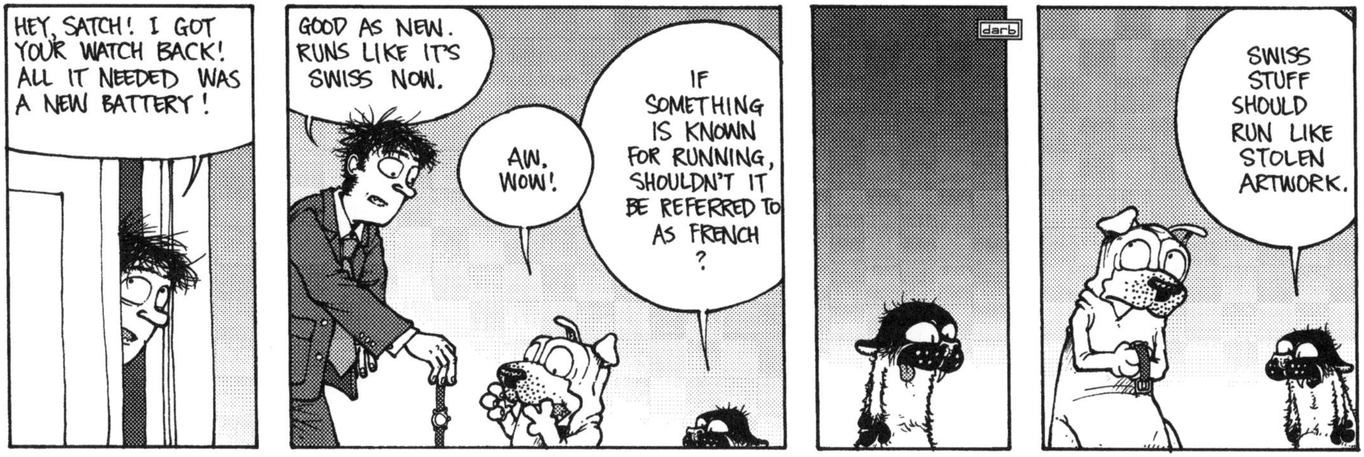
HEY, SATCH! I GOT YOUR WATCH BACK! ALL IT NEEDED WAS A NEW BATTERY!
GOOD AS NEW. RUNS LIKE IT'S SWISS NOW.
AW, WOW!
IF SOMETHING IS KNOWN FOR RUNNING, SHOULDN'T IT BE REFERRED TO AS FRENCH ?
darb
SWISS STUFF SHOULD RUN LIKE STOLEN ARTWORK.

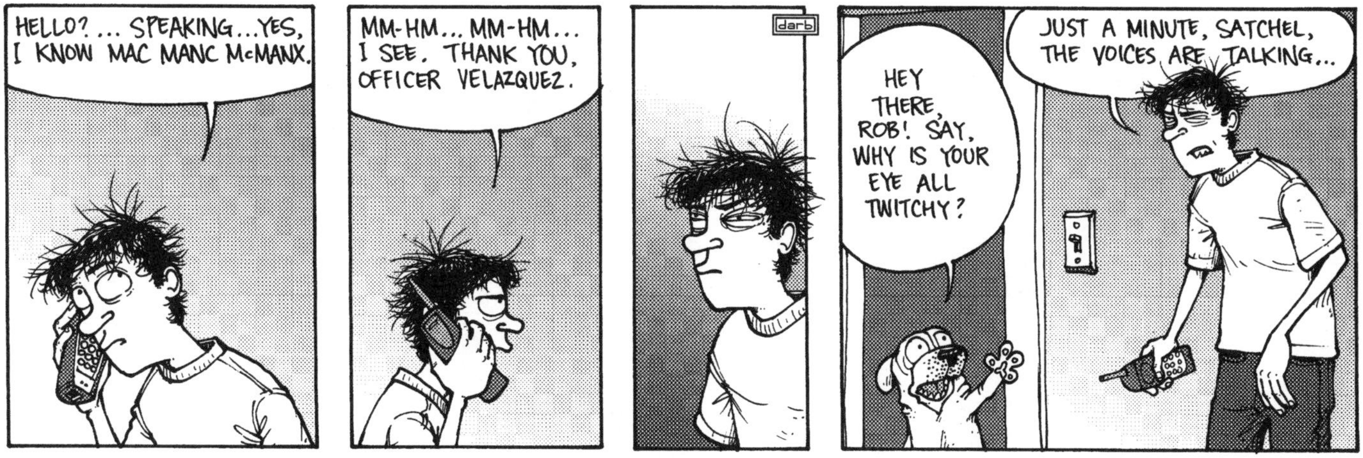
HELLO?... SPEAKING... YES, I KNOW MAC MANC McMANX.
MM-HM... MM-HM... I SEE. THANK YOU, OFFICER VELAZQUEZ.
darb
HEY THERE, ROB! SAY, WHY IS YOUR EYE ALL TWITCHY?
JUST A MINUTE, SATCHEL, THE VOICES ARE TALKING...

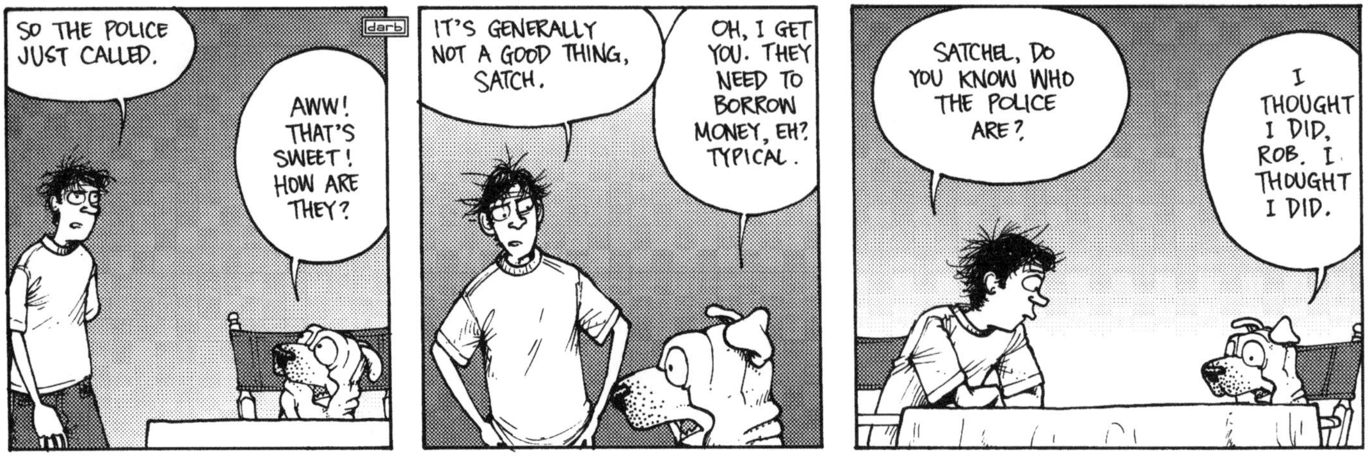
SO THE POLICE JUST CALLED.
AWW! THAT'S SWEET! HOW ARE THEY?
IT'S GENERALLY NOT A GOOD THING, SATCH.
OH, I GET YOU. THEY NEED TO BORROW MONEY, EH? TYPICAL.
SATCHEL, DO YOU KNOW WHO THE POLICE ARE?
I THOUGHT I DID, ROB. I THOUGHT I DID.

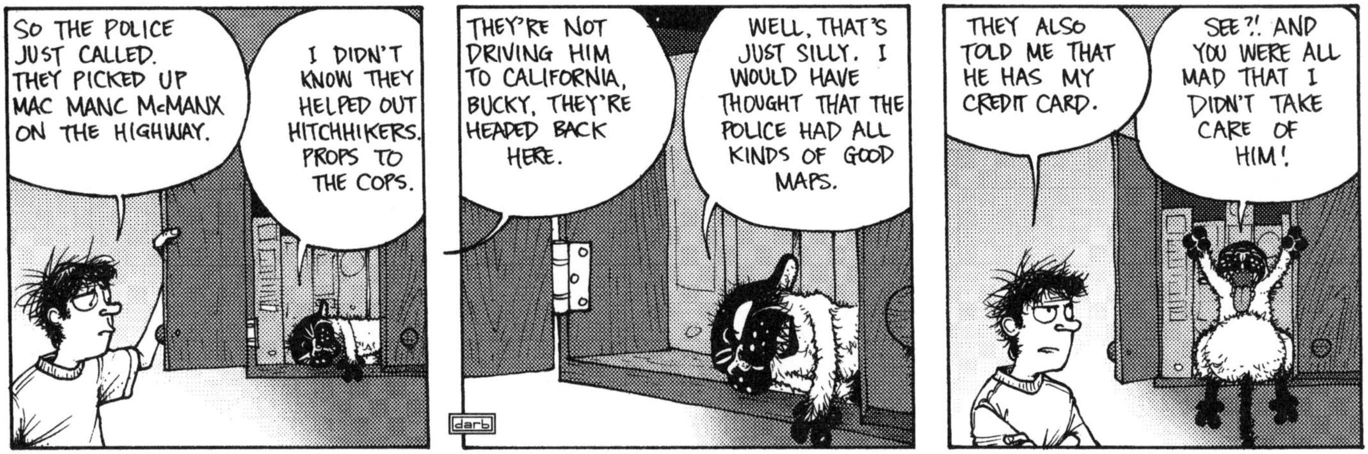
SO THE POLICE JUST CALLED. THEY PICKED UP MAC MANC McMANX ON THE HIGHWAY.
I DIDN'T KNOW THEY HELPED OUT HITCHHIKERS. PROPS TO THE COPS.
THEY'RE NOT DRIVING HIM TO CALIFORNIA, BUCKY, THEY'RE HEADED BACK HERE.
WELL, THAT'S JUST SILLY. I WOULD HAVE THOUGHT THAT THE POLICE HAD ALL KINDS OF GOOD MAPS.
THEY ALSO TOLD ME THAT HE HAS MY CREDIT CARD.
SEE?! AND YOU WERE ALL MAD THAT I DIDN'T TAKE CARE OF HIM!

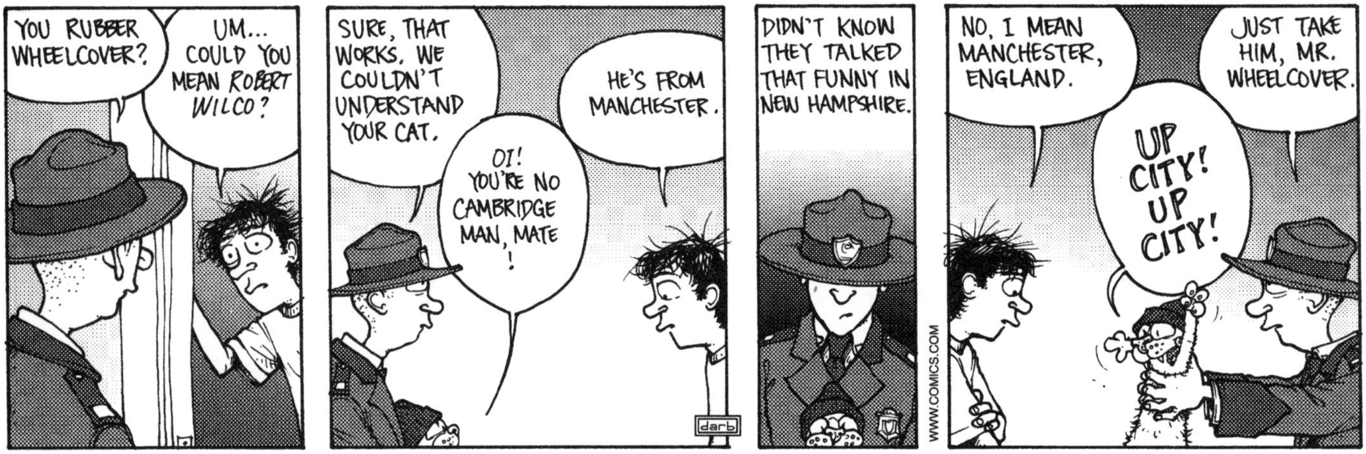
YOU RUBBER WHEELCOVER?
UM... COULD YOU MEAN *ROBERT WILCO*?
SURE, THAT WORKS. WE COULDN'T UNDERSTAND YOUR CAT.
OI! YOU'RE NO CAMBRIDGE MAN, MATE!
HE'S FROM MANCHESTER.
DIDN'T KNOW THEY TALKED THAT FUNNY IN NEW HAMPSHIRE.
WWW.COMICS.COM
NO, I MEAN MANCHESTER, ENGLAND.
JUST TAKE HIM, MR. WHEELCOVER.
UP CITY! UP CITY!

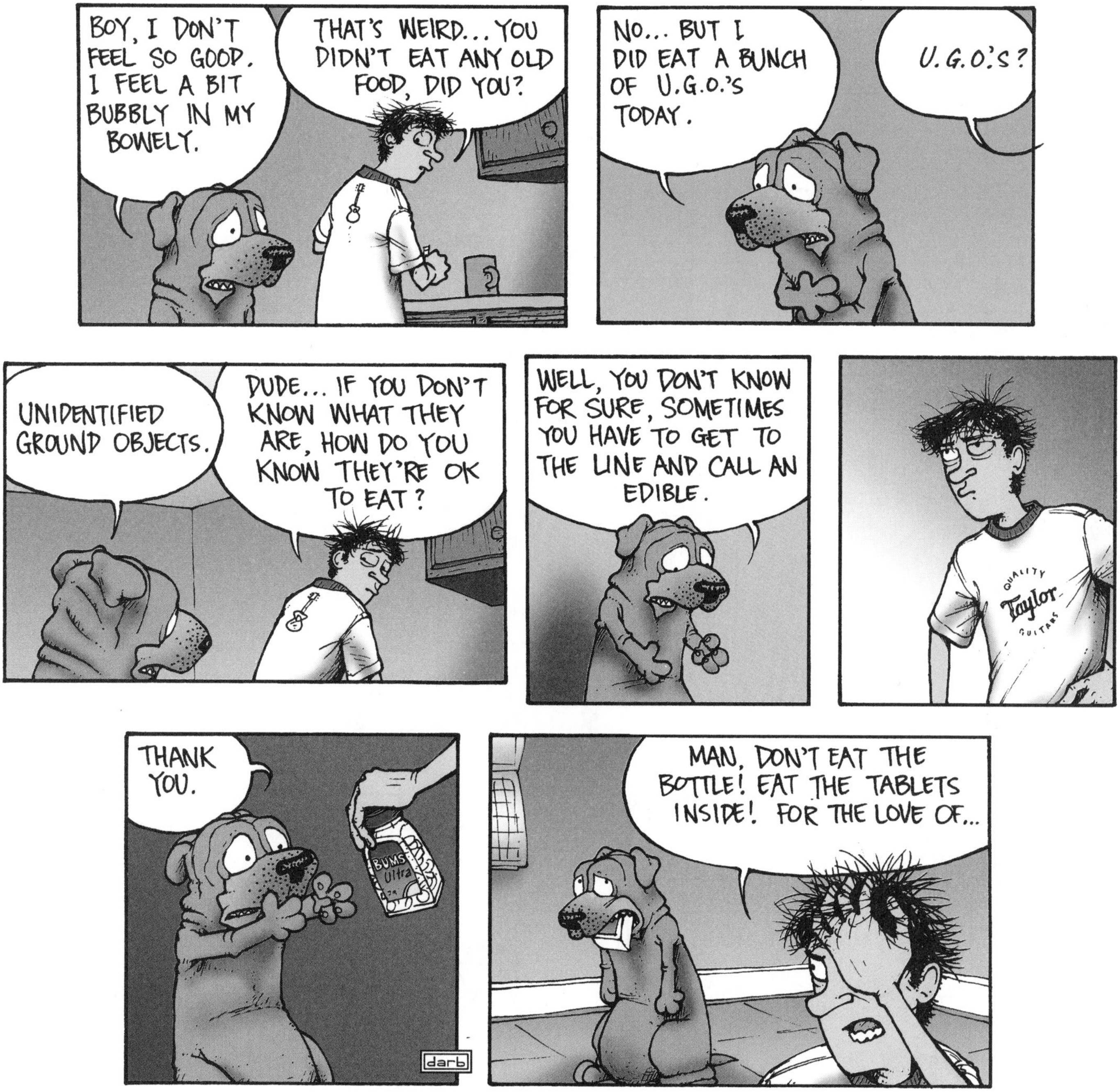
BOY, I DON'T FEEL SO GOOD. I FEEL A BIT BUBBLY IN MY BOWELY.
THAT'S WEIRD... YOU DIDN'T EAT ANY OLD FOOD, DID YOU?
NO... BUT I DID EAT A BUNCH OF U.G.O.'S TODAY.
U.G.O.'S?
UNIDENTIFIED GROUND OBJECTS.
DUDE... IF YOU DON'T KNOW WHAT THEY ARE, HOW DO YOU KNOW THEY'RE OK TO EAT?
WELL, YOU DON'T KNOW FOR SURE, SOMETIMES YOU HAVE TO GET TO THE LINE AND CALL AN EDIBLE.
QUALITY Taylor GUITARS
THANK YOU.
BUMS Ultra
darb
MAN, DON'T EAT THE BOTTLE! EAT THE TABLETS INSIDE! FOR THE LOVE OF...

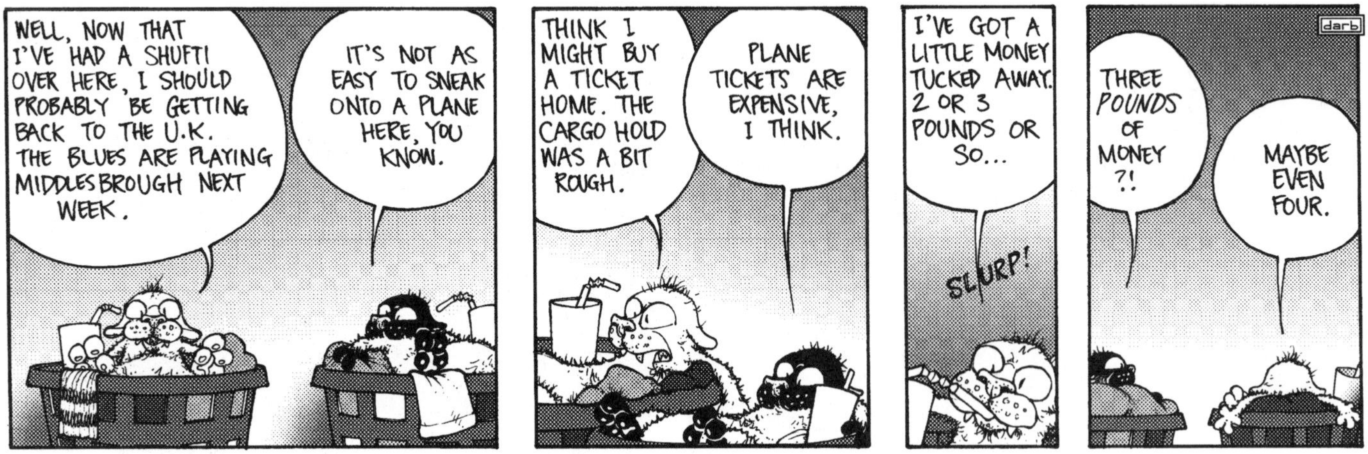
WELL, NOW THAT I'VE HAD A SHUFTI OVER HERE, I SHOULD PROBABLY BE GETTING BACK TO THE U.K. THE BLUES ARE PLAYING MIDDLESBROUGH NEXT WEEK.
IT'S NOT AS EASY TO SNEAK ONTO A PLANE HERE, YOU KNOW.
THINK I MIGHT BUY A TICKET HOME. THE CARGO HOLD WAS A BIT ROUGH.
PLANE TICKETS ARE EXPENSIVE, I THINK.
I'VE GOT A LITTLE MONEY TUCKED AWAY. 2 OR 3 POUNDS OR SO...
SLURP!
THREE *POUNDS* OF MONEY ?!
MAYBE EVEN FOUR.
darb

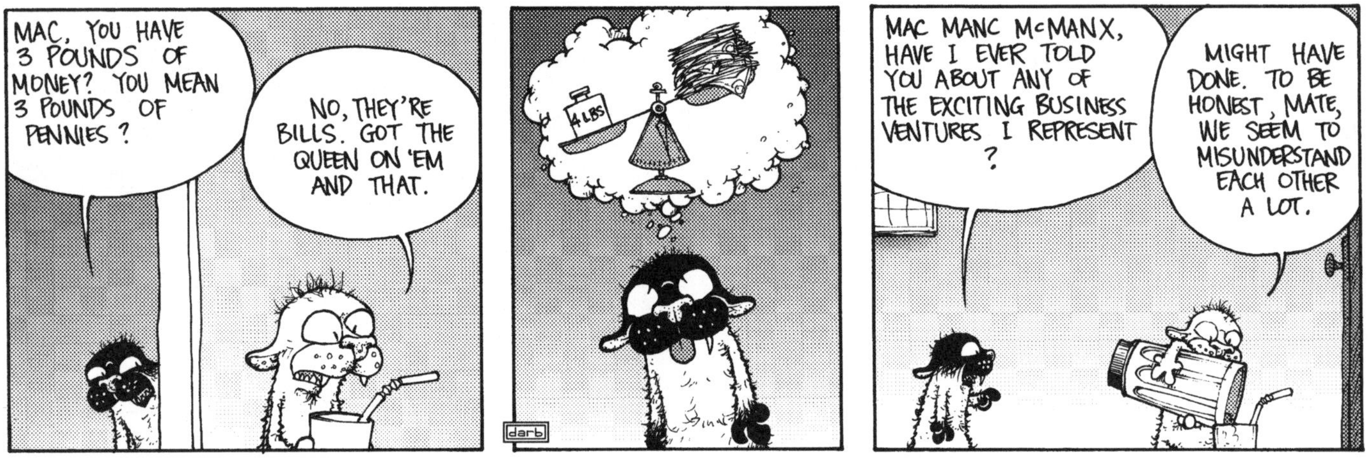
MAC, YOU HAVE 3 POUNDS OF MONEY? YOU MEAN 3 POUNDS OF PENNIES ?
NO, THEY'RE BILLS. GOT THE QUEEN ON 'EM AND THAT.
4 LBS
darb
MAC MANC McMANX, HAVE I EVER TOLD YOU ABOUT ANY OF THE EXCITING BUSINESS VENTURES I REPRESENT ?
MIGHT HAVE DONE. TO BE HONEST, MATE, WE SEEM TO MISUNDERSTAND EACH OTHER A LOT.

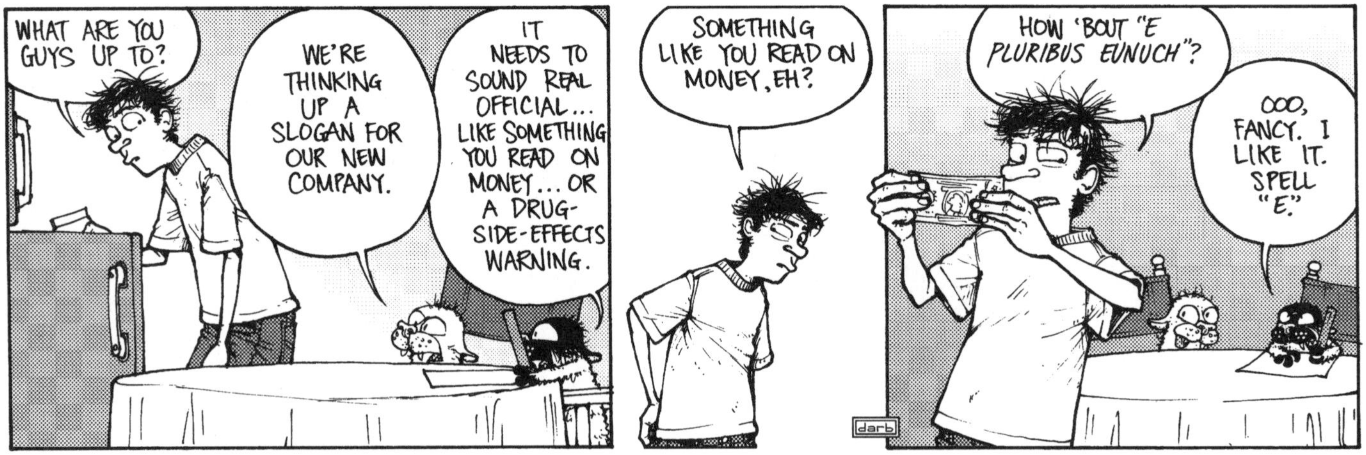
WHAT ARE YOU GUYS UP TO?
WE'RE THINKING UP A SLOGAN FOR OUR NEW COMPANY.
IT NEEDS TO SOUND REAL OFFICIAL... LIKE SOMETHING YOU READ ON MONEY... OR A DRUG-SIDE-EFFECTS WARNING.
SOMETHING LIKE YOU READ ON MONEY, EH?
darb
HOW 'BOUT "*E PLURIBUS EUNUCH*"?
OOO, FANCY. I LIKE IT. SPELL "E."

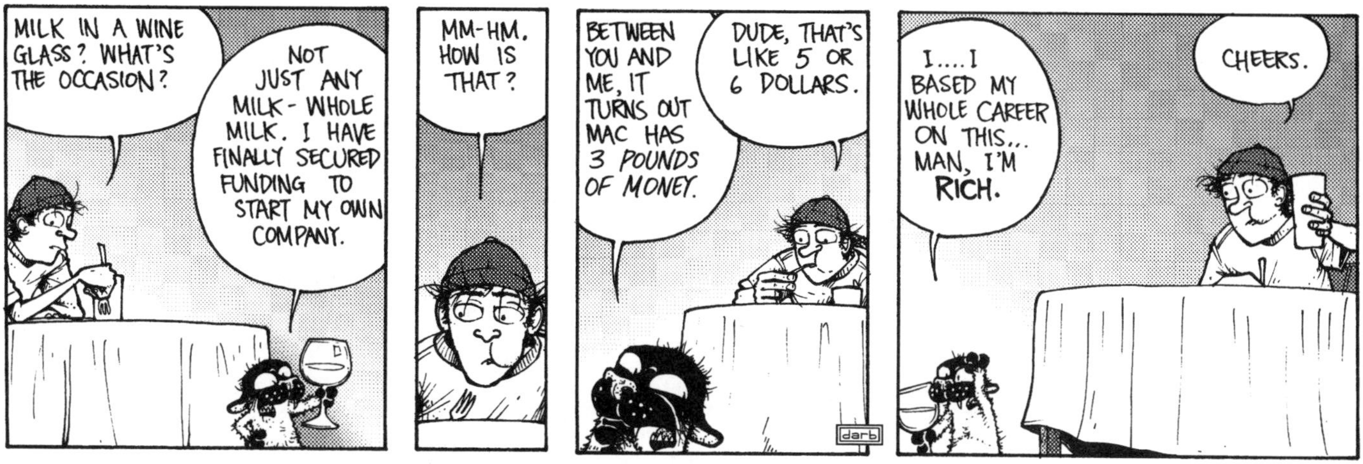
MILK IN A WINE GLASS? WHAT'S THE OCCASION?
NOT JUST ANY MILK- WHOLE MILK. I HAVE FINALLY SECURED FUNDING TO START MY OWN COMPANY.
MM-HM. HOW IS THAT?
BETWEEN YOU AND ME, IT TURNS OUT MAC HAS 3 *POUNDS OF MONEY.*
DUDE, THAT'S LIKE 5 OR 6 DOLLARS.
I....I BASED MY WHOLE CAREER ON THIS... MAN, I'M **RICH.**
CHEERS.
darb

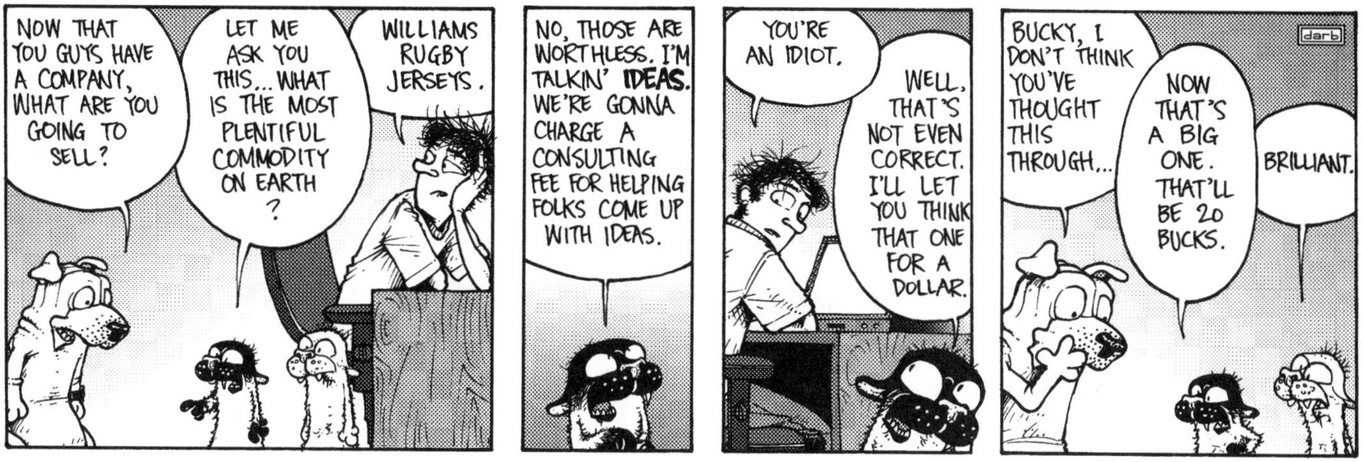
NOW THAT YOU GUYS HAVE A COMPANY, WHAT ARE YOU GOING TO SELL?
LET ME ASK YOU THIS... WHAT IS THE MOST PLENTIFUL COMMODITY ON EARTH?
WILLIAMS RUGBY JERSEYS.
NO, THOSE ARE WORTHLESS. I'M TALKIN' **IDEAS.** WE'RE GONNA CHARGE A CONSULTING FEE FOR HELPING FOLKS COME UP WITH IDEAS.
YOU'RE AN IDIOT.
WELL, THAT'S NOT EVEN CORRECT. I'LL LET YOU THINK THAT ONE FOR A DOLLAR.
darb
BUCKY, I DON'T THINK YOU'VE THOUGHT THIS THROUGH...
NOW THAT'S A BIG ONE. THAT'LL BE 20 BUCKS.
BRILLIANT.

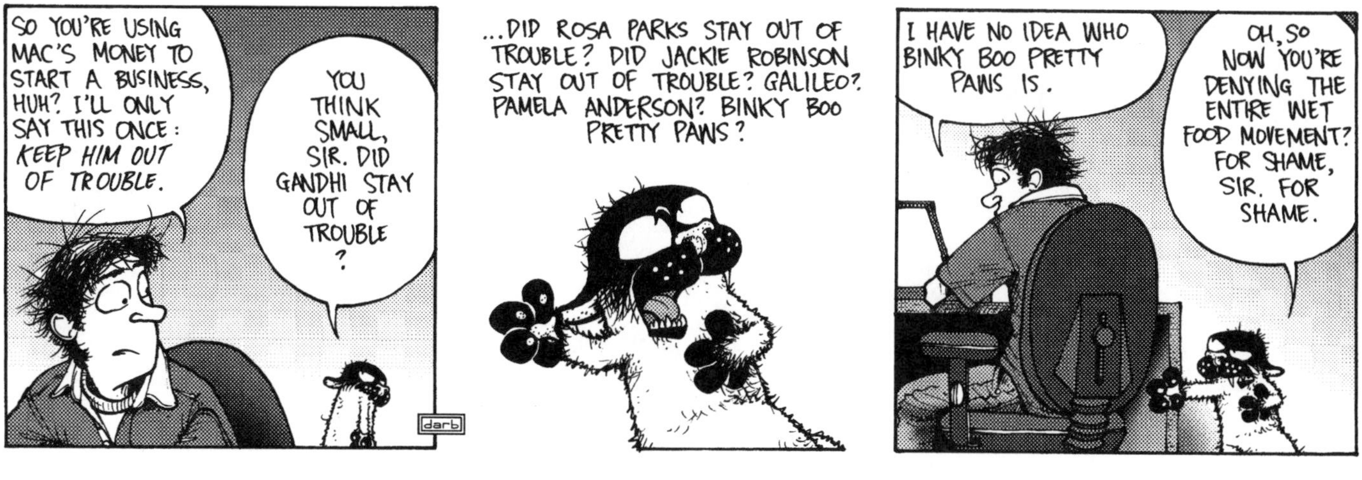
SO YOU'RE USING MAC'S MONEY TO START A BUSINESS, HUH? I'LL ONLY SAY THIS ONCE: *KEEP HIM OUT OF TROUBLE.*
YOU THINK SMALL, SIR. DID GANDHI STAY OUT OF TROUBLE?
darb
...DID ROSA PARKS STAY OUT OF TROUBLE? DID JACKIE ROBINSON STAY OUT OF TROUBLE? GALILEO? PAMELA ANDERSON? BINKY BOO PRETTY PAWS?
I HAVE NO IDEA WHO BINKY BOO PRETTY PAWS IS.
OH, SO NOW YOU'RE DENYING THE ENTIRE WET FOOD MOVEMENT? FOR SHAME, SIR. FOR SHAME.

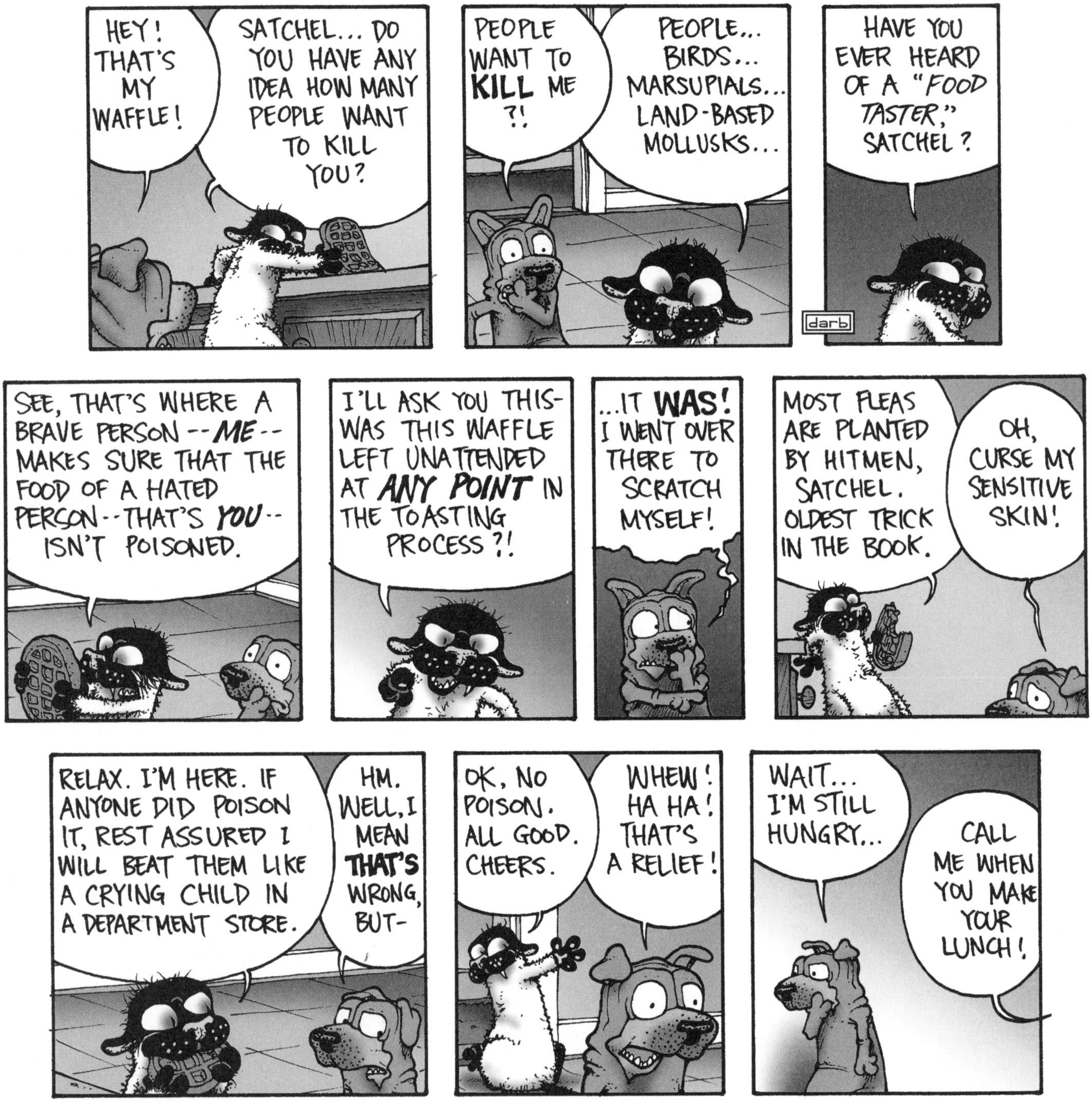
HEY! THAT'S MY WAFFLE!
SATCHEL... DO YOU HAVE ANY IDEA HOW MANY PEOPLE WANT TO KILL YOU?
PEOPLE WANT TO KILL ME ?!
PEOPLE... BIRDS... MARSUPIALS... LAND-BASED MOLLUSKS...
HAVE YOU EVER HEARD OF A "FOOD TASTER," SATCHEL?
darb
SEE, THAT'S WHERE A BRAVE PERSON --ME-- MAKES SURE THAT THE FOOD OF A HATED PERSON--THAT'S YOU-- ISN'T POISONED.
I'LL ASK YOU THIS- WAS THIS WAFFLE LEFT UNATTENDED AT ANY POINT IN THE TOASTING PROCESS?!
...IT WAS! I WENT OVER THERE TO SCRATCH MYSELF!
MOST FLEAS ARE PLANTED BY HITMEN, SATCHEL. OLDEST TRICK IN THE BOOK.
OH, CURSE MY SENSITIVE SKIN!
RELAX. I'M HERE. IF ANYONE DID POISON IT, REST ASSURED I WILL BEAT THEM LIKE A CRYING CHILD IN A DEPARTMENT STORE.
HM. WELL, I MEAN THAT'S WRONG, BUT-
OK, NO POISON. ALL GOOD. CHEERS.
WHEW! HA HA! THAT'S A RELIEF!
WAIT... I'M STILL HUNGRY...
CALL ME WHEN YOU MAKE YOUR LUNCH!

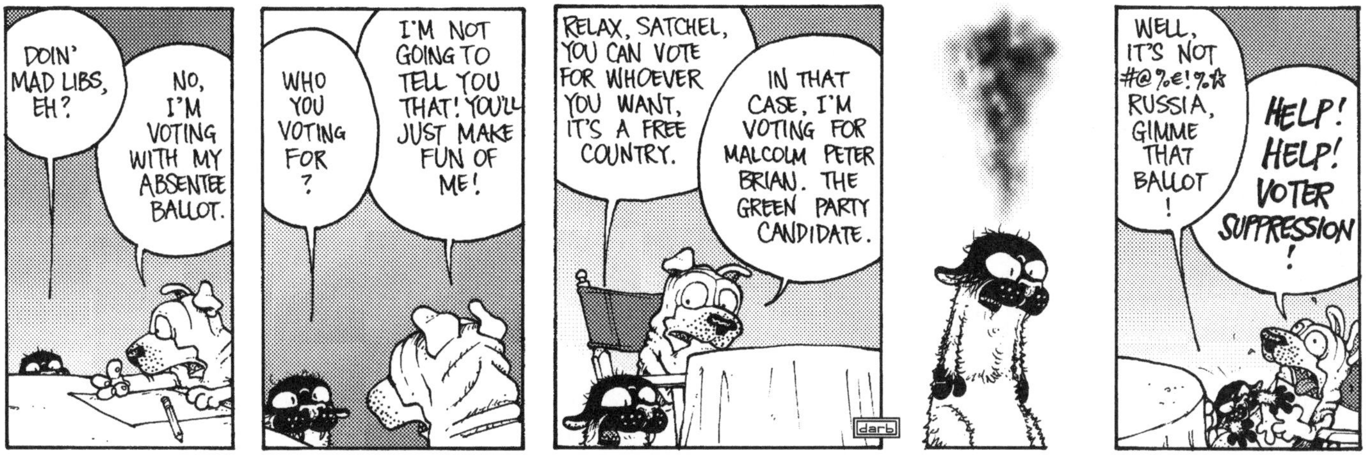
DOIN' MAD LIBS, EH?
NO, I'M VOTING WITH MY ABSENTEE BALLOT.
WHO YOU VOTING FOR?
I'M NOT GOING TO TELL YOU THAT! YOU'LL JUST MAKE FUN OF ME!
RELAX, SATCHEL, YOU CAN VOTE FOR WHOEVER YOU WANT, IT'S A FREE COUNTRY.
IN THAT CASE, I'M VOTING FOR MALCOLM PETER BRIAN. THE GREEN PARTY CANDIDATE.
WELL, IT'S NOT #@%€!%☆ RUSSIA, GIMME THAT BALLOT!
HELP! HELP! VOTER SUPPRESSION!
darb

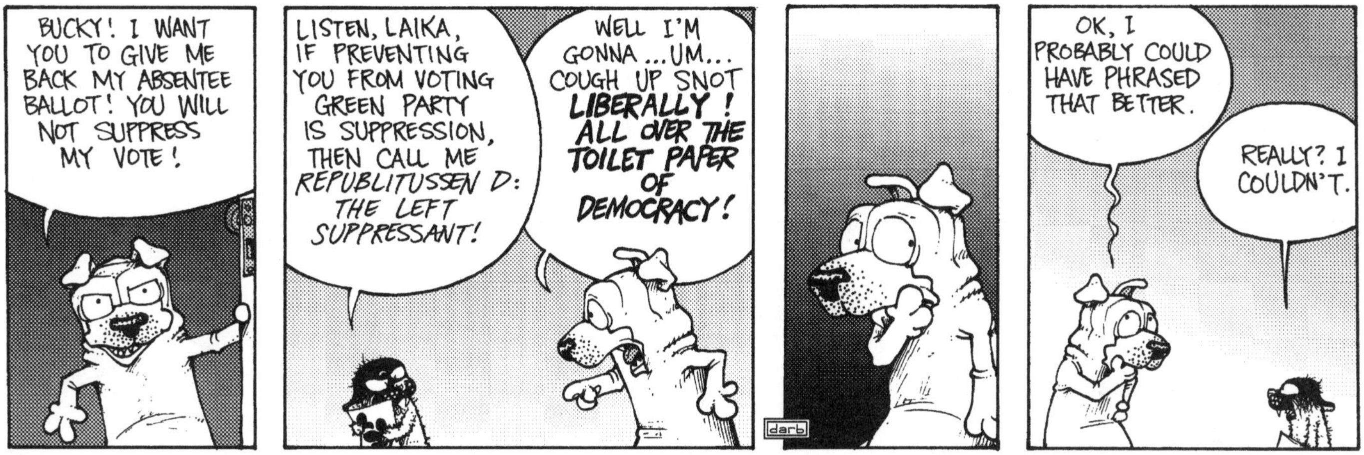
BUCKY! I WANT YOU TO GIVE ME BACK MY ABSENTEE BALLOT! YOU WILL NOT SUPPRESS MY VOTE!
LISTEN, LAIKA, IF PREVENTING YOU FROM VOTING GREEN PARTY IS SUPPRESSION, THEN CALL ME REPUBLITUSSEN D: THE LEFT SUPPRESSANT!
WELL I'M GONNA ... UM... COUGH UP SNOT LIBERALLY! ALL OVER THE TOILET PAPER OF DEMOCRACY!
darb
OK, I PROBABLY COULD HAVE PHRASED THAT BETTER.
REALLY? I COULDN'T.

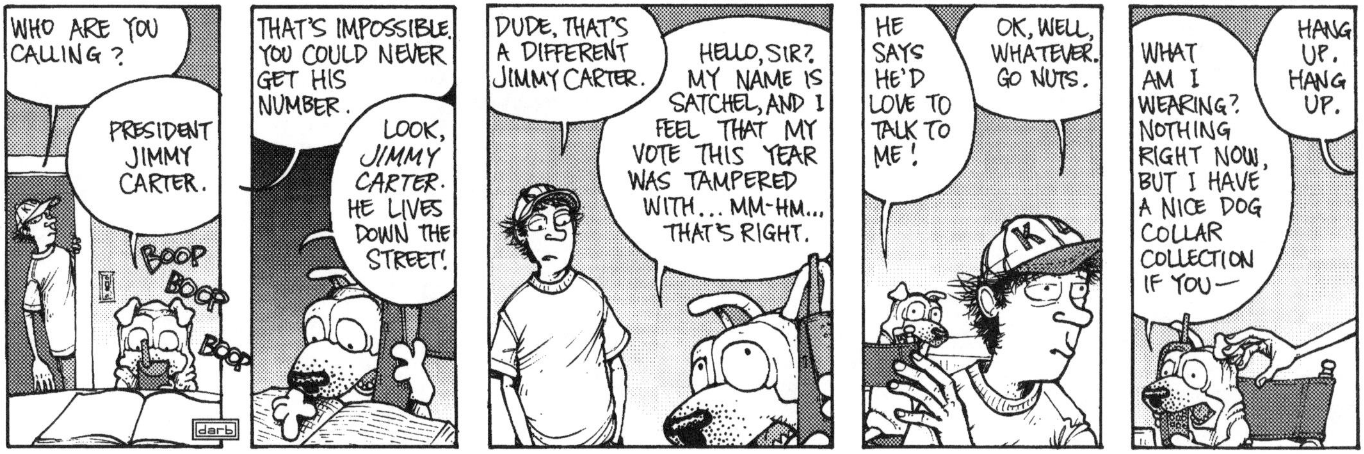
WHO ARE YOU CALLING?
PRESIDENT JIMMY CARTER.
BOOP BOOP BOOP
darb
THAT'S IMPOSSIBLE. YOU COULD NEVER GET HIS NUMBER.
LOOK, JIMMY CARTER. HE LIVES DOWN THE STREET!
DUDE, THAT'S A DIFFERENT JIMMY CARTER.
HELLO, SIR? MY NAME IS SATCHEL, AND I FEEL THAT MY VOTE THIS YEAR WAS TAMPERED WITH... MM-HM... THAT'S RIGHT.
HE SAYS HE'D LOVE TO TALK TO ME!
OK, WELL, WHATEVER. GO NUTS.
WHAT AM I WEARING? NOTHING RIGHT NOW, BUT I HAVE A NICE DOG COLLAR COLLECTION IF YOU—
HANG UP. HANG UP.

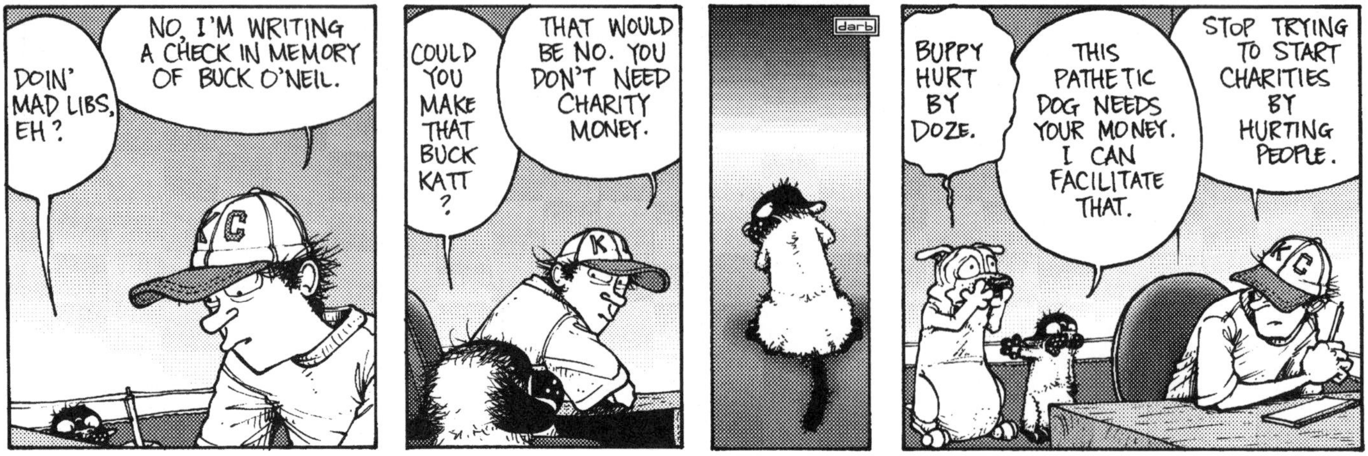
DOIN' MAD LIBS, EH?
NO, I'M WRITING A CHECK IN MEMORY OF BUCK O'NEIL.
COULD YOU MAKE THAT BUCK KATT?
THAT WOULD BE NO. YOU DON'T NEED CHARITY MONEY.
darb
BUPPY HURT BY DOZE.
THIS PATHETIC DOG NEEDS YOUR MONEY. I CAN FACILITATE THAT.
STOP TRYING TO START CHARITIES BY HURTING PEOPLE.

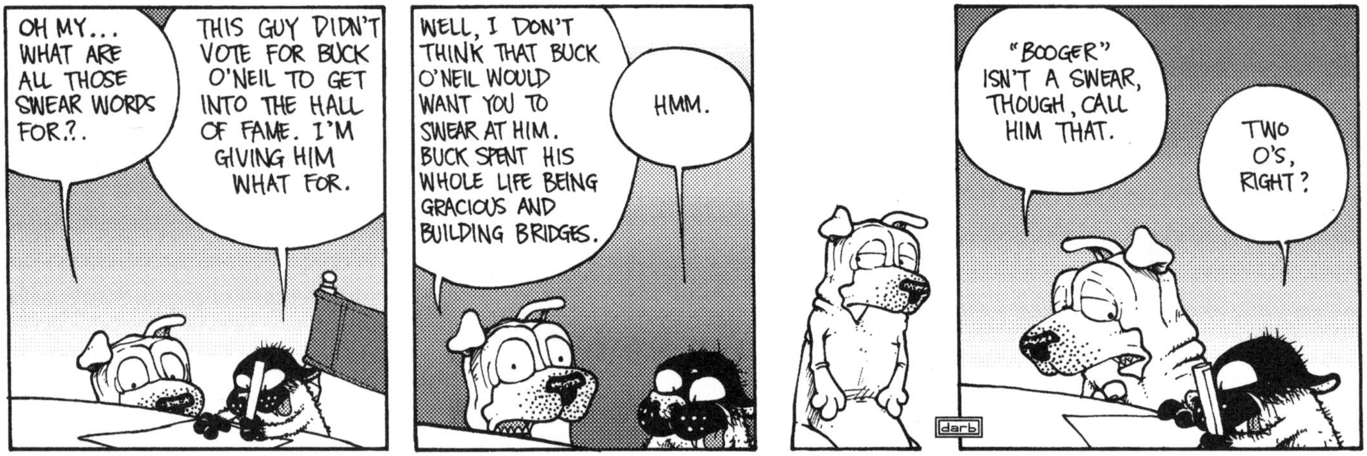
OH MY... WHAT ARE ALL THOSE SWEAR WORDS FOR?.
THIS GUY DIDN'T VOTE FOR BUCK O'NEIL TO GET INTO THE HALL OF FAME. I'M GIVING HIM WHAT FOR.
WELL, I DON'T THINK THAT BUCK O'NEIL WOULD WANT YOU TO SWEAR AT HIM. BUCK SPENT HIS WHOLE LIFE BEING GRACIOUS AND BUILDING BRIDGES.
HMM.
darb
"BOOGER" ISN'T A SWEAR, THOUGH, CALL HIM THAT.
TWO O'S, RIGHT?

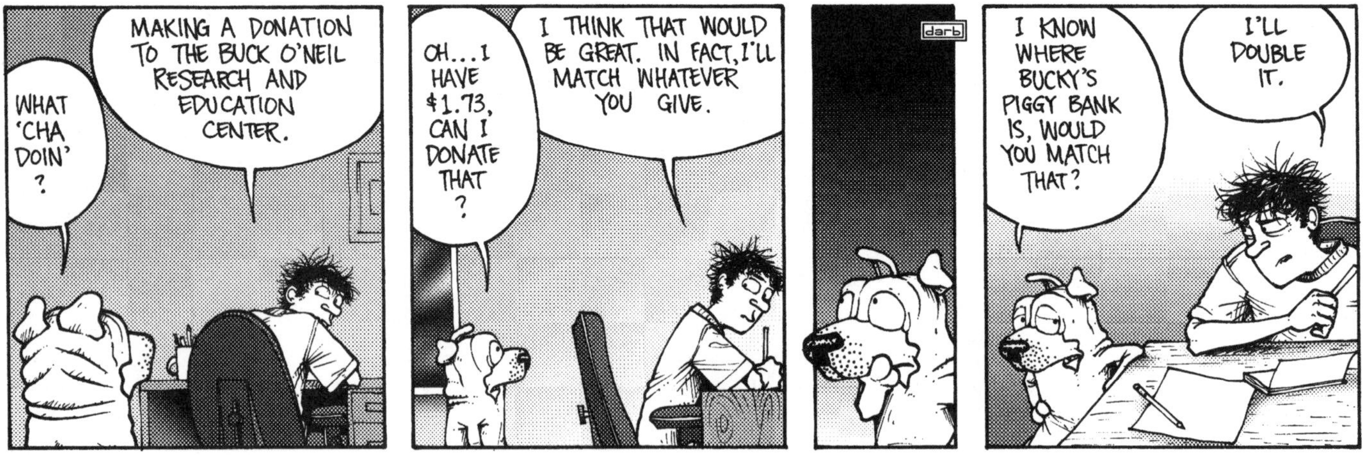
WHAT 'CHA DOIN'?
MAKING A DONATION TO THE BUCK O'NEIL RESEARCH AND EDUCATION CENTER.
OH... I HAVE $1.73, CAN I DONATE THAT?
I THINK THAT WOULD BE GREAT. IN FACT, I'LL MATCH WHATEVER YOU GIVE.
darb
I KNOW WHERE BUCKY'S PIGGY BANK IS, WOULD YOU MATCH THAT?
I'LL DOUBLE IT.

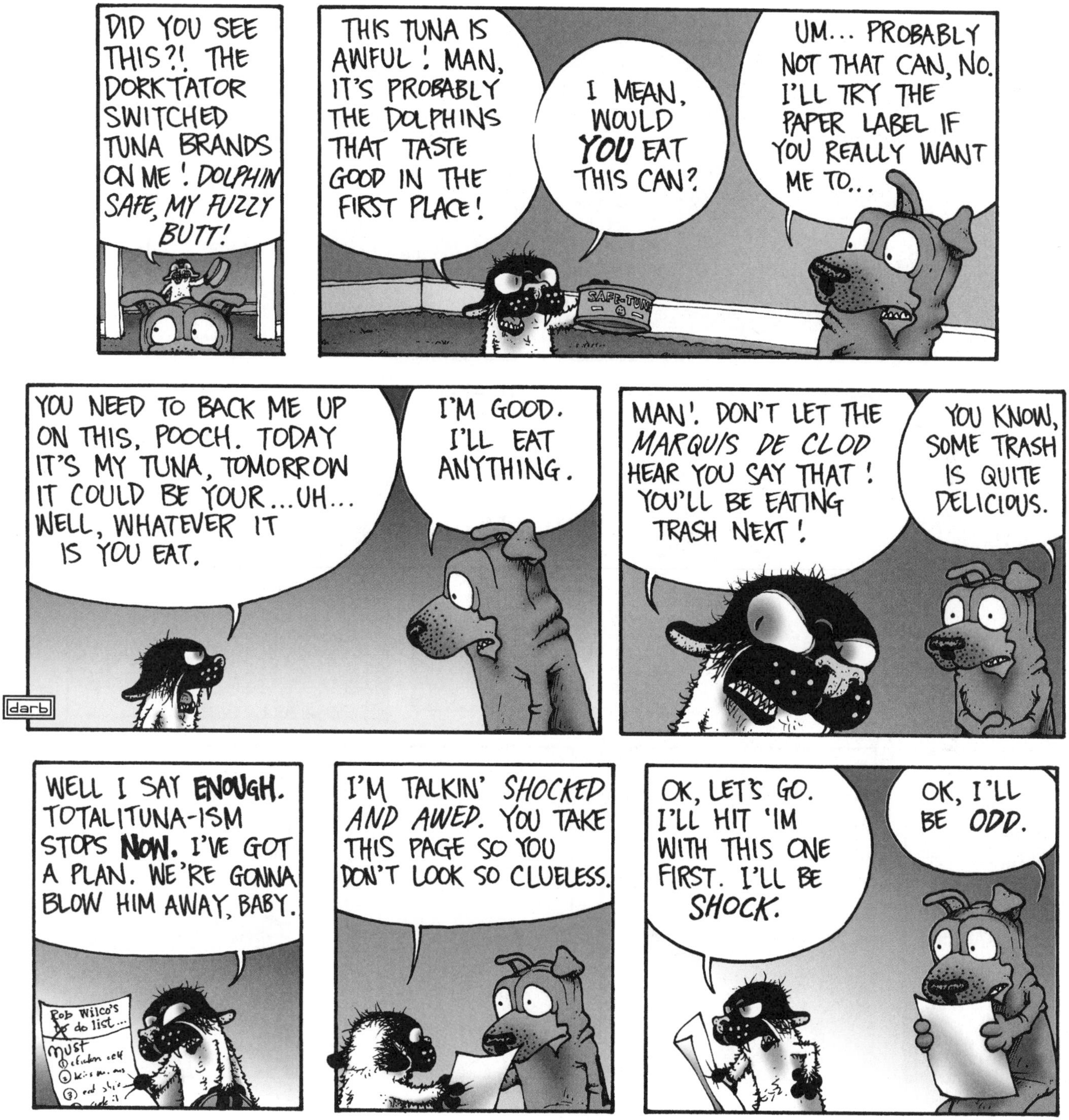
DID YOU SEE THIS?! THE DORKTATOR SWITCHED TUNA BRANDS ON ME! DOLPHIN SAFE, MY FUZZY BUTT!
THIS TUNA IS AWFUL! MAN, IT'S PROBABLY THE DOLPHINS THAT TASTE GOOD IN THE FIRST PLACE!
I MEAN, WOULD YOU EAT THIS CAN?
UM... PROBABLY NOT THAT CAN, NO. I'LL TRY THE PAPER LABEL IF YOU REALLY WANT ME TO...
SAFE-TUNA
YOU NEED TO BACK ME UP ON THIS, POOCH. TODAY IT'S MY TUNA, TOMORROW IT COULD BE YOUR...UH... WELL, WHATEVER IT IS YOU EAT.
I'M GOOD. I'LL EAT ANYTHING.
darb
MAN! DON'T LET THE MARQUIS DE CLOD HEAR YOU SAY THAT! YOU'LL BE EATING TRASH NEXT!
YOU KNOW, SOME TRASH IS QUITE DELICIOUS.
WELL I SAY ENOUGH. TOTALITUNA-ISM STOPS NOW. I'VE GOT A PLAN. WE'RE GONNA BLOW HIM AWAY, BABY.
Rob Wilco's do list...
MUST
I'M TALKIN' SHOCKED AND AWED. YOU TAKE THIS PAGE SO YOU DON'T LOOK SO CLUELESS.
OK, LET'S GO. I'LL HIT 'IM WITH THIS ONE FIRST. I'LL BE SHOCK.
OK, I'LL BE ODD.

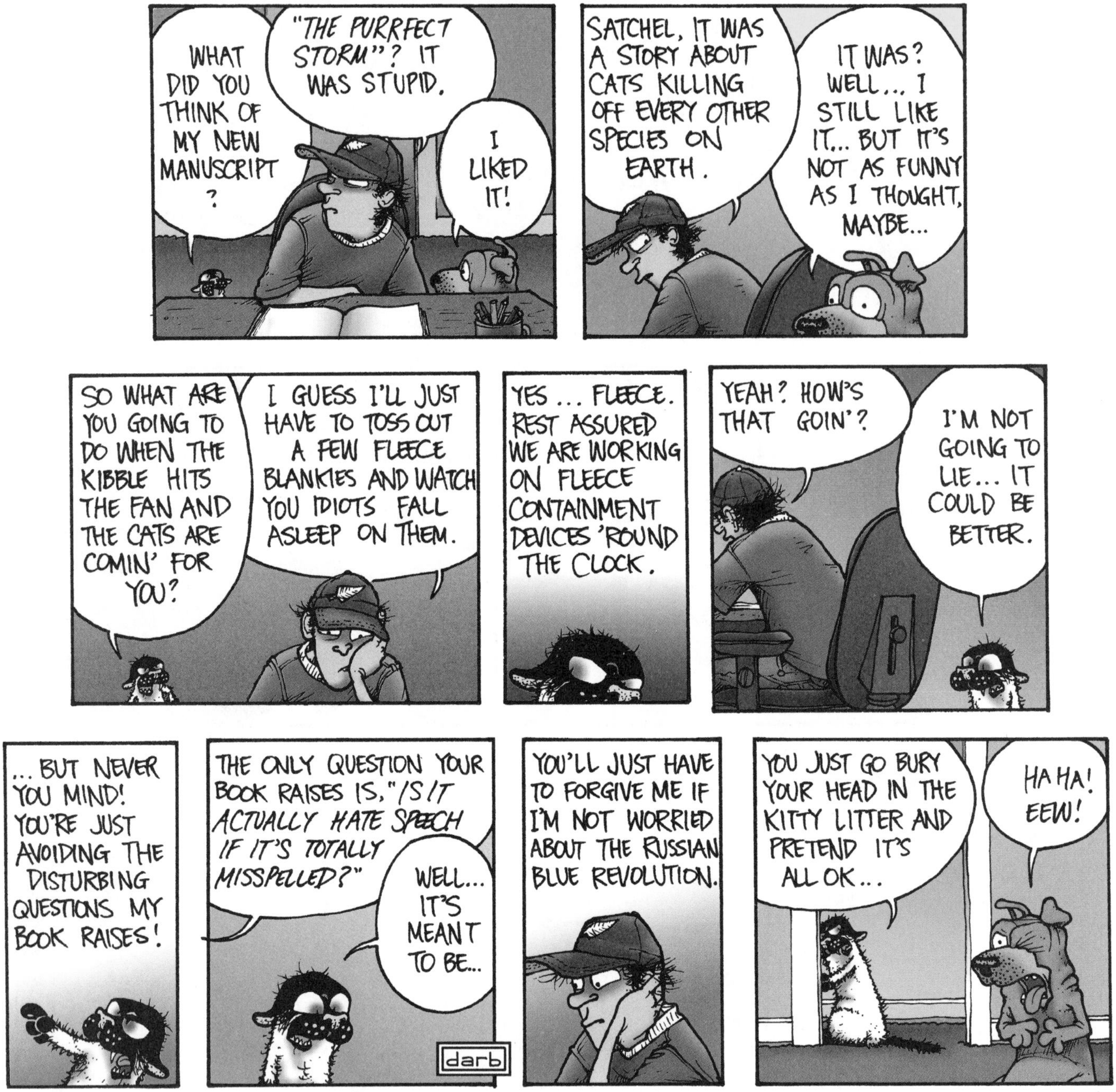
WHAT DID YOU THINK OF MY NEW MANUSCRIPT?
"THE PURRFECT STORM"? IT WAS STUPID.
I LIKED IT!
SATCHEL, IT WAS A STORY ABOUT CATS KILLING OFF EVERY OTHER SPECIES ON EARTH.
IT WAS? WELL... I STILL LIKE IT... BUT IT'S NOT AS FUNNY AS I THOUGHT, MAYBE...
SO WHAT ARE YOU GOING TO DO WHEN THE KIBBLE HITS THE FAN AND THE CATS ARE COMIN' FOR YOU?
I GUESS I'LL JUST HAVE TO TOSS OUT A FEW FLEECE BLANKIES AND WATCH YOU IDIOTS FALL ASLEEP ON THEM.
YES... FLEECE. REST ASSURED WE ARE WORKING ON FLEECE CONTAINMENT DEVICES 'ROUND THE CLOCK.
YEAH? HOW'S THAT GOIN'?
I'M NOT GOING TO LIE... IT COULD BE BETTER.
...BUT NEVER YOU MIND! YOU'RE JUST AVOIDING THE DISTURBING QUESTIONS MY BOOK RAISES!
THE ONLY QUESTION YOUR BOOK RAISES IS, "IS IT ACTUALLY HATE SPEECH IF IT'S TOTALLY MISSPELLED?"
WELL... IT'S MEANT TO BE...
darb
YOU'LL JUST HAVE TO FORGIVE ME IF I'M NOT WORRIED ABOUT THE RUSSIAN BLUE REVOLUTION.
YOU JUST GO BURY YOUR HEAD IN THE KITTY LITTER AND PRETEND IT'S ALL OK...
HA HA! EEW!

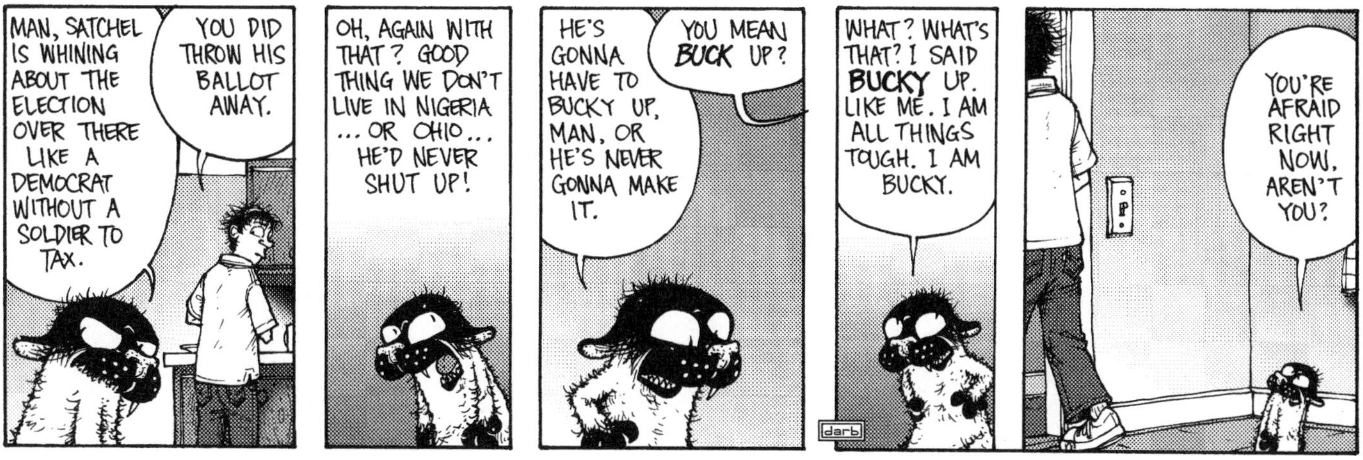
MAN, SATCHEL IS WHINING ABOUT THE ELECTION OVER THERE LIKE A DEMOCRAT WITHOUT A SOLDIER TO TAX.
YOU DID THROW HIS BALLOT AWAY.
OH, AGAIN WITH THAT? GOOD THING WE DON'T LIVE IN NIGERIA ... OR OHIO ... HE'D NEVER SHUT UP!
HE'S GONNA HAVE TO BUCKY UP, MAN, OR HE'S NEVER GONNA MAKE IT.
YOU MEAN BUCK UP?
WHAT? WHAT'S THAT? I SAID BUCKY UP. LIKE ME. I AM ALL THINGS TOUGH. I AM BUCKY.
darb
YOU'RE AFRAID RIGHT NOW, AREN'T YOU?

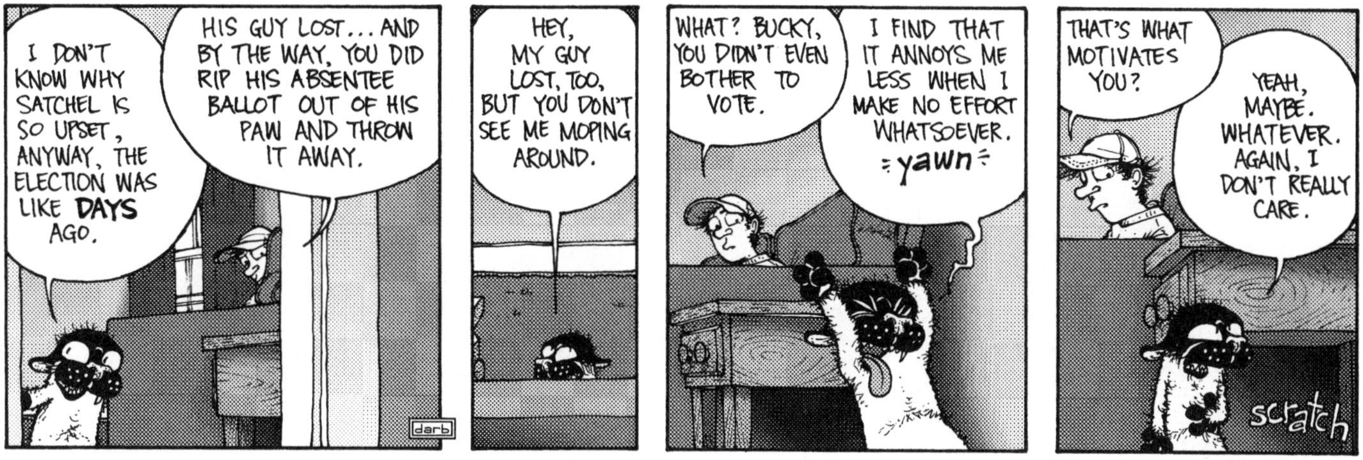
I DON'T KNOW WHY SATCHEL IS SO UPSET, ANYWAY, THE ELECTION WAS LIKE DAYS AGO.
HIS GUY LOST... AND BY THE WAY, YOU DID RIP HIS ABSENTEE BALLOT OUT OF HIS PAW AND THROW IT AWAY.
darb
HEY, MY GUY LOST, TOO, BUT YOU DON'T SEE ME MOPING AROUND.
WHAT? BUCKY, YOU DIDN'T EVEN BOTHER TO VOTE.
I FIND THAT IT ANNOYS ME LESS WHEN I MAKE NO EFFORT WHATSOEVER. yawn
THAT'S WHAT MOTIVATES YOU?
YEAH, MAYBE. WHATEVER. AGAIN, I DON'T REALLY CARE.
scratch

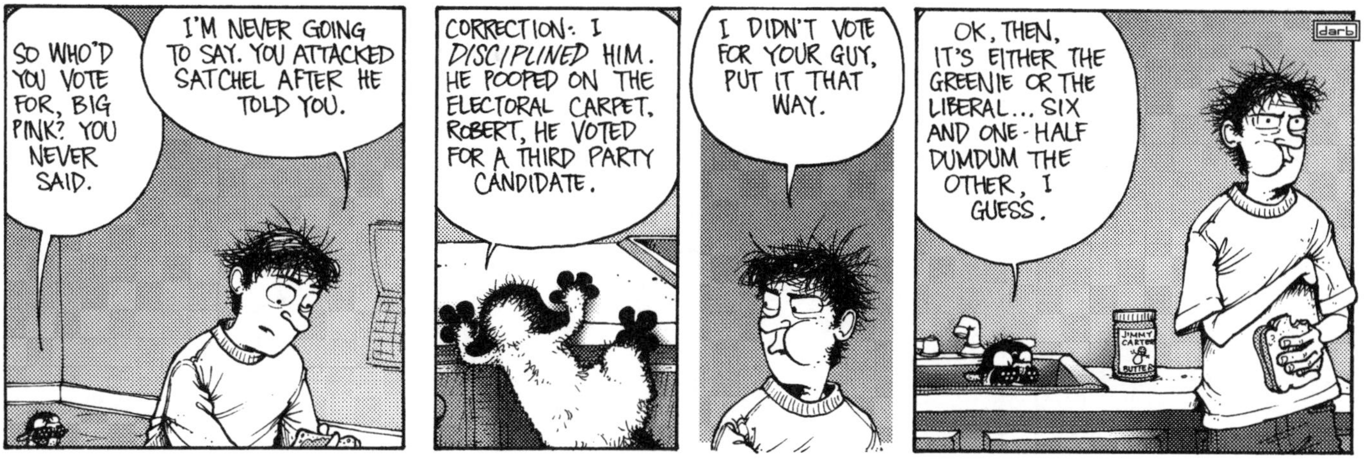
SO WHO'D YOU VOTE FOR, BIG PINK? YOU NEVER SAID.
I'M NEVER GOING TO SAY. YOU ATTACKED SATCHEL AFTER HE TOLD YOU.
CORRECTION: I DISCIPLINED HIM. HE POOPED ON THE ELECTORAL CARPET. ROBERT, HE VOTED FOR A THIRD PARTY CANDIDATE.
I DIDN'T VOTE FOR YOUR GUY, PUT IT THAT WAY.
darb
OK, THEN, IT'S EITHER THE GREENIE OR THE LIBERAL... SIX AND ONE-HALF DUMDUM THE OTHER, I GUESS.
JIMMY CARTER BUTTER

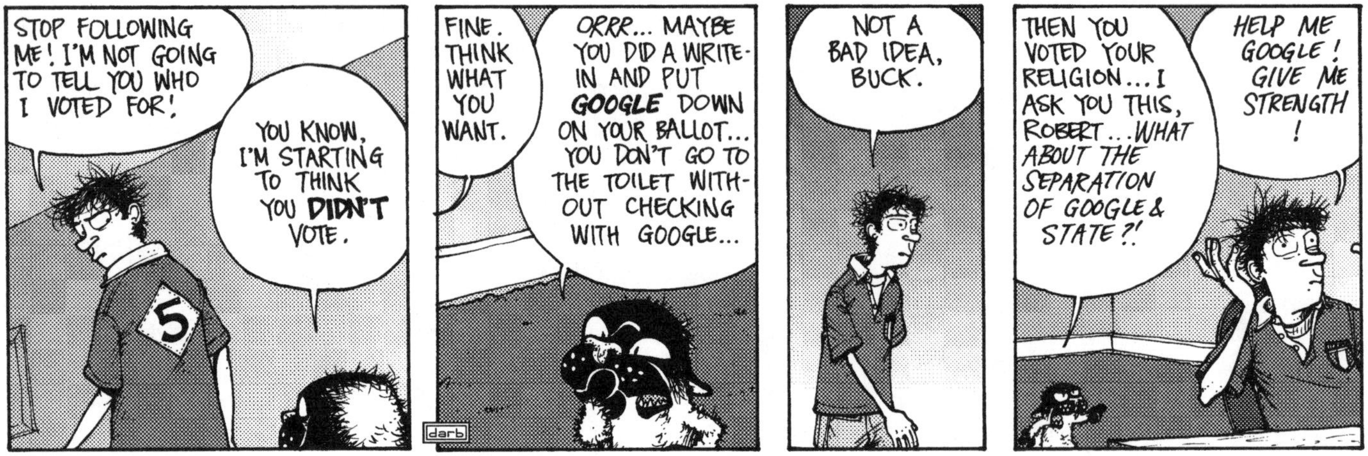
STOP FOLLOWING ME! I'M NOT GOING TO TELL YOU WHO I VOTED FOR!
YOU KNOW, I'M STARTING TO THINK YOU **DIDN'T** VOTE.
FINE. THINK WHAT YOU WANT.
ORRR... MAYBE YOU DID A WRITE-IN AND PUT **GOOGLE** DOWN ON YOUR BALLOT... YOU DON'T GO TO THE TOILET WITH-OUT CHECKING WITH GOOGLE...
NOT A BAD IDEA, BUCK.
THEN YOU VOTED YOUR RELIGION... I ASK YOU THIS, ROBERT... *WHAT ABOUT THE SEPARATION OF GOOGLE & STATE?!*
HELP ME GOOGLE! GIVE ME STRENGTH!
darb

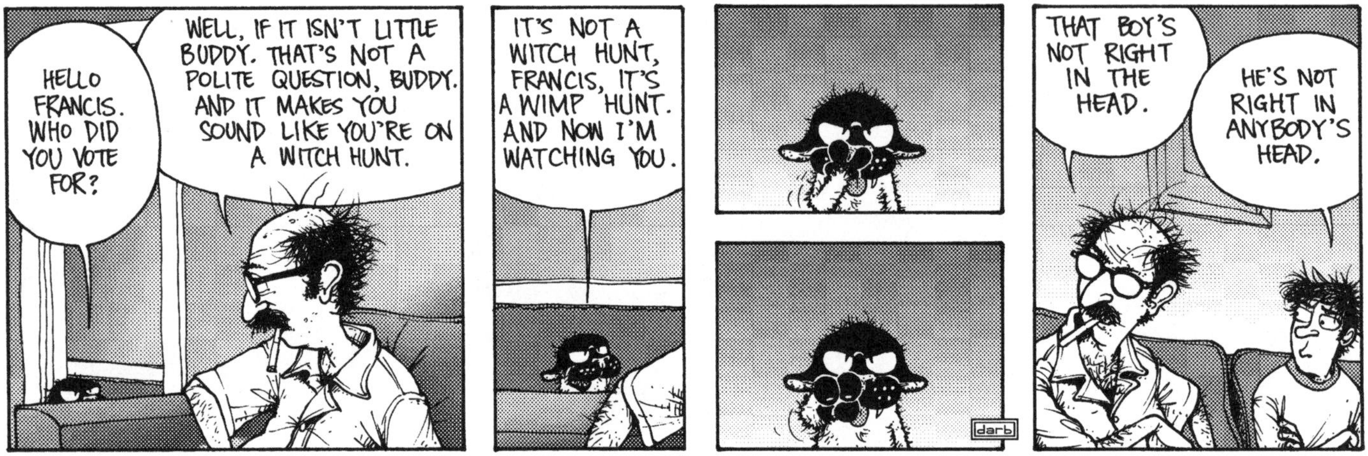
HELLO FRANCIS. WHO DID YOU VOTE FOR?
WELL, IF IT ISN'T LITTLE BUDDY. THAT'S NOT A POLITE QUESTION, BUDDY. AND IT MAKES YOU SOUND LIKE YOU'RE ON A WITCH HUNT.
IT'S NOT A WITCH HUNT, FRANCIS, IT'S A WIMP HUNT. AND NOW I'M WATCHING YOU.
darb
THAT BOY'S NOT RIGHT IN THE HEAD.
HE'S NOT RIGHT IN ANYBODY'S HEAD.

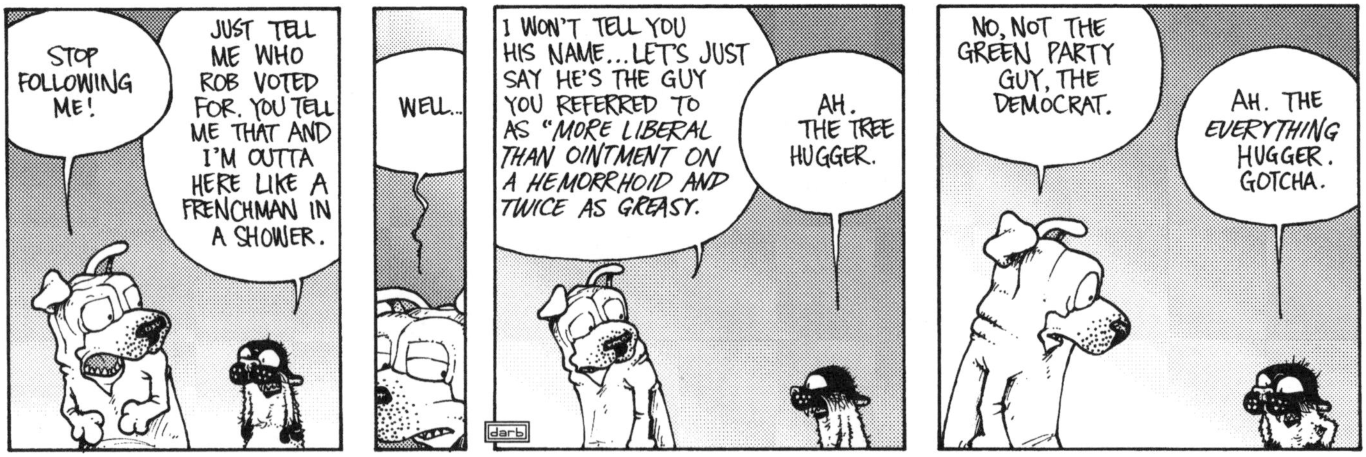
STOP FOLLOWING ME!
JUST TELL ME WHO ROB VOTED FOR. YOU TELL ME THAT AND I'M OUTTA HERE LIKE A FRENCHMAN IN A SHOWER.
WELL...
darb
I WON'T TELL YOU HIS NAME... LET'S JUST SAY HE'S THE GUY YOU REFERRED TO AS "*MORE LIBERAL THAN OINTMENT ON A HEMORRHOID AND TWICE AS GREASY.*
AH. THE TREE HUGGER.
NO, NOT THE GREEN PARTY GUY, THE DEMOCRAT.
AH. THE *EVERYTHING* HUGGER. GOTCHA.

MAN, THIS DARFUR SITUATION IS UNBELIEVABLE... WHAT'S WRONG WITH PEOPLE, ANYWAY?

DON'T GET ME STARTED ON **PEOPLE**! AND WHAT IS DARFUR?

THE PLACE ON TV RIGHT NOW! IT'S A WORLD CRISIS, DUDE, LIKE 400,000 PEOPLE HAVE DIED THERE!

YES, BUT DOES IT AFFECT THE PRICE OF CATNIP? SEE, *THAT'S* HOW YOU GET PEOPLE TO CARE.

OK, I'M GONNA LEAVE BEFORE THIS TURNS INTO A BIG FIGHT.

PERHAPS IF THERE WERE A DARFUR *VIDEO* GAME...

OK, NOW YOU'RE GROUNDED. YOU'RE GROUNDED FOR APATHY.

darb

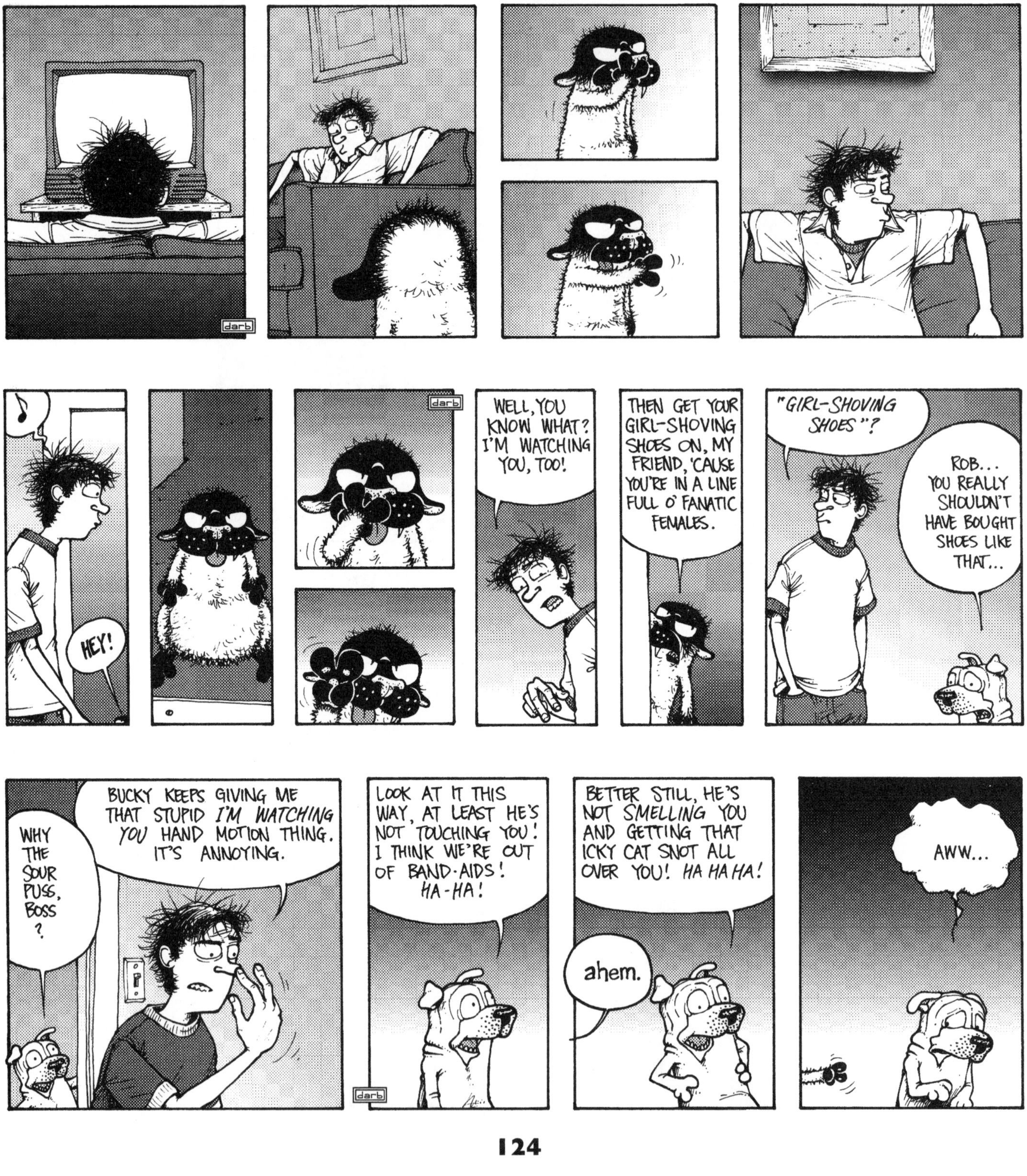
darb
darb
HEY!
WELL, YOU KNOW WHAT? I'M WATCHING YOU, TOO!
THEN GET YOUR GIRL-SHOVING SHOES ON, MY FRIEND, 'CAUSE YOU'RE IN A LINE FULL O' FANATIC FEMALES.
"GIRL-SHOVING SHOES"?
ROB... YOU REALLY SHOULDN'T HAVE BOUGHT SHOES LIKE THAT...
WHY THE SOUR PUSS, BOSS?
BUCKY KEEPS GIVING ME THAT STUPID *I'M WATCHING YOU* HAND MOTION THING. IT'S ANNOYING.
darb
LOOK AT IT THIS WAY, AT LEAST HE'S NOT TOUCHING YOU! I THINK WE'RE OUT OF BAND-AIDS! HA-HA!
BETTER STILL, HE'S NOT *SMELLING* YOU AND GETTING THAT ICKY CAT SNOT ALL OVER YOU! *HA HA HA!*
ahem.
AWW...

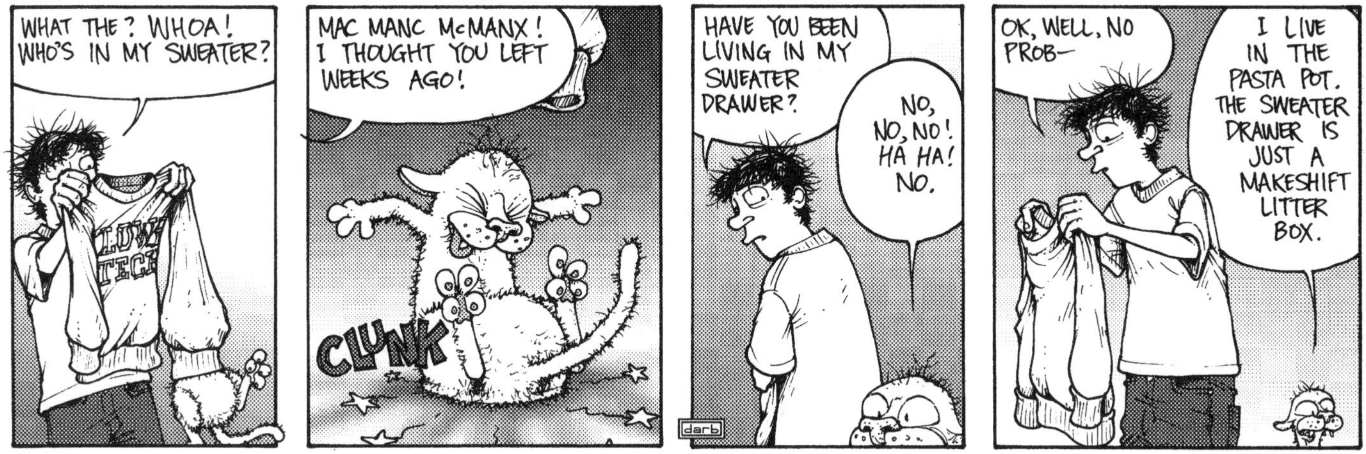
WHAT THE? WHOA! WHO'S IN MY SWEATER?
MAC MANC McMANX! I THOUGHT YOU LEFT WEEKS AGO!
CLUNK
HAVE YOU BEEN LIVING IN MY SWEATER DRAWER?
NO, NO, NO! HA HA! NO.
OK, WELL, NO PROB—
I LIVE IN THE PASTA POT. THE SWEATER DRAWER IS JUST A MAKESHIFT LITTER BOX.
darb

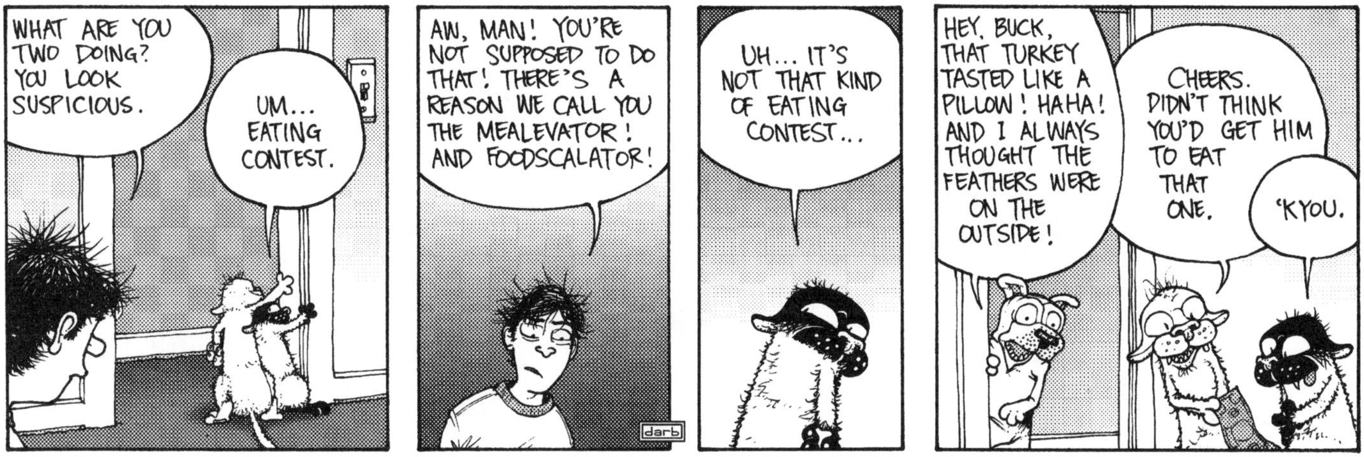
WHAT ARE YOU TWO DOING? YOU LOOK SUSPICIOUS.
UM... EATING CONTEST.
AW, MAN! YOU'RE NOT SUPPOSED TO DO THAT! THERE'S A REASON WE CALL YOU THE MEALEVATOR! AND FOODSCALATOR!
UH... IT'S NOT THAT KIND OF EATING CONTEST...
HEY, BUCK, THAT TURKEY TASTED LIKE A PILLOW! HAHA! AND I ALWAYS THOUGHT THE FEATHERS WERE ON THE OUTSIDE!
CHEERS. DIDN'T THINK YOU'D GET HIM TO EAT THAT ONE.
'KYOU.
darb

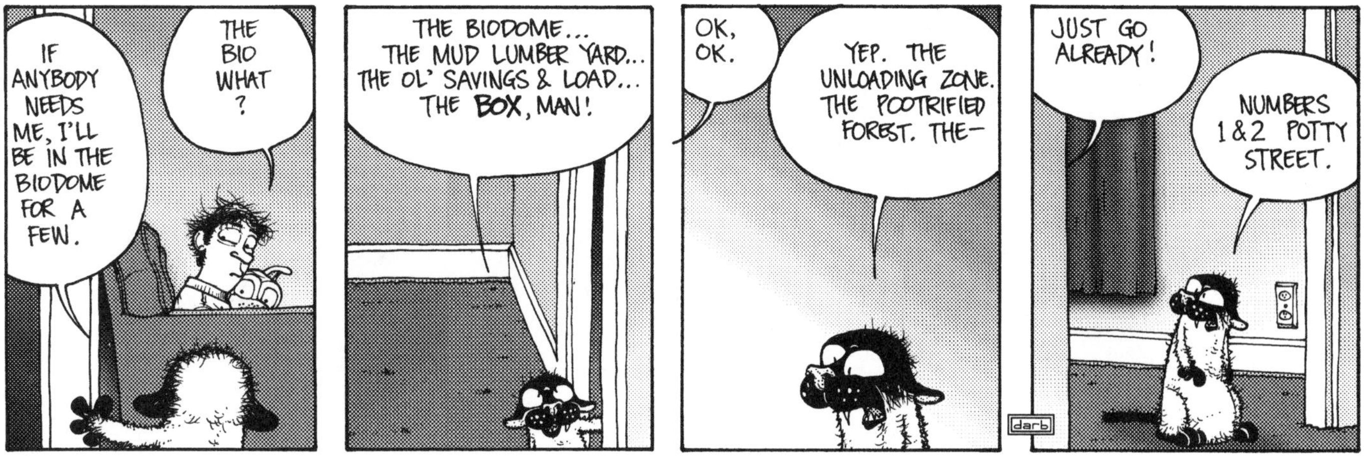
IF ANYBODY NEEDS ME, I'LL BE IN THE BIODOME FOR A FEW.
THE BIO WHAT?
THE BIODOME... THE MUD LUMBER YARD... THE OL' SAVINGS & LOAD... THE BOX, MAN!
OK, OK.
YEP. THE UNLOADING ZONE. THE POOTRIFIED FOREST. THE—
JUST GO ALREADY!
NUMBERS 1&2 POTTY STREET.
darb

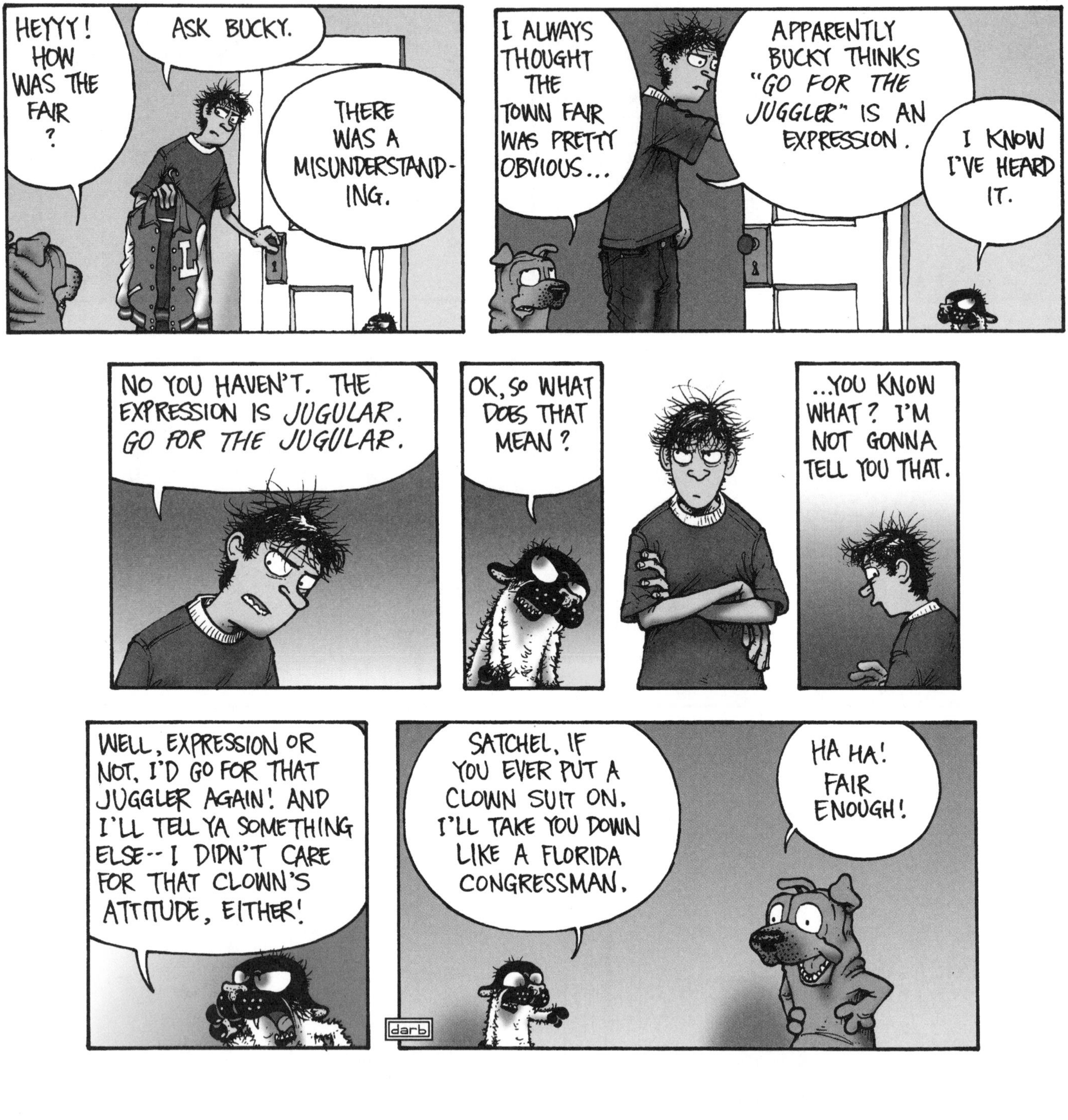
HEYYY! HOW WAS THE FAIR?
ASK BUCKY.
THERE WAS A MISUNDERSTANDING.
I ALWAYS THOUGHT THE TOWN FAIR WAS PRETTY OBVIOUS...
APPARENTLY BUCKY THINKS "GO FOR THE JUGGLER" IS AN EXPRESSION.
I KNOW I'VE HEARD IT.
NO YOU HAVEN'T. THE EXPRESSION IS JUGULAR. GO FOR THE JUGULAR.
OK, SO WHAT DOES THAT MEAN?
...YOU KNOW WHAT? I'M NOT GONNA TELL YOU THAT.
WELL, EXPRESSION OR NOT, I'D GO FOR THAT JUGGLER AGAIN! AND I'LL TELL YA SOMETHING ELSE-- I DIDN'T CARE FOR THAT CLOWN'S ATTITUDE, EITHER!
SATCHEL, IF YOU EVER PUT A CLOWN SUIT ON, I'LL TAKE YOU DOWN LIKE A FLORIDA CONGRESSMAN.
HA HA! FAIR ENOUGH!
darb

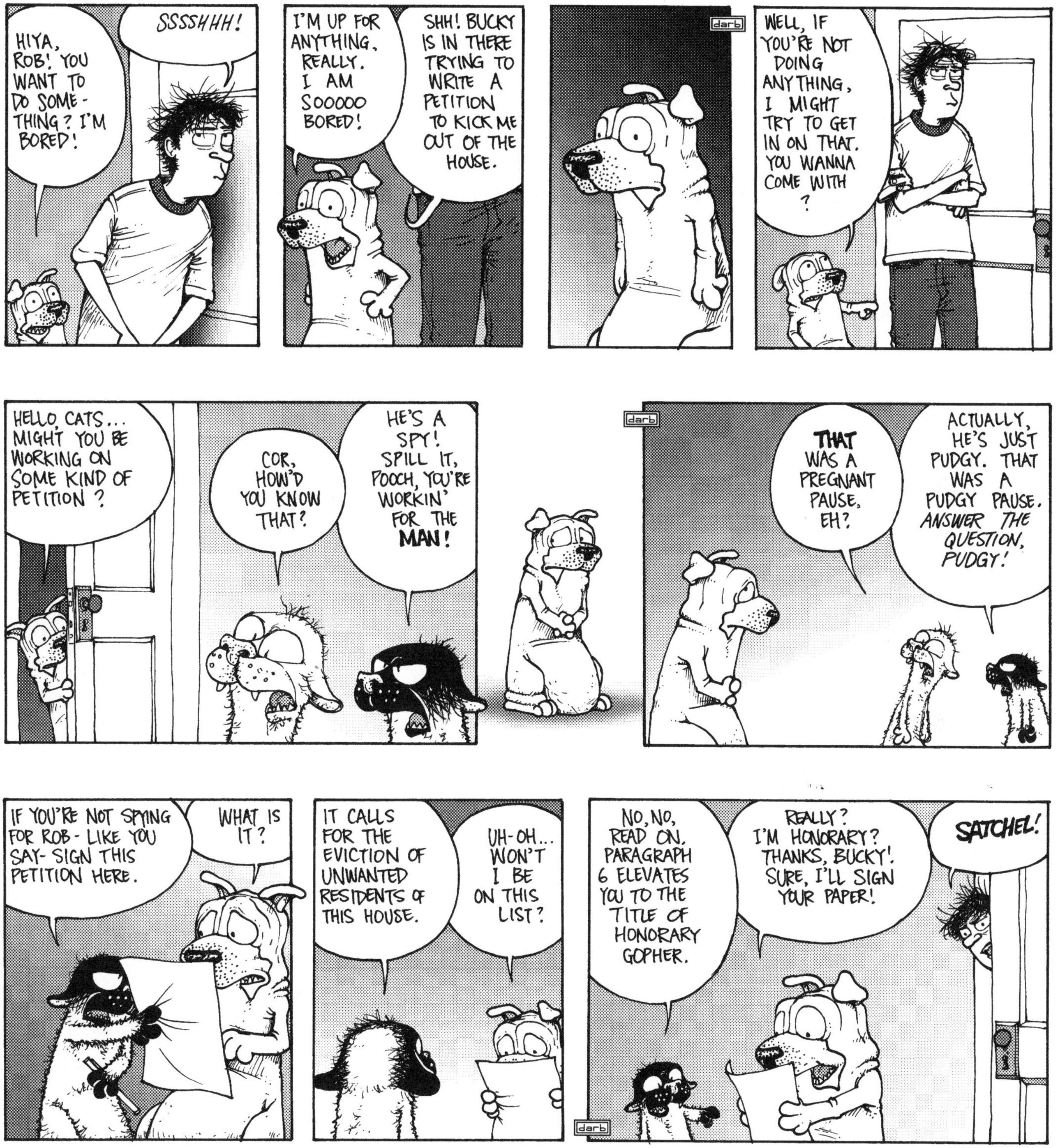
HIYA, ROB! YOU WANT TO DO SOME-THING? I'M BORED!
SSSSHHH!
I'M UP FOR ANYTHING, REALLY. I AM SOOOOO BORED!
SHH! BUCKY IS IN THERE TRYING TO WRITE A PETITION TO KICK ME OUT OF THE HOUSE.
darb
WELL, IF YOU'RE NOT DOING ANYTHING, I MIGHT TRY TO GET IN ON THAT. YOU WANNA COME WITH?
HELLO, CATS... MIGHT YOU BE WORKING ON SOME KIND OF PETITION?
COR, HOW'D YOU KNOW THAT?
HE'S A SPY! SPILL IT, POOCH, YOU'RE WORKIN' FOR THE MAN!
darb
THAT WAS A PREGNANT PAUSE, EH?
ACTUALLY, HE'S JUST PUDGY. THAT WAS A PUDGY PAUSE. ANSWER THE QUESTION, PUDGY!
IF YOU'RE NOT SPYING FOR ROB- LIKE YOU SAY- SIGN THIS PETITION HERE.
WHAT IS IT?
IT CALLS FOR THE EVICTION OF UNWANTED RESIDENTS OF THIS HOUSE.
UH-OH... WON'T I BE ON THIS LIST?
darb
NO, NO, READ ON. PARAGRAPH 6 ELEVATES YOU TO THE TITLE OF HONORARY GOPHER.
REALLY? I'M HONORARY? THANKS, BUCKY! SURE, I'LL SIGN YOUR PAPER!
SATCHEL!

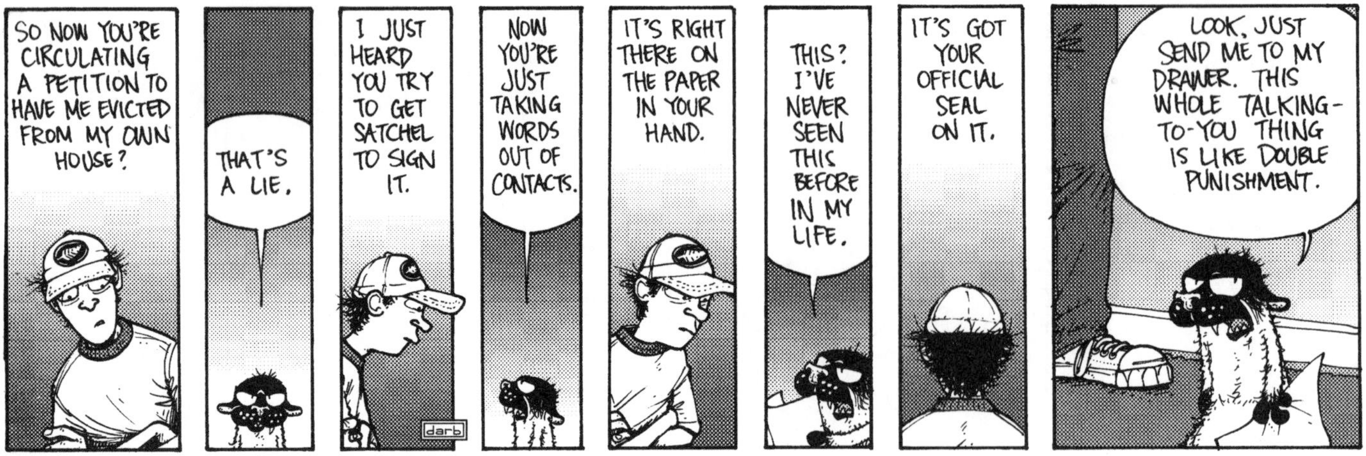
SO NOW YOU'RE CIRCULATING A PETITION TO HAVE ME EVICTED FROM MY OWN HOUSE?
THAT'S A LIE.
I JUST HEARD YOU TRY TO GET SATCHEL TO SIGN IT.
NOW YOU'RE JUST TAKING WORDS OUT OF CONTACTS.
IT'S RIGHT THERE ON THE PAPER IN YOUR HAND.
THIS? I'VE NEVER SEEN THIS BEFORE IN MY LIFE.
IT'S GOT YOUR OFFICIAL SEAL ON IT.
LOOK, JUST SEND ME TO MY DRAWER. THIS WHOLE TALKING-TO-YOU THING IS LIKE DOUBLE PUNISHMENT.
darb

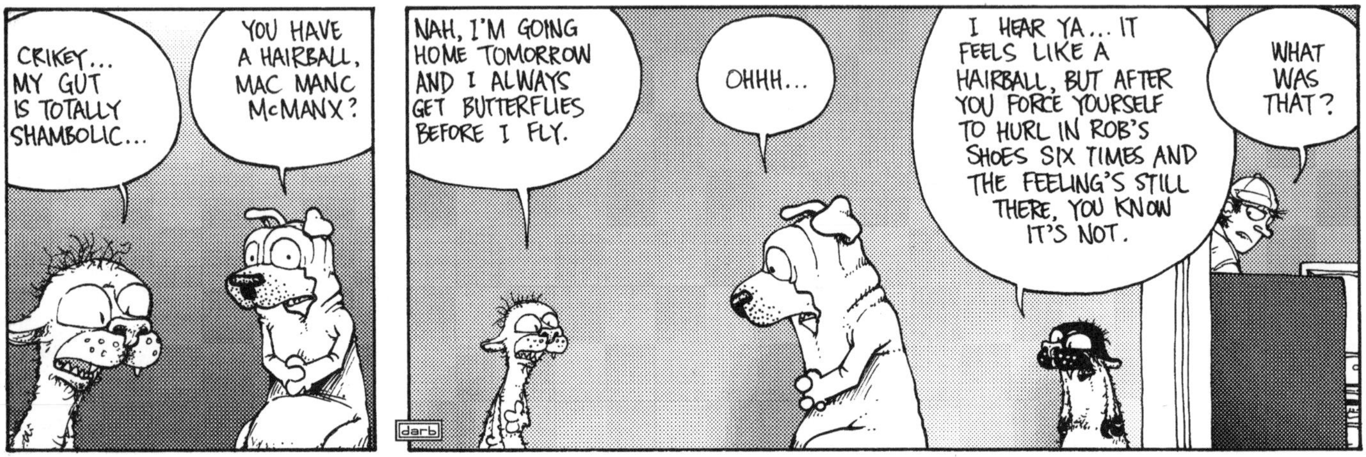
CRIKEY... MY GUT IS TOTALLY SHAMBOLIC...
YOU HAVE A HAIRBALL, MAC MANC McMANX?
darb
NAH, I'M GOING HOME TOMORROW AND I ALWAYS GET BUTTERFLIES BEFORE I FLY.
OHHH...
I HEAR YA... IT FEELS LIKE A HAIRBALL, BUT AFTER YOU FORCE YOURSELF TO HURL IN ROB'S SHOES SIX TIMES AND THE FEELING'S STILL THERE, YOU KNOW IT'S NOT.
WHAT WAS THAT?

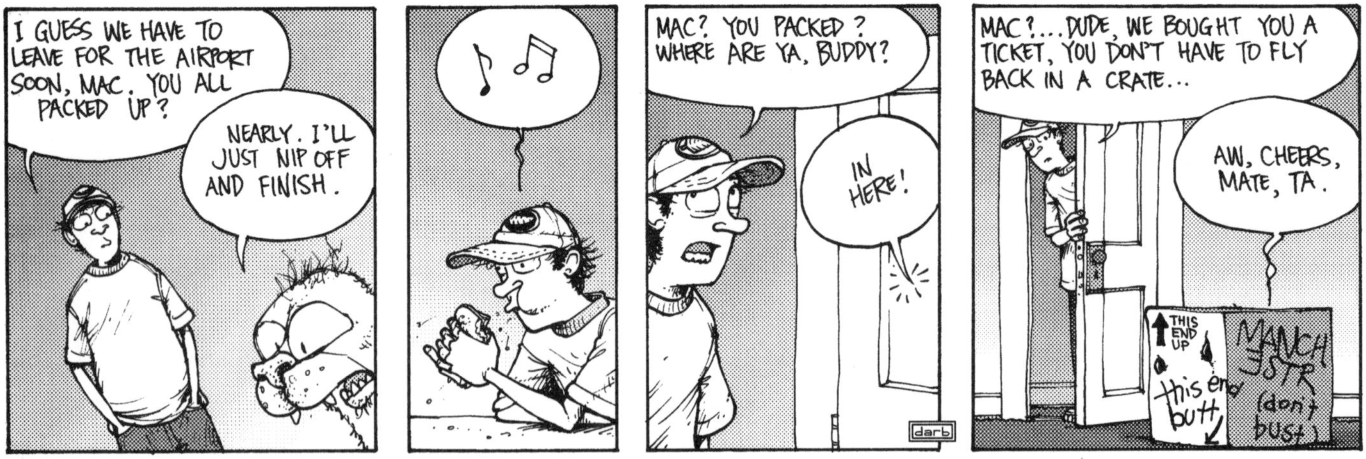
I GUESS WE HAVE TO LEAVE FOR THE AIRPORT SOON, MAC. YOU ALL PACKED UP?
NEARLY. I'LL JUST NIP OFF AND FINISH.
MAC? YOU PACKED? WHERE ARE YA, BUDDY?
IN HERE!
darb
MAC?...DUDE, WE BOUGHT YOU A TICKET, YOU DON'T HAVE TO FLY BACK IN A CRATE...
AW, CHEERS, MATE, TA.
THIS END UP
this end butt
MANCH ESTR
(don't bust)